U.S. Immigration
in the 1980s

Published in cooperation with
the Center for Immigration Studies,
Washington, D.C.

U.S. Immigration
in the 1980s

Reappraisal and Reform

EDITED BY
David E. Simcox

Westview Press
BOULDER & LONDON

Center for Immigration Studies
WASHINGTON, D.C.

LIBRARY
COLBY-SAWYER COLLEGE
NEW LONDON, NH 03257

This Westview softcover edition is printed on acid-free paper and bound in softcovers that carry the highest rating of the National Association of State Textbook Administrators, in consultation with the Association of American Publishers and the Book Manufacturers' Institute.

Published in 1988 in the United States of America by Westview Press, Inc., 5500 Central Avenue, Boulder, Colorado 80301

Library of Congress Cataloging-in-Publication Data
U.S. immigration in the 1980s.
  Includes index.
  1. United States—Emigration and immigration.
2. United States—Emigration and immigration—
Government policy. I. Simcox, David E. II. Title:
US immigration in the 1980s. III. Title: United States
immigration in the 1980s.
JV6493.U18 1988   325.73   88-17231
ISBN 0-8133-7542-8

Printed and bound in the United States of America

⊗ The paper used in this publication meets the requirements of the American National
     Standard for Permanence of Paper for Printed Library Materials Z39.48-1984.

6   5   4   3

CONTENTS

LIST OF TABLES

PREFACE

Immigration is a major transforming social force in American society and culture. Since the changes it brings tend to be slow and subtle, the size and direction of immigration's reshaping force is not always apparent to most Americans. The contribution of immigration to America's industrial and agricultural might and its rich cultural diversity are inarguable and well documented in a vast literature. But like every other enriching social phenomenon, from industrialization to trade unionism to feminism and automation, immigration brings costs in terms of social divisions, economic disruptions, urban tensions and individual anxieties. Grafting, in society as in the human body, is rarely without pain and is not always successful. America no less than the immigrant shares in the discomfort of the adjustment process.

This book seeks to add balance to the current literature on immigration by examining it first in terms of its effects on the United States and the problems or advantages it brings to a rapidly changing society. The book looks at the unrest and demographic forces at work beyond our borders and considers the options, prospects and obstacles for effective and humane management of immigration into the United States in the service of clear national goals. While attentive to the past, the contributors to this volume look more to the future, to the American society of tomorrow that the immigration of our era is relentlessly reshaping.

The time and thought of scores of talented and committed associates went into this book. It would be futile to try to name them all. But four tireless workers deserving special mention are: Susan Subak who worked closely with the editor and the authors in editing the manuscripts; Anna Scruggs, who bore with good humor the task of typing the manuscripts and entering the numberless revisions; Richard Estrada who helped design the project and keep it moving in the initial stages; and Connie Suwalsky who did the final editing.

Special acknowledgement goes also to Greg Curtis, who conceived the idea of a broad review of immigration, and who followed up with the support, encouragement and patience needed to make it a reality. Otis Graham and Roger Conner merit special gratitude for their solid ideas on the book's structure and content and for their perceptive editorial suggestions.

Other members of the Board of the Center for Immigration Studies who read and commented on manuscripts, invariably for their improvement, were. Liz

Paddock, Gene Katz and George Grayson. Two other board members, Leon Bouvier and Malcolm Lovell, gave freely of their time in preparing or adapting articles for inclusion in this volume.

We are indebted to the Urban Institute, the American Immigration Lawyers Association, and Popular Mechanics for their permission to reprint materials and to the Immigration and Naturalization Service, Department of State, Bureau of the Census and other public institutions from whom we gathered much of the data that appears here.

ABOUT THE AUTHORS

—Gerda Bikales is a former Executive Director of U.S. English, a national public interest organization supporting the designation of English as the official language of the United States.

—Leon Bouvier, a demographer, has been Professor of Sociology at the University of Rhode Island and is now Adjunct Professor of Sociology at Old Dominion University. Formerly Vice President of the Population Reference Bureau, Bouvier is a frequent author on immigration and demographic change.

—Richard Estrada, a journalist and historian from El Paso, Texas, was formerly Director of Research at the Federation for American Immigration Reform.

—Lawrence Fuchs was the Executive Director of the Select Commission on Immigration and Refugee Policy from 1979–1981. He is now Professor of American Civilization at Brandeis University.

—Otis Graham is Distinguished University Professor of History at the University of North Carolina at Chapel Hill and former Program Director of the Center for the Study of Democratic Institutions. Dr. Graham is now Chairman of the Policy Board of the Center for Immigration Studies.

—Lindsey Grant, during a lengthy career in the State Department, worked on international environmental and population issues. He is now a freelance writer and consultant.

—Gary Imhoff, a Washington freelance writer on immigration, assimilation and minority issues, is coauthor with former Colorado Governor Richard Lamm of *The Immigration Time Bomb*, published in 1985.

—Dr. Jacquelyne Jackson is Professor of Sociology at Duke University and an author on social issues affecting black Americans.

—Malcolm R. Lovell, Jr. was Assistant Secretary of Labor for Manpower from 1970 to 1973 and Under Secretary of Labor from 1981 to 1983. He now directs the Labor and Management Institute of the George Washington University.

—Dr. Ray Marshall was U.S. Secretary of Labor from 1977 to 1980. He is now Professor of Economics and Public Affairs at the Lyndon B. Johnson School of Public Affairs at the University of Texas.

—Philip Martin is Professor of Agricultural Economics at the University of California at Davis and a former staff member of the Select Commission on Immigration and Refugee Policy.

—Mark Miller is Professor of Political Science at the University of Delaware, specializing in research on migration, labor and nationality themes in Europe. Dr. Miller is co-editor of the book *The Unavoidable Issue: U.S. Immigration Policy in the 1980s*, published in 1983.

—Eric Sevaried, a long-time national correspondent and commentator for CBS, also has had extensive international experience. He served as a war correspondent during World War II and was stationed in the Asian and European bureaus.

—David Simcox is Director of the Center for Immigration Studies. During a twenty-nine year career in the State Department he worked on Latin American migration and labor issues. He was Director of State's Office of Mexican Affairs from 1977 to 1979.

—Barnaby Zall, a Washington attorney, is legal counsel for the Federation for American Immigration Reform. In 1986 he was the recipient of the American Bar Association's prize for the best essay on U.S. asylum policy.

I

INTRODUCTION

Overview—A Time of Reform and Reappraisal

By David Simcox

The border patrol [in the San Diego sector] picked up 4,000 lawless migrants back in 1965; in 1985 the number was 421,000 . . . The farmers, wanderers, smugglers, pregnant mothers, drug peddlers do not seem like the stuff of crisis, but they are.

—Theodore H. White,
Time, August 25, 1986

The Maturing of U.S. Immigration Reform

American immigration's watershed event in the 1980s was the enactment in November 1986 of the Immigration Reform and Control Act (IRCA) after some fifteen years of off-and-on congressional deliberations. But rhetoric comparing its significance to the 1965 overhaul of our legal immigration system is overdrawn. The new act aims at strengthening the enforcement of existing law and, through amnesty, erasing some of two decades' accumulation of enforcement neglect. Left intact is the 1965 regime for legal immigration, with its heavy emphasis on family reunification. Also left standing is the convoluted structure of regulations, court decisions and interpretations dating from the 1952 law for excluding or deporting aliens or awarding them immigration benefits.

THE ROOTS OF COMPASSION FATIGUE

The immigration reforms of 1986 had their origins in glacial changes over the years in public attitudes, but in the 1980s, in particular, Americans came to care more. The period was marked by increasing public awareness of the cumulative impact of legal and illegal immigration on national life, and by a more questioning attitude toward immigration's social contribution and—as the 1980s progressed—a rising unease over its magnitude and seeming immunity to government control.

Probably no event of the period did more to crystalize these concerns than the 1980 Mariel Boatlift. The traditional humanitarian impulse of many Americans to welcome refugees was tempered in that case by a sense of affronted nationalism, by a disturbing feeling that a fraying American immigration policy was being made not in Washington, but in a foreign land.

But this was only one event, although perhaps the culminating one, of a series of developments and trends since the mid-1970s that spotlighted the disorderliness of the nation's management of immigration and conditioned the public to ponder more the social costs of heavy immigration along with its benefits. Other trends and events helped reshape public perceptions and nourish a sense of what Senator Alan Simpson (R-WY) called "compassion fatigue:"

—The resettlement at public expense of more than one million refugees after 1975, 800,000 of them from Southeast Asia, and the attendant problems of high federal and state outlays, persistent welfare dependency exceeding 70 percent in several states, frictions in the assimilation process and secondary migration leading to heavy clustering in California and a few other preferred areas of settlement.

—The surge in apprehensions of Mexican illegal aliens, which broke the one million threshold in 1976, remained high during the peak of Mexico's oil

3

boom prosperity, and jumped by another 25 percent in 1983 with Mexico's economic collapse. More sensitive to job competition in times of unemployment, many Americans were more inclined to take notice of the continuing high flows of illegals in 1982 and 1983 when joblessness in the United States approached 10 percent. The growing public perception of things in disarray was confirmed by the admission of Attorney General William French Smith in 1981—echoing the findings of the Select Commission on Immigration and Refugee Policy—that "we have lost control of our borders." Increasing lawlessness on the border, with frequent attacks on Border Patrol officers peaking in 1986 with 150 recorded assaults, added resonance to Smith's warning.

—The headline grabbing political agitation in 1979 among the 60,000 Iranian students in the United States left many Americans offended by the insouciance of the Iranian visitors, and dismayed by the INS's inability to locate many of them or hold them to the terms of their visas.

—The increasing signs that immigrants—including illegal ones—were not free of attendant public and social welfare costs. The 1981 Supreme Court Decision in *Doe v. Plyler*,[1] which assured illegal alien children free public education, jolted the prevalent assumption that the illegal alien was a non-revenue consuming taxpayer and further heightened the sense of immigration policies adrift.

—Rising public concern over crime among immigrants and refugees, given sharper focus by high crime rates among Mariel boatlift migrants, sensational drug-related crime in South Florida's foreign community, and complaints from local officials in the southwest about increased crime and drug smuggling and rising criminal justice costs among illegal aliens. Even though ethnic and other immigrant advocacies stressed that crime among aliens was not disproportionate, much of a public conditioned to expect zero social costs from foreign newcomers found even that was still too much.

—The spread of bilingualism and multilingualism in the 1970s in U.S. communities, and rising political resistance to it in the 1980s, further exposed the American public to the pervasive transforming effects of rapid immigration.

Public opinion, in poll after poll in the late 1970s and early 1980s, showed that a majority of Americans opposed illegal immigration, supported the notion of punishing employers who knowingly employed illegal aliens, and opposed amnesty for illegal aliens. In 1983 in the first major poll on black and Hispanic opinion on immigration, it was confirmed that both groups solidly favored employer sanctions and better efforts to control the border. But polling questions on broad public interest issues such as "Do you favor disarmament or rigorous collection of taxes?" can often elicit a heavy favorable response that may be difficult to translate into solid backing for specific action. Favorable public opinion needed to be brought together with effective and committed congressional leadership. The departure of the indifferent James Eastland from control of the Senate Judiciary Committee, and the accession of the energetic Senator Simpson to the leadership of the Senate Subcommittee on Immigration and Refugees was the needed catalyst.

Final passage of a reform package in 1986 was a legislative miracle—but one long in coming. Employer sanctions have been pending since the major immigration law revisions of 1952. In that year Congress stiffened penalties for harboring or transporting illegal aliens. However, at the insistence of Texas growers, Congress added the notorious Texas Proviso: "However, the normal incidents of employment shall not be deemed harboring."[2] So it was an offense to illegally enter the United States, but it was perfectly legal for an employer to knowingly employ illegal aliens, a situation once described by Congressman Romano Mazzoli (D-KY) as "Hanging up a 'help wanted' sign at the Border."[3]

For some years after 1952, illegal immigration was held in check by massive and sometimes indiscriminate deportations combined with an agricultural migrant labor or bracero program with Mexico from 1942 to 1965. The 1965 legal immigration reforms left the problem of illegal immigration untouched, and may have contributed to it by opening new migration channels to nationalities previously excluded. In 1965, when the bracero program ended, the Immigration and Naturalization Service (INS) apprehended a mere 110,371 illegal aliens. From 1965 illegal immigration continually increased, and began to involve much more than temporary Mexican entrants in the fields. Mexican illegals, increasingly joined by Central Americans and Caribbean citizens migrated illegally and entered urban occupations in increasing numbers.

Many explanations have been offered for the sharp climb in the 1960s: 1) the end of the bracero agreement in 1965, which simply drove much of what had been legal labor migration underground; 2) the after effects of the twenty-two-year bracero agreement, which created networks and migration channels that gave illegal immigration a momentum of its own; 3) the explosive growth of the Mexican labor force stemming from the post-war surge in population, with rising education levels nurturing new expectations; 4) the demand for cheap flexible labor in the booming U.S. economy of the Vietnam era, when unemployment averaged below 5 percent between 1965 and 1974.

Changes inside Mexico in the 1960s were also beginning to push out more migrants. While the Mexican economy was registering impressive growth rates statistically through much of the 1960s and 1970s—over 6 percent per year—Mexico's agriculture was beginning to stagnate, driving more small farmers and day workers into the cities or to the United States in search of work. The Mexican labor force in the 1970s was growing at an unprecedented 4.4 percent annually, but the poor education and training of millions of new job seekers limited their utility to Mexico's changing economy. For much of its impressive growth numbers, Mexico's industrial sector was relying increasingly on capital-intensive processes: Jobs added did not match the growth of output. The labor force grew at about 750,000 a year, but new jobs approached only 400,000 a year through most of the 1970s. The gap between new workers and jobs was proportionally even greater in troubled Central America.[4]

As the problem became more apparent, as employers exploiting illegals began taking over entire local occupations, organized labor began pushing for "employer sanctions," prohibition of knowing employment of illegal aliens. Similar laws were already being adopted by such states as California in 1971, but effective enforcement was blocked or slowed by litigation and weak compliance machinery.

Led by liberal Democrats, the U.S. House of Representatives resoundingly passed employer sanctions in 1972 and again in 1973, each time only to have the notion killed in the Senate at the behest of agricultural growers reliant on an illegal labor force, showing the same political clout that had helped push through the Texas Proviso in 1952.

In 1977 President Jimmy Carter introduced an immigration reform package that would impose employer sanctions, provide a limited amnesty and improve border security. This moderate consensus plan featuring employer sanctions and amnesty was not seriously entertained by Congress. But a new complicating factor surfaced: Young Hispanic activists reared in the confrontational politics of the 1960s began gaining leadership, particularly in the Mexican-American Legal Defense and Education Fund (MALDEF) and the League of United Latin American Citizens (LULAC). These activists opted to oppose employer sanctions as inherently discriminatory. Some Hispanic spokesmen professed support in principle for ending illegal immigration, but claimed the remedies lay in better enforcement of labor standards or overcoming the social and economic "push" factors in Mexico. In their opposition, Hispanic groups found themselves aligned with growers, small and medium business interests, civil rights proponents and the Congressional Black Caucus. While black advocacy groups such as NAACP and the Urban League feared the job displacement of blacks and supported sanctions, black congressmen unanimously opposed them. Shaping the black legislative position was the desire for solidarity with Hispanic colleagues, the heavy Hispanic presence in many of their districts, the suspicion of any measures smacking of discrimination, and the growing influence of West Indian immigrants in black leadership and political life. (Duke University Sociologist Jacquelyne Jackson examines black attitudes toward immigration later in this volume.)

Confused by opposition from both left and right, Congress in 1978 set up the Select Commission on Immigration and Refugee Policy (SCIRP), headed by civil rights leader the Reverend Theodore Hesburgh, president of Notre Dame University. The Commission was charged with investigating the facts and making policy recommendations on immigration reform. The Select Commission reported in 1981, recommending employer sanctions. After conducting its own fact-finding, the new Reagan Administration in 1981 endorsed many of the Commission's findings on enforcement. Commission Member Senator Alan Simpson became chair of the Senate Immigration Subcommittee, and after consultations in late 1981 introduced a bipartisan bill with House Immigration Subcommittee Chair Romano Mazzoli in early 1982.

Where before the conservative Senate had killed reform, now it was the liberal House which failed to act. The Senate followed Simpson, but House leaders thwarted consideration until the final days of the 97th Congress in 1982, when the bill was crushed under the weight of three hundred amendments. Bills were reintroduced in the 98th Congress, but again stalled at the desk of House Speaker Thomas P. (Tip) O'Neill (D-MA). After some public outcry, O'Neill relented, the bill passed the House in late 1984, but then foundered in conference committee. The major impasse was the states' insistence on full reimbursement of social services costs.

RECOVERY FROM APPARENT DEATH IN 1986

As the 99th Congress drew to a close in the autumn of 1986, immigration reform again seemed doomed. The formidable challenge of reconciling so many conflicting interests to pass new legislation led one congressman to christen immigration reform "a metaphor for governance." So passage of IRCA, literally at the last minute, was a stunning legislative surprise. Everyone had some disappointment with one or more of its provisions, but there was widespread relief that Congress had finally acted.

Since 1981 there had been no greater impediment to immigration reform legislation than the Democratic leadership of the House of Representatives. Throughout the 99th Congress Speaker O'Neill and House Judiciary Committee Chairman Peter W. Rodino (D-NJ) either stalled the initiative or did nothing to advance it. O'Neill in particular was wary of permitting his party to take the lead on the bill. Since the early 1970s Rodino had been a leading proponent of employer sanctions, but with the passage of time the New Jersey congressman appeared to have become more interested in legalization. This shift in emphasis may have been a response to the growing number of Hispanic and other minority immigrants in his Newark district and to the same forces that influenced many liberal congressmen to oppose the legislation altogether. Joining liberals in opposition were a growing immigrant aid and service-provider constituency, important business interests, libertarian and civil liberties groups.

House Majority Leader Jim Wright (D-TX), while privately expressing no opposition to immigration reform (he would ultimately vote for the bill), nonetheless expressed concern over the prospect that the proposed legislation would be considered during a congressional election year. It is unclear whether Wright was under pressure from Texas business leaders opposed to the bill. The slow progress prompted the pro-reform *New York Times* to alert the nation in an editorial that O'Neill, Wright and Rodino knew "how to strangle a bill without leaving fingerprints."

Just as many members of Congress danced a minuet around the bill, so too did the White House gingerly address the proposed legislation. Aware of President Reagan's influence and popularity, Senator Simpson repeatedly sought his endorsement of the immigration reform package. At one point Chairman Rodino declared that the bill had received little meaningful support, "least of all" from the President. Reagan met with Senator Simpson to assert his support for the legislation in March 1986, but he never brought to bear the full measure of his influence on its behalf. Instead, the President repeatedly sent out mixed signals to Congress and the nation. Congressman Mazzoli reported that the Administration did not "conspiciously" lobby House members prior to a key House vote on the bill. Even after Simpson-Rodino had been passed by both houses of Congress, the President, unsure of how his signing of the legislation might affect the prospects of Republican candidates in a host of state and congressional races—the all-important control of the Senate hung in the balance—withheld comment on IRCA immediately after its passage and signed it only after the November 4th Congressional elections. The signing ceremony itself on November 6 was distinctly low-key.

The President's ambivalence toward the legislation reflected the countervailing pressures of different allied interest groups. Prominent Republicans such as former President Gerald Ford and ex-Attorney General William French Smith supported immigration reform along with a majority of the American people, according to polls. Yet, influential business interests in the border states strongly opposed it. Proponents of deregulation opposed it as a paperwork burden or an interference with the free market.

A COMPROMISE FOR AGRICULTURE

Any bill seeking to capture the support of both the western growers and the Farm Workers Union, which carried the AFL-CIO's proxy on farm labor issues, needed to provide for an adequate supply of agricultural workers and at the same time reduce their exploitability. On June 10 Congressman Charles Schumer of New York announced that he, along with Congressmen Howard Berman and Leon Panetta, both fellow Democrats from California, had crafted a plan designed to reconcile these conflicting interests. The original Schumer proposal called for the Attorney General to grant permanent resident status to any illegal alien who could prove that he had been working in agriculture in the United States for at least twenty full days from May 1, 1985 to May 1, 1986, while those aliens arriving in subsequent years to work on farms would also be eligible for permanent resident status. Congressman Rodino supported the plan only after seeing that his expressed desire to have a bill with no agricultural provision at all—a "lean and clean" bill—would not materialize. As the plan gathered momentum, other interest groups that had rigidly opposed the bill began to rethink their position.

Among the revisionists were five members of the Hispanic Caucus who bolted and voted yes when the bill came to a final vote. This was significant: the solid opposition of the Hispanic Caucus to the bill had often been cited by other congressmen and interest groups as a justification for their own opposition, which though often based on economics, benefitted from the added patina of loftier motives. Veteran Hispanic representatives such as Henry Gonzalez (D-TX), Edward Roybal (D-CA), Kika de la Garza (D-TX), Matthew Martinez (D-CA) and Robert Garcia (D-NY) continued to claim that employer sanctions would discriminate against Hispanic Americans and other "foreign-looking" persons, a rallying point for Hispanic Caucus opposition in 1982 and 1984.

Other explanations have been offered for the last-minute passage of the bill. Many congressmen believed the immigration issues would not be addressed again for several years if the bill were defeated. Others invoked the prospect of draconian measures if the immigration situation worsened appreciably. A feeling persisted that Congress would pass an employer sanctions provision sooner or later and that opposition to the entire bill based on this provision alone was inadvisable if other concessions could be obtained in return. In addition, the large vote against the legalization amendment strongly implied that the "amnesty" provision contained in the final bill represented the most liberal one that could be passed. A stern resistance to this provision had been growing among the voters since 1984.

The attitudes of the Hispanic American rank-and-file cannot be overlooked in seeking to explain the switch by some Hispanic congressmen. Congressman Esteban Torres (D-CA) and Albert Bustamante (D-TX), chairman and vice-chairman of the Hispanic Caucus respectively, stated that the status quo was hurting their Hispanic constituents, especially those long resident in the country; these Hispanics were telling their representatives to vote for immigration reform. Bustamante also expressed fear of a backlash against all Hispanics if the immigration status quo were permitted to continue. Congressman Richardson and Ortiz expressed more interest in the legalization provision of the bill, but they nonetheless voted for the entire package. (A more detailed analysis of Hispanic political views appears in Richard Estrada's article "Hispanic Americans: The Debased Coin of Citizenship" later in this volume.)

A number of black congressmen also switched to support for the bill, thus damaging a solid black-Hispanic alliance against the bill that had existed since the 1970s. Opposition to Simpson-Mazzoli had been a key feature of the Jesse Jackson campaign to build a "Rainbow Coalition" behind his bid for the Democratic presidential nomination in 1984, just as it had been the position of the eventual Democratic presidential nominee, former Vice President Walter Mondale. But polls had also repeatedly shown that black respondents were concerned about the negative impact of illegal immigration upon the black community, particularly job competition.

As adjournment neared, time, or the lack of it, became the engine that powered the bill. Congressmembers despaired of finishing quickly for an early return to their districts for last-minute re-election campaigning. On September 26, however, the House failed to agree on the "rule" for debating the bill, and Chairman Rodino lost no time in declaring the legislation dead. Senator Simpson seemed to agree, and said he was not prepared to manage it in the Senate in a future session. Eulogies for the bill appeared in the media.

Nevertheless, a handful of representatives felt a workable compromise could yet be struck. Led by Brooklyn liberal Charles Schumer of the Immigration Subcommittee, they worked closely with grower and labor interests for several days. On October 14 a House-Senate conference committee reached agreement on a compromise.[5] On October 15, the House voted for the bill, 238-173. On October 17, the Senate followed suit by 63-24.

Almost exactly two years before, in October 1984, a similar conference committee had been unable to resolve the issue of federal reimbursement for costs attendant with extending social services to aliens, and the bill had died.

An analysis of the vote shows that support for and opposition to the bill did not break on liberal/conservative lines. Senate liberals Howard Metzenbaum (D-OH) and Paul Simon (D-IL) backed it, as did conservative Lloyd Bentsen (D-TX), moderate Republican Charles Mathias (MD) and, of course, Wyoming's Republican conservative Alan Simpson. In the House, four young liberal Hispanic Democrats supported the legislation along with conservative Republic Congressmen such as House Minority Leader Robert Michel (IL), Dan Lungren (CA) and Trent Lott (MS).

Lawmakers agreed that the revival of the bill was miraculous, a testimonial to the power of public opinion and constituent pressure, effective lobbying and congressional perseverance. Moreover, given the mounting frustration the bill had produced since 1982, it may have been that no one really wanted to assume responsibility for killing yet another version of immigration reform.

A clear factor in the bill's passage was wide recognition that the problem was getting worse. The INS apprehended 1.7 million illegal aliens in federal fiscal year 1986, a 30 percent increase over 1985's record figure, and a 70 percent increase over 1982. The deterioration of Mexico's economy, a visible increase in illegal immigrants in most portions of the country, growing concern over the smuggling of drugs, and a helpless feeling of rising stress along the southern border all worked to force a decision.

What the vote confirmed is that illegal immigration is no longer seen as a border or agricultural problem, but has become a problem affecting every corner of the nation. Such propositions as: illegal aliens only take jobs Americans won't do, or that cheap, flexible labor is good for the economy had lost some of their power to convince.

HOW EFFECTIVE IS THE NEW LAW?

The law could be the turning point in regaining control of the borders, or it could usher in vast additional waves of immigration. The price paid for employer sanctions—turning off the "job-magnet" that draws illegal aliens here—was a controversial amnesty provision that grants permanent residence to illegal aliens who have resided continuously in the United States since January 1, 1982, and the Schumer farm worker legalization plan that gives eventual citizenship to those who worked for ninety days in the fields in 1986. Growers displayed their clout by winning other concessions: the right to "replenish" the supply of agricultural workers by further foreign recruiting, an expansion of temporary agricultural worker entries; a two-year moratorium on enforcement of employer sanctions in agriculture; and a further curb on INS operations against field workers.

The law also builds in elaborate machinery to monitor and act against employment discrimination stemming from the new law, including procedures for congressional review of employer sanctions after three years and their repeal if warranted.

Employer sanctions can work, but only if enforced. Congress authorized a 50 percent increase for immigration enforcement, but in early 1987 it faced the task of appropriating the funds to pay for it. Most of the funding for the legalization of up to 3.9 million aliens who entered before 1982 will be gained through fees. ($175 per adult applicant and $50 per child to a maximum of $420 per family.) Genuine concern over deficits will work in favor of those who seek to starve enforcement of the law.

Most employers will probably comply voluntarily with the hiring prohibition, but the potential for profit in exploiting labor will tempt some to defy it. To enter the culture of our country as a respected law, the sanctions must be rigorously enforced from inception. But just the enactment of employer sanctions has been a statement with symbolic deterrent effect. Removed from the law is a debilitating contradiction that made it illegal for aliens to enter unbidden, but permitted employers to hire them without penalty. The laws send a message to all Americans and to major migration source countries of a greater will to bar illegal immigration. The deterrent value of this message played a part in the 25 to 30 percent decline in illegal border crossings noted by the INS in the early months of 1987.

SCIRP concluded by a narrow vote in 1981 that, for both fairness and effectiveness, employer sanctions should be accompanied by some form of secure but nonintrusive identification system. A secure system would remove any subjective factor from an employer's hiring decision, and would forestall document fraud. The law disavows any authority for a national ID card, but calls for study and experimentation. Early in 1987 the Social Security Administration (SSA) began a pilot call-in program to verify the validity of social security numbers. The current law's reliance on existing civil documents for identification is a major weakness, an invitation to fraud and counterfeiting and a troublesome paperwork burden on employers.

Legalization, too, provides both a policy dilemma and a potential administrative tangle. Any alien who can prove continuous unlawful residency in the United States from January 1, 1982 is eligible to apply for temporary resident status, and eighteen months later, for adjustment to permanent resident status. After five years in permanent resident status, the legalized alien can apply for citizenship.

Illegal-alien amnesties in other developed countries have experienced low participation rates. But the United States, being large and diverse, with relatively open borders, and a large illegal population, may experience the opposite problem. If the amnesty is strictly applied as intended in the law, problems could be minimal. If administrative funding is denied to INS, or if the amnesty system is jammed by frivolous or massive litigation, the legalization could become a mere rubber stamp for masses of questionable applications.

Clearly, it is in the country's best interests that the law be strictly enforced.

NOTES

1. *Plyler v. Doe*, 50 U.S.L.W. 4650 (1982).
2. 8 USC 1324.
3. Unpublished remarks at an address April 8, 1987, Washington, D.C.
4. Leon Bouvier and David Simcox, *Many Hands, Few Jobs: Population, Unemployment and Emigration in Mexico and the Caribbean*, CIS 2 (1986).
5. Almost exactly two years before, in October 1984, a similar conference committee had been unable to resolve the issue of federal reimbursement for costs attendant with extending social services to aliens, and the bill had died.

Legal Immigration:
The Ceiling That Does Not Seal

Legal immigration in the 1980s maintained the steady long-term growth trend it has displayed since 1966, when the current system of uniform, non-racial country ceilings went into effect. Total legal immigration reached 601,700 in 1986, 86 percent above the 1966 figure of 323,000. Legal immigration between 1980 and 1986 has brought an average of 570,000 newcomers each year (see Tables 1.1 and 1.2).

In the twenty years since the 1965 reforms, that opened the United States to sizable immigration from Asia, Asian countries have supplanted European nations as the chief sources of legal immigration. During the 1980s Asian countries annually supplied 48.4 percent of legal immigration; Latin America was the second largest source, with 32 percent. Europe and Canada in the 1981–1985 period accounted for 14.8 percent of total immigration, continuing a long-term decline (see Table 1.3).

The steady growth in the numbers of close family members entitled to enter the United States exempt from the law's numerical ceiling of 270,000 underlies much of the continuing rise in total numbers as well as the increases in the Asian and Latin American components. In 1986, 334,740 were admitted outside the ceiling; nearly two-thirds of these were spouses, fiances, parents or children of U.S. citizens and 31 percent were refugees and asylees. (Table 1.4)

Immigration of immediate relatives exempt from the ceiling doubled between 1966 and 1986, with about 60 percent of the total annually going to spouses and fiances. The INS has estimated that as many as 30 percent of all marriages involving an immigration benefit are fraudulent. INS produced these figures in support of additional legal barriers against marriage fraud legislation which was adopted at the close of the 99th Congress.[1]

Looking ahead, unless there are changes in the apportionment of immigration, overall legal immigration is likely to continue its vigorous growth, fed by the prospective rise of entries of close relatives of U.S. citizens exempt from the ceiling. The list of visa registrants waiting abroad for one of the 270,000 annual ceiling spaces continues to show regular growth. It is concentrated among those countries already supplying most of the immigrants, and is heavily weighted to family preferences. (See Table 1.5) The cumulative process of chain migration steadily enlarges the pool of potential immigrants with family preferences or who are exempt from the ceiling while increasingly concentrating the immigrants selected among those countries that have the largest pools of recent immigrants in the United States.

The waiting list for visas to immigrate to the United States grows steadily, reaching 2 million in January 1987, an increase of 7.8 percent over 1986. Much

14

Table 1.1

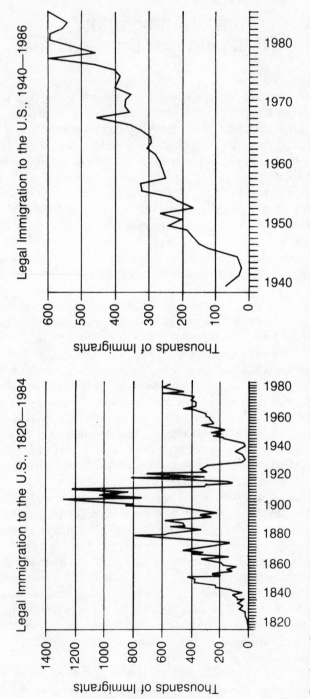

Legal Immigration to the U.S., 1940—1986

Legal Immigration to the U.S., 1820—1984

Thousands of Immigrants

Reprinted from Leon F. Bouvier and Robert Gardner, "Immigration to the U.S.: The Unfinished Story," *Population Bulletin*, Vol. 41, No. 4, November 1986, by permission of Population Reference Bureau, Inc., Washington, D.C.

Table 1.2   Legal immigration to the United States 1820–1986.
(From 1820 to 1867, figures represent alien passengers arrived;
from 1868 to 1891 and 1895 to 1897, Immigrant aliens arrived;
from 1892 to 1894 and to the present time, Immigrant aliens
admitted.)

Year	Number of Persons	Year	Number of Persons
1820–1986	53,122,058	1850	369,980
1820	8,385	1851–1860	2,598,214
		1851	379,466
1821–1830	143,439	1852	371,603
1821	9,127	1853	368,645
1822	6,911	1854	427,833
1823	6,354	1855	200,877
1824	7,912	1856	200,436
1825	10,199	1857	251,306
1826	10,837	1858	123,126
1827	18,875	1859	121,282
1828	27,382	1860	153,640
1829	22,520		
1830	23,322	1861–1870	2,314,824
		1861	91,918
1831–1840	599,125	1862	91,985
1831	22,633	1863	176,282
1832	60,482	1864	193,418
1833	58,640	1865	248,120
1834	65,365	1866	318,568
1835	45,374	1867	315,722
1836	76,242	1868	138,840
1837	79,340	1869	352,768
1838	38,914	1870	387,203
1839	68,069		
1840	84,066	1871–1880	2,812,191
		1871	321,350
1841–1850	1,713,251	1872	404,806
1841	80,289	1873	459,803
1842	104,565	1874	313,339
1843	52,496	1875	227,498
1844	78,615	1876	169,986
1845	114,371	1877	141,857
1846	154,416	1878	138,469
1847	234,968	1879	177,826
1848	226,527	1880	457,257
1849	297,024		*(continued)*

Table 1.2 Continued

Year	Number of Persons	Year	Number of Persons
1881–1890	5,246,613	1916	298,826
1881	669,431	1917	295,403
1882	788,992	1918	110,618
1883	603,322	1919	141,132
1884	518,592	1920	430,001
1885	395,346		
1886	334,203	1921–1930	4,107,209
1887	490,109	1921	805,228
1888	546,889	1922	309,556
1889	444,427	1923	522,919
1890	455,302	1924	706,896
		1925	294,314
1891–1900	3,687,564	1926	304,488
1891	560,319	1927	335,175
1892	579,663	1928	307,255
1893	439,730	1929	279,678
1894	285,631	1930	241,700
1895	258,536		
1896	343,267	1931–1940	528,431
1897	230,832	1931	97,139
1898	229,299	1932	35,576
1899	311,715	1933	23,068
1900	448,572	1934	29,470
		1935	34,956
1901–1910	8,795,386	1936	36,329
1901	487,918	1937	50,244
1902	648,743	1938	67,895
1903	857,046	1939	82,998
1904	812,870	1940	70,756
1905	1,026,499		
1906	1,100,735	1941–1950	1,035,039
1907	1,285,349	1941	51,776
1908	782,870	1942	28,781
1909	751,786	1943	23,725
1910	1,041,570	1944	28,551
		1945	38,119
1911–1920	5,735,811	1946	108,721
1911	878,587	1947	147,292
1912	838,172	1948	170,570
1913	1,197,892	1949	188,317
1914	1,218,480	1950	249,187
1915	326,700		*(continued)*

Table 1.2 Continued

Year	Number of Persons	Year	Number of Persons
1951–1960	2,515,479	1971–1980	4,493,314
1951	205,717	1971	370,478
1952	265,520	1972	384,685
1953	170,434	1973	400,063
1954	208,177	1974	394,861
1955	237,790	1975	386,194
1956	321,625	1976	398,613[a]
1957	326,867	1976, TQ	103,676[b]
1958	253,265	1977	462,315
1959	260,686	1978	601,442
1960	265,398	1979	460,348
		1980	530,639
1961–1970	3,321,677		
1961	271,344	1981–1986	2,864,406
1962	283,763	1981	596,600
1963	306,260	1982	594,131
1964	292,248	1983	559,763
1965	296,697	1984	543,903
1966	323,040	1985	570,009
1967	361,972	1986	601,700
1968	454,448		
1969	358,579		
1970	373,326		

[a]The INS Changed its format for computing statistical data from a fiscal year ending June 30 to one ending September 30.
[b]The "transitional quarter" covers the period July through September 1976.
Source: Immigration and Naturalization Service.

Table 1.3   Where U.S. legal immigrants have come from

Country of Birth	Period of Immigration			
	1981–85	1971–80	1961–70	1951–60
Europe and Canada	14.8%	20.4%	45.9%	70.2%
Latin America and Caribbean	32.0%	40.3%	39.0%	22.5%
Asia	48.4%	36.4%	13.4%	6.2%
Other	4.8%	2.8%	1.8%	1.1%

Source: Immigration and Naturalization Service.

Table 1.4 Legal immigration by category in the 1980s

Immigration Category	1980	1981	1982	1983	1984	1985	1986	Percent Change 1980–86
TOTAL	530.6	596.6	594.1	559.8	543.9	570.0	601.7	+13%
Subject to ceiling	289.5	330.4	259.7	269.2	262.0	264.2	267.0	− 8%
Family references	229.1	226.9	206.1	213.5	212.3	213.3	212.9	− 7%
Occupational preferences (and dependents)	44.4	44.3	51.2	55.5	49.5	50.9	53.6	+21%
Other	16.0	59.2	2.5	0.3	0.2	0.1	0.4	−98%
Exempt from ceiling	241.2	266.2	334.4	290.6	281.9	305.8	334.7	+39%
Immediate relatives of U.S. citizens	151.1	147.1	163.0	172.0	177.8	204.4	223.5	+39%
Spouses & fiances	96.9	92.0	104.2	112.7	116.6	129.8	137.6	+42%
Parents	33.7	34.2	35.4	34.7	34.6	39.0	45.2	+34%
Children	20.6	21.0	23.3	24.6	26.6	35.6	40.6	+97%
Refugees & asylees	88.1	107.6	156.6	102.7	92.1	95.0	104.4	+19%
Other	8.2	7.1	9.9	10.5	7.0	6.9	6.9	−16%

Source: Immigration and Naturalization Service Statistical Annual.

of the growth in numbers of active visa registrants occurs in those countries that are the major senders of immigrants because of the workings of family reunification. The waiting list is only a partial indicator of actual visa demand, since only those intending immigrants with an approved petition from a relative or sponsor in the United States are formally registered.

The following charts show the growth in registration in 1986–1987 by immigration preference categories and by the top twelve immigration source countries. Immigration preference categories under current law are: (First) unmarried sons and daughters of U.S. citizens—20 percent; (Second) spouses and unmarried children of permanent resident aliens—26 percent; (Third) professionals or persons of exceptional ability in sciences and arts—10 percent; (Fourth) married sons and daughters of the U.S. citizens—10 percent; (Fifth) brothers and sisters of U.S. citizens over age 21—24 percent; (Sixth) skilled and unskilled workers in short supply—10 percent.

Some indication of the possible size and chief sources of future immigration of close family members can be glimpsed in the current trends in naturalization.

Table 1.5   Legal immigration by preference category during the late 1980s

Category	January 1985 Totals	January 1986 Totals	January 1987 Totals
First	9,848	11,764	15,800
Second	320,698	346,728	367,465
Third	27,588	28,460	31,442
Fourth	81,382	95,851	107,021
Fifth	1,142,107	1,210,656	1,305,119
Sixth	49,915	48,740	58,442
Nonpreference	146,383	161,276	167,387
Total	1,777,931	1,903,475	2,052,676

Growth of waiting lists for U.S. visas in major immigration source countries.

January 1986		January 1987	
Mexico	366,820	Mexico	381,530
Philippines	362,695	Philippines	380,244
India	142,734	India	176,966
Korea	134,778	Korea	139,984
China (mainland born)	112,843	Vietnam	109,054
Vietnam	97,539	China (mainland born)	100,246
China (Taiwan born)	69,397	China (Taiwan born)	79,572
Jamaica	52,909	Jamaica	49,162
Dominican Republic	37,332	Dominican Republic	44,422
Guyana	37,133	Hong Kong	37,127
Hong Kong	34,059	Guyana	35,282
Pakistan	30,234	Pakistan	34,974

Source: Visa Office, Department of State.

Total naturalizations increased some 157,938 in 1980 to an all-time high of more than 280,000 in 1986. Increasing naturalizations mean more citizens entitled to petition for the immigration of their close family members exempt from the ceiling or to confer a preference on non-immediate family members who are subject to the 270,000 ceiling.

During the 1980s an estimated 2.2 million adult immigrants will be naturalized, acquiring the right to petition for the admission of close family members. The legalization and special farm worker admissions programs enacted in 1986 will begin conferring permanent resident status on two to four million formerly illegal aliens or temporary workers by 1989. When those legalized become permanent legal residents (after eighteen months of temporary resident status) they will have the right to confer second preference for their wives and unmarried children. By late 1993 the amnestied aliens will begin becoming eligible for citizenship and the right to bring in spouses or fiances, children and parents outside the ceiling. The immigrants with the highest propensity to seek prompt naturalization are in most cases from those countries with highest immigration demand. Mexico, which has had a relatively low rate of naturalization for the many immigrants it sends, sharply increased its naturalizations in 1985. The trends are apparent in a listing of the leading countries of origin of immigrants and newly naturalized citizens between 1983 and 1985 (see Table 1.6).

Table 1.6   Naturalization of immigrants according to country of origin 1983–1985

Country	Naturalization (1000s)			Legal Immigrants (1000s)		
	1983	1984	1985	1983	1984	1985
Philippines	22.1	23.4	28.9	41.5	42.7	47.9
Mexico	12.5	14.5	23.0	59.0	57.5	61.0
Korea	12.8	14.0	16.8	33.3	33.0	35.2
Vietnam	11.1	11.0	18.0	37.5	37.2	31.8
China	9.3	9.1	11.7	25.7	23.3	24.7
India	8.8	8.2	10.3	24.4	24.9	26.0
Cuba	10.3	15.7	10.4	8.9	10.5	20.3
USSR	2.8	7.6	8.9	5.2	6.0	3.5
UK (includes Hong Kong)	7.8	7.6	8.8	14.8	13.9	13.4
Dominican Republic	4.8	4.8	5.8	22.0	23.1	23.7
Jamaica	3.9	4.6	4.8	19.5	19.8	18.9
Greece	3.4	3.0	4.2	2.9	2.8	2.5
Colombia	2.9	3.5	4.1	9.6	11.0	11.9

Source: Immigration and Naturalization Service.

WHERE IMMIGRANTS SETTLED

The preferred destination of about one of every six legal immigrants in the 1980s was the New York City metropolitan area. California was easily the preferred state, with 28 percent of the new permanent residents in 1986 planning to reside there, concentrating in Los Angeles, Orange County, San Francisco-Oakland and San Jose. Immigration per capita was highest in 1985 in Jersey City, which had 13.5 immigrants per thousand inhabitants. Other communities popular among new immigrants were Chicago, Washington, D.C. and the Miami-Hialeah area.

Preferences for settlement varied with the nationality of immigrant groups. Caribbean and Colombian immigrants showed a marked preference for the New York-New Jersey area, except for Cubans who maintained a preference for Miami followed by New Jersey. Mexican and Central American newcomers favored the Los Angeles area and other major California cities, though Houston, Dallas, El Paso and the Texas border area were selected by a large number of Mexicans, along with Chicago. Asian immigrants, though somewhat more dispersed, also showed a preference for settlement in California cities. Studies of 1980 Census figures suggest illegal immigrants tend to cluster in the same areas of heavy legal alien settlement with California estimated to be host to almost half of the illegal alien population of 2.2 million identified by the Census Bureau in 1980.

The legal immigration for the 1980s confirms the trend in recent years of steady growth of the share of total immigration used for the family reunification category in 1985. The figures since 1977 have shown a steady decline in the percentage of immigrants other than refugees entering without family preferences from 32 percent in 1977 to about 9 percent in 1986. But even this percentage includes dependents of immigrants selected for skills or special job abilities.

Table 1.7 Top ten urban areas of settlement for 1986 immigrants

City	Number (1000s)	1986 Immigrants (per 1000 population)
1. New York City	94.8	11.4
2. Los Angeles/Long Beach	62.8	8.0
3. Chicago	21.7	3.5
4. Miami/Hialeah	20.8	12.1
5. San Francisco	16.4	10.8
6. Washington, D.C.	15.8	4.7
7. Anaheim/Santa Ana, CA	13.3	6.4
8. San Jose, CA	12.3	9.0
9. Oakland	10.1	5.4
10. Boston	9.7	3.4

Source: Immigration and Naturalization Service.

Immigrants actually skills-tested represented 4 percent of total legal immigration in 1985. The priorities categories for refugee admissions also give some preference for resettlement to those who have family connections in the United States.

Twenty years of emphasis on family reunification have increased the percentages of aged parents and children and reduced the average skills of recent cohorts of legal immigrants. In 1985, 56 percent were minor children and retired persons. The snow-balling effect of chain migration is likely to produce continuing displacement of prospective skilled immigrants by the very young, the aging and the less skilled family members. This trend toward lower skilled immigrants may be reinforced by the legalization proffered by the 1986 immigration reforms. Illegal aliens tend to be less skilled, and legalization will make larger numbers of them a permanent feature of the labor market. They in turn, on achieving permanent resident status and ultimately citizenship, confer immigration preference on family members in Latin American countries.[2]

NOTES

1. House Subcommittee on Immigration, Refugees and International Law, *Oversight Hearing on the Immigration and Naturalization Service*, 99th Cong., 2nd sess., GPO, 1987.

2. Barry Chiswick, "The Declining Quality of Immigrants," *New York Times*, December 21, 1986.

Illegal Immigration: Counting the Shadow Population

Maintaining a trend that quickened in the mid-1970s, illegal immigration by all available indicators spiraled further in the first half of the 1980s. Apprehensions at the Mexican border (98 percent Mexican nationals), arrests of deportable aliens, deportations and visa overstays all showed an upward trend.[1]

Clandestine entry ("entry without inspection") remained the predominant mode of illegal presence in the United States, accounting for an estimated 60 percent of all illegal entries. Overstays of non-immigrant visas (visa abuse) and the use of fraudulent documents or statements accounted for most of the remaining 40 percent.

Fueling the rise in illegal immigration are the rapid growth of the working age population and the accompanying economic stagnation in many Third World countries, including major migrant source countries in the Caribbean basin. With economic decline in source countries has often come political unrest, further boosting out-migration. Some non-oil producing Caribbean and Central American sending countries such as El Salvador, Jamaica, Nicaragua and Haiti, which have long been heavy suppliers of migrants to the United States, suffered devastating economic slumps as early as the mid-1970s, accelerating an already sizable outflow of their people northward. Mexico experienced an economic slowdown in 1976, but recovered rapidly by 1978, posting some of its best economic growth figures ever between 1978 and 1981 because of strong demand for its oil exports at peak prices. The Mexican government invested its new found wealth heavily in social welfare programs, food and energy subsidies and rapid capital-intensive industrialization.

Apprehensions surpassed one million a year for the first time in 1977. During Mexico's 1978–1981 economic boom, during which the Mexican government claimed to have created an average of over 750,000 jobs a year, apprehensions of Mexicans at the border leveled off but remained high at just below one million yearly in 1980–1982. The figures resumed climbing sharply in 1983 after Mexico's 1982 economic collapse under the weight of nearly $100 billion in international debt and plummeting oil prices. With unemployment or underemployment afflicting 50 percent of Mexico's labor force, apprehensions reached nearly 1.7 million in 1986 (Table 1.8), a 24 percent increase over 1985 and a jump of 71 percent over 1981.

The continued sizable outflow of Mexican migrants during the 1979–1982 period when Mexico was enjoying an unprecedented economic boom with rapid job creation, and boasting a strong peso relative to the dollar raises questions about the assumed relationship between economic opportunity in the sending country and out-migration. The trend suggests that Mexican migration to the

Table 1.8   Illegal immigrants apprehended 1965–1986

Period	Number of Apprehended Illegal Immigrants
1965	110,371
1966	138,520
1967	161,608
1968	212,057
1969	283,557
1970	345,353
1971	420,126
1972	505,949
1973	655,968
1974	788,145
1975	756,819
1976	866,433
1977	1,033,427
1978	1,047,687
1979	1,069,400
1980	910,361
1981	975,780
1982	970,000
1983	1,251,000
1984	1,246,000
1985	1,348,000
1986	1,670,000

Source: U.S. Department of Justice Annual Reports of the Immigration and Naturalization Service.

United States has acquired a dynamic of its own not always entirely propelled by economic forces. Family migration customs, ethnic recruiting networks, desire for the urban lifestyle, family reunification and thirst for U.S.-quality social services have become powerful non-economic migration incentives in Mexico and throughout the Caribbean basin.[2] (David Simcox examines the social and economic forces driving migration from Mexico and Central America later in this volume.)

INS apprehension and deportation figures and studies of visa abuse indicate that the Central American countries, particularly El Salvador, have become the major source of illegal immigrants after Mexico. Rapid population growth and the diminishing availability of land began spurring heavy emigration from El Salvador and to a lesser extent Guatemala in the late 1960s. The State Department in 1985 estimated illegal immigration from El Salvador and Guatemala in 1977 at 25,000 and 15,000 a year respectively; with 350,000 Salvadorans already in the United States illegally by 1980 when civil strife in that country began spurring the outflow.

A mid-1985 survey of the Urban Institute placed the total of Central American immigrants in the country (including legal immigrants) at 750,000 to 1.3 million (see Table 1.9).

HOW MANY ILLEGAL IMMIGRANTS?

Estimates abound of the number of illegal immigrants in the United States. They are often exercises in speculation based on fragmentary data applying elusive definitions. Of the many estimates made since the middle 1970s of the total population of illegals and its annual rate of growth, none has emerged as a clear consensus figure, though Census Bureau 1980 findings are now most frequently used as a point of departure. All approaches share certain weaknesses in data, definition or method:

—The clandestine nature of the illegal alien population makes it extremely difficult to count. Illegal aliens themselves prefer it that way.

—Just who is an illegal alien? Should the count be limited to the relatively permanent population or "settlers" who entered originally without inspection or overstayed nonimmigrant visas? This group has the greatest labor market and demographic effect. Or should the count include all forms of irregular status, however technical and brief: The illegal alien who has applied to change his status and has received work authorization; the holder of a valid nonimmigrant visa who is violating his status by working; or the possessor of a valid border crossing card who enters the United States each day for a few hours of illegal work.

—Duration of stay and time of year: Since some illegal immigration is seasonal, estimates will vary with the time of year and the migration cycle. Those illegal aliens that are settled are more likely to be counted in the census. Two other possible counting methods would yield higher figures:
  a) A count of the number of persons in irregular status on "any given day" would embrace the seasonal worker, the commuter and those in brief periods out of status;
  b) A count of the number of illegal alien "person-years" would aggregate all periods spent illegally by seasonals and commuters, along with settlers, into "full-time equivalents" as a measure of impact on labor markets and public services.

—Difficulty in adjusting estimates of the illegal population to account for the numbers leaving that population through death, emigration or attainment of legal status.

—INS apprehension statistics, which is one of the few empirical indicators available may point at best to general trends in migration flow, but they

Table 1.9 Central American migrants in the U.S., by place of current residence and country of origin

Place of Current Residence (Includes Entire Metropolitan Area)	El Salvador	Guatemala	Nicaragua	Honduras	Total
Estimated US total	500,000–850,000	100,000–200,000	40,000–80,000	50,000–100,000	750,000–1.3 million
Los Angeles	250,000–350,000	60,000–80,000	N/A	15,000	325,000–500,000
San Francisco	60,000–100,000	5,000–10,000	N/A	N/A	75,000–125,000
Phoenix/Tucson[a]	4,000–8,000	1,000–3,000	N/A	N/A	5,000–15,000
Texas[b]					
Dallas	10,000–15,000				
Other		10,000–40,000	5,000–15,000	N/A	100,000–200,000
Rio Grande Valley	15,000–25,000				
Houston[c]	30,000–60,000				
Chicago	20,000–40,000	10,000–20,000	N/A	N/A	30,000–60,000
New Orleans[c]	20,000–40,000	1,000–5,000	N/A	30,000–60,000	50,000–100,000
New York City	60,000–100,000	10,000–30,000	N/A	N/A	75,000–150,000
Washington, D.C.	80,000–150,000	10,000–30,000	N/A	N/A	100,000–200,000
Miami[d]	5,000–15,000	1,000–2,000	30,000–45,000	N/A	35,000–60,000

Source: Ruggles et. al., "Profile of the Central American Population in the United States," The Urban Institute, June 1985.
Notes: N/A indicates no estimate is available. In most cases, however, population is believed to be relatively small.
[a]Includes 1,000–2,000 migrants in rural Arizona.
[b]Estimates for Texas are particularly difficult to make because immigrants in Texas are not generally part of an established community, but rather are in transit to other areas.
[c]City not included in survey; estimates based on reports from those in other areas and documentary sources.
[d]Includes some migrants in rural Florida.

are far from precise indicators of degrees of change. Changes in the scale and direction of the INS enforcement effort, such as by increasing or decreasing forces on the Mexican border, or by technological changes, can significantly affect raw numbers. INS apprehensions decreased significantly in 1980 in large part because of manpower diverted to management of Mariel entrants and temporary restraints on enforcement to permit an accurante 1980 census count. Apprehensions increased from 1.3 million to over 1.6 million between 1985 and 1986. Clearly the flow of migrants was up, but the number must be discounted to some extent for increases in the Border Patrol and better detection equipment beginning in 1985.

The following is a selection of better known studies or assessments that illustrate the range of estimates of the illegal population in the 1970s and 1980s (see Table 1.10).

In the absence of a precise consensus number, estimates of public officials, journalists and observers are most frequently based on Bureau of Census findings.

Census Bureau researchers initially concluded from 1980 census data that just over two million illegal aliens were counted in the 1980 Census. Census specialists subsequently concluded that the illegal population had been "undercounted" and estimated it at 2.5 to 4 million in 1980, with an estimated annual growth of 100,000 to 300,000—see below. Of that base number, census found that:[3]

—54.9 percent of illegal aliens came from Mexico (2 million to 2.8 million in 1986) and 22 percent from other Latin American countries;
—49 percent were between fifteen and twenty-nine;
—53.2 percent were males;
—49.8 percent were in California, with New York (11.4); Texas (9.1), and Illinois (6.6) the next most important states of illegal residence;
—32.0 of all illegals lived in the greater Los Angeles-Long Beach area.
—Other major cities of illegal alien residence were:

	Percent
New York	10.3
Chicago	6.0
Orange County, CA	3.8
Washington, D.C.	3.4
San Francisco	2.7
Houston	2.5
San Diego	2.4
Miami	2.4

The absence of a clear consensus number, understandable in view of the weak data, has not been allowed to paralyze policymaking, as the enactment of 1986

Table 1.10 Some estimates of illegal alien population in the United States since 1973

Source and Date		Date of Estimate	Estimate (millions)
Lancaster and Scheuren (1978)	For limited group. Matched samples of IRS tax returns, social security contributions and beneficiary data with Current Population Survey of 1973. Considered by some to be soundest study methodologically. Range of 67% confidence limits: 2.9–5.7 million.	1973	3.9 (age 18–44)
Lesko Associates (1975)	Comparison and average of estimates by immigration specialists using Delphi techniques of iterative informed guesswork. About half of estimate thought to be in labor force. Included an estimated 5.2 million illegals of Mexican-origin.	1975	8.2
U.S. Immigration Service (1974) (1976)	(a) 1974/75 report to House Subcommittee on Legal and Monetary Affairs. (b) Survey by immigration districts based on rough estimates by experienced immigration border patrol and local law enforcement officers. 1976 survey estimated 3.7–3.9 illegals in U.S. labor force.	1975	(a) 4–12 (b) 5.5–6.0
Corwin, Arthur (Author on Mexican Immigration)	Based on broad survey of estimates by immigration and foreign consular officers, immigrant groups, and on alleged 1980 census undercounts, and congressional hearings. Estimated 4.5–5.5 million illegals in U.S. labor force, depending on season.	1981	8.6–11.3

Source	Description	Year	Estimate (millions)
Select Commission on Immigration and Refugee Policy (SCIRP) (1981)	Speculative estimate by Census Bureau demographers of illegal alien population done for the SCIRP based on assessment of other studies.	1978	3.5–6.0
U.S. Inter-Agency Task Force on Immigration and Refugee Policy (1981)	Review of SCIRP findings and agency estimates.	1981	6.25
Dr. Charles Keeley, Population Specialist (1981)	Estimates for SCIRP.	1981	4.0
Congressional Budget Office	Study of the Costs of Legalization.	1983	4.5
National Research Council	Study by Demographer Dr. Kenneth Hill, based on six existing studies of illegal population.	1985	1.5–3.5
U.S. Census Bureau	Using 1980 Census data, Census Bureau demographer Jeffrey Passell placed undocumented population in 1980 at 2.5 to 4 million, with annual growth of 100,000 to 300,000. Extrapolation from 1980 figures would yield a population of 3.1 to 5.8 million in 1986.	1985	2.5–4.0 (in 1980)
Immigration and Naturalization Service	For purposes of planning legalization, INS estimated total illegal population of 6 million, 3.9 million of which came before January 1, 1982. INS estimates annual increase of 500,000.	1986	6.0
Daniel R. Vining University of Pennsylvania	Study of international air passenger arrivals and departure statistics 1959–1978. Found net migration to the U.S. by air alone was 500,000–700,000 a year. Concluded that addition of net migration by sea and land would easily bring total annual net migration above 800,000. No estimate made of total population of illegals.	1979	

immigration reforms shows. Unknowns confront policymakers as well when they deal with Soviet intentions, extent of tax fraud and the amount of drugs being smuggled into the United States. But they recognize the dangers of withholding action while awaiting definitive data that may never come. Clearly the upsurge in the last twenty years of apprehensions, deportations, document fraud and admissions of non-immigrants leaves little doubt that the volume of illegal immigration has been rising. Vernon Briggs, professor of economics at Cornell and authority on immigration, stated concisely the reasoning that came to be accepted by legislators in 1986 in enacting reforms:

> The character of the entire process precludes the possibility that an actual tabulation of persons who immigrate illegally will ever be made . . . we should realize this is also the case with most of the other social problems of the day and in all these other vital areas of public concern the lack of data has not precluded the adoption of major policy initiatives to meet perceived needs. Furthermore, it makes little conceptual difference whether the number of illegal immigrants in the nation is three million, six million, nine million or twelve million. The precise number is irrelevant if we concede the number is substantial and is increasing annually.[4]

NOTES

1. *Statistical Yearbooks of the INS 1975–1985*.

2. Leon Bouvier and David E. Simcox, *Many Hands, Few Jobs: Population, Unemployment and Emigration in Mexico and the Caribbean*, CIS 2 (1986).

3. Bureau of the Census, Statement of Dr. Jeffrey S. Pessel before the U.S. House of Representatives Subcommittee on Immigration, Refugees and International Law, September 11, 1985.

4. Vernon Briggs, *Immigration Policy and the American Labor Force* (Baltimore: Johns Hopkins University Press, 1984), p. 137.

Immigration and the Labor Market: The Repeal of Supply and Demand

By the conservative estimates of the Census Bureau, as many as 2.1 million illegal aliens entered the United States to settle in the period of 1980–1986. More expansive estimates place the number at about 3.5 million in the first seven years of the decade joining nearly four million legal aliens who settled here in the same period. Three-quarters of all legal immigrants and refugees settled in seven states, with just under half going to California and New York. Most available data indicates a similar clustering of illegal aliens.

The participation rate of adult legal aliens in the U.S. labor force at least matched that of the general population; local studies suggest that illegal aliens participated at a rate higher than the national rate, but aggregate data is scarce. Illegal aliens tended to concentrate, as did the legal aliens, in the labor markets of major cities: Los Angeles, New York, Miami, Chicago, San Francisco, Washington, D.C. and Orange County, California. Evaluations of the labor market effects of immigrants, particularly in areas of concentration on the wages, working conditions and employment prospects of the previously settled population burgeoned as an industry in the past decade. The 1980s were replete with conflicting studies, claims and counterclaims, and speculation whether the influx of aliens displaced American and legal resident workers or depressed their wages and working conditions.

A historical premise of American immigration law is that immigrants can have a major effect on local and national labor markets. The law bars the entry of aliens to perform skilled or unskilled labor unless is is shown that sufficient qualified workers are not available at the time and place where the alien seeks to work or that the wages and working conditions of U.S. workers similarly employed will not be affected.[1] Even temporary foreign workers can be imported legally only if determined by the Department of Labor through a rigorous process that the foreign workers will not adversely affect the wages, working conditions or employment prospects of American workers in the area.

In fact, however, the law demands no test of labor market effects for the 95 percent of immigrants entering the United States with family preferences or as refugees, or as dependents. The long-standing assumptions about the effect of immigration on the labor market—present in varying forms in U.S. immigration laws since the 1885 prohibitions against foreign contract labor—are now under question as never before. As immigration has grown in the 1970s so has the voice and influence of a school of academic "immigration expansionists," social scientists and economists whose claims involve varying combinations of the following assertions:

31

—Immigrants create more jobs than they take through their entrepreneurial drive and the creative synergism of their interaction with each other and with the host society;

—Their effective demand for goods and services spurs business activity and the creation of new jobs;

—Added to the labor supply, immigrants increase national wealth and improve everyone's real wages by helping decrease overall production costs.

—Immigrants, with higher employment rates and lower dependency levels, pay more in taxes than they receive in public services.

—Most immigrants complement the existing work force rather than substitute for it, thus increasing productivity without significant displacement, ultimately creating more jobs for everybody.

—If immigrants are not complementary and there is displacement of American workers, it is at worst a transitory phenomenon; those displaced ultimately benefit with better paying jobs as a result of the long-term economic growth stimulated by immigration;

—The labor market is "segmented;" most immigrants take jobs in the "secondary" labor market, handling dirty, dangerous, low wage jobs spurned by native workers.

Advancing one or more variants of these positions are social scientists such as Julian Simon, Wayne Cornelius, Michael Piore, Frank Bean, Mexican scholar Jorge Bustamante and Beryl Sprinkel, Chairman of the Council of Economic Advisors (CEA).

But many other economists, social scientists and opinion leaders are loathe to repeal so readily the law of supply and demand as it applies to labor. Most Americans as well assume that immigrants entering a loose labor market can cause job displacement and force down wage levels. Poll after poll shows most white, black citizen respondents—and in some polls, Hispanic citizens—see a connection between immigration and loss of jobs.

During the last decade there has been no lack of serious scholarship supporting this traditional point of view. Few studies, however, now hold that the number of jobs in the economy is fixed, with immigrants and native workers in a zero-sum competition for them. Such scholars as Michael Wachter, Philip Martin, Vernon Briggs, Joseph Nalven, former Labor Secretary Ray Marshall and Donald Huddle have developed fresh analytical approaches showing that displacement of native workers is rarely one-for-one and that it occurs in immigrant-impacted labor markets through more subtle, gradual processes involving such previously overlooked factors as employer preconceptions about the desirability of different ethnic groups as workers; the displacing effects of ethnic recruiting networks; and the dampening effect of abundant and cheap flexible labor on upgrading and mechanizing jobs of native workers. (Philip Martin and Ray Marshall discuss these factors in job displacement in detail in their articles later in this volume.)

California scholar Richard Mines, for example, denies that displacement as such occurs, defining the process instead as employer "abandonment" of veteran citizen workers for recent immigrants as a way of holding down labor costs, recruiting the new immigrants through ethnic networks and intermediaries. Mines notes that although nationwide immigration may have created more jobs than it is removing, this often does not help individual "abandoned" workers, who often have low skills.

The running debate over displacement has suffered from some lack of precision over long term versus short term labor market consequences of immigrant flows, or over aggregate versus regional and local effects, and from a tendency to discount short term and local displacement.

A 1987 study by George Borjas and Marta Tienda, whose past studies have tended to discount immigration's displacing effects, illustrates how overall labor displacement that may be negligible when measured at the national level can be of serious dimensions among highly impacted regions or sub-groups of the labor force. Borjas and Tienda note that one group of workers that is strongly and negatively affected by an increased supply of new immigrants is the stock of foreign workers already in the United States, adding data showing that "a 10 percent increase in the number of new immigrants reduces the average wage of resident foreign workers by 2 to 9 percent."[2]

Even the recent findings of U.S. government authorities lack unanimity on the issue of displacement. A 1986 report of the CEA affirms the expansionist view that displacement is negligible or of brief duration. While conceding that some initial displacement of native workers may occur when immigrants are substitute rather than complements for the existing work force, the CEA sees the net effect of the increased labor supply is to raise the aggregate income of the native-born population. The CEA report claims:

> Studies that take a broad view of the labor market have found no significant evidence of unemployment among native-born workers attributable to immigration. Any direct effects of immigration on domestic employment have either been too small to measure or have been quickly dissipated with job mobility.[3]

But the U.S. Department of Labor has consistently taken a less benign view of the labor market effects, at least of illegal immigration. In 1983 testimony in support of the Simpson-Mazzoli legislation, Deputy Undersecretary of Labor Robert Searby cited labor economist Michael Wachter's "cautious calculation" of a 20 to 30 percent displaced out of the labor force altogether, becoming "discouraged workers" who no longer show up in the unemployment statistics. Noting the high cost to the taxpayers, Searby added that by Wachter's conservative estimate 500,000 illegal alien workers entering the United States each year will increase unemployment by 100,000 annually with a cost to the treasury for benefits of $700 million a year.[4]

A 1986 review by the General Accounting Office (GAO) of fifty-one studies of the labor market effects of illegal aliens led to a qualified finding that illegal alien workers appear to displace native or legal workers. Noting the past tendency of many studies to focus on Mexican illegal workers in the southwest and on agriculture, GAO states that ". . . illegal aliens have been found in all major categories of industry and occupation, although many are in agriculture and manufacturing. This suggests that the possibility of widespread displacement is greater than formerly believed."[5]

Perhaps the most exhaustive and oft-cited study in the 1980s of the impact of heavy immigration on a regional labor market was The Urban Institute's 1985 publication, *The Fourth Wave: California's Newest Immigrants* by Thomas Muller and Thomas Espenshade.[6] The study documents the considerable costs as well as the benefits to California of the arrival in the decade of the 1970s of more than 1.8 million immigrants, nearly a million of them Mexican and more than 60 percent illegal. The authors conclude that the heavy immigration stimulated economic growth and significant job creation in the region. Of the 645,000 new jobs created in Los Angeles County during the 1970s, two-thirds of them went to immigrants.

The presence of Mexican immigrants in southern California did not cause unemployment to rise among non-Hispanic minorities, particularly blacks, according to the Urban Institute. It finds that Mexican immigrant workers typically do not compete directly with native workers for the same jobs. Rather, the availability of plentiful low-wage labor contributed to an economic expansion during the 1970s—often in industries that were stagnant elsewhere in the United States—that resulted in the creation of 52,000 manufacturing jobs that would have not otherwise existed.

DISPLACEMENT OF BLACKS

Urban Institute cites statistics showing higher-than-average job participation rates and lower-than-average unemployment rates for blacks as evidence job displacement was negligible and that blacks were "not harmed" by the heavy migration.

From 1970 until 1983 there continued to be a net in-migration of blacks to California, though the volume of their in-migration slowed appreciably as the period progressed. (At the same time, there was a net out-migration of whites and settled Hispanics.) More than 90 percent of the net increase in black employment was in white-collar fields. Noting that only a small percentage of Mexican immigrants received white-collar jobs, the Urban Institute concludes that job "complementarity" rather than competition exists between blacks and Mexicans in Los Angeles County. But the Urban Institute's report does acknowledge that blacks and immigrants do compete for jobs in food services, retail trade, building maintenance and hotel service. It expects this competition to continue, concluding that some blacks and others who are unable to improve their occupational status will find fewer job opportunities as a result of immigration.

The decade's net out-migration of whites and settled Mexicans and Hispanics from California, together with the declining net in-migration of blacks, is a major demographic and labor market trend highlighted by the Urban Institute which points to a high level of indirect displacement or "abandonment" of less-skilled American workers. Worth noting here is that black in-migration exceeded out-migration by 102 percent from 1970 to 1975, and then declined to 62 percent from 1975 to 1980, and to 11 percent from 1980 to 1983. If the pattern continues, net black migration from California will exceed in-migration in the next decade, with the out-migrants largely from less-skilled categories. The Urban Institute notes that Mexican immigration may have become a "substitute" for internal in-migration.

Rising out-migration of blue-collar Americans may help explain why job displacement was not reflected in the area's relatively favorable employment and labor market participation rates and why "complementarity" has seemingly developed between black and Mexican workers. California appears to be exporting—or no longer importing from the other forty-nine states—the less-skilled workers that most directly compete with Mexican workers. Thus, those who become unemployed or "discouraged workers" often appear in the statistics of other states. California's labor market practices may affect unemployment in the other forty-nine states in two ways difficult to document statistically: (1) the number of unemployed California has exported; and (2) the unemployed in other states who remain in that status because of potential employment opportunities foreclosed in California.

COMPLEMENTARITY OR INDIRECT DISPLACEMENT

Blacks are well represented nationally in such production fields as metal and plastic working, textile and apparel machine operation, and fabrication and assembly, occupations that registered significant growth in Los Angeles during the 1970s. However, new black migrants to California in the 1970s have mainly gone into white-collar occupations, while the black presence in such low-wage industries as apparel has declined.

As Urban Institute sees it, increasing numbers of blacks are no longer competing for the less-skilled industrial jobs in southern California. "Complementarity" may well be the blacks' acceptance of the realities of the southern California industrial labor market. Heavy immigration has produced declining wages and standards in those occupations in which blacks are well-represented nationally. Ethnic network job recruitment and non-English-speaking work forces are conditions that have combined with declining wages to help shut lower-skilled black and other American workers out of major sectors of industry.

The Urban Institute's report acknowledges only briefly that ". . . some blacks (and others) who are unable to improve their occupational status or move to areas with less immigrant competition will find fewer job opportunities as a result of immigration."[7] If the Urban Institute had developed this finding further, it might have given a more troubling picture of immigration's effect on black workers. Abandonment of U.S.-born black workers by employers in certain industries and their substitution by lower-wage Mexicans is common, though one-for-one job displacement may not be apparent. The process can be seen in the Urban Institute's figures showing that 24,000 immigrants have taken jobs in Los Angeles' service economy, while that sector itself was losing 7,400 jobs.

In sum, the impressive economic performance of southern California has benefitted the black workers possessing white-collar skills, a group that would enjoy favorable employment prospects in many other U.S. labor markets. But southern California in recent years has become less congenial to low-skilled black residents; and less inviting to those blue-collar blacks in declining industries elsewhere in the United States that, absent heavy immigration, would have found migration to California a more attractive option.

NEEDED: A NEW CONCEPT OF DISPLACEMENT

The widely differing interpretations among analysts of what constitutes job displacement is again pointed up acutely in these reports, suggesting that new analytical concepts of labor market effects of immigration are needed. Obscured by favorable local unemployment statistics, job upgrading for some native workers, and the subtle effects of out-migration is the core fact that, despite the creation of an impressive 645,000 new jobs, fewer American workers had jobs in Los Angeles County with heavy immigration than would have had them in the absence of immigration. Clearly there has been a "net displacement," though indirect, gradual and definitely not one-for-one.

NOTES

1. Immigration and Nationality Act, Sec. 212(a)(14).
2. George J. Borjas and Marta Tienda, "The Economic Consequences of Immigration," *Science*, February 6, 1987.
3. *Annual Report of the Council of Economic Advisers*, "The Economic Effects of Immigration," (Chapter 7); GPO (1986), p. 18.
4. U.S. Congress House Committee on Judiciary. Subcommittee on Immigration and Refugees. *Hearings on the Immigration Reform and Control Act of 1983*. 98th Cong., 1st sess. (1983), pp. 1214–1216.
5. General Accounting Office, "Limited Research Suggests Illegal Aliens May Displace Native Workers," (GAO/PEMD-86-9BR), April 1986.
6. Thomas Muller and Thomas J. Espenshade, *The Fourth Wave: California's Newest Immigrants* (Washington, D.C.: The Urban Institute Press, 1985).
7. *The Fourth Wave*, p. 102.

Immigration and Social Welfare: The Notion of the Non-Revenue Consuming Taxpayer

Along with the growth of public unease in the 1980s about uncontrolled immigration, came heightened concern over illegal aliens' use of social welfare programs and more skepticism about the proposition that the illegal alien was a non-revenue consuming taxpayer. These changing attitudes sprang in part from greater press and media coverage of the complaints of state and local governments about rising support costs for illegal aliens,[1] and from some studies showing that illegal aliens' welfare and services use was rising proportionally. Also increasingly apparent in the last decade is that the illegal alien population was no longer predominantly young male seasonal workers; it now included far larger numbers of women and children, and thus was more inclined to permanent settlement and greater use of social programs.[2]

These trends found confirmation in immigration-intensive areas in the rising numbers of infants born to illegal alien mothers in public hospitals, rapidly increasing school enrollments of illegal alien children,[3] and the higher incidence of welfare dependency among the settled illegal population in areas of high concentration.[4] Another conditioning factor for public opinion was the shifting perception, because of the rapid inflation and high unemployment of the late 1970s and declining international competitiveness, that the United States was changing from a society of abundance to one of limits. Cost control and budget cutting in government programs regained respectability. Control of welfare fraud won new backing as the amounts to be allocated to the legally entitled shrank.

In the early 1970s Congress began enacting laws to bar illegal aliens from social welfare programs, beginning in 1972 by limiting Supplemental Security Income (SSI) to citizens and legal residents. By 1981 undocumented illegal aliens had been excluded from most major federal assistance programs: Aid to Families with Dependent Children (AFDC), food stamps, unemployment compensation and student financial loan programs.[5] Congress also denied federal housing assistance to illegal aliens in 1981 but the implementing regulations have never been issued (see below). Illegals were barred by regulation rather than by statute from Medicaid, a prohibition overturned by the New York Federal District Court in 1986.

Rising evidence that legal aliens, who are screened for their likelihood of becoming "public charges," have also been major users of social welfare programs prompted Congress to enact further restrictions for new legal residents in the 1970s. The so-called "deeming" amendments to social welfare legislation sought to insure that the resources of the sponsors of legal immigrants were applied first in meeting the legal immigrant social welfare needs during the first three years of his residency in the United States.[6]

But while Congress was moving toward tighter limits on the access of aliens to welfare, the courts, advancing the doctrine of "communitarianism," have been expanding the eligibility of illegal aliens for the publicly funded benefits of American society.[7] Many of the landmark cases were initiated by civil rights and ethnic advocacies, or by legal aid attorneys. Some state governments, in their efforts to comply with federal guidelines limiting access of illegal aliens, have found themselves challenged by huge class action suits. Or the states themselves have supported litigation to liberalize federal entitlements to ease the burden of illegals on purely state resources.

A milestone of the 1980s was the Supreme Court's 1982 decision in *Doe v. Plyler*[8] that required the states to provide free public education to children of illegal aliens. The Supreme Court decision overturned a Texas law that required school districts either to deny enrollment to children of illegals or to charge tuition.

Some other trend setting cases in recent years are:

—A 1986 consent order by the State of Texas and 1984 Oregon court ruling granting unemployment benefits to illegal aliens who are not permitted to work under the terms of the immigration law. (*Ibarra v. Texas Unemployment Commission*—E.D. Final Consent Decree Filed, August 22, 1986.)
—A decision by the Alameda County (California) Superior Court in July 1985 requiring the enrollment of illegal aliens in taxpayer supported colleges and universities at tuition rates paid by other California residents.
—A decision by the federal court of the Eastern District of New York in July 1986 holding that illegal aliens are entitled to Medicaid. (*Lewis v. Gross*, No. 79-C-1740—E.D.N.Y., July 14, 1986.)
—In 1985 a New York federal court prohibited an effort by federal agencies to correct a previous mistaken policy that gave Supplemental Security Income to illegal aliens. Other courts have begun using this decision to expand the categories of aliens eligible for various forms of welfare. (*Berger v. Hechler*, 771 F.2d 1556 (2nd Cir. 1985)

The stop and start efforts of the federal government since 1980 to deny illegal aliens housing assistance illustrate the tough judicial and political gamut such proposals must run. Congress voted in 1981 to prohibit any financial assistance under U.S. housing legislation for the benefit of aliens who were not lawful residents.[9] The Department of Housing and Urban Development was blocked from issuing implementing regulations first, by landlords and then by Congress itself in 1983. HUD again prepared to issue the final rules in mid-1986 which would require the removal of illegal aliens from public housing or subsidy rolls or require them to pay for use of the properties at market rates.

No comprehensive national studies of illegal alien use of public housing exist. In April 1986 Val Coleman, press spokesman for the New York City Housing

Authority, called the number of illegals among the Authority's 600,000 tenants "substantial." Testifying at the Los Angeles City Council Committee on Public Health and Human Resources in April 1986, Los Angeles public housing officials said illegal aliens could be living in 30 percent to 100 percent of southern California's 500,000 units. The New York City Bar Association, which has opposed the HUD regulation, has cited estimates that 35 percent to 40 percent of tenants in public housing—four to five million people—could have a live-in illegal alien in the family and thereby be subject to removal.

Protest from ethnic and immigrant interest groups was immediate and strident. Charging that the proposed regulations were inhumane, these groups claimed that they discriminated against Hispanics. They argued that it was common for immigrant families receiving housing assistance to have members who were legal residents or citizens along with illegals. They also warned that many foreign born housing clients who are in fact entitled would have difficulty documenting their status.

At the insistence of sympathetic congressmen, HUD delayed enactment of the rule on two occasions in 1986. Congress in October 1986 attached a restriction to HUD's appropriation barring appropriated funds for implementing the proposed 1986 alien rule. Meanwhile a federal court in California also issued an injunction against implementation of the rule, and in November 1986 extended the injunction to a nationwide class of public housing tenants. (*Yoland-Donnelly Tenant Assoc. v. Pierce*, No. Civ. S-86-0846 MLS—E.D. Cal., November 14, 1986)

The November 1986 immigration reform law includes subsidized and public housing among federal entitlement programs requiring a verification of legal resident status under INS's Systematic Alien Verification for Entitlements program (SAVE). Congress applied SAVE to public housing benefits in the Housing and Community Development Act passed in late 1987. In the same legislation, however, Congress gave local housing agencies the discretionary authority (a) to continue housing assistance to illegal aliens to avoid dividing families; and (b) to continue assisting ineligible aliens for up to three years while they seek affordable housing elsewhere.

Until made mandatory for the states by the immigration reform law, (giving an exception to those states that can show it is redundant or not cost effective), SAVE had been a voluntary program of the INS for screening public assistance rolls in cooperation with the state governments. It began as a pilot program in 1984. The SAVE program provides the participating states with direct automated access to INS computer files for verifying the status of aliens who apply for such benefits as unemployment insurance, food stamps, student grants and loans, and housing subsidies. If the computer check on an alien applicant indicates a discrepancy, or if no record is found, a follow-up investigation is done by mail. In 1985 INS claimed the SAVE system helped U.S. agencies avoid more than $100 million in payments to ineligible welfare applicants. INS estimates that

SAVE could ultimately yield more than $2.8 billion in savings on unjustified welfare claims. The agency bases this estimate on the assumption that about six million people or 2.5 percent of the population are illegal aliens and their share of the $112 billion paid out in 1980 for programs vulnerable to alien claims would be $2.8 billion.[10]

Not surprisingly, the SAVE program is less than popular with immigrant interests and service providers and even with some state and local governments. Concerned local and state governments have felt that the program draws too much political fire, or will result in costly lawsuits. Some claim the program is not cost effective since there are not many illegal aliens in their states, that it would be redundant, or that the removal of those aliens from federal assistance rolls would leave their judisdictions to bear more of the aid burden. Civil rights and ethnic groups charge that the savings claimed are exaggerated, that the INS data is not accurate enough, or that it will be used by INS to round up thousands of illegal aliens. Because of the many objections, the legislation mandating SAVE for the states permits concerned federal agencies to waive it under certain conditions and requires a GAO study of it before large scale implementation can begin, which must be no later than October 1, 1988. By January, 1988 more than twenty states had entered the SAVE program. Under the new law, SAVE will screen aliens applying for: 1) Aid to Families with Dependent Children; 2) Medicaid; 3) unemployment compensation; 4) food stamps; 5) possibly, housing assistance, and 6) educational loans and grants.

A doctrine increasingly asserted by immigrant interest groups and legal aid to justify social welfare benefits for illegals is PRUCOL—Permanent Resident Alien Under Color of Law. Those interpreting PRUCOL liberally claim that an illegal immigrant is in the United States lawfully unless the INS is actively deporting him. In recent years the term "permanently residing under color of law" has been expanded by courts to apply to nearly any alien seeking some form of immigration benefit from within the country. If present judicial trends continue, the term may soon expand to include virtually any alien who has made an application that could lead to permanent residence, suspension of deportation, asylum or withholding of deportation. Also likely to be included under the expanded concept would be aliens in the process of pursuing any form of administrative or judicial relief or those who have extended voluntary departure.[11]

In Congress's debates on an immigration amnesty since 1981, the prospect of massive social welfare costs for millions of newly legalized aliens was a major stumbling block. Who should pay those costs was a critical issue, with the House-Senate conference in 1984 foundering on the issue of appropriate reimbursement to the States. The 1986 reforms deny eligibility to newly legalized "temporary resident aliens" for five years to AFDC, Medicaid and food stamps, though allowing plentiful exceptions for such categories as Cuban-Haitian entrants, the aged, blind and disabled, those eligible for emergency services and pregnant women. Amnestied aliens remain eligible for an array of other federally-funded programs including SSI, school feeding, job training and educational assistance. They are entitled as well to general assistance in most states. In deference to growers, Congress made legalized special agricultural workers immediately eligible for food stamps. Congress softened the "who pays?" issue by providing $1 billion a year for four years, beginning in 1988, to state and local governments for legalization costs.

Having long asserted that illegal aliens make minimal use of social assistance programs, immigrant advocacies have fought hard and with considerable success for a "flexible" interpretation of the reform law's "public charge" provision as grounds for denying legalization. They have contended that social insurance programs such as unemployment compensation should not be considered cash assistance. A central argument has been that past receipt of public cash assistance of itself should not bar an applicant from legalization, but is relevant only to the extent it may reflect on the individual's future self-sufficiency. INS accepted this concept of "prospective" application of the public charge test in its final regulations in April, 1987, and excluded a wide range of assistance "in-kind" (e.g. housing and food stamps) or "work-related" compensation, such as unemployment compensation.[12]

Immigration status and entitlements to social services are likely to remain contentious and tangled policy issues. An increasingly economy-minded Congress, and an executive branch moved by interests of economy and ideology, will persist in efforts to keep social welfare costs down and turn off the magnet of illegal immigration. Many important state governments share these objectives.

But a diverse coalition of interests with varied motives will continue pushing to make social services more, not less, accessible. Animated by the spirit of "communitarianism," the Courts remain quick to interpret any ambiguity over entitlements in social welfare legislation in favor of the immigrant. Troublesome questions of due process, equal protection and privacy rights will be no less persuasive in the courts' approach. Adding to the complexity of the task of the courts and the executive branch rule makers has been the proliferation of "mixed families," requiring solomonic decisions to safeguard the entitlements of children of U.S. citizens in households in which there are alien parents or siblings who are illegal or otherwise ineligible.

Lobbying and litigating for the newcomer with increasing elan and effectiveness is a congeries of ethnic group, immigrant and civil rights advocacies, service providers and legal services, often funded by public revenues or by wealthy foundations such as Ford. The powerful lobby of colleges and universities also resists encroachment on the entitlements to educational aid and other forms of assistance to foreign students, an increasingly important market with U.S. citizen enrollments trending downward. Receding but still important is the clientelist tendency within the federal and state welfare and service agencies.

Nurtured in the period of budgetary bounty of the 1960s and early 1970s, the clientelists see their mission of meeting basic human needs as overriding such technical concerns as immigration status that might disqualify potential clients.

Effective enforcement of employer sanctions will, if anything, intensify the debate, as the safety net of public assistance will become vital to many illegal immigrants barred from the workplace. Finally, confronting Congress and the states amid the day-to-day tactical forays is the enduring task of determining policies that both economize and dissuade without doing violence to U.S. society's broader self-interest in preserving minimum standards of public education and health for all.

NOTES

1. See "Surge of Illegal Aliens Taxes Southwest Towns' Resources," *New York Times*, March 9, 1986.

2. Roger Conner, *Breaking Down the Barriers: The Changing Relationship Between Illegal Immigration and Welfare*, Federation for American Immigration Reform, Washington, D.C., September, 1982.

3. *The Fourth Wave*, Chapter 5, pp. 88–90.

4. Maurice D. Van Arsdol, Jr., et al., *Non-Apprehended and Apprehended Undocumented Residents in the Los Angeles Labor Market: An Exploratory Study* (Los Angeles: University of Southern California, Department of Sociology, May 1979).

5. Congressional Research Service, *Alien Eligibility Requirements for Major Federal Assistance Programs* (Report No. 83-209 EPW), Washington, D.C., 1983.

6. Ibid.

7. Peter Schuck, "Immigration Law and the Problem of Community" in Nathan Glazer, ed., *Clamor at the Gates* (San Francisco: Institute for Contemporary Studies, 1985).

8. 457 U.S. 202 (1982).

9. 42 U.S.C. 1426a.

10. Immigration and Naturalization Service, "SAVE Program," Washington, D.C., 1986.

11. Dan Stein and Steven Zanowic, "Permanent Resident Alien Under Color of Law: The Opening Door to Alien Entitlement Eligibility," *Georgetown Immigration Law Review*, Vol. 1, No. 2, Spring 1986.

12. Letter of February 13, 1987 from Congressman Peter Rodino, Chairman of the House Judiciary Committee, to Attorney General Edwin Meese; and 8 CFR 245a.1 and 245a.2.

Immigration Enforcement: A Finger in the Sluice Gates

Twenty years of rising educational levels and enhanced transport and communications have spurred worldwide mobility. Legal immigration has doubled from less than 300,000 in 1965 to 600,000 in 1986. Admissions of non-immigrant visitors have jumped fivefold since 1965—to more than ten million a year. The number of persons, foreign and American, entering the United States and subject to inspection now approaches a third of a billion yearly. Petitions for naturalization have nearly tripled in that two-decade period. The number of foreign students in the United States has increased four times since 1965. And perhaps what is the most resource-demanding phenomenon of all, apprehensions of illegal aliens, a mere 110,000 in 1965, by 1986 had increased fifteen times over.[1]

The budget of the Immigration and Naturalization Service (INS) increased eight times over in the two decades since 1965—from 73 million to 576 million in 1985. These seemingly impressive figures obscure the fact that INS, relative to the spiraling growth of its work load and responsibilities, has suffered a resource drought during most of that period that devastated its ability to meet its requirements under the law. At the same time, the period since 1965 has been one of rapid and often dizzying changes in American immigration laws and attitudes and, more importantly, in social, economic and demographic changes beyond our border over which the United States has little control.

The 1970s and early 1980s brought still more resource-intensive obligations to the INS. Beginning in 1975 the agency had to manage huge new flows of refugees, administering the selection and admission of some one million between 1975 and 1985. The 1980 refugee legislation, which liberalized the definition of asylum, sparked an explosion of asylum claims among migrants from troubled countries in the early 1980s which burdened the agency with more than 160,000 cases for adjudication. Discounted for inflation, the INS budget had increased two and one half times in the twenty years following 1965, but the agency share of the overall federal budget had actually fallen by almost 2 percent in that period. Personnel growth also lagged behind work load and new responsibilities.

INS authorized positions have grown from 7,000 in 1965 to 11,600 in 1986, an increase of two-thirds, but much of that growth did not begin until the late 1970s. At the beginning of the decade, with the accession of the Reagan administration, the INS was the ''stepchild'' of the U.S. government. Understaffed, underfunded, missing permanent leadership through part of the Carter administration, lacking a natural constituency among the American people and bereft of high-level interest or support either in the Justice Department or in the Executive Branch, the agency was struggling to conduct a monstrous law enforcement task with its overall mission clouded by ambivalent legislation and court decisions and congressional dithering.

Table 1.11   INS Resources, 1977–1987 (in millions)

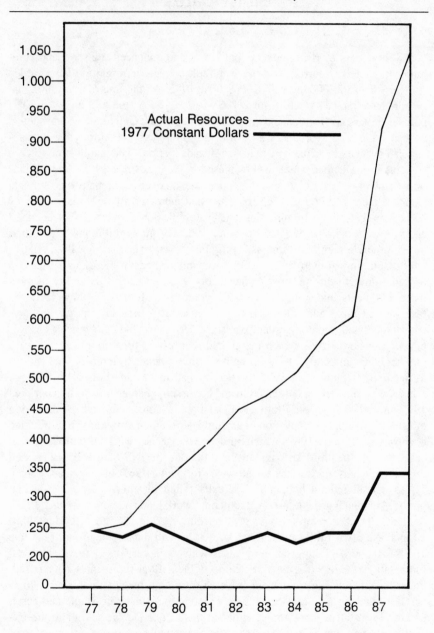

Table 1.12 INS resources, 1969–1988

Year	1969	1970	1971	1972	1973	1974	1975	1976	1977	1978
Authorized INS positions	6,703	6,920	7,230	7,682	7,682	7,982	8,082	8,832	9,473	10,071
Total INS budget (in 1000's)	89,726	105,798	121,940	130,944	137,184	155,186	181,320	214,609	244,615	254,490
Authorized border patrol positions	1,690	1,782	1,859	2,030	2,005	2,122	2,236	2,434	2,427	2,480
Total apprehensions	283,557	345,353	420,126	505,949	655,968	788,145	766,600	875,915	1,042,215	1,057,977

Year	1979	1980	1981	1982	1983	1984	1985	1986	1987	1988*
Authorized INS positions	10,997	10,943	10,886	10,604	10,933	10,605	11,692	11,694	13,321	15,453
Total INS budget (in 1000's)	309,285	349,031	370,078	440,557	495,694	509,355	674,539	609,303	927,600	1,057,000
Authorized border patrol positions	2,741	2,915	2,876	2,890	3,069	2,857	3,707	3,707	3,842	4,500
Total apprehensions	1,076,415	910,361	975,780	962,687	1,251,000	1,246,000	1,300,000	1,670,000	1,158,030	—

*Projected

Enforcement was fragmentary and uneven. Ethnic groups and immigrant interests, at times echoed by high-placed appointees in the administration and INS itself, pressed the agency to concentrate more on its services functions— presumably to the further neglect of its enforcement mission. The seeming impossibility of the enforcement task made for low morale or even apathy among career employees. The agency had fallen seriously behind in modernizing its procedures for handling the masses of data to keep records on millions of immigrants, visitors, petitioners and smugglers. A 1980 GAO report concluded that INS "has not been able to adequately enforce immigration laws and the prospects for its doing so are dim. It has neither the legal means nor sufficient resources to stem the growing number of illegal aliens entering the United States."[2]

While apprehensions on the Mexican border mounted steadily, exceeding one million for the first time in 1977, INS spokesmen could only speculate that at best only one out of every two or three aliens entering were actually being caught. The agency's efforts in November 1979 to track down some 60,000 Iranian students in the country shed public light on INS's record-keeping deficiencies. The control system for non-immigrants, intended to track their whereabouts, status and departure, was in a state of near collapse. A 1979 test of a sample of 3,700 aliens believed to have overstayed their visas was unable to account for fully two-thirds of them.[3] Interior enforcement was becoming token as the undocumented population swelled beyond the capabilities of the small and diminishing number of investigators. In many cases, the agency lacked funds to detain or repatriate these aliens they did locate. Citing apprehended aliens with a Form 210, which orders their voluntary departure on an honor system arrangement, has been the common and mostly ineffective substitute for detention and removal. Similarly, aliens subject to deportation have most often been released on bond or on their own recognizance. A 1984 study showed 76 percent of these failed to show when ordered to report for deportation.[4]

In many ways the INS budget was captive during the late 1970s and early 1980s to the general uncertainty in Washington over future immigration policy. The Office of Management and Budget, the Congress and Justice Department were reluctant to push major new initiatives for an INS buildup in the absence of a clearer statement of the national will on immigration. The lack of employer sanctions, under debate in the Congress off and on since 1971, was the single most important source and symbol of confusion and ambiguity in enforcement policy.

Taking office in early 1981, the Reagan administration initially maintained this policy of keeping INS on short rations until it could evaluate the agency's needs rationally and sort out its own immigration priorities. But there were already signs of a subtle change in the political climate that would be more supportive of immigration enforcement and INS. The Reagan administration had not failed to notice the political damage inflicted on the Carter administration by its handling of the Mariel Boatlift. The administration's sensitivity to such issues as drugs, terrorism and general law enforcement, and its relatively lower concern for third world reactions abroad or the demands of minorities and immigrant constituencies within the United States made it more willing to accept the political risk of tighter immigration enforcement.

Changing attitudes were apparent in the findings of the administration's 1981 Task Force on Immigration and Refugee Policy, which evaluated and accepted a number of the recommendations of the Select Commission established in 1979. Acknowledging that the United States had lost control of its borders, President Reagan voiced determination to apply the immigration laws with more rigor in mass asylum situations.[5] Along with its own bill for employer sanctions and other immigration reforms, in 1981 the administration unsuccessfully sought legislation for additional powers to deal with immigration emergencies like Mariel and deployed the Coast Guard in the Caribbean to interdict the seaborne flow of illegal Haitian migrants into South Florida. Some additional powers, such as an immigration emergency fund and tougher penalties for conveying unlawful aliens to the United States, were subsequently enacted. Sparking a controversy which continues, the administration decided to make more use of its existing powers to detain or otherwise control increasing numbers of asylum seekers arriving at ports of entries without legal documents.

The appointment of Alan Nelson as Commissioner of Immigration, an attorney with management experience, was the first step in a process of reordering the immigration bureaucracy and rationalizing its resource needs.

Following a careful review of INS's material and personnel needs beginning in 1981, the agency proposed—and received—major increases in its budget and staff in 1984 and 1985. Much of the increase went to the Border Patrol which grew in 1985 to almost 3,500 positions, an increase of 850 over the previous year. The agency increased its overall personnel strength by more than 1,000, with most of the increases going for enforcement. This was INS's largest single-year personnel increase in its history. Commissioner Alan Nelson spoke of the increases as a "down payment" on the additional resources that would be needed with immigration reform, ultimately passed in late 1986. INS improved its budget prospects by playing up its contribution first to the struggle against drugs and more recently against terrorism, both causes that enjoy immense public and congressional backing.[6] INS released frequent information showing that the Border Patrol was making two-thirds of all drug seizures at the border, far exceeding the take of Customs or the Drug Enforcement Agency. The value of drugs that the Border Patrol seized rose from $10.2 million in 1981 to $150 million in 1986.[7]

The 1986 immigration reform legislation has ushered in further major increases in the INS budget. The act called for an additional 50 percent increase in the Border Patrol by the end of 1988 and an increase of more than $900 million in the overall budget. The cost of legalizing illegals in the country before 1982 will add about $125 million to the 1987 budget and nearly $150 million in 1988 but the INS proposes to recover most of this amount through fees for legalization.

Even with the reduced rations presented by the administrator, the agency's available funds will climb to over $900 million in 1987 and over a billion in 1988—an increase of 140 percent in the eight years of the Reagan administration. The work force of INS in 1980 will show similar growth, rising from 10,800 in 1981 to some 15,400 in 1988.

But notwithstanding Congress's good intentions, the administration, fighting serious deficits, has not sought the full increases endorsed by the Reform Act. These sizable increases are at best only a start toward equipping INS to enforce fully the existing laws and to handle the many responsibilities added by the 1986 reform legislation. INS has asked for only a little more than half the number of the additional border patrol positions suggested in the law, bringing the Border Patrol to more than 4,200 by 1988. While border enforcement has become better manned since 1984, the 1986 reforms add a number of new enforcement provisions that both increase INS's arsenal against immigration abuses and load heavy new burdens on its staff, particularly its investigators for internal enforcement.

Important among the 1986 enforcement initiatives that will impose added obligations on the INS staff are:

—Employer sanctions, requiring compliance officers to monitor credibly the estimated six to seven million employers covered by the 1986 Act and to investigate the accompanying fraud and misrepresentations.
—Legalization for pre-1982 entrants and for agricultural workers, which could produce two million to four million cases, entails frequent investigations of fraud and counterfeiting by claimants or employers.
—Provisions in the reform act for prompt apprehension and removal of criminal aliens, and similar measures for drug offenders in the 1986 Narcotics Traffickers Deportation Act, significantly increase caseloads for INS investigators, attorneys, immigration judges of the Executive Office of Immigration Review and support staff. Until passage of the Act, INS had been able to deport only about 30 percent of the deportable criminal aliens that law enforcement agencies refer to them each year.
—The 1986 legislation to combat marriage fraud, which INS estimates now taints 30 percent of all marriages involving an immigration benefit, will require investigator time.
—Alien smuggling continues to grow, taxing the limited time of investigators. The new law further tightens penalties and mandates stronger border controls. In 1986 alone the INS arrested some 22,000 smugglers, continuing a steady upward trend. Of those, 7,999 were prosecuted and 6,579 convicted. Nearly 14,000 smugglers' vehicles were seized with a value of $31 million of illegal drugs.

INS has lost investigators since the mid-1970s. At the beginning of 1987 the agency was struggling to meet old and new demands with only 680 investigators nationwide. INS's response has been to concentrate investigators' efforts on notorious cases of fraud or illegal alien employment, large scale rackets, welfare benefit abuse and criminal aliens.[8] With the new legislation investigator strength will grow to nearly one thousand nationwide, an amount some law enforcement experts note is still only one-third the number needed for truly effective enforcement with the added responsibilities.

Even so, there are signs that the sharp increases in funding along with strong congressional interest and the long-delayed passage of employer sanctions have reinvigorated INS, evoking confidence among agency professionals that the United States can gain control over illegal immigration. They note that a good part of the nearly 50 percent increase in apprehensions at the southern border between 1985 and 1986 is due to the increase in border patrolmen and their more sophisticated supporting equipment—aircraft, sensors, night scopes and low-light TV. Sophisticated equipment and better training is also helping INS inspectors to detect more fraudulent documents at ports of entry. Special fraud intercept lenses, using high-tech laboratory equipment, now support regular inspection at high-fraud ports of entry.

Further progress in border enforcement is still impeded by the "it-can't-be-done" syndrome in Congress and the public, many of whom oppose effective border controls in any event. INS must continue to stress that controlling the 2,000-mile border with Mexico depends on effective patrolling of barriers along segments totalling less than 200 miles in length that are now the major corridors of illegal entry.

Successful implementation of employer sanctions is absolutely critical to restoring credible immigration controls. Even with the full increase of more than six hundred additional border patrol and investigator positions for this task by 1988, INS faces a mammoth task of persuading or compelling the nation's seven million employers not to hire illegals. It will have to deploy its limited resources carefully, concentrating on notorious violators to deter others by example, using past experience and intuition to ferret out likely violators. INS must be backed by a non-intrusive but foolproof system for verifying aliens' eligibility to work. The agency must be able to count on a continuing flow of resources beyond 1988 and high level support in the executive branch and in Congress. If INS enforces employer sanctions effectively, there are likely to be counter pressures from interest groups to go easy or to make exceptions.

For success INS must also have more support from other involved government agencies. In the reform act Congress cited the importance of the Department of Labor in deterring illegal immigration by rigorous enforcement of labor standards and federal contract compliance. But without additional resources—and the Labor Department asked for little in 1987—Labor's Employment Standards Administration is unable to meet its responsibilities under existing legislation, even without the addition of employer sanctions to its already overburdened agenda. INS will need to cooperate closely with the Social Security Administration (SSA), the Internal Revenue Service (IRS) and state and local governments. Recent history of interagency cooperation is not encouraging. Many agencies have proved reluctant to deviate from their established missions or to take on activities they see as having a low payoff which may cost them the trust of their clientele. High-level executive branch leadership and continuing congressional support will be essential to overcome these handicaps. (See Chapter 16 by Malcolm R. Lovell on requirements for successful enforcement of employer sanctions.)

While the INS shows promise of gaining strength from additional resources and stronger legislation, the nation's outermost screen against illegal immigration, the consular service of the State Department, remains exceedingly hard-pressed to provide any rigor in issuing an average of six million visas a year during the last five years. Some 40 percent of the illegal aliens now in the United States are estimated to have originally entered with valid visas issued by the State Department and then overstayed or violated the terms of their admission, or entered using counterfeit visas or passports.[9] A 1986 study by INS's statistical analysis branch based on data on non-immigrants who should have departed during the six-month period between October 1984 and March 1985, concluded that 4.5 percent, or 182,000, overstayed. Not surprisingly, countries with high demand for U.S. residence visas such as the Philippines, Haiti, Jamaica and Mexico have high overstay rates. The most frequent overstayers were those who came in the category of temporary visitors for pleasure, the so-called tourist visa. Another category of frequent abuse, the student visa, was not included in the survey.[10] The age of high tech has made counterfeit passports and supporting documents steadily more difficult to detect.

The dollar's decline may further increase the flow of tourism to the United States and in 1987 and 1988 the State Department embassies and consulates abroad expect the applications of seven to eight million foreign nationals seeking to visit the United States. To winnow out those who are non-bonafide non-immigrants, or who are ineligible under any of the other thirty-three provisions of the immigration law, there are fewer than 350 American consular officers, supported by about 1,100 foreign service national supporting staff. This small worldwide staff, which issues immigrant as well as non-immigrant visas, has not increased during the past two years and expects no increase in the immediate future. They will be called on to issue close to seven million additional visas in 1987. The size of the work load means that each consular officer has less than three minutes to make a judgment on the validity of the documents and statements of each applicant.[11]

The 1986 legislation will add additional burdens on over-worked consular staffs at certain posts abroad in administering the expanded temporary agricultural workers provisions (H-2A) and accepting applications for legalization under the special agricultural workers program.

Struggling to cope with an impossible work load, the State Department has opted for visa practices abroad that emphasize economy but reduce their effectiveness as a screen. Large numbers of visas are issued without personal interviews. The State Department issues an increasing number of non-immigrant visas with longer periods of validity, and still more with no expiration date at all. Because of this, while only about six million visas are issued yearly, the actual number of valid visas in circulation and available at any one time for use to apply for entry into the United States (or for transfer to unauthorized parties) may be as high as twenty-five to thirty million.[12]

Finally, in performing the visa function, the State Department continues to labor under the long-standing conflict between its mandate for rigorous application of the immigration law on one hand and its interest in trouble-free relations and easy interchange with foreign countries. From time to time professional consuls face pressure even from within the U.S. government to bend the laws governing issuance of non-immigrant visas to admit persons who are really intending immigrants or refugees, who cannot accept the delays or inconvenience entailed by the correct provisions of the law.

NOTES

1. *Statistical Yearbooks of the INS, 1975–1985.*

2. General Accounting Office, "Prospects Dim for Effectively Enforcing Immigration Laws," (GAO, 1980), p. i.

3. Ibid.

4. House Subcommittee on Immigration, Refugees and International Law; *Oversight Hearings on Immigration and Naturalization Service*, 99th Cong., 2nd Sess. (GPO, 1987), p. 197.

5. See statement of President Ronald Reagan, July 30, 1981.

6. Attorney General William French Smith, "Apart from repelling an invader, there appears no clearer test of a nation's will to exercise its sovereignty than its ability to control its borders against illegal entry of persons and goods. Our sovereignty is being assaulted directly by the movement of illegal aliens and drugs into our national territory." U.S. Department of Justice Press Release, February 1, 1984.

7. INS Press Statement, February 20, 1986.

8. INS, Prepared Statement of Commissioner Alan Nelson before the Senate Appropriations Subcommittee of the Department of Justice, May 7, 1987.

9. "Prospects Dim for Effectively Enforcing Immigration Laws," GAO.

10. Robert Warren, "The INS Nonimmigrant Information System: Assessing the Statistics on Nondeparture," Statistical Analysis Branch, INS, 1986.

11. David S. North, *Enforcing the Immigration Law: A Review of the Options* (WDC: New Transcentury Foundation, 1980).

12. Estimates provided orally by Visa Office Statistical Branch, Department of State, 1986.

Refugees, Asylum and Sanctuary:
National Passion vs. National Interest

After five years' heavy flow of Southeast Asian refugees, Congress in 1980 enacted the Refugee Act with the intent of imposing order and consistency on the admission of refugees and asylees into the United States while taming the executive branch's use of the parole power. That Act brought the United States into conformity with, and even broadened the international definition of a refugee: "A person who is outside his country of nationality and who is unable or unwilling to return to that country because of persecution or well-founded fear of persecution on account of race, religion, nationality, membership in a particular social group or political opinion." The Act also established a domestic policy for federally-funded resettlement assistance which was to be the same for all groups of refugees. With the Act, Congress sought to affirm a clear role for itself, through the House and Senate Judiciary Committees, in determining the numbers to be admitted.

In 1980 refugee admissions reached an all time high of 207,000. The 1980 admissions would bring total refugee entries since 1975, when the Republic of Vietnam collapsed, to about 550,000, 94 percent of them from Southeast Asia alone. Refugee admissions stayed high for the following year at 159,000, but began dropping off sharply as the decade progressed. Between 1975 and 1986 the United States had received for resettlement more than a million refugees, more than 800,000 of them from Southeast Asia, in what may be one of the largest government-financed mass movements of people ever. (See Table 1.13) These figures do not include some 125,000 Cubans who left their country for the United States in the 1980 Mariel Boatlift and perhaps as many as 40,000 Haitians who entered in their own boatlift between 1972 and 1981. The Mariel Boatlift began in April 1980 shortly after enactment of the 1980 Refugee Act and constituted a classic mass asylum. But the Carter Administration was reluctant to declare the Cubans refugees and chose not to use the act's budget-burdening provisions for dealing with it. The Cubans and Haitians were paroled under a new and vague ad hoc category, "Cuban/Haitian entrant," and ultimately offered permanent residence under either the Cuban Refugee Act of 1966 or the 1986 immigration reform act.

Following the initiation of consultation with Congress in 1981, the U.S. government began to manage down the number of refugees for resettlement in the United States. Refugee policymakers began to give more emphasis to repatriation in place of resettlement for most refugees, reserving the option of resettlement in the United States for those with the strongest ties to the United States under a six-category worldwide priorities system. Admissions were reduced to below 100,000, and since 1983 have been held at 70,000 or lower, but still 40 percent higher than the 50,000 the Refugee Act calls "normal flow."

The reduction in intake stems in part from a drying up of the priority cases in Southeast Asia, those refugee candidates who had close ties to the U.S. government or with close family members in the United States. But other factors were also working for reduction. Congress and public opinion had wearied of the financial cost and social stresses of massive resettlement. Key congressional leaders, such as Senator Alan Simpson became increasingly concerned that heavy U.S. refugee resettlement was itself becoming a magnet for continuing out-migration, particularly in Southeast Asia, among many whose claims to refugee status were dubious.[1]

The enormous cost of the domestic resettlement programs—totalling more than $3 billion federal dollars by 1986, at times sparked resentment among domestic minorities and the poor who saw the programs as overly generous. Finally, there was rising concern over the high degree of welfare dependency among refugees, particularly among those Southeast Asian refugees entering after 1978. In mid-1986 55 percent of the refugees who had arrived in the last three years were on public assistance. In California 90 percent were on welfare, while Massachusetts, Washington and Hawaii all had dependency rates over 70 percent. A federal refugee resettlement official told Congress in 1986 that the refugee program had become something it was never meant to be: a long-term service, training and education program.[2]

Table 1.13   Refugee admissions 1975 to 1987

Fiscal Year	Africa	East Asia	Eastern Europe	Soviet Union	Latin America	Near East/ South Asia	Total
1975	0	135,000	1,947	6,211	3,000	0	146,158
1976	0	15,000	1,756	7,450	3,000	0	27,206
1977	0	7,000	1,755	8,191	3,000	0	19,946
1978	0	20,574	2,245	10,688	3,000	0	36,507
1979	0	76,521	3,393	24,449	7,000	0	111,363
1980	955	163,799	5,025	28,444	6,662	2,231	207,116
1981	2,119	131,139	6,704	13,444	2,017	3,829	159,252
1982	3,326	73,522	10,780	2,756	602	6,369	97,355
1983	2,648	39,408	12,083	1,409	668	5,465	61,681
1984	2,747	51,960	10,285	715	160	5,246	71,113
1985	1,953	49,970	9,350	640	138	5,994	68,045
1986	1,315	45,454	8,713	787	173	5,998	62,440
1987	232	7,383	2,235	297	0	2,250	12,397
Total	15,295	816,725	76,271	105,481	29,420	37,382	1,080,574

Source: U.S. Department of State/ Bureau for Refugee Programs.

Generous welfare and cash assistance plans may have added to the program's magnetism for prospective economic migrants in Southeast Asia. Refugees' propensity for secondary migration, leading to heavy clustering in southern California and the gulf coast of Texas, made them more visible as political targets. According to U.S. Department of Health and Human Services figures, 320,000 of the more than 800,000 Southeast Asian refugees arriving since 1975— 40 percent—now live in California, with Orange County the preferred area of resettlement. Secondary migration has tended to further concentrate refugees in states with high welfare benefits.[3] Large scale admissions become associated in the public mind with its concern over the nation's seeming lack of a grand design for immigration in general.

In fact, refugee policymakers and resettlement agencies have worked hard and so far successfully to fence off refugee programs from overall immigration policy and to emphasize the distinctions between the two in the public mind. They have stressed that the acute vulnerability of refugees to persecution and their often urgent need for immediate protection are conditions that the immigration process with its delays, ceilings and emphasis on family connections often cannot assuage. At the same time, policymakers and refugee advocates have themselves blurred the distinction between immigrants and refugees by assigning presumptive refugee status to broad classes of people on the move in the Soviet Union, Eastern Europe and Southeast Asia, with less concern for assessments of individual risk of persecution. (See Chapter 14 by Barnaby Zall) Since the initial removal of high risk political refugees before 1978, arriving Southeast Asian refugees have displayed the hallmarks of economic migrants as much as fugitives from persecution.

The legislative architects of the 1980 refugee law's asylum procedures did not foresee that vast numbers of desperate intending immigrants would seek to use asylum claims as an alternative route to permanent residence in the United States or as a delaying device in deportation proceedings. The criteria for granting asylum are similar to those for granting refugee status. While refugees are examined and selected abroad, asylum is given or denied to persons either already in the United States or at the port of entry.

For the determined entry seeker, the adjudication of asylum has often assured prolonged delays during which the applicant can work and develop other "equities" for remaining permanently. Further appeals in the federal courts of unfavorable decisions by immigration judges may drag on for up to several years. The landmark March 1987 Supreme Court decision in *Cardoza-Fonseca*[4], which mandated a more liberal criteria for the government's assessment of "well-founded fear," is illustrative; it completed an adjudication process that began eight years earlier.

INS Commissioner Alan Nelson calls those entering the United States illegally and then filing frivolous asylum claims "Queue Jumpers." The administration in 1981 opted for a tough policy of detaining some asylum seekers who enter illegally, requiring bonds, denying them work authorization, or interdicting Haitian migrants on the high seas. The policy remains under attack by immigrant interests.[5] The Administration argues that if asylum seekers are simply released pending a decision, as immigrant advocacies demand, many disappear, local communities are burdened and intending migrants abroad are encouraged to try the same.

Before 1980 the INS received only a few thousand asylum claims each year. With the 1980 act claims jumped to 50,000 the first year. By mid-1983 there were more than 170,000 pending asylum cases, and Cubans initiated two-thirds of them. Other major source countries of asylum seekers were El Salvador, Iran, Nicaragua and Haiti. With greater experience, better training and increases in personnel, INS was able to whittle down the backlog of cases to 126,000 by late 1985. Pending asylum cases under INS jurisdiction again declined sharply during 1986, as extra staff cut into the backlog. In early 1987, INS had no backlog except Cuban cases and was almost current in handling the some 18,000 new applications a year. The estimated 80,000 Cuban applications would be resolved by the special legalization provisions in the 1986 reform act for Cubans and Haitians. Few figures, however, are available on a large number of cases decided by INS district directors, immigration judges or the Board of Immigration Appeals that are now under appeal in the federal courts. INS's increasingly rapid handling of new asylum claims has diminished their usefulness as a delaying device.

The Sanctuary Movement began in late 1981 when a handful of churches began sheltering Central American illegal migrants. Its proponents' motives ranged from the purely humanitarian concern for illegal aliens from troubled countries to a desire for actions to oppose U.S. foreign policies in Central America. Its spokesmen argued that the United States was illegally deporting Central Americans under the Refugee Act and under the 1949 Geneva Convention.[6] Another strand of Sanctuary's rationale affirmed the tradition of "civil disobedience" in confronting laws seen as unjust, although by no means all Sanctuary activists submitted themselves to arrest.

Sanctuary proponents have argued that migrants from Central America are fleeing repression and violence in their home countries. They charge that the United States is responsible for much of the injustice, unrest, poverty and violence in those countries, or is allied to repressive regimes there. Thus, they claim, U.S. denials of 97 percent for Salvadorans and 99 percent of Guatemalans for asylum petitions are seen as politically motivated. Sanctuary advocates have argued that 3,000 to 4,000 illegal aliens that the INS returned to El Salvador each year face real danger—some even say "certain death." But investigations conducted by human rights organizations, by the State Department, and in 1986 by the Intergovernmental Committee on Migration (ICM), have yielded little evidence of a pattern of persecution against returning Salvadorans.[7]

Only about 350 churches and synagogues out of the nation's total of more than 300,000 have joined the Sanctuary Movement. Some twelve cities and two states, Wisconsin and New Mexico, declared themselves sanctuary areas, although two of the cities, Seattle and Los Angeles, withdrew their declarations in the face of heavy public opposition. In 1986 New Mexico's newly inaugurated Governor Garrey Carruthers rescinded former Governor Toney Anaya's 1985 declaration of that state as a sanctuary.

But if the primary goal of the Sanctuary Movement is to publicize its political case, it has been successful. A six-month trial of five members of the Sanctuary Movement in 1986 in the U.S. District Court at Tucson on charges of conspiracy to smuggle aliens into the United States also gained the movement wide coverage. The five activists were convicted of alien smuggling and given probation. The case is now under appeal. A 1984 conviction of two sanctuary activists was subsequently upheld by the 5th Circuit of the U.S. Court of Appeals and the Supreme Court refused to review the 5th Circuit's ruling.[8]

A proposed legislative alternative to sanctuary has been to grant displaced Central Americans a period of safe haven by authorizing Extended Voluntary Departure (EVD)—a suspension of deportations—while the General Accounting Office carries out an eighteen-month study of conditions in their home countries and Congress considers its findings. (As of October, 1987 EVD legislation had been approved by the House and was awaiting action in the Senate). EVD has been solely a discretionary authority of the Attorney General, acting on the recommendation of the State Department. In effect it is a special permission for non-permanent resident aliens from particularly troubled countries to remain for a determined period in the United States until the situations in their home countries ease. EVD originated as an immigration law enforcement procedure, but it has increasingly been used to make up for the absence of any temporary safe haven provisions in the law. Since 1960 the Attorney General has granted EVD to nationals of sixteen countries, including such troubled groups as Afghans, Iranians, Nicaraguans, Lebanese, Ugandans and Ethiopians. Four of the countries designated so far are Warsaw Pact members, while six others are communist or communist-dominated, buttressing critics' charges that the government's decisions are ideologically biased.

Through the first half of 1987 the Reagan administration had consistently opposed EVD legislation on the grounds that Salvadoran illegal aliens were predominantly economic migrants from a country with a tradition of heavy illegal immigration.

The debates over EVD and Sanctuary highlight some of the critical differences among U.S. policymakers and within public opinion concerning refugee and asylum definitions and procedures. The administration argues that it is the Attorney General who has the authority to award refugee and asylum status following a rigorous examination of claims of individuals to have a well-founded "fear of persecution"—an assertion upheld in the Federal District Court convictions in 1986 of five sanctuary activists. The burden is on the claimant to satisfy U.S. officials that his fear is well-founded that he would be persecuted in his home country because of his race, religion, nationality or membership in a particular social group or political opinion. While *Cardoza-Fonseca* eases this test somewhat it does not circumscribe the Attorney-General's discretionary authority. Thus, those leaving their home countries because of economic deprivation or generalized conditions of violence do not qualify as refugees or asylees for those reasons alone. The administration also takes into account such factors as past illegal immigration flows from the region in question and alternative places of refuge the migrant may have entered before seeking asylum to the United States.

Countering this view is a growing insistence among immigration lawyers, ethnic groups, international refugee interests and some congressional officials that the United States and other receiving states are obligated to extend protection to those fleeing life-threatening conditions such as generalized violence, war or even natural disasters, even though they may not be able to establish that they are singled out as individuals for mistreatment, a doctrine affirmed in the 1969 Convention of the Organization of African Unity. In this view evidentiary proof of specific threats is less important than the credibilty of the subjective fears of those fleeing.[9] They argue that the reality of contemporary refugee movements is that the majority of people who are afraid to return to their home countries fear the dangers of civil war and violent internal upheavals, but they do not necessarily fear individual persecution. Seeming economic migrants, they assert, may also qualify as refugees since adverse economic measures may be directed against a group for social, religious or political reasons.[10]

Adoption of EVD legislation for Central Americans (Nicaraguans were added to the bill's coverage in early 1987) would be a significant precedent for U.S. immigration policy as well as another run around the 1980 Refugee Act. EVD would grant de facto resident status and work authorization to several hundred thousand Central Americans who will not otherwise qualify for the legalization included in the 1986 immigration reform law.

While the bill's grant of protection would be temporary until conditions changed in homelands and the migrants can return, there is likely to be little desire among the majority of the migrants to return to the economic privation of the region when peace returns. Moreover, INS enforcement will be unable to track such large numbers and compel their return. With enactment of EVD for Central Americans, Congress would add one or more ad hoc patch to the current crazyquilt of immigration procedures that has confounded overall rational management of immigration and refugee intake.

NOTES

1. Senate Committee on the Judiciary, "Annual Refugee Consultation." *Hearing before the Subcommittee on Immigration and Refugee Policy*, 99th Cong., 1st sess., September 17, 1985. (GPO, 1986), pp. 1–2.

2. House Subcommittee on Immigration and Refugee Policy. Hearing, "Mid-year Consultation on U.S. Refugee Programs for Fiscal Year 1986," 99th Cong., 2nd sess., June 20, 1986. (GPO, 1986), pp. 36–37.

3. U.S. Coalition for Refugee Affairs, Proposed Refugee Allocations for Fiscal Year 1987—*Report to Congress for Fiscal Year 1987.* (Washington, D.C., September 1986).

4. *Immigration and Naturalization Service v. Luz Marina Cardoza-Fonseca*, 107 S.CT 1207.

5. See William Shaw Gross, "Refugees Fleeing Violence Find Few Signs of Welcome," *Los Angeles Times*, July 27, 1986 and Arthur C. Hilton, "The Imprisonment of Refugees in the United States," in Lydio F. Tomasi, ed., *In Defense of the Alien*; (New York: Center for Migration Studies, 1987).

6. Ignatius Bau, "Sanctuary," *New Catholic World*, (May/June 1985).

7. Roger Conner, "Extended Voluntary Departure for Salvadorans." Statement before the Senate Subcommittee of Immigration and Refugee Policy, April 22, 1985, (WDC: Federation for American Immigration Reform, 1985); and Chris Hedges, "Study Finds No Harm to Deportees," *Dallas Morning News*, July 13, 1986.

8. *Merkt v. U.S.* No. 86-1089 and U.S. v. Phillip M. Willis Cong., Sister Darlene Nigorski et. al. CR.85-008-Phx. ehc Tuscon.

9. Astri Suhrke: "Global Refugee Movements and Strategies of Response," in Mary M. Kritz, ed., *U.S. Immigration and Refugee Policy: Global and Domestic Issues* (Lexington, MA: Lexington Books, 1983).

10. UN High Commissioner for Refugees, *Handbook on Procedures and Criteria for Determining Refugee Status* (Geneva, 1979), Articles 63 and 64.

Unfinished Business in American Immigration Policy

Demographic and social forces both within the United States and in the international environment will continue to stimulate intense immigration pressures for the remainder of this century. Within the American body politic there are sharply conflicting political demands on future immigration quantities. On one side is a congeries of determined special interests that, though representing a minority, press effectively for more immigration. On the other side is a sizable but unfocused majority of the electorate that favors restricting immigration and harnessing it more rationally to agreed national needs. This deep division will continue to roil policymaking. While legislators might prefer to feel that the 1986 reforms have put immigration issues back on the shelf, Congress will find little relief from rising public debate or the demands of increasingly clamorous immigrant special interests.

THE ENVIRONMENT

The social and economic forces in the Third World propelling the heavy migration of the 1970s and 1980s are likely to be part of the domestic and international landscape for the remainder of this century. World population reached five billion in 1987 and will add another billion by the turn of the century, with 85 percent of the total in the Third World. The burgeoning working-age populations of immigrant source countries will turn out job seekers faster than their weak economies can produce jobs. Even the return of those countries to the robust levels of growth of the 1960s and 1970s would in most cases reduce but not end the jobs deficit.

Political instability, fanned by economic despair and the rising demands of youth on sluggish political systems, will also continue driving large numbers to seek physical security and economic betterment in western industrial countries. Major immigration source countries with high risks of political turmoil are the Philippines, Columbia, Korea, Nicaragua, El Salvador, Guatemala and Honduras, Haiti and Nigeria.[1]

The major question mark for the migration future is the future stability and economic viability of Mexico, source of half of all illegal immigration to the United States. By 1987 Mexicans had suffered six consecutive years of economic slump and a 37 percent drop in real income since 1982. Mexico is now adding a million persons a year to its labor force, and its authoritarian, single-party political structure is showing increasing brittleness under economic stress. (David Simcox discusses demographic and social forces in Mexico affecting emigration in an article later in this volume.)

The sharp decline of the dollar's value beginning in early 1985 has not appreciably narrowed earning differentials between the United States and less developed immigrant exporting countries. The value of the currencies of most source countries has fallen at the same rate as the dollar or, as in the case of Mexico, El Salvador, the Dominican Republic and Columbia, many times faster. Even rapid job creation in many of the source countries has restrained immigration demand only modestly. For the intending migrant from Mexico and the Caribbean, the prospective gain of working in the United States far exceeds the dollar value of most jobs at home. But the continued high flow of Mexican migrants northward during Mexico's boom years of 1978–1981 illustrates that economics alone does not drive individual migration choices. The presence of large welcoming family networks and ethnic enclaves, quality schools and social services are an important and growing attraction.

Trends within the United States as well are making some key interest groups more insistent on higher levels of immigration. As the United States matures demographically and its economy continues shifting toward services, demand mounts for new workers in the labor-intensive low-wage services sector. With employer sanctions going into effect in 1987, employers were more alert to the possibility of labor shortages. Apprehension over a scarcity of labor has been reinforced by the growth of convictions among some demographers and social commentators that the United States, with its maturing population and declining fertility rates, faces a shrinking pool of younger citizens and long-term population decline. Accepting this diagnosis, more abundant immigration becomes an option for solving such presumed future problems of scarce labor, declining military manpower and payment of social welfare costs of rising numbers of aging Americans.[2]

The pronounced humanitarian strain in America's outlook on migration and refugees remains a powerful driving force. The growth of legal and illegal resident populations from troubled countries, their allied legal service providers an associated advocates of specific foreign policies, have now gained a grip on the levers of congressional influence. The public, which feels more restrictionist, is poorly organized. And Congressmen have shown that their responsiveness often depends little on whether the petitioners are citizens or even in the country legally.

A diverse range of prospective conflicts over specific policy issues within Congress, the executive branch and the courts can be grouped in the following major issue categories:

1. The Enforcement of Immigration Reform and Control

The perception of impending labor shortages, fears of overregulation, humanitarian impulses and simple greed are likely to stiffen resistance to effective enforcement of employer sanctions. The commitment of Congress and the executive to sustained effective enforcement cannot be assumed. A key test is their readiness to fund and apply the increases needed by enforcement agencies such as INS and Labor to make employer sanctions more than a symbolic law. Congress will also face continuing efforts to condemn sanctions to an early death by showing that they are inherently discriminatory against Hispanics and the foreign born. If sanctions begin working as intended, both Congress and the executive must expect a more virulent backlash from some employers and special economic interest who will demand relief or ad hoc exemptions.

2. Legal Immigration

Legal immigration which exceeded 600,000 in 1986, has acquired a momentum that will assure continued growth, as increasing numbers of newly naturalized immigrants of the late 1970s and early 1980s exercise their right to bring in close family members free of the law's numerical restrictions. Chain migration may gain further steam in the mid-1990s as two million or more illegal aliens estimated to be legalized by the amnesty and special farm worker provisions of the 1986 law reach eligibility for citizenship and with it the right to bring in close family members free of the ceiling.

Some legislators and immigrant interests maintain even higher levels of legal immigration are desired! The 1986 curbs on illegal immigration have triggered arguments that the United States, having closed the "back door" of illegal immigration, must now open wider the "front door" of legal immigration. (See the article by Laurence Fuchs later in this volume.)

3. Quasi-Legal Immigration

Policymakers can also expect continuing proposals for ad hoc arrangements through legislative tinkering or liberalized interpretation of existing law and regulations that will have the effect of expanding de facto immigration. Refugee interests are still unreconciled to administration's policy since 1981 of "managing down" the refugee ceiling from their six-digit peaks of the late 1970s to current ceiling of not more than 70,000. Voluntary agencies providing services under contract for refugee resettlement have themselves become a powerful lobby for expanded ceilings, some even arguing for an assured annual "floor" of refugee intake.[3]

At the same time, there is little prospect that pressures will ease to expand alternative arrangements to the refugee process for migrants from troubled countries, such as Extended Voluntary Departure (EVD), "parole" and conditional entrant status, and for further liberalization of asylum criteria. Also likely are further initiatives by immigrant interests to institutionalize some form of temporary safe haven for migrants from troubled countries and their dependents as an alternative to EVD.

Immigrant religious and civil rights interests remain determined to bring forward the January 1982 cutoff date for amnesty stipulated in the 1986 reforms. While pressures continue for Congress to legislate a later cut-off date, INS will be pressed to administer the legalization program with leniency, particularly in cases where rigorous application might divide families. As the aliens amnestied under this 1986 act attain permanent resident status in 1989 and 1990, their petiitions to bring in family members could sharply increase the waiting period in the 2nd and 5th preference categories, confronting Congress with demands for expediated admissions in those categories in the interest of the always politically compelling family reunification. The courts will become even more important as battlegrounds for many of these issues.

Varied and intense pressures will continue meeting counter-pressures from increasingly vocal groups advocating a more rational management of immigration and tight controls on illegal entry. Near the top of the agenda of immigration reformers is full funding for enforcement of employer sanctions, backed up by a secure identification process for verifying worker eligibility. They can be expected to press for a phasing out of the 1986 law's special legalization and recruitment program for foreign agricultural workers, and for rigorous application of the legalization provisions of the 1986 law as written.

On refugee policy, immigration reformers will continue pressing for limitations on resettlements closer to the 50,000 normal flow specified in the act and for vigorous individual application of the 1980 act's criteria in selecting refugees. Refugee advocacies and restrictionists could converge in support of new humanitarian measures for safe haven in the United States to replace the bureaucratic mechanism of EVD. But while immigration expansionists seek such safe haven features as an add-on to a continued high level of refugee resettlement, some reformist view it as a possible alternative to permanent resettlement if legal and enforcement measure could be developed to ensure the prompt repatriation of haven seekers when conditions improve back home.

The concept of a comprehensive immmigration "budget" or ceiling will remain high on the agenda of those concerned over runaway migration. The steady growth of the close family member category, plus the demonstrated weakness of Congress and the executive for "quick fix" arrangements, demonstrated in the creation of a new category of "entrants" for Mariel Cubans, argue for a built-in legislative discipline. What has evolved in the United States is an immigration system that often responds blindly to such shifting demands as increased low-cost labor, gratification of family and ethnic groups for admission of their kin and colleagues and humanitarian impulse to provide a haven to the world's afflicted. Since all these goals have enjoyed considerable political appeal, until now there has been little support for the concept of trade-offs among them within an overall global ceiling. Congress displayed some interest in variations of this approach during the six-year debate over Simpson-Mazzoli.[4] Senator Alan Simpson proposed a ceiling of 565,000—465,000 for family immigrants and 120,000 for independent immigrants—in a legal immigration reform bill introduced in December 1987. Critics warned that it would pit immigrants against refugees and one ethnic group against another. With real immigration rising and special interest pressures more insistent, Congress might now find a ceiling a useful device for insulating itself from unending demands.

Immigration reformers will continue to seek a variety of possible alternatives to the current law's emphasis on family reunification, which now accounts for 95 percent of all non-refugee legal immigration. While family reunification retains considerable political sanctity, there is more willingness to recognize its tendency to concentrate migration among a handful of nationalities with abundant family connections, deny opportunities to the highly skilled and other needed seed immigrants and assure steadily rising immigration levels through the phenomenon of chain migration.

NOTES

1. "South American Turmoil Forecast: 1987 Business Survey Looks at Factors Influencing Trade," *Miami Herald,* November 28, 1986.

2. Ben Wattenberg, *The Birth Dearth* (New York: Pharos Books, 1987).

3. Dennis Gallaher et al, *Of Special Humanitarian Concern: US Refugee Admissions Since the Passage of the Act;* Refugee Policy Group (Washington, D.C., 1985), pp. 33–34.

4. Senate Subcommittee on Immigration and Refugee Policy; *Hearing on the United States as a Country of Mass First Asylum,* 97th Cong., 1st sess. (GPO, 1981).

II

IMMIGRATION AND U.S. WORKERS

"Undocumented workers, if not used directly to undercut the bargaining position of citizen and documented labor, can be used politically and organizationally to fragment labor at several levels. First, they can be brought into competition with negatively privileged citizen labor, most particularly blacks, Latinos, women and youths. As competitors for the same category of jobs (e.g. in service and retail trade), undocumented workers provide the equivalent of a decrease in the overall wage levels associated with those jobs or a diminution of minimum wage laws in that sector. The latter strategy provides the equivalent of a reduction in the guarantees of citizenship without directly expressing the battle in those terms."

—Robert J. Thomas
"Citizenship, Gender and Work":
Social Organization in Industrial Agriculture
(Berkeley: University of California Press, 1985)

Network Recruitment and Labor Displacement
By Philip Martin

By conservative estimates the American economy has absorbed three to six million illegal immigrant workers over the past ten years. How has this flow of illegal immigrant workers into the American labor market since the mid-1970s affected the wages and job prospects of U. S. citizens and legal immigrants? What should we expect in its future impact on the nature and availability of jobs, assuming the 1986 immigration reforms do not appreciably slow the illegal flow?

Three prevailing theories provide a convenient starting point for inquiry:

—one-for-one displacement assumes that illegal aliens and American workers compete for the same jobs, with the aliens winning out because they work "hard and scared" for less.

—segmented labor market theories assume that there is no labor market competition because illegal aliens and American workers look for different kinds of jobs.

—"triage" theory recognizes that some one-for-one displacement occurs, that most jobs can be upgraded to attract Americans, and that some jobs exist only because illegal alien workers are available. None of these theories takes fully into account the process of network recruitment of illegal aliens and its significant role in the process of labor displacement.

In 1978 and 1979 when six million Americans were unemployed and the Border Patrol was finding over one million deportable aliens each year, some argued that unemployment would vanish if the then estimated five to six million illegal aliens could somehow be removed—an application of the theory of one-for-one displacement.[1]

Unlike proponents of one-for-one displacement, segmented labor market theorists argue that illegal alien workers only compete for jobs that American workers shun, such as hotel cleaning or tomato picking. The "segmentation" theory further holds that if illegal aliens have any effect on the job and wage prospects of American workers, it is positive, since hotel cleaning and tomato picking make possible the continuation of better jobs for Americans as clerks, waiters, truck drivers and food processors. According to this line of argument, the major "problem" associated with illegal immigration is violation of labor standards laws, suggesting that an alternative to border enforcement is more workplace inspections of wages and working conditions.

One-for-one displacement and segmentation occupy the two extremes in the debate over competition between American and other workers. In between is the familiar and more reasonable triage assumption: that for a given number of jobs held by illegal aliens, some might be filled by American workers if vacated;

some might be filled by American workers only after the employer improves wages and working conditions; and some jobs might disappear because they would not be worth doing at higher wages, such as the housewife who resumes doing her own cleaning instead after the departure of an illegal alien maid or the farmer who decides that wages are too high to re-pick a field a third time.

Of the three different perspectives on how illegal alien workers and Americans compete in the labor market, "triage" provides the most convincing explanation of the dynamic process in which illegal workers come to dominate certain work forces. In many occupations most workers find jobs through tips passed along by friends and relatives. Awareness of this network recruitment system, which has become highly developed by illegal aliens and their employers, is a key to understanding how illegal aliens displace American workers.

Most American businesses hire American workers—there are 107 million workers employed, including the estimated three to six million illegal aliens. Most mainstream American businesses such as steel and auto manufacturers; finance, insurance and real estate firms; and government do not knowingly hire illegal aliens. And they have few problems recruiting and retaining American workers.

But the businesses that depend heavily on illegal alien workers typically experience a high turnover of American workers. A hotel cleaning staff, a light manufacturing operation or a landscape service may have to hire up to thirty American workers each year to keep ten job slots filled. Many of these jobs pay relatively low wages, are physically demanding or require work at nights or on weekends. American workers often switch employers if they dislike a supervisor or get laid-off and turn to unemployment insurance.[2]

Illegal alien workers from Mexico, Latin America and Asia gained a foothold in these jobs in the 1960s and early 1970s in regions where immigrants concentrated. Some of these illegal aliens stayed only until reaching a savings target and eventually quit and returned home. For example, some of the Mexicans (braceros) who stayed illegally after the migrant labor agreement ended in 1964 later returned to Mexico. However, some opened restaurants or garment shops in the United States, and many of these pioneer migrants found entry-level employment in U.S. hotels, factories and service firms in major urban areas.

In the 1970s two events turned this pioneer immigrant foothold into a dominant presence in many firms. First, the Civil Rights movement raised the expectations of many unskilled American workers, while the War on Poverty programs provided previously unavailable employment and training options or a better economic safety net for some of the American workers who had traditionally accepted hotel cleaning, restaurant and light manufacturing jobs. Second, illegal aliens began coming to the United States in greater numbers and a diverse group of labor-intensive businesses expanded after the economy recovered from the 1973–1974 energy and food price hikes. Many of these small businesses had pyramid job structures: a few optimistic professionals with a concept or idea employed local clerical and sales workers in the front office and unskilled illegal aliens in the backroom warehouse or factory. Other small businesses, such as ethnic restaurants and landscape services, were begun by immigrant entrepreneurs who employed friends and relatives.

The proliferation of such small businesses further increased the demand for unskilled workers. However, as American workers continued to quit low-wage jobs or demand higher wages, some employers turned to the immigrant workers who had stayed with the firm, promoted them to supervisory positions, and left it to them to recruit new workers. These ethnic supervisors—some of whom had acquired legal status—turned to their friends and relatives to fill vacant jobs.

In California, the Southwest and a growing number of midwestern cities, as American workers quit, their replacements were drawn increasingly from Mexican villages. Small businesses that had suffered from the high turnover of American workers soon realized that illegal immigrant workers gave them, at least for a while, the same reliable work forces as those enjoyed by mainstream businesses, but without raising wages or improving labor standards.

The low-cost illegal immigrant workers hired and supervised by ethnic foremen were a welcome relief to the often shaky businesses that depended on them. A furniture or shoe manufacturer in high-cost Los Angeles could be assured of a virtually unlimited supply of eager minimum wage workers who could be trained in one day and closely supervised to assure quality work. A restaurant or hotel could offer its customers superior back room service without increasing its production costs because illegal immigrants proved to be more loyal and dependable than the mixed crews of Americans they replaced. Businesses became dependent on illegal immigrants because they realized that they could get the employee loyalty and reliability of high-wage and mainstream businesses, even at minimum wages and without fringe benefits and investment in professional personnel management.

The secret to such work force changes lay in the employer's decision to turn work force recruitment and supervision over to an ethnic foreman who could recruit illegal alien friends, relatives and countrymen as workers. Once an initial ethnic work crew was assembled, the workers' information network perpetuated the recruitment and training of new workers with no advertising, screening or training costs to the employer.

As illegal immigrants learn more about the U.S. labor market, they are more prone to quit one low-skilled job for another because wages are higher or the work is easier. As settled immigrant workers acquire some of the traits of American workers, employers must either upgrade wages and working conditions or tap into a more recent immigrant network. The more recent recruits usually spend from several months to a few years on the job before they too begin to get restless.

Network recruitment and ethnic supervision change the nature of the work place, making it even less congenial to the American worker. The language of the work place changes from English to Spanish or Chinese. Most of the illegal immigrant workers are friends and relatives, and the workplace culture changes to reflect their shared experiences, such as growing up in a Mexican village. Frequently, the business owner loses touch with the workers because he or she cannot speak their language and comes to depend on a bilingual supervisor to be an intermediary.

The network recruitment and ethnic supervision system is an efficient way to hire low-cost workers. New employees can be recruited quickly, trained at little or no cost to the employer by friends and relatives already employed, and laid-off during business downturns. As long as ethnic supervisors remain employed, the work force can be reassembled or a new work force recruited if business picks up. If an entire work force is apprehended by the INS or discharged an employer can pay a coyote (labor smuggler) $300 to $1,000 per worker for a new work force to establish a new network recruitment system.

Field research confirms the existence of kinship and village networks that educate workers abroad about U.S. job opportunities and wages.[3] These networks provide information and sometimes financing for the trip across the U.S. border, acting as private employment agencies and training schools for new arrivals.

Initially, the pioneer migrants from abroad are young men who come to the United States as target earners, hoping to save enough money for economic advancement back home. As migrant networks "mature," however, pioneer migrants find better jobs and gradually help friends and relatives move up in the U.S. labor market. Better U.S. jobs are harder to give up, and some migrants send for their families. The arrival of women and children extends job networks into new workplaces, encouraging more families to come to the United States.

The pace of network maturation varies considerably: some networks make the transition from farm to factory within five years, others continue to link Mexican villages and U.S. farms as they have done for two generations. Most field research, however, suggests that more and more illegal workers are bypassing low-wage farm jobs and going directly to urban areas, where immigrant families have gained a foothold, persisted and now fill jobs in a variety of workplaces.

As different Mexican villages get linked with particular American work places, the network recruitment system increases the dependency of Mexican villages on the American labor market.[4] Instead of adopting public and private policies to create jobs that would reduce emigration pressures in the future, the Mexican government often neglects areas that can live off remittances and traditionally concentrates its own resources on capital-intensive development. The village itself looks to its workers in the United States for income instead of developing its own limited resources. The recruitment network erects an umbrella over American workplaces, reserving these jobs for workers from a particular Mexican village or region. This network is the primary asset of many Mexican villages; it increases the wealth of the village, because village workers can obtain jobs in the United States and send back remittances. Particular villages "own" the jobs in various American farms, hotels and factories.

Decades of such cross-border dependency have made these recruitment networks an integral part of the fabric of Mexican village economies and Mexican workers key parts of some U.S. industries. As these labor migration networks become more entrenched, the economic impacts of illegal immigrant workers change. Some illegal workers settle with their families in the United States and their attitudes and workplace behavior change. Indeed, both the Mexican villages and the U.S. firms in many cases come to depend on a constant migration of new workers across the border: the villages to continue the remittances, and the firms to keep their migrant workers flexible. As European nations discovered with their legal foreign workers, time spent in the country more than extension of citizenship or political rights to foreigners determine the economic impacts of migrant workers.[5] Network recruitment not only excludes American workers from certain jobs, it also builds a dependency relationship between U.S. employers and Mexican sources that requires a constant infusion of new workers.

Ethnic recruitment networks are not a recent feature of American labor markets. A turn-of-the-century study of labor markets concluded that "most white immigrants secured employment directly or indirectly through compatriots . . . employers had quite definite ethnic preference in hiring . . . over time, these ethnic employment patterns solidified still further and social networks provided the new foundation for recruitment . . . these networks rarely crossed ethnic boundaries."[6] As in the past, today's ethnic networks make it difficult for a single public agency, such as the employment service, to collect and disseminate job-matching information to all workers because the private job information networks are considered better by both employers and alien workers. Established employers are dependent on the system. Prospective new entrepreneurs open businesses in those areas and are assured that network recruitment will provide them abundant low-cost, flexible labor.

Network recruitment and ethnic supervision yield three workplace ironies for American workers:

—Unemployed English-speaking workers are excluded from categories of U.S. jobs because they do not speak the "right" workplace language, do not fit in culturally or do not have the "right" contacts to learn about these nonadvertised job vacancies.

—Employers using the network, for whom wages are 30 to 60 percent of production costs, typically can get by with small personnel offices or none at all—in sharp contrast to the large personnel departments maintained by businesses elsewhere that are highly dependent on people.

—Illegal alien workers replace Americans because they work cheaper and harder and because they are readily available as American workers quit. Periodic INS raids, paradoxically, may make such immigrant work forces even more reliable because they permit the employer to weed out trouble-makers without seriously disrupting production schedules.

These work place realities can be illustrated with case studies of several businesses.

The American workers who were once recruited for low-wage, high-turnover jobs have lost the bridge that used to connect them to such jobs. Poorly educated and trained American workers who do not have friends and relatives already employed in such work places are less likely to obtain jobs and learn even rudimentary work skills such as coming to work every day and listening to a supervisor's instructions. Many observers have emphasized the effect of un-employment on this missing bridge to jobs. Charles Murray notes that in the 1970s low-income youths became "decoupled from the mechanism whereby poor people in this country historically have worked their way out of poverty,"[7] although Murray blames the availability of welfare, not immigrant workers, for destroying the job bridge.

Restaurants and hotels include in their work forces some citizens or legal workers, because they need English-speaking clerks and waiters. Most illegal aliens are usually confined to kitchen and cleaning jobs. A major hotel may have several hundred cleaning and kitchen jobs, but few are available when the ethnic supervision and network recruitment system is in place. Instead of advertising vacant jobs or posting vacancies at the Employment Service, the friends and relatives of immigrant workers are recruited privately. Since these recruitment networks operate efficiently within ethnic enclaves in the United States and villages abroad, unemployed Americans who scan the want ads and visit the Employment Service seldom learn about such job vacancies. An unemployed American who tries to apply for such jobs directly is sometimes referred to a supervisor who speaks little or no English, and many then give up the search. The cross-border recruitment system provides illegal alien workers with a more sophisticated job-search network than is available to many unemployed American workers.

Fruit and vegetable farming is an $18 billion a year business (at the farm level). Wages are 30 to 60 percent of the cost of producing oranges, strawberries and grapes.[8] A strawberry farmer, for example, can incur wage costs of $12,000 to $15,000 per acre and aim to obtain $25,000 for the strawberries. Fruit and vegetable farming is a high-cost, high-risk and potentially high-profit enterprise. If everything goes right the farmer may reap a profit of $5,000 per acre, a sharp contrast to the average gross revenue of $100 per acre for a Kansas wheat farmer and profits in a good year of $10 to $20 per acre.

High-value farm commodities are often perishable—to obtain the best quality and price, fruits and vegetables should be picked within windows of three to seven days.

Given the high-potential profit and high risk nature of strawberry production, a 100-acre strawberry farmer with an annual payroll of $1.2 million could seemingly benefit from a personnel department that would carefully screen workers, develop programs to attract and retain the best harvesters and ensure productivity. The typical strawberry farm, however, has no such personnel department. Most growers assume that a harvest work force will be available when it is needed. Most growers simply hire everyone who shows up to pick, pay them piece-rate wages so that the cost of harvesting is about $1.25 per twelve-pint tray whether the strawberries are picked by a fast worker or a slow one, and lay workers off from day to day during the season and at the end of the season. Ethnic crew leaders and farm labor contractors assume the farm's personnel management function, recruiting and supervising harvest workers. By relying on the ethnic recruitment and supervision system, growers do not have to devote themselves to personnel management.

Network recruitment can stabilize low-wage employment, encouraging employers accustomed to high worker turnover to establish work rules that make jobs even more unattractive to American workers and reduce pressures from the more settled illegals for improved wages and conditions. Some hotels and restaurants for example, have put more of their work forces on "on-call" status. Workers are expected to be available, but they are paid only if they are actually needed. Other businesses have adopted split shifts: some janitorial firms have converted an eight-hour shift into two four-hour shifts, lessening the attractiveness of jobs. Unionized hotels and restaurants have resisted on-call and split-shift policies that increase worker turnover, but employers with long waiting lists of job applicants or with access to an efficient recruitment network feel free to make such changes.

Illegal alien workers are often valued more than Americans because of lower absenteeism rates. If employers want a reliable low-wage work force, then periodic INS raids presumably should make illegal aliens less reliable and encourage employers to turn to Americans. Periodic INS raids, however, can help increase the reliability of an illegal alien work force because the benefits of permitting an employer to winnow out "troublemakers" can outweigh the costs of disrupted production.

As illegal immigrant workers learn about American society and their workplace rights, some workers become union activists and demand wage and fringe benefit improvements. An ethnic supervisor may not want to risk the unlawful step of firing workers solely because of union activities. Firing may also boomerang by encouraging the friends and relatives of the fired worker to become pro-union. An easier way for some employers to rid themselves of immigrant troublemakers is to wait for, or even request, an INS raid and then selectively rehire apprehended workers when they return. Selective rehiring—even though it too is unlawful—is one reason why employers of illegal alien workers frequently report that they have "a good relationship" with the INS.[9]

Legal and illegal immigrants are a double-edged sword for American unions. Most unions are opposed to large-scale illegal immigration because a larger work force reduces union bargaining strength. Illegal immigrant workers, however, tend to concentrate in goods-producing industries that have traditionally been union strongholds but have shed workers in the 1970s and 1980s. Some unions recruit illegal workers to maintain their bargaining power; since nonunion firms using illegal workers could soon undercut established unionized firms. Union leaders at times are trapped between employers seeking wage concessions to stay in business and immigrant workers whose presence generated or preserved the business, forcing difficult decisions on where to draw the line on concessions to save jobs. Unions representing work forces that are 50 percent illegal are reluctant to call strikes because illegal alien strikebreakers from other village networks are readily available and because employers often ask the INS to check the legal status of strikers.

Network recruitment and ethnic supervision explain how illegal aliens gain a foothold with certain businesses and then exclude unemployed English-speaking workers from job vacancies. Unlike the one-for-one displacement hypothesis, network recruitment allows the low-wage employer to have at his disposal a reliable work force without having to weigh the merits of two or more workers competing for a single job slot. Unlike the segmented theory, network recruitment emphasizes the initial mingling of American and immigrant workers in the work place and the tendency of the recruitment system—and the nature of the job— to eventually exclude Americans. Reinforcing these economic barriers are the cultural and linguistic isolation the minority English-speaking American worker feels in breaking into or adjusting to a workplace dominated by non-English speaking immigrants.

Network recruitment helps to explain why illegal aliens eventually dominate the work forces of particular farms and factories. But why don't unemployed Americans replace the illegals apprehended in well-publicized raids such as the 1982 Operation Jobs? The answer is complex and varies from firm to firm: illegals usually work harder than American workers; unlike U.S. workers, illegals lack an alternative to low-wage jobs; illegals may be able to better evade U.S. taxes; and illegals are less likely to insist that employers obey labor standards laws—all characteristics making them preferred in the eyes of employers.

Anecdotal and survey evidence suggests that many illegal aliens at least initially work harder than similar American workers. Many of the jobs filled by illegals are physically demanding, and American workers hoping to eventually find a better job are more likely to complain. Illegal aliens, on the other hand, often have a savings target and are willing to work very hard to keep their jobs. Such workers maintain a fast pace under piece-rate wages to maximize their earnings. Illegal alien workers often accomplish more during each hour worked in certain jobs and often work more hours per week or year than American workers.[10] In some instances, the availability of illegal alien workers makes it unnecessary to spend money to make the work environment better.

Why are illegal alien workers satisfied with the relatively low wages that American workers would complain about? The most important reason is expectations: American workers, raised in a culture that emphasizes high consumption and upward mobility, realize that low wages will not buy them the American dream. For young American workers, high turnover farm and factory jobs offer only temporary employment until a "real" job becomes available. American workers also have easier access to safety net programs such as welfare and unemployment insurance, and are thus not forced to accept "immigrants' jobs."

Many illegal aliens similarly regard their U.S. farm and factory jobs as temporary, but the illegal alien workers see U.S. wages of five to ten times their earnings at home as a temporary bonanza, not a temporary purgatory. However, just as many young American workers get trapped into low-wage jobs for a lifetime, so many illegal alien workers eventually settle in the United States instead of returning.

Different expectations are the most important reason that illegal alien workers are satisfied while American workers fret about the same jobs. However, there are also economic reasons for the illegal workers' satisfaction. Employers concern themselves with the total costs of hiring labor: wages, payroll taxes for social security and unemployment insurance, and fringe benefits such as health insurance and pension benefits. In contrast, many of the young illegal workers in low-wage jobs are concerned primarily with their take-home pay. In some instances, illegals can be paid a lower overall hourly wage than American workers but still obtain more take-home pay.

For most workers, hourly wages are only 75 percent of total wage costs because employers must also pay social security, unemployment insurance and disability coverage. Many employers also voluntarily provide fringe benefits such as health insurance and pension benefits. Since illegal workers are less concerned about fringe benefits than American workers, employers can eliminate fringe benefits and save money. Some employers go further and illegally fail to make required contributions for social security or disability insurance, saving up to 20 percent of their wage costs. These employers gamble that this failure to pay mandatory taxes will go unnoticed because illegal alien workers will be afraid to apply for benefits.

Sometimes employers and illegal alien workers cooperate to avoid taxes by dividing up the 7 percent worker and 7 percent employer contribution to social security. No income taxes are withheld from the farmworkers unless the worker requests withholding, and many nonfarm workers claim large numbers of dependents to minimize the income tax withheld and then fail to file income tax returns.

Employers sometimes hire workers as "independent contractors" so that the workers are responsible for making their own tax payments. In agriculture, this "independent contractor" status permits the worker to employ his children legally as farmworkers. In construction and services, "independent contractors" frequently change job sites to hamper detection and prosecution. Finally, some employers hire only "casual" workers, since an employer is not required to withhold income or social security taxes from workers employed less than thirty days. "Casual" workers are sometimes re-employed month after month.

Illegal alien workers may willingly cooperate with employers to avoid income and payroll taxes, or they may often be unwilling or uninformed parties to it. But, illegal workers are almost always the victims of employer attempts to reduce costs by violating laws regulating minimum wages and maximum hours, safety and health standards in the workplace, and the right to organize and bargain. The underfunded and undermanned Department of Labor inspection staff often relies on complaints to determine which of the six million business establishments to inspect. An illegal alien work force is less likely to complain. Employers in industries prone to work place accidents such as agriculture and construction are inclined to prefer illegal workers to minimize the potentially high costs of complying with safety and health standards.

Can employers distinguish between legal and illegal workers? Many employers assert they "know" who is legal and illegal. A San Diego farmer had used this reasoning: "Since we've got about 99 percent undocumented in the field, I consider anybody who shows up to be undocumented."[11] A study of hiring by Los Angeles manufacturing plants found that a worker's legal status "was deduced from his speech (use of Spanish) and references. Often jobs went to friends or family members of the undocumented production workers." Thus, after illegals gain a foothold, employer knowledge, preferences, and immigrant recruitment networks reinforce each other to yield concentrations of illegal immigrant workers. In eleven Los Angeles manufacturing firms making auto parts and plastics with thirty five to 1,000 workers, seven surveyed had work forces that were at least 90 percent immigrant workers.

BUSINESS COMPETITION AND WAGE DEPRESSION

A frequent claim is that illegal aliens depress wages because employers know their vulnerability weakens their bargaining power relative to American workers. Although there are instances of such unequal pay for equal work, network recruitment often produces over the longer term illegal alien or American work forces, but not a mixture, in job categories such as kitchen staff, assembler or farm hand.[12] If enterprises in an industry tend to divide into those with mostly legal and those with mostly illegal workforces, then competition between them can depress wages, or it can displace American workers, or both. In most industries, the competitive process that ultimately displaces American workers is complex. Some examples might clarify it:

Subcontracting and Displacement

California and Arizona produce most of the nation's fresh citrus on farms that typically are owned by corporations or absentee investors. The packinghouses that sort and sell oranges and lemons to retail stores coordinate the citrus harvesting. Citrus harvest crew leaders must deal with these packinghouses to coordinate the flow of fruit from the grove to the supermarket. Harvest crews are organized by labor contractors, employer associations, packinghouses and individual growers or farm managers.

The southern California lemon industry provides an unusually clear illustration of how competition between employer associations (which tried to avoid hiring illegal aliens) on one hand and labor contractors (who depend on illegal aliens) on the other depressed wages and displaced American workers.[13] The employer associations hired bilingual managers in the early 1970s to establish professional and legal lemon harvesting crews. These managers then developed a standard wage and fringe benefit package that was among the best in agriculture. By 1978 the employer associations had stabilized the harvest work force at one-eighth its previous size and the average worker at the largest co-op earned $5.63 hourly and $3,400 for seasonal work that lasted ten to thirty weeks.

Lemons are overproduced. Only a carefully selected 25 to 40 percent of those harvested are sold to consumers as fresh lemons. Most lemons are diverted to the money-losing processing market. Farmers are usually required to harvest all of their lemons to receive the money-making price for the 25 to 40 percent sold as fresh lemons.

Several years of low lemon prices coincided with a union-organizing drive in 1978 and 1979 to yield union election victories among lemon harvesters, already among the best paid farm workers in the United States. Growers resisted unionization by encouraging labor contractors to come into the area and harvest lemons. The contractors relied on illegal alien workers, who did not demand increased wages or fringe benefits. Meanwhile, the union won wage increases and refused to make concessions because it needed the wage gains to increase its appeal to unorganized workers. These wage increases proved to be a Pyrrhic victory. Labor contractors soon took market share away from the unionized co-ops. While they had harvested 80 percent of the area's lemons in 1979, the co-ops harvest less than 10 percent today. Contractors increased their market share from 10 to 80 percent.

Contractors dependent on illegal aliens displaced American workers and depressed wages, even though it's hard to find these effects in labor statistics. Some of the unionized workers are still employed, but for fewer weeks and with more use of unemployment insurance. The lower wages paid by labor contractors rarely get reported in labor statistics. When contractor wages are reported, they tend to be misleadingly high because they do not include overcharges for transportation, housing, meals and work equipment.

Labor contractors and illegal alien workers replaced labor co-ops and U.S. citizen and legal immigrant workers over five years ago. Now that labor contractors harvest most of the lemons, the lemon industry can assert that "without illegal aliens we will go out of business," since the co-ops, their work forces, and their infrastructure are disappearing. It was not the nature of the job that made the lemon industry dependent on illegal aliens, it was a series of decisions to reduce harvesting costs and to turn to labor contractors that replaced American workers with illegal aliens.

A similar displacement process occurred in San Diego agriculture. In the mid-1970s the fear of union activity in southern San Diego county and the advantage of the inaccessibility to the Border Patrol of the hilly rural northern area encouraged producers of tomatoes and strawberries to, in the words of one grower, "look for a farm that has a certain amount of inaccessibility."[14] The United Farm Workers (UFW) union charged that one large tomato grower deliberately discriminated against the legal farmworkers who wanted UFW representation, most of whom were Mexican legal residents or commuters. An appellate court summarized the displacement process:

> Before 1975 factors favoring legals had included their relative permanence and immunity from deportation, while the illegals had in their favor their willingness to do more work for less money . . . after 1975 [the employer] admittedly began preferentially hiring from the illegals.[15]

San Diego agriculture illustrates both how illegal workers displaced legal workers and how this displacement process has impeded mechanization, since the hills inaccessible to the Border Patrol also work against the use of machinery.

Subcontractors and immigrant workers have displaced construction workers in a similar fashion. Michael Piore, immigration specialist, drew a distinction between the role of immigrant workers in Europe and the United States:

> Construction is the most intensive employer of immigrants throughout Northern Europe. In a good part of the United States, however, construction crafts are the aristocracy of blue collar work; positions are reserved for native workers, and the minorities . . . have been carefully excluded.[16]

Piore's argument that the strength of unions and high skill requirements made it difficult for American contractors to employ immigrant workers is a contention not supported by recent trends.

The construction industry shares many of agriculture's features: it is an important sector of the economy; there are thousands of contractors and even more subcontractors, but a few firms account for much of the new building in a region;

and construction employment is seasonal. Wages are typically half of the total costs of building.

The construction industry has three major subsectors: general builders and commercial construction, new home building and rehabilitation of existing buildings. Unions are strongest in the general construction of downtown offices and major projects such as dams and bridges, in part because governments are often buyers of such projects. On such projects, most workers satisfy Piore's definition of blue-collar aristocrats.

The work forces of new home builders are more diverse. While many union workers are employed on home sites, contractors and subcontractors also turn to illegal immigrant workers to fill both skilled and unskilled jobs and to blunt union organizing efforts.

Home-building and "rehab" work are often dominated by financially-strapped subcontractors who reduce labor costs to help them bid low on jobs and then make the work profitable. A study of labor in the Manhattan construction industry found that illegal immigrant workers, often trained by their fathers in Jamaica or the Dominican Republic and recruited by kinship networks, dominate the "rehab" work forces of subcontractors.[17] Most of the employers had fewer than ten workers, and many of the building permits listed a much smaller rehab task than was actually undertaken, concealing the spread of illegal immigrant workers in this sector.

A similar story of subcontracting and competition among businesses with different degrees of dependence on illegal aliens explains how flexible and lower cost contract janitorial services have displaced direct hire janitors and have encouraged the subcontracting of garments and computer assembly jobs. In many cases, a mainstream business seeking to lower production costs seeks savings by subcontracting particular operations: examples are the building owner who can either hire a janitorial staff or rely on a janitorial service or the apparel company that can hire seamstresses directly or subcontract sewing. The search for lower costs pushes such businesses to subcontractors who recruit illegal immigrants as workers.

The use of illegals by subcontractors has two pernicious effects. First, if subcontractors really are cheaper, most businesses are forced eventually to switch to them to compete. Different businesses will feel different degrees of pressure: mainstream vegetable farms paying hourly wages of $10 or more to U.S. citizens and legal immigrants are hurt by the subcontracting of competitors, as are unionized garment shops that must compete with sweatshops. Janitorial service is a relatively small cost of building ownership. But when vacancies reduce rents, building owners seek to cut costs. No business is an island. If one business can save by subcontracting to an illegal work force, other businesses face competitive disadvantages if they do not follow suit.

Business competition can promote the spread of subcontracting across an industry, change the structure of jobs and discourage American workers from taking jobs that might have once been acceptable. An unskilled American worker might be willing to start as a janitor for a major bank or insurance company and hope to work up the job ladder. But the same worker may shun what he sees as a dead-end job with a janitorial service that only cleans buildings. Similarly, an American worker willing to join a major building contractor or manufacturer as an unskilled worker may turn down a job with a subcontractor who only handles low-wage cleanup or assembly operations.

The availability of illegal alien workers and the search for lower costs link up to promote subcontracting, which then selectively lowers some production costs and transfers others to society as a whole, while it discourages American workers from seeking certain jobs.

Subcontracting and illegal alien work forces are no longer confined to established immigrant sectors such as agriculture, footwear and garments. Subcontracting and illegal alien workers also sustain more glamorous high tech industries such as computers, plastics and telecommunications.[18] In the semiconductor and electronics industry, unskilled operators outnumber engineers eight to one. Many of these operators are immigrant workers stuffing circuit boards on traditional assembly lines. These assembly line jobs have been migrating abroad; the so-called "Atari-Democrats" of 1983 needed to change the descriptive adjective associating them with high tech employment after Atari moved several thousand low-wage assembly jobs from California to lower-wage Asian nations.[19] Low-skill high-tech jobs that do not move abroad are often automated in the United States.

As high-tech manufacturers have been increasing their employment, established smokestack manufacturing firms in autos, steel and rubber are laying off experienced American workers. But there has been little transference of workers from the shrinking industries to the growing ones. Most new high tech workers are immigrants and American women who have never had manufacturing jobs before. *Business Week* quotes observers who note that most government planners have failed to realize that displaced manufacturing workers "spurn high tech jobs as menial and demeaning," although these officials persist in unrealistic plans to lure high-tech firms to shore up their local economies.[20]

The movement of unskilled manufacturing jobs abroad raises trade and productivity questions. Even with low wage immigrant workers, many American firms still cannot compete with imports. For example, the electronics trade deficit was $7 billion in 1984. Most electronic production processes involve engineering and scientific conception as well as manufacturing and assembly, and distribution and maintenance. Some argue that without the low wage (immigrant) workers, the higher skilled "good" technical and professional jobs held by American workers will be lost to overseas competitors. But with the United States as the world's largest market-place, distribution and maintenance jobs are likely to remain near consumers. Even if manufacturing and assembly line jobs migrate abroad, the United States will still retain most of the concept creative jobs that accompany new products.

Immigration Enforcement and Business Failure

Subcontracting often lowers wage costs and decreases the attractiveness of jobs to American workers. Subsequent INS enforcement of immigration laws against such subcontractors is then wrongly blamed for destroying a business. During the 1970s, for example, low wage manufacturing employment expanded in California despite escalating housing prices. Some of these new and expanding businesses are now dependent on a flexible and low cost immigrant work force. If the INS conducts truly disruptive raids, business owners assert that their existence is threatened.

These business owners are probably correct—most of them will go out of business. But many of these marginal businesses will close in any event. Immigration enforcement is wrongly blamed for putting a firm out of business while the real reasons for business failure remain less clear.

A food processing example illustrates how enforcement can be blamed falsely for business failure. Processing chicken for the California market is a messy job done by black and white American workers in the Southeast, by Mexican-Americans in central California, and by illegal alien workers in the urban areas of northern California. Several of the northern California poultry processing firms were raided during the 1982 INS Operation Jobs. The poultry firms quickly claimed that Americans wouldn't do such work for the $5 to $6 an hour they were paying and that higher wages would put them out-of-business because of competition from the Southeast and central California.

The northern California poultry firms were being honest when they asserted that without illegal alien workers they would go out of business. What they failed to add was that even with such workers they could not survive because the poultry industry had changed and left them isolated.

Feed is about three-fourths of the cost of raising broilers. Northern California farmland that can grow grapes is too expensive to use for wheat and corn. Rising energy prices in the 1970s encouraged poultry production to shift to southeastern states—which produce 88 percent of U.S. broilers—that are closer to the midwestern corn fields. It takes two pounds of feed to produce one pound of poultry, making it cheaper to ship poultry instead of chicken feed to California. The INS Operation Jobs was a convenient target for the frustrations of northern California poultry processors, but the "real villains" are OPEC, the southeastern competitors who built modern processing facilities, and investors in vineyards—not the INS. Operation Jobs became a more visible target than the underlying economic reasons for business failure.

This example illustrates a basic feature of a dynamic economy: every business is buffetted constantly by changing economic forces. Many businesses do not survive: fully one-third of the 500,000 to 600,000 new businesses started each year in the United States soon fail. The Small Business Administration reports that 80 percent of all new businesses fail within ten years.[21] Even well established firms can find that they are in shrinking or sunset industries—as recently as the 1920s, there were over eighty American companies manufacturing cars. An illegal alien work force cannot buffer firms against the underlying economic forces that are affecting an industry, although it may preserve sunset business for a few more years. Illegal aliens are thus a selective subsidy to certain employers and industries. An employer who "needs" alien workers to fill $4 per hour jobs when American workers demand $5 hourly is simply asserting that the firm cannot operate without a wage subsidy.

The American economy is creating new businesses and jobs at an unprecedented rate, some of which will depend on the immigrant wage subsidy. The number of new businesses started annually has increased more than fivefold in three decades, from 90,000 to over 500,000 annually. This spurt in business activity has created jobs for professionals and managers and generated a great deal of praise for the entrepreneurial spirit of the U.S. economy. But even boosters such as John Naisbitt acknowledge that "most new jobs tend to fall on the no-skill, low-pay side" of the labor market,[22] jobs such as food service worker, custodian, clerk and attendant.

How many of these new unskilled and low wage jobs were created because illegal immigrant workers were available? An overall guess is difficult to make, but it is clear that during the 1970s, some industries expanded despite economic trends that should have made them contract. Low-wage garment manufacturing employment expanded in New York and Los Angeles, two of the urban areas where housing is most expensive. Other labor intensive manufacturers also expanded in those areas in defiance of the gap between low wages and high living costs, such as furniture and luggage, shoemaking and computer assembly. These mobile manufacturing industries, however, are poised to automate and/or move abroad if wages rise, so the United States simply gains a few years of sweatshop profits for its toleration of their employment practices.

Immigrant Workers: Benefits and Costs

By conservative estimates the American economy has absorbed three to six million illegal alien workers over the past ten years. Economic theory suggests that the presence of additional workers—be they teenagers, married women or immigrants—tends to depress wages, hold down consumer prices and increase business profits. These profits can then underwrite business investment that results in new firms and factories, new jobs, higher wages and productivity and a growing economy.[23]

This scenario of extra people-lower wages, lower prices-higher profits-faster economic growth rests on two critical assumptions: 1) the availability of idle resources such as land and capital (including technology), and 2) economies-of-scale in production. The "idle resources" argument was true for the first 150 years of American history—the United States had unexploited land and mineral resources that were developed with immigrant workers and both European and American capital.[24] Today the U.S. economy does not have resources that are idle because there is not enough unskilled labor. Solving the challenges on technology's frontiers might be expedited with the help of additional scientists and engineers, but no one seriously argues that a shortage of unskilled labor is slowing down technological progress.

The economic justification for more immigrant workers often rests on the presumed advantages of economies-of-scale. Immigration, it is argued, provides both more workers and more consumers. The additional workers make possible larger industries with greater output at lower unit cost; the increased volume of low-cost products is then consumed and made profitable in a market expanded by immigration.

Dissenting economists argue that economies-of-scale can be obtained with even greater efficiency through international trade and investment. Large-scale, low-cost production can better be achieved by taking the workplace to the labor rather than by bringing the labor to the workplace. Similarly, consumers of an American product can be spread throughout the world and still contribute to the ability of the U.S. consumers to buy that product at lower cost.

A second objection to the proposition that "immigrants don't cost—they pay" is that the lower wages-higher profits claimed are not necessarily translated into business investment that leads to more economic efficiency and lower consumer prices. It is one thing to have profits to invest—it is another to have an incentive to invest. The history of development of industrialized countries shows that rising wages were an incentive for both technological advances and for entrepreneurs to invest in the labor-saving machinery they made possible. These changes increased worker productivity and lowered consumer prices. Higher profits enable businesses to make productivity-increasing investments. The availability of low-wage labor deprives entrepreneurs of incentives to make such investments. As Ray Marshall noted in his dissent to the Final Report of the Select Commission on Immigration and Refugee Policy, "Additional supplies of low-skilled alien workers with third-world wage and employment expectations can not only lead employers to prefer such workers, it can also lead to outmoded labor-intensive production processes, to the detriment of U.S. productivity."[25]

Lower wages and higher profits can become a double-edged sword affecting economic growth. Higher profits enable firms to invest more, but lower wages can discourage firms from buying costly equipment when cheap labor is readily available. Low wages, uncertain economic prospects and high interest rates can discourage productivity-increasing investment despite high profits: as the *Wall Street Journal* notes: "Labor is a relatively cheap and flexible expenditure for companies to make, especially when you compare it with the price of capital and energy."[26] Low wages, uncertainty and high interest rates encourage many firms to hire easily laid-off workers instead of committing themselves to buy equipment which must be paid for whether it operates or not, helping to explain why parts of the American economy remain more labor-intensive in the 1980s. Like other forms of subsidy, illegal immigration has distorted the optimum allocation of resources in developing the economy.

Even though wages have been rising slowly in the 1980s, some U.S. businesses have been investing in labor-saving production methods because their managers believe that over the long haul the United States cannot compete with foreign producers on wages. A rubber company president is quoted as asserting that "We'll never have labor rates [in the U.S.] comparable to developing countries . . . we've got to out-innovate or out-automate the world if we're to have a chance of competing."[7] Even with wages rising slowly, the prospect of rising real wages can be an incentive for businesses to invest in labor-saving innovations. Businesses whose owners depend on immigrant workers and who believe that "cheap labor" will always be available, often fail to plan for higher cost labor in the future. They then echo agriculture's traditional lament that proposed immigration reforms will "put us out of business."

The U.S. economy must first absorb American minorities, teenagers and women—they are already here, and the country has already made a commitment to provide jobs for all Americans who want to work. Controlling the level of immigration is one of the few policy choices universally recognized as a sovereign right of nation-states. As Vernon Briggs emphasizes, immigration affects the number of workers in the United States, the operation of U.S. labor markets and business planning, so the U.S. government can and should regulate the number and kind of immigrants it admits in a way that maximizes the well-being of American workers already here.[28]

The unskilled illegal immigrants who entered the United States labor market over the past decade lowered overall wages, and have had marked effects on wages in particular labor markets.[29] American teenagers and women are spread throughout the country, and their varying levels of education and skill prevent locally concentrated impacts. Immigrants, however, are concentrated in particular industries, areas and occupations, and once they gain a foothold, ethnic network recruitment fills job vacancies and excludes unemployed Americans.

DOES THE AMERICAN ECONOMY NEED IMMIGRANT WORKERS?

There are two opposing positions on the American economy's "need" for immigrant workers. Some economists review the 1970s rapid growth in workers and jobs and assert that the United States faces labor shortages in the 1990s. At this time the percentage of elderly will grow, the participation of women in the work force will level off and the number of teenagers who enter the labor market will shrink. Other economists assert that labor-saving machinery, the growing use of part-time workers and flexible hours, later retirements and the shifting of low wage jobs overseas may lead to a surplus of unskilled workers. The "labor shortage" proponents believe that today's immigrants will be tomorrow's answer to labor shortages; while the "labor surplus" school argues that today's immigrants will add to tomorrow's unemployment problems.

An article of faith for many economists is that a market economy cannot suffer long from shortages because prices and wages change to eliminate them.

A shortage, by definition, requires adjustments. Economists expect the responses of businesses and consumers to higher "shortage" prices and wages to yield adjustments. For example, if the price of gasoline rises, consumers buy smaller cars and take fewer trips, decreasing the demand for gasoline while the higher prices encourage producers to search for more oil and scientists to develop efficient engines and alternative fuels. Similarly, rising wages set in motion forces that will eliminate labor shortages: Investors include labor-saving machines in their plants instead of assuming that workers will be readily available; some employers build overseas or import some labor-intensive components; and firms offer self-service options for cost-conscious consumers. The pace and ease of adjustment will vary from firm-to-firm and industry-to-industry, but the expectation is that when businesses believe there will be fewer low cost unskilled workers available in the future, they start to adjust.

Almost all Americans gained appreciation for how the economy adjusts to changing prices and wages by witnessing the reactions to rising energy and land prices during the 1970s. It is one thing, however, to say that the economy will adjust, and another to say how it should adjust. It is clear that rising wages for unskilled workers will force more adjustments on some firms and businesses than others. For example, labor-intensive businesses such as restaurants, hotels and other service establishments that employ a high-proportion of minimum wage workers may have to raise their prices if there are fewer unskilled workers. Consumers might go to restaurants less often if prices are raised, so volume and profits might drop. Understandably, many labor-intensive businesses do not welcome a decline in the flow of unskilled workers. Makers of labor-saving machinery, however, would see increased demand. Self-service establishments would benefit, as would the suppliers of automated banking and shopping machines.

Should Americans welcome a future with more or fewer immigrant workers? The answer to this question depends on what kind of economy we want. With more immigrants, there will be lower wages and more jobs; fewer immigrants mean higher wages and more machines. These alternative futures involve other non-economic national concerns such as population, environmental quality and democratic institutions. Whichever future is chosen, many production processes will still be mechanized or disappear in the United States, since other countries will mechanize and Americans will turn to cheaper imported goods. For example, the United States does not have to automate its auto factories, but if it does not, Americans will increasingly switch to lower-cost Japanese cars produced in automated factories. Some Americans lament the mechanization of farm production, but without it most consumers would buy bread made with mechanically-harvested Canadian or Argentine wheat.

The debate over future labor shortages or surpluses cannot be answered without asking what kinds of adjustments American society can and should make. One approach is to ask if the jobs and businesses created and preserved by the availability of illegal immigrant labor should exist in the American economy. Many observers assume that all jobs offered by employers should be filled: Michael Piore says that the jobs taken by foreign workers . . . "are critical to the functioning of an industrial society . . . any wholesale attempt to end the migration is, therefore, likely to be exceedingly disruptive to the operation of society and to the welfare of various interest groups within it."[30]

However, many of the jobs filled by immigrants are "artificial" in the sense that they are low in value-added and would disappear if wages rose slightly. The U.S. government has promised full employment for Americans. But admitting immigrant workers is a "privilege" that can be revoked. If the government opens the border gates to create and preserve jobs and businesses, then Americans should ask whether the resulting economic activity is worthwhile, and whether it balances the costs to society as a whole.

Most of the eighty million U.S. homes are cleaned by their occupants. This private housecleaning does not count in statistics as a job, business or as part of the GNP. Since there are vast numbers of workers in Latin America who would be eager to clean American houses for $2 an hour or less, the United States could, by opening its gates even more widely, create perhaps ten million new housecleaning jobs and several hundred thousand new cleaning businesses. The underlying reality—cleaning houses—would be unchanged, but the availability of low-wage immigrant workers would create jobs and businesses that would be counted in economic statistics as a gain. The Americans who used to clean their own homes would have more time available for work or leisure. If cleaning wages, however, were to rise to $4 or $5 hourly and immigrant cleaners were not available, many Americans would revert to cleaning their own homes. Many Americans might have been better off with the immigrant cleaning help, but the additional immigrant cleaning jobs and businesses, would have been "artificial" in the sense that they would disappear if the immigrant wage subsidy disappeared.

Many of the jobs and businesses currently created and preserved by illegal immigrants share some of this "artificiality" in the sense that they would disappear if illegal workers were not available. Many of the new landscaping and janitorial services would disappear, as would a variety of light manufacturing operations. The disappearance of some sunset enterprises, such as the northern California poultry processing industry, would be hastened.

Would the economy be hurt by the evaporation of these jobs and businesses? The answer is that all inevitable adjustments are costly, but that policies which promote necessary adjustments are in the best interest of the nation. The end of the bracero program in 1964 forced farmers to adjust. Some of those who did not turn to illegals mechanized, while others formed co-ops and developed settled and local work forces. Stopping illegal immigration in the 1980s would also require adjustments.

Evaporating jobs do not necessarily mean disappearing industries or declining output. During the 1930s there were seven million farmers. Today one-third as many farmers produce twice as much food and fiber. A business that sheds jobs and adopts productivity- improving technologies is more likely to survive in a dynamic economy than a business that resists labor-saving changes in an interdependent world.

It has been suggested that the United States should continue to import unskilled workers to avoid tariffs, quotas or other protectionist policies.[31] This argument recognizes that immigrant workers will for a time work at wages low enough to compete with imports. However, many of the industries clamoring for protection from imports, such as shoes, textiles and apparel, also employ illegal immigrants. A policy of "importing workers to avoid protection" often fails to head off pressures for further subsidies in the form of tariffs and quotas.

THE URGENCY OF REFORM

Immigration reform was fifteen years in coming in large part because employers who use illegals and businesses and private organizations that serve them acquired a strong vested interest in the status quo.

One way delay made reform more difficult was that the availability of low-wage immigrant workers becomes a resource that got capitalized into the values of land and business assets. A prospective farmer values land by examining its potential revenues and costs,[32] just as a buyer of an established janitorial and landscape service wants to know about revenues and costs. One of the most important costs in such businesses is wages, and low immigrant wages soon get capitalized into the prices of land and business assets. Old and new owners and their banks expect these assets to retain their value. Businesses may forget how much the value of their assets depends on the availability of low-wage labor until the source is threatened.

The longer a business has been dependent on a subsidy such as illegal immigrant labor, the better organized and more determined it becomes to resist changes that might reduce the subsidy, thus raising wage costs and reducing the value of business assets. Southwestern farmland is a prime example. Fifty years ago, the lack of water and labor uncertainties made much of the Southwest's farmland almost worthless. However, federal irrigation projects and Mexican farm workers have made southwestern farmland some of the most valuable in the United States. Owners of irrigated southwestern farms have organized themselves to prevent the loss of subsidies of both water and labor that are viewed after fifty years as their "God-given right." Their impressive organization and clout were evident in special arrangements for agricultural labor included in the 1986 Reform Act as a condition for its passage.

The longer illegal immigration persists, the more low wages will be incorporated into the values of business assets and the longer entrepreneurs will ignore options for less labor-intensive forms of production. Some of the service establishments, factories and farms of the most sophisticated economy in the world have depended on remote Mexican or Central American villages for unskilled labor. These dependencies distorted economic development in both the United States and Mexican economies: the U.S. economy has been importing large numbers of workers, along with goods and capital, despite unemployment of about 6.5 percent and idle industrial capacity; Mexico has been allowing the export of workers to the United States, thus increasing its dependency on and vulnerability to U.S. policies, while concentrating its own investment on the development of its own capital-intensive industries.

Without immigration reform, a more unequal society would continue to develop in the United States unabated, with troublesome separations. For example, some projections indicate that the California work force will be mostly immigrants or their descendants by 2010. These working immigrants, mostly non-white, will be supporting mostly white pensioners with their payroll contributions. Is American society resilient enough to handle the resulting tensions? Most of the immigrants have been concentrating in or near the urban areas of only five states, with attendant environmental and economic consequences for those areas.

The American economy may well have more jobs and businesses if, in the short run, illegal alien workers are allowed to enter freely and work in the United States.[33] But the number of jobs and businesses alone is not an accurate measure of the soundness of economic development or quality of life. Tolerating heavy illegal immigration introduces distortions into the economy that are difficult to remedy, while imposing environmental and social costs that must be borne by the society as a whole.

NOTES

1. Donald Huddle estimates that there is a 65 percent displacement ratio, i.e., "for every one hundred illegals employed, sixty-five U.S. workers are displaced or kept out of the job markets." Huddle's estimates are probably too high for the entire economy: most of his examples are from high-wage construction, where jobs do not yet have the stigma of being "immigrants jobs." See Donald Huddle, Arthur Corwin and Gordon MacDonald, *Illegal Immigration: Job Displacement and Social Costs* (Alexandria, Va: American Immigration Control Foundation, 1985), p. 2.

2. A Houston survey of unemployed American workers who might have been interested in the jobs vacated by the 1982 Operation Jobs project emphasizes the "undesirable" traits of such American workers. Of 122 workers who expressed an interest in these vacant jobs, 8 percent had no telephones and were thus hard to contact. The 100 workers interviewed were high school graduates with a mean age of twenty-seven who had earned an average of $7.06 hourly, had been unemployed 3.3 months, and were willing to work for $4.84 hourly. Most employers confronted with unemployed workers who had experienced such downward wage mobility would realize that they would quit for better-paying jobs as soon as possible, so these employers often prefer illegal alien workers. See Donald Huddle, "Jobs: Do Illegal Aliens Take Them and Do U.S. Workers Want Them," *The Mexican Forum* (Vol. 5, No. 1, January 1985), p. 5.

3. See the contributions by Richert and Massey; Mines; Jones, Harris, and Valdez; Guttierrez; and Dagodag in Richard Jone's, ed., *Patterns of Undocumented Migration: Mexico and the U.S.* (Totowa, NJ: Rowan and Allenheld, 1984).

4. One such network is documented in Richard Mines and A. deJanvry, "Migration to the U.S. and Mexican Rural Development," *American Journal of Agricultural Economics* (Vol. 64, No. 3, August 1982).

5. Mark Miller and Philip Martin, *Administering Foreign Worker Programs: Lessons from Europe* (Lexington, MA: Lexington Books, 1981).

6. Suzanne Model, "Ethnic Bonds in the Workplace," *Russel Sage Foundation Newsletter*, Vol. 6 (May 1985), pp. 6–7.

7. Charles Murray, "Welfare: Promoting Poverty or Progress," *Wall Street Journal*, May 15, 1985.

8. Philip Martin, *Seasonal Workers in American Agriculture: Background and Issues*, (Washington, D.C.: National Commission for Employment Policy, 1985).

9. INS enforcement is disruptive and is usually not welcomed by employers. However, many employers have adapted to standard enforcement practices so that proposed immigration reforms may have fewer effects than is often assumed. For example, a frequently-voiced employer assertion is that "good workers have good identification," and many employers already request identification before hiring.

Standard enforcement practice is to concentrate limited resources on the largest employers with the most employees. However, larger employers are most likely to hire the most legal workers and the most well-established illegals, since they tend to pay higher wages and offer more fringe benefits. If the INS and the Labor Department rationally concentrate enforcement on larger firms, they:

—apprehend the established illegals most likely to return to the United States.

—also interview legal workers who complain of discrimination.

—disrupt the larger businesses and generate vocal protests.

Smaller competitors who tend to hire more illegals at even lower wages are investigated less often because enforcement resources are limited. Thus, standard and rational enforcement practices can fragment employers into smaller units that are harder to detect. This fragmentation appears to be occurring in farm labor contracting, janitorial and landscape services, and other urban services.

10. Many illegal aliens are employed only part of the year in the United States, but the tendency of illegals to work more than forty hours per week (if the hours are available), has been documented in most recent empirical studies, buttressing a 1976 finding of David North and Marion Houstoun, *The Characteristics and Role of Illegal Aliens in the U.S. Labor Market: An Exploratory Study*, (Washington, D.C.: New Transcentury, 1976).

11. Joseph Nalven and C. Frederickson, *The Employer's View: Is There a Need for a Guestworker Program?* (San Diego: Community Research Associates, 1982), p. 29.

12. Rebecca Morales, "Transitional Labor: Undocumented Workers in the Los Angeles Automobile Industry," *International Migration Review*, Vol. 17, No. 4, p. 582.

13. Large-scale immigration has historically generated concentrations of foreign workers in certain occupations and industries. Walter Fogel notes that in 1910 "foreign-born workers were especially numerous in a few occupations . . . tailors . . . bakers, mine and apparel operatives, and laborers in manufacturing, transportation and utilities: . . . Foreign-born workers were found to be 58 percent of all workers in iron and steel manufacturing, 61 percent in meatpacking, 62 percent in bituminous coal mining and 69 percent in cotton mills." See "Immigrants and the Labor Market: Historical Perspectives and Current Issues" in Demetrios Papademetriou and Mark Miller, eds., *The Unavoidable Issue: U.S. Immigration Policy in the 1980s* (Philadelphia: ISHI, 1983), p. 73.

14. Richard Mines and Philip Martin, "Illegal Immigration and the California Citrus Industry," *Industrial Relations* (Vol. 23, No. 1, Winter 1984), pp. 139–149.

15. *The Employer's View*, p. 28.

16. Ibid, p. 25.

17. Michael Piore, *Birds of Passage: Long-Distance Migrants and Industrial Societies* (New York: Cambridge University Press, 1979), p. 18.

18. Diana Balmori, "Hispanic Immigrants in the Construction Industry: New York City 1960-1982," *New York University Occasional Paper 38*, 1983.

19. The Bureau of Labor Statistics considers 36 of the 977 industries with standard industrial codes to be high tech because their R & D expenditures and number of technical employees are at least twice the average for all U.S. manufacturing. Such industries include makers of drugs, computers, electronic components, aircraft and laboratory equipment.

20. Some Democrats reportedly endorsed the overseas migration of standard production jobs. Walter Mondale reportedly endorsed Robert Reich's call to recognize that production and jobs "which make routine the solution of older problems are coming to be the special province of developing nations." *The Next American Frontier* (New York: Time Books,1983).

21. *Business Week*, March 28, 1983, p. 90.

22. The United States has 2.5 to 3 million small businesses with 50 or fewer employees, and these small businesses account for most new jobs. However, the U.S. treasury estimates that small businesses underpaid their taxes by $27 billion in 1985. *Wall Street Journal*, May 20, 1985.

23. John Naisbitt, "Reinventing the American Corporation," *New York Times*, December 23, 1984.

24. In the words of Melvin Reder, ". . . an increased labor supply would reduce the real wage rate which, in turn, would increase the rate of return on capital (other things equal), leading to an increased rate of investment." Reder "The Economic Consequences," p. 222.

25. Indeed, Alan Olmstead notes that in the 1820s and 1830s new farmland was often more productive than established farmland—"it was common for grain farmers moving to the northern midwest to obtain twice the yield per acre than they achieved in their eastern homelands. The key point here is that bringing new land into production not only increased total output, it also resulted in higher output per person." See *Issues in American Economic Growth: Past, Present, and Future*, UCD Agricultural History Center Working Paper 16, 1984, p. 2.

26. Statement by Commissioner Ray Marshall, *Final Report of the Select Commission on Immigration and Refugee Policy*, Washington 1981, Appendix B, p. 365.

27. "Total Jobs Keep Rising Despite Many Layoffs and Talk of Recession," *Wall Street Journal*, March 24, 1980.

28. Quoted in *Business Week*, July 15, 1985, p. 57.

29. Vernon Briggs, *Immigration Policy and the American Labor Force*, (Baltimore: John Hopkins University Press, 1984).

30. Immigrant workers lowered the rate of increase in wages—in many instances, nominal wages continued to increase, but inflation-adjusted or real wages declined.

31. Michael Piore, "Illegal Immigration to the U.S.: Some Observations and Policy Suggestions," in *Illegal Aliens: An Assessment of the Issues*, (WDC: National Council for Employment Policy, 1976), p. 26.

32. J. N. Bhagwati, "Shifting Comparative Advantage, Protectionist Demands, and Policy Response Options." Paper presented to an NBER Conference May 8–11, 1980.

33. The availability of labor at predetermined wages affected the price of farmland through history. For example, Indians in Guatemala were forced to supply a certain number of workdays to hacienda owners until 1946, and "each piece of cultivated land enjoy(ed) the traditional, if not legal, right to an Indian work force. Indeed, the number of Indians determined the value of certain farms." Miles L. Wortman, *Government and Society in Central America: 1680–1840* (New York: Columbia University Press, 1982) p. 14.

34. The United States may be unwittingly "overbuilding" low-wage industries because immigrant workers are available, much as the U.S. economy got accustomed to cheap energy and was thus vulnerable to the OPEC price hikes. Tax laws and low-wage labor may, for example, lead to overcapacity and persistent profit squeezes in agriculture and hotels.

Seeking Common Ground for Blacks and Immigrants
By Jacquelyne Johnson Jackson

Economic competition between blacks and immigrants in the United States is not new. In an early example, the artisans in Philadelphia between 1790 and 1820 were mostly black, but they were largely displaced by whites. In the words of W.E.B. DuBois, this phenomenon was due to "the sharp competition of the foreigners and the demand for new sorts of skilled labor of which the Negro was ignorant, and was not allowed to learn.[1] The heavy influx of European immigrants between 1830 and 1860 also displaced many black workers.[2]

Booker T. Washington, the most prominent black leader of his era, questioned the preference for foreign workers in the southern labor market. Speaking before the Cotton States and International Exposition in Atlanta, Georgia, in 1895, he said:

> To those of the white race who look to the incoming of those of foreign birth and strange tongue and habits for the prosperity of the South, were I permitted I would repeat what I say to my own race, 'Cast down your bucket where you are.' Cast it down among the eight millions of Negroes whose habits you know. . . . As we have proved our loyalty to you in the past. . . . so in the future, in our humble way, we shall stand by you with a devotion that no foreigner can approach, ready to lay down our lives, if need be, in defence of yours, interlacing our industrial, commercial, civil, and religious life with yours in a way that shall make the interests of both races one.[3]

Despite Washington's plea, shortly after the turn of the century, seven southern states organized "immigration bureaus" to try to meet the South's labor needs with whites and to accelerate the Negro exodus to the North.[4] But the "Great Migration" of blacks from the South between 1916 and 1935 and their increasing employment in northern industries was in part a consequence of the drop in immigration during World War I and the tighter restrictions on both immigration and the use of temporary "nonimmigrant" workers after World War I.

But two decades of heavy immigration beginning in the 1960s, much of it by unskilled and uneducated workers, has given Washington's concern a new timeliness. A critical but at times neglected issue in the debates on immigration reform of the past decade and a half is the impact of legal and illegal immigration on the socioeconomic conditions of native blacks and other minorities, particularly those in the secondary, or low-skilled, labor market.

While blacks are affected in many ways, deserving special attention are: (1) the impact of legal and illegal immigrants on blacks in low-wage jobs in the secondary labor market, (2) the attitudes of blacks toward immigration reform before passage of the immigration act, (3) the voting positions of black congressmembers on the immigration reform and control bills of 1984 and 1986, and (4) the likely impact of the act on blacks living in areas with high concentrations of recent immigrants and refugees.

JOB DISPLACEMENT AND WAGE DEPRESSION

Anecdotal data, labor market statistics and simple observation show a pronounced trend during the past two decades of immigrant and refugee workers replacing many native black unskilled, semi-skilled and supervisory workers in such businesses as hotels, restaurants, fast food outlets, light manufacturing firms, construction firms and taxicab companies in metropolitan areas with heavy concentrations of recent immigrants and refugees. Indications of these trends have been confirmed by sectoral and regional studies during the past decade that suggest that undocumented workers displace low-skilled native workers and depress wages.

In the last few years, however, these conclusions have been challenged by studies that have received a great deal of attention although their methods are questionable.[5] Studies by Kevin McCarthy and Burciago Valdez for The Rand Corporation in 1985 and by Thomas Muller and Thomas Espenshade for the Urban Institute in 1984 contend that immigrants generally do not affect the employment opportunities or earnings of black Californians.[6] Their studies, while acknowledging the vulnerability of the least skilled, address incompletely the issue of job displacement of blacks by undocumented workers.

A major flaw, for example, in the McCarthy and Valdez study is its comparison of the earnings of year-round, full-time workers in 1969 and 1979 in reaching their conclusion that black earnings had outpaced that of Hispanics. The authors thereby ignored the competition that takes place between blacks and undocumented workers who are not year-round, full-time workers. In addition, they did not take full account of the blacks who were discouraged from looking for work, many of whom were abandoned by their employers in favor of undocumented workers.

The Muller and Espenshade report also suffered from using too simple a model for the labor market. Their analysis tested a linkage between the black unemployment rate and the percentage of Hispanics in the total population. The percentage of Hispanic immigrants of all ages, however, is clearly an inappropriate measure of their proportion in the labor force. If Muller and Espenshade had determined the relationship between black unemployment rates and the percentage of Hispanic immigrants in the local labor markets, their results may not have supported their claim that rising proportions of Hispanic immigrants in the local markets reduced black unemployment.

One of the most widely disseminated studies of the job displacement issue, which was prepared by George Borjas and Marta Tienda, concludes that immigrant workers rarely lower the earnings of native workers. However, even they acknowledged that their conclusions are based on "aggregated data for large and diverse groups of native workers" rather than on data for specific local markets and therefore does not represent what actually happens in local labor markets with large numbers of immigrant workers.[7]

Illegal immigrants, of course, are not evenly spread over the United States, but are concentrated in the major urban areas also favored by black citizens and in industries and occupations where blacks have been overrepresented. Five of the top ten urban black population centers (i.e., Chicago, Houston, Los Angeles, New York and Washington, D.C.) are also the areas where most illegal immigrants have settled.[8] Even several scholars who believe that immigrants don't displace a significant number of native workers on a nationwide scale, agree that in areas heavily populated by immigrants, steep competition between similarly skilled immigrants and native workers can be significant.[9]

Philip Martin has convincingly demonstrated that illegal workers tend to dominate certain work forces because immigrants eventually gain control of mid-level supervisory positions and job recruitment (See Chapter 2). Martin's analysis of network recruitment may well be the best explanation for the demise of black occupational kinship networks in job sectors where blacks once functioned as the primary recruiters and supervisors. In addition, Robert Ainsworth, in his study published by the National Commission for Employment Policy also concluded that undocumented workers often cause job displacement through the use of occupational kinship networks.[10]

Richard Mines, who studied the effects of undocumented Mexican workers on labor markets in California between 1977 and 1985, has revealed how employment sectors once filled by black workers, became dominated by immigrants receiving low wages. In the early 1980s, for example, employers in the high-rise office districts of Los Angeles began to use new contractors who had tapped into networks of recent immigrants to hire janitors. The rising proportion of immigrant janitors was accompanied by a substantial decline in the number of native black janitors and hourly janitorial wages plummeted from an average of about $13.00 an hour (including benefits) to just over the minimum wage. Mines also reported that employers replaced their veteran workers with recent immigrants in the frozen food industries in Watsonville, construction clean-up jobs in Orange County and janitorial work in San Jose.[11]

The proliferation of job networks that are controlled by immigrants and in turn hire other immigrants has particularly harmed the employment prospects of blacks who look for jobs by using their friends and relatives. Almost one-fifth of unemployed blacks typically use fewer than two job seeking methods; again most often rely upon their friends and relatives.[12]

In addition, blacks have been increasingly shut out of jobs because of "linguistic" discrimination. In Florida for instance, many hotels and other service employers now hire only Spanish-speaking or bilingual workers. These employers often perceive a lack of "fit" between blacks and their Spanish-speaking employees and customers. A growing number of local school districts and public agencies in areas with heavy concentrations of immigrants are hiring fewer monolingual professionals. Many black professionals fluent only in English are now losing out to bilingual competitors.

Blacks might even agree that immigrants create some jobs. But too often the jobs created are not for domestic minorities but for the next wave of immigrants recruited through ethnic networks, whether it be Miami's Cuban enclave, the garment industries of New York and New Jersey or the light industries of Los Angeles.

The controversy about the effects of immigrants and refugees on native black employment and earnings will persist until definitive data are available. But in the absence of such data, blacks and other vulnerable minorities deserve the benefit of the doubt: public policies should be shaped by values that promote economic equity for all citizens, including those Americans whose slave ancestors did not come to U.S. shores in search of freedom.

ATTITUDES ABOUT IMMIGRATION REFORM AND CONTROL

Whatever the studies show, polls show blacks perceive serious job competition with Hispanic workers as a fact. The most representative poll of black and Hispanic attitudes about immigration prior to the act is the 1983 telephone poll of a nationally representative sample of 800 blacks and 800 Hispanics. The public opinion poll was conducted by V. Lance Tarrance and Associates and Peter D. Hart Research Associates. Almost 96 percent of the black and 59 percent of the Hispanics respondents were born in the United States, and 98 percent of these black and 76 percent of these Hispanic respondents were American citizens.

A comparison of the black and Hispanic responses reveals both considerable similarities and some differences. Hispanics were substantially more likely than blacks to regard immigration reform and control as a most important or very important national issue, to favor admitting more legal immigrants and to support milder laws for illegal aliens. They were, however, less likely to consider it a major problem when illegal immigrants harmed unemployed Americans or lowered American wages. Blacks and Hispanics were similar in the percentages supporting penalties against employers hiring illegal aliens. But the Hispanics were far more supportive of amnesty for undocumented workers. Both groups tended to favor amnesty for undocumented workers who had resided in the United States for at least five years. Hispanics were substantially more likely to support public school and bilingual education for illegal immigrants. Both groups tended to oppose welfare benefits, except Medicaid, for illegal immigrants. They also strongly agreed that ballots should be printed in both English and Spanish.

Attitudes among the black respondents in the Tarrance-Hart poll did not differ substantially. Age and sex variations were slight. Compared to naturalized black

Table 3.1   Blacks' and Hispanics' views on immigration: Tarrance-Hart Poll, 1983

Interview Item	Blacks	Hispanics
Immigration is a most important or very important national issue.	56.3	72.4
U.S. should admit "fewer" or "a lot fewer" legal immigrants.	73.1	49.6
There should be tougher laws for illegal immigrants.	69.8	47.2
Illegal immigrants are a major harm to U.S. jobless.	69.2	45.9
Illegal immigrants lowering American wages is a major problem.	60.8	38.6
Restricting immigration is bad for the American economy.	47.9	50.9
Favor penalties against employers knowingly hiring illegal immigrants.	65.8	59.2
Favor amnesty for long-time undocumented workers.	57.2	74.1
Favor amnesty for those in the U.S. 5+ years.	59.9	59.2
Favor increasing border controls.	69.0	60.8
Favor free education for illegal immigrants.	55.6	70.1
Support educational instruction in English only.	66.4	43.2
Oppose illegal immigrants receiving welfare.	59.1	56.6
Favor illegal immigrants receiving Medicaid.	50.0	51.6
Support ballots printed in English and Spanish.	75.8	79.9

citizens and non-citizens, native blacks were far more supportive of tougher restrictions against illegal and legal aliens and much more likely to believe that undocumented workers displaced American workers and depressed their wages and working conditions. Compared to those respondents who did not complete college, most college graduates favored tougher enforcement penalties to curb illegal immigration, but were somewhat less likely to support enforcement. The same pattern was true of respondents in upper white collar jobs as compared with all other respondents, and of those with household incomes of $25,000 or more, as compared with lower-income respondents. In their support of free education, the black respondents did not differ significantly by income. Respondents whose incomes were under $10,000 were substantially more likely to believe that illegal immigrants should be eligible for welfare benefits and Medicaid. Opposition to illegal aliens receiving welfare was positively correlated with income.

The Tarrance-Hart findings for blacks generally match the findings in other national and regional polls about immigration reform. For example, in a 1983 telephone survey of 1,031 English-speaking respondents in six urban counties of southern California by the Field Research Corporation, Thomas Muller and Thomas Espenshade reported that 91 percent of the black respondents believed that the problem of illegal immigrants in their area was very serious or somewhat serious. Most also believed that illegal immigrants displaced area residents (*especially blacks*), and depressed wages. Both the Field poll and a 1983 *Los Angeles Times* poll found that more than 80 percent of the blacks surveyed, a higher percentage than for whites, supported penalties against employers hiring undocumented workers.[13] A 1986 poll by the *San Francisco Chronicle* reported that 48 percent of its black respondents believed that undocumented workers take jobs from Californians.[14] This percentage was only four percentage points higher than that reported in a 1986 *New York Times/CBS News Poll.*[15] However, the results of these two polls and the Tarrance-Hart poll are not directly comparable, owing to their sampling and instrumental differences. Therefore, it cannot be assumed that the proportion of blacks who believe that undocumented workers take jobs away from native workers has diminished over time. The results of these polls suggest that a strong plurality of blacks continue to believe that undocumented workers adversely affect many American workers.

A *Miami Herald* poll taken shortly after the 1980 Miami riots found that black attitudes towards specific immigrant groups tended to divide along ethnic lines. About 85 percent of the black respondents in Dade County (which includes Miami) believed that the Cuban refugees had "hurt black chances," while only 47 percent believed that the Haitian presence was harmful.[16] Black resentment towards Cuban refugees in Miami, whose numbers rapidly increased after the Mariel Boatlift, may have helped to precipitate the 1980 riots in that city. Moreover, in other cities, some blacks aired their resentment towards Asian small shopowners in black neighborhoods or resisted Southeastern Asian settlement in some previously racially segregated black neighborhoods.

Some black resentment of immigrants and refugees has also surfaced in the media, and especially on talk and call-in shows about immigrants and refugees. But a primary cause of this resentment has been typically overlooked by the media and the non-black public. The stark differences in the American reception of Cuban and Haitian refugees were far too discriminatory for Congressman George W. Crockett, Jr. In his House speech he spoke for millions of black Americans and other fair-minded Americans in protesting:

. . . [the] determined effort [of the INS and the Department of State] to exclude the first significant class of black refugees to come to our shores. The result has been racist in effect, regardless of intent . . . There has been much discussion that the [approximately 15,000] Haitian refugees are simply economic refugees and therefore not entitled to refuge in our country. This simplistic and distorted assertion emanates from a theoretical assumption that economics and politics are separable. This was not asserted nor could it be in the case of the Indochinese refugees.[17]

Crockett believes strongly, as do most black Americans, that due process and equal protection under the law, as well as economic assistance, must also be accorded to non-white refugees. Black resentment against preferential treatment given to non-black refugees, such as most of the Cubans, can only be understood within this context.

In general, recent polls of black views on immigration, coupled with periodic reports in the media of certain black behavior towards immigrants and refugees, suggest strongly that most blacks favor immigration reform to halt illegal immigration and to reduce legal immigration. The view is based largely on their belief—rightly or wrongly—that many blacks have been and will continue to be harmed by the growing presence of immigrants, and because they tend to view native blacks and immigrants and refugees as prospective competitors who will increasingly gain an edge over them if history repeats itself.

POSITIONS OF BLACK CONGRESSIONAL REPRESENTATIVES

Until 1986 curbs on illegal immigration had virtually no support among blacks in Congress. In 1984 only one member of the Congressional Black Caucus, Harold Ford, voted for the Simpson-Mazzoli bill, despite the polls showing that a majority of American blacks supported employer sanctions.

Many observers were surprised when most black representatives failed to support fully the immigration bills of 1984 and 1986. Some of their surprise came from their assumption that the constituents of black representatives are black and that those representatives should vote the views of their constituents. But in fact only 60 percent of the blacks in the 99th Congress represented predominantly black districts; the majority of blacks in the United States do not reside in those districts. Another false assumption is that American blacks are politically monolithic and that they are the sole or primary constituents of black representatives in the Congress.

Some believe that the lack of support in 1984 and 1986 for immigration reform among black representatives was due to a presumed alliance with Hispanic congressmembers and with Hispanic political leaders in their districts. Five of the six black representatives with the largest proportion of Hispanics in their districts (over 20 percent) voted against the conference report of the 1986 bill. In contrast, four of the five representatives with the lowest percentages of Hispanics in their districts (1 percent or less) voted for the report, indicating that the presence or absence of Hispanic constituents was a factor in the representatives' voting patterns. But the rhetoric of the floor debate suggests a different story. Only one black representative referred explicitly or directly in the hearings or debates to the Hispanics' position as a reason for his opposition to the bill. Judging by the debate, the black congressmembers were more concerned with what they considered substantial flaws in the bill than they were with voting in tandem with some of their Hispanic colleagues.

Another factor in black opposition to the bill was the perception that the bill discriminated against Haitian refugees. The lack of provisions favorable to Hai-

Table 3.2 Voting patterns of black representatives on the 1984 and 1986 immigration reform legislation

Representative	State	(1984) H.R. 1510	(1986) H.R. 3810
William L. Clay	Mo.	Nay	Yea
Cardiss Collins	Ill.	Nay	Yea
John Conyers, Jr.	Mich.	Nay	Not Voting*
George W. Crockett, Jr.	Mich.	Nay	Not Voting
Ronald V. Dellums	Cal.	Nay	Nay
Julian C. Dixon	Cal.	Nay	Yea
Mervyn M. Dymally	Cal.	Nay	Nay
Harold E. Ford	Tenn.	Yea	Yea
William H. Gray III	Pa.	Nay	Yea
Katie Hall	Ind.	Nay	—
Augustus F. Hawkins	Cal.	Nay	Nay
Charles A. Hayes	Ill.	Nay	Nay
Mickey Leland	Texas	Not Voting	Nay
Parren J. Mitchell	Md.	Nay	Not Voting*
Major R. Owens	N.Y.	Nay	Yea
Charles B. Rangel	N.Y.	Nay	Yea
Gus Savage	Ill.	Nay	Nay
Louis Stokes	Ohio	Nay	Yea
Edolphus Towns	N.Y.	Nay	Nay
Alton R. Waldon, Jr.	N.Y.	—	Yea
Alan Wheat	Mo.	Nay	Yea

Sources: Congressional Record, June 20, 1984; Congressional Record, October 9, 1986.
*Not voting, but paired against passage of bill.

tian refugees in the 1982 version of the bill prompted the Congressional Black Caucus to form a Task Force on Haitian Refugees. H.R. 1510 provided for the legalization of all eligible Cuban and Haitian entrants in the United States, but Congressmember George Crockett was still seriously concerned that the choice of a cut-off date of January 1980, instead of a January 1982, was anti-Haitian as most Haitians arrived after January 1980.[18]

In 1986 several Black Caucus members objected to the provisions for temporary agricultural workers and special agricultural workers. In a speech before the House, Representative George Crockett explained: "The paradox of using significant numbers of undocumented farmworkers during a time of intolerably high domestic unemployment in the agriculture industry only sustains the unjust system of low wages, substandard working conditions, and high profit margins that have produced such misery on our farms in the past."[19] Congressmembers John Conyers, Jr., Ronald V. Dellums and Mickey Leland also opposed these provisions and what they saw as a lack of enforceable sanctions in the bill.

Most of the black representatives favored generous amnesty and believed that it was the most important part of the bill. Although he was also troubled by the probability that legalization would harm American workers, Congressman Major R. Owens supported amnesty (but not blanket amnesty), even though he believed that it was not favored by his constituents.[20]

A majority of the black representatives supported amendments to the 1986 bill that would hold employers responsible for verifying applicant eligibility (73.7 percent), delete criminal penalties against employers who knowingly and willfully continued to violate the law by hiring undocumented workers (55.6 percent), require the INS to obtain search warrants for open farmlands (82.4 percent) and permit illegal aliens to live in public housing (88.2 percent). They unequivocally voted to: prohibit employment discrimination on the basis of alienage, with enforcement by a Special Counsel in the Department of Justice; and to delete EVD for undocumented Salvadorans and Nicaraguans. Many of the amendments favored by most black representatives, however, were deleted from the final version of the bill.[21]

It is clear that black opposition to immigration reform in 1984 and, partially, in 1986 was not due to any single set of causes. Some were concerned that the flawed legislation would neither end the use of easily exploited foreign agricultural workers nor secure the border and be fair and just for many illegal aliens. The reasons for the shift from almost blanket opposition in 1984 to a slim majority favoring the bill in 1986 varies among individual representatives, but includes such factors as constituent pressure to support legalization and pressure from non-black congressional colleagues to favor a much-needed bill. Most likely too, there was underlying concern about job displacement and depressed wages and working conditions of American workers who were forced to compete with foreign workers.

LIKELY IMPACTS OF THE ACT ON BLACKS

It is too early to determine precisely what effects the act will have on blacks, particularly those in metropolitan areas with large concentrations of lower-class blacks and recent immigrants, refugees and illegal aliens. The greatest impact is likely in the areas of employment, education and public welfare services. Unless the INS rigorously enforces the provisions for employer sanctions, including the rules to combat casual hiring and loopholes for general contractors, few blacks will gain the jobs left by undocumented workers. Even if sanctions do prevent employers from hiring undocumented aliens, they may, for a time, opt to employ refugees and recent immigrants to the extent possible instead of native blacks. The possible relocation of more low-wage American businesses abroad may also harm the employment prospects of some blacks. But if wages and working conditions improve nationwide in the secondary labor market, blacks should come out ahead overall.

Public schools are sites of increasing tension and conflict among poor minorities and whites. Among the major challenges are achieving the proper racial and ethnic composition of administrators and faculty and distributing resources between bilingual and remedial programs. The increasingly frequent hiring of bilingual staff tends to decrease the number of black teachers and to deplete the resources available for remedial courses. An increase in the number of persons eligible for public welfare services, such as health care and public housing, will undoubtedly burden certain local and state governments, leading to increased taxes, reduced services or both.

While Congress in the act mandated a triennial comprehensive immigration impact report, it unfortunately did not provide for specific reports of the effect of the act on native blacks and other groups who most often compete with recent immigrants, refugees and illegal aliens. While blacks share a responsibility for monitoring the impacts and lobbying for public policies to reduce them, the major responsibility for effective leadership in assimilating these newcomers lies with the federal government.

Given the racial and ethnic polarization which could increase as a consequence of legalization, black and other American citizens must work harder to improve intergroup relations. Concerned citizens should urge Congress to support better border control, a higher minimum wage and adequate federal funding to ease the burden to state and local governments charged with delivering health, educational and human welfare services to the newcomers. In addition, citizens should urge their representatives to make sure our immigration laws are enforced in a non-discriminatory way and perhaps reconsider EVD status for Salvadorans and Nicaraguans. Furthermore, blacks and Hispanics should heed Congressman Crockett's warnings against an agribusiness policy which would use hiring methods that foster job displacement and wage depression for many U.S. workers. They should urge American employers to first "cast down their buckets" for willing native workers.

NOTES

1. W.E. Burghardt Du Bois, *The Philadelphia Negro, A Social Study* (Philadelphia: University of Pennsylvania, 1899), p. 33.

2. See, e.g., Du Bois, *The Philadelphia Negro*, Sterling D. Spero and Abram L. Harris, *The Black Worker* (New York: Columbia University Press, 1931), and William Julius Wilson, *The Declining Significance of Race, Blacks and Changing American Institutions* (Chicago: The University of Chicago Press, 1978).

3. Quoted in Francis L. Broderick and August Meier, eds., *Negro Protest Thought in the Twentieth Century* (Indianapolis, Indiana: The Bobbs-Merrill Co., Inc., 1965), pp. 5–6.

4. John Higham, *Strangers in the Land: Patterns of American Nativism, 1860–1925* (New York: Atheneum, 1978), p. 114.

5. See, e.g., L.F. Chapman Jr., *Annual Report of the Immigration and Naturalization Service* (GPO, 1974), pp. iii–iv, Kingsley Davis, "The Migrations of Human Populations," *Scientific American*, Vol. 231, 1974, pp. 93–105, David North and Marion Houstoun, *The Characteristics and Roles of Illegal Aliens in the U.S. Labor Market: An Exploratory Study* (WDC: New Transcentury, 1976), Jacquelyne J. Jackson, "Illegal Aliens: Big Threat to Black Workers," *Ebony*, Vol. 34 (1979); pp. 33–36, 38 and 40, John Reid, *Black America in the 1980s* (WDC: Population Reference Bureau, Inc., December 1982), Briggs, Immigration Policy, John K. Hill, "The Economic Impact of Tighter U.S. Border Security," *Economic Review* (Federal Reserve Bank of Dallas, July 1985), pp. 12–20, James E. Pearce and Jeffery W. Gunther, "Illegal Immigration from Mexico: Effects on the Texas Economy," *Economic Review* (Federal Reserve Bank of Dallas, September 1985), pp. 1–11, and Philip Martin, *Illegal Immigration and the Colonization of the American Labor Market* (WDC: Center for Immigration Studies, 1986).

6. Kevin F. McCarthy and R. Burciago Valdez, *Current and Future Effects of Mexican Immigration in California: Executive Summary* (Santa Monica, California: The Rand Corporation, 1985) and Thomas Muller and Thomas J. Espenshade, *The Fourth Wave, California's Newest Immigrants* (WDC: The Urban Institute Press, 1985).

7. George Borjas and Marta Tienda, "The Economic Consequences of Immigration," *Science*, February 6, 1987, p. 647.

8. This estimation is based on a variety of reports about the geographical distribution of undocumented aliens. Approximately 2.1 million undocumented aliens were counted in the 1980 census and the annual net increase since then has been estimated at about 200,000 annually [U.S. Bureau of the Census, *Current Population Reports*, Series P-25, No. 1000, *Estimates of the Population of the United States, by Age, Sex and Race: 1980 to 1986* (GPO, 1987)]. Also see Jeffrey S. Passel and Karen A. Woodrow, "Georgaphic Distribution of Undocumented Immigrants: Estimates of Undocumented Aliens Counted in the 1980 Census by State," *International Migration Review*, Vol. 18 (1984), pp. 642–671.

9. Vernon M. Briggs, *Immigration Policy and the American Labor Force* (Baltimore: Johns Hopkins Press, 1984) and Borjas and Tienda, "The Economic Consequences of Immigration."

10. Robert G. Ainsworth, *Illegal Immigrants and Refugees—Their Economic Adaptation and Impact on Local U.S. Labor Markets: A Review of the Literature* (WDC: National Commission for Employment Policy, Research Report Series, RR-86-22, October 1986), pp. vii–viii.

11. Richard Mines, "Undocumented Immigrants and California Industries: Reflections on Research," for Hearings of the Intergovernmental Relations Committee, November 15, 1985.

12. See, e.g., U.S. Department of Labor, Bureau of Labor Statistics, *Handbook of Labor Statistics*, Bulletin 2217 (GPO, June 1985), pp. 85 and 88.

13. *Los Angeles Times*, July 15, 1983.

14. *San Francisco Chronicle*, October 2, 1986.

15. *New York Times/CBS News Poll*, 1986.

16. The *Miami Herald* poll of May 11, 1980, as cited in John F. Stack Jr., ed., *The Primordial Challenge: Ethnicity in the Contemporary World* (Westport, CT: Greenwood Press, 1986), p. 10.

17. *Congressional Record*, Vol. 130, No. 185, June 20, 1984, p. H 6126.
18. *Congressional Record*, Vol. 130, No. 85, pp. H 6126 and H 6127.
19. *Congressional Record*, Vol. 132, No. 139, October 9, 1986, p. H 9733.
20. *Congressional Record*, Vol. 130, No. 84, June 19, 1984, p. H 6054.
21. *Congressional Record*, Vol. 132, No. 139, October 9, 1986.

Hispanic Americans: The Debased Coin of Citizenship
By Richard Estrada

Although the status of Hispanic Americans in the United States since World War II has featured neither an unbroken rise nor a continuous decline, in recent years a serious and not-easily reversible descent may have begun.[1]

Despite dramatic gains in the number of Hispanic American elected officials, government appointees, educators and other professionals, various negative trends are threatening the well-being of the group as a whole. For example, Hispanic Americans are becoming more impoverished, not less. They are becoming less educated, not more. And if one looks closely at public life, it is clear that burgeoning numbers of Hispanics have not won political power commensurate with their numbers. The media is filled with encouraging stories of Cuban American success, but the sober rejoinder from the scholarly community is that Cuban Americans are not representative of Hispanics as a group. In sum, trends indicate that the future of Hispanic Americans is not a bright one, and some observers believe they may actually comprise America's next major underclass.

How can this be after more than two decades of massive social programs designed to remove those impediments believed to be preventing Hispanics and other minorities from entering the American mainstream? The traditional answers—racism and discrimination—were the very obstacles that the civil rights legislation and social programs of the 1960s (and later) were supposed to overcome. Now, even black scholarship has begun to question the importance of race in explaining black-white socioeconomic differentials.[2]

In 1987 many serious observers believe that the civil rights struggle is a thing of the past, and that racism and discrimination can no longer be viewed as the primary roadblocks to Hispanic American progress. Discrimination is obviously much reduced by the social and legal changes of the past few decades. However, even if it were still exerting a strong influence, other minority populations—Asians, as a prominent example—have also suffered the effects of prejudice, and yet they are model achievers of contemporary American society. (The argument that cultural differences among different ethnic cultures account for achievement differentials merits further investigation, but lies beyond the scope of this article.)

There is never any single answer to differential rates of apparent socioeconomic progress among groups in a society. This essay posits the following: A major constraint upon Hispanic American advancement lies in the conjuncture of trends in economic structure and in U.S.-bound immigration. As I will argue, structural change now underway in the American economy is diminishing the number of those entry-level manufacturing jobs that have proved so vital to the socioeconomic advancement of previous generations of Americans. The rungs on the ladder of socioeconomic progress are proving harder and harder to climb. Simultaneously, economic dislocation and a changed political climate have weakened the political will to maintain, let alone extend, social programs of special assistance to the disadvantaged.

These factors, of course, affect other ethnic groups as well. Yet Hispanic Americans are especially vulnerable to another phenomenon. More than any other group, Hispanic Americans are suffering the effects of massive immigration, especially illegal immigration. It is important to note that the new immigration commenced in the mid-1960s, simultaneously with the birth of reforms that promised to help minorities enter the mainstream. The impact of immigration becomes more apparent when we note that unlike all other advanced industrial nations, the United States chooses to annually admit hundreds of thousands of legal immigrants while tolerating massive illegal immigration as well.[3] As the levels of immigration, especially illegal immigration, have risen, Hispanic American socioeconomic indicators have fallen. Just as Hispanics are projected to overtake blacks in sheer numbers, so too are they projected to outstrip blacks in the category of poverty rates.

The basic impact of illegal immigration on Hispanic Americans seems clear enough. Illegal aliens from Mexico and other Latin American countries settle in Hispanic American communities, which are already heavily populated and economically disadvantaged. Then, the illegal aliens proceed to compete with citizens and legal resident aliens for limited employment opportunities, social services and affordable housing. Illegal immigration does not cause problems in these areas; it does, however, worsen them. The presence of the illegal aliens also distorts, insidiously, society's and the government's perception of the needs of the Hispanic American community.

HISPANICS IN THE U.S.: WHO AND HOW MANY?

Hispanic demographic growth is phenomenal among ethnic groups in America, and immigration is a key factor in that phenomenon. The nearly nineteen million persons of Hispanic origin in the United States today comprise about 7 percent of the total population, making them the second largest minority group in the country, after blacks. Between 1980 and 1987 the Hispanic population grew by 700,000, or 30 percent. At the same time, the non-Hispanic population increased by only 6 percent. According to the Census Bureau, the number of Hispanics could more than double shortly after the year 2000. The Hispanic growth rate of 3 to 5 percent annually is projected to remain at that level for the next three decades because of relatively high fertility and immigration, both legal and illegal. If present trends continue, Hispanics may become America's largest minority within a few decades.

Persons of Mexican descent are by far the largest Hispanic group, numbering 11.8 million, or 63 percent of all Hispanics. Of that number, however, it is astonishing to note that perhaps as few as five million are actually U.S. citizens, or Mexican Americans.[4] The rest are permanent resident aliens and illegal aliens. By themselves, persons of Mexican origin comprise the second largest minority group in the United States. But among Hispanics in the United States, Puerto Ricans make up the second largest category, with some 2.3 million persons according to the Census Bureau. This represents 12 percent of all Hispanics. Third in Hispanic demographic ranking (cumulative national origins) are persons of Central and South American origin, who are estimated to number 2.1 million, or 11 percent of the Hispanic population. In fourth place are persons of Cuban origin, who are believed to number one million, or 5 percent of all U.S. Hispanics. And in fifth place (cumulative national origins) are persons of "other" Hispanic origin, predominantly from Spain. These number 1.6 million or 8 percent of the Hispanic population.

DIFFERENTIAL IMPACTS OF IMMIGRATION FROM HISPANIC SOURCE COUNTRIES: THE OLD AND THE NEW

We have seen that the United States is currently experiencing the largest surge of immigration pressures in the nation's modern history, in absolute terms. The majority of these immigrants derive from Spanish-speaking nations. Combined legal and illegal immigration levels are at or above the highest levels recorded in our history, and despite early indications that it is having the desired deterrent effect. it is too early to determine if the Simpson-Rodino reform law will on balance enlarge or shrink the heavy influx of migrants of the past decade or more. Legal migration will certainly rise in the short run, due to the amnesty provision, and to family reunification petitions following that amnesty. A large agricultural worker program features substantial potential for enlarging legal flows. At least in the short run, as enforcement measures fall short of the massive border control and workplace enforcement assignment given to the underfunded INS, large-scale illegal immigration is likely to continue. A monograph published by the Center for Immigration Studies, *Many Hands, Few Jobs*, authored by Leon Bouvier and David Simcox, presents sobering estimates of the immigration pressures from Mexico, Central America and the Caribbean in the next generation, given burgeoning populations and faltering economic growth.[5]

How does this high rate of Spanish-speaking immigration affect Hispanic Americans?

Some assume that rising numbers of Hispanics automatically work to the advantage of Hispanic Americans. It would be better, they reason, to be a larger segment of American society, and immigration (along with high birth rates) advances that goal. Although this conception is true to a certain extent, there is much that cuts the other way.

The expansion of the Hispanic population and cultural influence within the United States has in recent years proven a bane as well as a boon to Hispanic Americans. U.S. Hispanics do enjoy growing political and social influence as their size increases—though it has been disappointing that the influence has not been proportionate to the size for reasons to be discussed below. While no minority group can fail to appreciate the advantages apparently brought on by larger proportional influence, it must also be kept in mind that other groups in the polity must experience diminished proportional influence when other groups enlarge their own, and this development may produce social strains which qualify the gains from growing sub-groups.

Whatever the advantages of the growth of the Hispanic segment of American society, there is a paradoxical result to which this essay directs attention. There is evidence that continued rapid expansion through *illegal* immigration impedes the socioeconomic advance of Hispanic Americans as a whole.

CHANGED ECONOMIC CIRCUMSTANCES

To understand why this is so, we must note the fundamental changes which have taken place since the last great wave of virtually uncontrolled immigration prior to World War I. Over the four decades of large-scale immigration to the United States which had begun in the 1880s and was interrupted only by World War I and restrictionist legislation (in 1921), there was no single linguistic-cultural component of overwhelming dominance. Immigrants came from southern Italy, from Poland and from the multiethnic region of the Balkans. They included Jews from Central Europe, with diminished numbers from Ireland and Western Europe. They spoke different languages, each group established its own cultural enclave and, as with immigrants everywhere, attempted to retain the traditional culture intact.

But the dominant American culture proved too powerful for such impulses toward cultural isolation. A mass-production system of manufacturing was coming into robust maturity in the United States, and the great industrial cities and regions of the nation were powerful magnets of jobs and opportunity. They also served as melting places—though groups of immigrants did not melt entirely. This industrial engine offered entry-level jobs to the unskilled, as well as rising wages and a ladder for individual and family advancement. Assimilation was always a complex process, a continuous compromise between giving up and retaining; still, a growing industrial economy carried all groups (not necessarily at the same speed) toward greater economic and linguistic-cultural assimilation in the English-speaking mainstream. American culture was enriched by many durable elements of language, religion and custom derived from roots abroad, but assimilation went forward, and was the key to group advancement among immigrants from outside Western Europe.

Today's circumstances are fundamentally different. For the first time in our national history, a majority of immigrants derives from a common cultural background and speaks a common language, which happens to be Spanish. The nation shares a nearly 2,000-mile land border with an entire region characterized by economic under-development, rapid population growth, high unemployment and political unrest. Hispanic migration runs in a swelling torrent, and cuts deep channels of habit and replenishment. In the border regions of the United States, and in some interior metropolitan areas, the Hispanic linguistic-cultural component of the immigrant population exerts an overwhelming dominance. Patterns of return travel and of media transmissions across borders reinforce the older culture in the American milieu. No other immigrant group in the United States pursued its assimilative destiny in such a setting.

This historical moment is unique and offers no precedents.

Today's economic circumstances also differ from those of the past. The United States in the 1980s is a nation in a rapid transition of a complex kind, in which both industrial employment and the portion of GNP deriving from manufacturing are declining. The rapid industrialization of areas of the lesser-developed world, along with the postwar recovery and industrial surge of Japan and Western Europe, exert competitive pressures upon 70 percent of the American internal marketplace for goods. Labor-intensive, low-skilled manufacturing sectors shrink or move overseas, and all skilled manufacturing moves toward higher technologies, higher value-added production in which only a skilled labor force has a future. U.S. manufacturing no longer offers a growing economic arena where unskilled and low-skilled workers in the millions may find a foothold on the ladder of upward mobility. Agriculture is completing its historic mechanization, and will employ no more Americans. The service sector expands, but real economic opportunities there are also tied to high levels of education and technical skills.

Thus Hispanics in the United States are undergoing an experience no other immigrant group knew. They seek economic and social advancement, in large and growing numbers, in an economy undergoing rapid structural change which reserves high-wage jobs for scientifically and technically educated workers. Yet Hispanics as a group derive from lower-class urban or rural backgrounds where low educational levels are endemic. As they achieve education, master English and advance economically and socially, the group's ranks are constantly replenished from source countries predominantly rural and underdeveloped. As a result of population growth, there were 24 percent more Hispanic families below the poverty level in 1986 than in 1981.[6] Hispanic Americans have not had the benefit of curtailment of large-scale immigration from their countries of origin, as did the various European and African groups before them. This is a major difference between the old and the new immigration.

What are the dynamics of this new set of circumstances in which Hispanic Americans find themselves?

Illegal Alien Impact on Jobs and Working Conditions: Job Displacement

In a recent survey of fifty-one studies, the GAO concluded that available information, although limited, shows that "illegal alien workers appear to displace (or take away jobs from) native or legal workers."[7] There is little disagreement that the adverse effects of illegal immigration in the job market are greatest upon those who most closely resemble the illegal aliens themselves— Hispanic Americans and Hispanic legal resident aliens.

In recent years illegal aliens have been very successful in finding work in the United States, although this trend has begun to undergo dramatic reversal as employer sanctions begin to be enforced under the new immigration law. For example, during the massive Hispanic immigration into California in the 1970s, some 645,000 jobs were created in Los Angeles County. Immigrants, of whom over a million were illegal aliens, filled no less than two-thirds of them.[8] In recent years illegal aliens in southern California have virtually colonized industries such as furniture making and apparel.[9]

In the northeastern United States, illegal alien workers probably adversely affect Puerto Ricans more than any other group. (There is, however, no such thing as a Puerto Rican illegal alien, as the United States granted all Puerto Ricans citizenship in 1917). Professor Frank Bonilla has written that "while the Puerto Rican presence in the total U.S. work force is minuscule, its concentrations at the bottom of the labor market in strategic locales within the United States is longstanding."[10] Among the 750,000 to 1,000,000 illegal aliens who reside in the New York metropolitan area are many from Latin America, some of whom attempt to pass as Puerto Ricans precisely because they are U.S. citizens, and as such are entitled to an array of benefits eagerly sought after by the illegal aliens.[11] Employers in New York City value Dominican illegal aliens in particular because they work more cheaply and are more docile than legal workers. In part because of such competition Puerto Ricans have labor force participation rates six to eight points below those of other Hispanic groups in the United States.[12] Illegal immigration also harms those Puerto Ricans living on the island, where illegal aliens from the Dominican Republic and other Spanish-speaking countries enter Puerto Rico either to work or to jump off into the major cities of the United States, especially New York City. Out of a total population of 3.3 million on the island, there are an estimated 150,000 to 200,000 illegal aliens.

Wages—The earnings of white immigrants who are not Hispanic usually equal those of native whites within ten to fifteen years after arrival in the United States. Yet, such is not the case for Mexican male immigrants who reside in this country for an equal period of time. They take about fifteen years before they enjoy significantly higher wage rates than the most recent immigrants. For Puerto Ricans, the wait is twenty-five years.[13]

Two scholars have recently argued that while a 10 percent increase in the number of new immigrants reduces the average wage of resident foreign workers by only 2 to 9 percent, the true impact of such a labor supply increase is significantly greater for those who work in the same labor markets as the immigrants.[14] As Dominican illegal aliens, who are known to compete with Puerto Ricans, often make under $1.00 an hour in their home country, they are willing to work for less than the minimum hourly wage of $3.35 an hour in New York City and Puerto Rico. Mexican illegal aliens earn less than illegal aliens of any other nationality, a condition that further aggravates the depressing effect of illegal immigration on the labor standards of Mexican Americans. The 1985 Rand Report observes that the wages of "Latino" workers in Los Angeles have been growing 40 percent more slowly than the wages of "Latino" workers elsewhere in the nation. While a decade before, Hispanic wage levels in Los Angeles were 25 percent above the national average, by 1985 wage levels had declined to the average.[15] A likely explanation is that during the 1970s the arrival of several hundred thousand mainly, but not exclusively, Mexican immigrants (legal and illegal) to the area expanded the labor force and either depressed the wages of Mexican Americans or inhibited salary increases. Some idea of the extent of this impact can be inferred from the fact that 50 percent or more of all illegal aliens residing in the United States are believed to be Mexican, who of course settle in Mexican American communities.

Social Services—On the subject of illegal aliens and social services, Michael Teitelbaum wrote in 1980:

> . . . the available evidence . . . suggests that publicly financed health services . . . are widely employed; educational services used substantially; unemployment insurance used but not disproportionately; welfare less so; and social security retirement benefits very little. At the same time, immigrants both legal and illegal do pay taxes to support such services, though in the case of the low-paid workers who apparently predominate among illegal immigrants, such taxes are of course very low.[16]

The evidence since 1980 indicates that social service usage by illegal aliens has grown, perhaps significantly, in some areas of the country more than others.

The pressure that illegal aliens exert on social services is greatest in those communities located in the region from Texas to California, along with the states of Florida, New York, New Jersey and Illinois. There appear to be four major factors that explain the increased burden: (1) There are more illegal aliens than ever before; (2) a higher percentage of women and children are entering illegally; (3) over time, illegal aliens are "learning the ropes" of the social service system; and (4) the law and the courts have extended greater entitlements to the illegals.

Illegal aliens come to the United States for jobs, not social services. However, as they become more successful in obtaining those services, the prospects for such assistance may become an additional incentive in the minds of would-be illegal aliens.[17] For a succinct argument of this position see Senator Alan K.

Simpson, "Mining 'The Golden Mountain'," Letter-to-the-Editor, *Wall Street Journal*, September 3, 1987.

Housing—The available number of low-cost housing units in the United States is falling, and the number of homeless individuals is increasing. For poor Americans residing in urban areas, especially minorities, the declining availability of affordable housing will be an even greater challenge at the turn of the century, according to recent projections.

The shortage is most dramatic in the nation's two largest metropolitan areas, which feature high concentrations of Hispanics. Between 1970 and 1980 the Hispanic population of Los Angeles increased from 17 to 27 percent of the county's entire population, largely because of massive immigration, much of it illegal.[18] Yet during the same period there was virtually no increase in the amount of housing available in the principal Hispanic neighborhood, Boyle Heights. Intense competition for housing between Hispanic Americans and Hispanic illegal aliens was the result. In southern California, managers of federally subsidized housing projects have testified that illegal aliens may be residing in from 30 to 100 percent of the 200,000 units currently housing 500,000 people.[19] The lack of conventional affordable housing has given rise to the phenomenon of "garage people" in Los Angeles County, where one survey indicates that around 200,000 people in mainly low-income Hispanic neighborhoods are finding shelter in about 42,000 garages.[20]

In New York City, where 1.4 million Hispanics comprise 20 percent of the population, the lack of adequate, affordable housing for this minority has been termed an emergency, and recent trends indicate the problem will go from bad to worse. Impoverished Puerto Ricans have been found to "pay more rent as a proportion of their income, than any other ethnic group in the city." Hispanic families are being forced by circumstances to double or triple up. A trend toward more expensive housing holds true even for the region's middle class. Between 1982 and 1986 the median price of existing single-family homes in the New York-New Jersey metropolitan region rose 127 percent, from $70,500 to $160,000, at a time when the national median increased by only 21 percent.[21]

The problem of social service usage among immigrants is giving rise to serious political consequences in other parts of the industrial world. Gary P. Freeman, professor of government at the University of Texas, asserts that growing migration from poor countries to Western Europe has placed a severe strain on European welfare-state politics. The intense debate in the United States over the legalization provision of the new immigration law in part reflects a serious anxiety among the American people over the issue of immigrant use of social services, and the fear among citizen taxpayers that they will bear the brunt of the costs.[22] If their concern grows as immigration levels rise, the possibility of significantly increased anti-immigrant sentiment looms very real indeed. This may represent yet another cost to Hispanic Americans stemming from immigration.

POLITICS: NUMBERS BUT NOT NECESSARILY POWER

The phenomenal numerical growth of Hispanics in America has positive implications for their political power. Prior to the passage of Simpson-Rodino, it was estimated that there were nearly three million registered Hispanic voters in the United States and that an additional four million would register during the 1980s.[23] Some experts view the amnesty provision of the new law as a harbinger of significantly increased voting power among Hispanics, to be realized perhaps within the next decade.

Yet, their numbers have been growing for years, and the complaint has persisted that Hispanics participate in the U.S. political process at a disappointing rate. Why? One possible explanation is that Hispanics are a youthful population, and youth of all ethnic backgrounds tend to exhibit low levels of voting participation. Another possible explanation is a growing poverty rate that likewise militates against political participation. But a more basic reason is that a significant number of Hispanics are not citizens and are therefore ineligible to vote. Except for Cubans, Hispanic permanent resident aliens have shown less inclination than non-Hispanic immigrants to become citizens and participate fully in the American political process. They appear to be torn between the economic inducements of Americanization on the one hand and identification with their Hispanic homelands, which often feature political cultures of non-participation, on the other. For instance, in Texas, Hispanics represented 8 percent of actual voters in 1986, although they comprised nearly 25 percent of the State's registered voters.[24]

HISPANIC AMERICAN ATTITUDES TOWARD IMMIGRATION

Contrary to a widespread misconception, most U. S. Hispanics do not favor illegal immigration. Instead, the preponderance of the available evidence indicates they want it curtailed. The dichotomy of opinion that does exist is between, on the one hand, Hispanic leaders, ethnic advocates and more affluent Hispanics who favor large-scale immigration and, on the other, the far more numerous rank-and-file who oppose it.

Hispanic Americans as a group worry about the impact of illegal aliens on the labor market. A 1982 Gallup Poll found that 75 percent of U.S. residents of Hispanic descent favored "restrictions on hiring illegal aliens and requiring worker identification cards."[25] In 1983 Peter D. Hart Research Associates and V. Lance Tarrance & Associates found that 66 percent of Hispanic citizens expressed a concern that illegal aliens displaced American workers, and an equal percentage supported penalties and fines for employers who hire illegal aliens.[26] In a 1984 exit poll that the Spanish International Network (SIN) conducted among Texas Hispanic voters, 60 percent favored employer sanctions.[27] In 1986 *The Texas Poll* found that 63 percent of Texas Hispanic respondents agreed it should be illegal to hire illegal aliens.[28]

CONCLUSION

While massive immigration has not caused the basic social and economic problems facing the Hispanic American community, the chronic influx of illegal aliens has nonetheless exacerbated them. The impact of immigration on Hispanic Americans has been particularly severe as the United States proceeds through a period of structural economic change and dislocation. It is not immigration per se that is so problematical to the current and future status of Hispanic Americans, but rather the unusually large number of immigrants, the predominance of a single source country or of various source countries featuring a common source culture, the illegal (and, therefore, more exploitable) status of many of the immigrants and, most significantly, the rate of their entry.

Those Hispanic Americans who have long favored an employer sanctions law to curtail the presence of illegal aliens in the work force now have such a provision in the Immigration Reform and Control Act of 1986. However, there is uncertainty as to how effectively the legislation will be enforced. The second major provision, that dealing with amnesty for illegal aliens present in the United States since before 1982, may also hold problems for those Hispanic Americans concerned with immigration.

One recent scholarly article on Mexican immigration concludes that "an appreciation of the social nature of immigration . . . suggests that Mexican migration to the United States will persist and that it will be more difficult and costly to control than many Americans believe."[29] Given the low educational and skills level of the average Hispanic immigrant to the United States, and given the decline in the number of well-paying manufacturing jobs in the country, a combination of continued illegal immigration and heightened legal immigration may further impede Hispanic American attempts to ascend the socioeconomic ladder. For Hispanics in the United States, more is proving to be less.

NOTES

1. The Center for Budget Priorities has recently projected that Hispanic rates will outstrip those of blacks by 1990. *CBPP News Advisory*, September 1986.

2. See, for example, William Julius Wilson, *The Declining Significance of Race*, (Chicago: The University of Chicago Press, 1978).

3. Vernon M. Briggs, Jr., "The Growth and Composition of the U.S. Labor Force," *Science*, October 1987, p. 179.

4. Some scholars argue that Mexican illegal aliens are Hispanic Americans or Mexican Americans, but aliens are in fact Mexican citizens even as they are not American citizens. See Frank Bean, "The Mexican Origin Population in the United States: A Demographic Overview," in *The Mexican American Experience: An Interdisciplinary Anthology* (Austin: University of Texas Press, 1985), pp. 57–58. The population figures for Hispanics presented in this section are from the *Current Population Reports*, "The Hispanic Population in the United States: March 1986 and 1987" (Advance Report).

5. Leon Bouvier and David Simcox, *Many Hands, Few Jobs: Population, Unemployment and Emigration in Mexico and the Caribbean*, CIS Paper No. 2, (Center for Immigration Studies, Washington, D.C., 1986).

6. *Current Population Reports*, "The Hispanic Population in the United States: March 1986 and 1987" (Advance Report).

7. GAO Report, *Impact of Illegal Immigration and Background on Legalization: Programs of Other Countries*. Prepared for the use of the House Committee on the Judiciary, 99th Congress, first session, November 1985.

8. David Simcox, "Two Views of California Immigration," CIS Review No. 1 (unpublished), (Center for Immigration Studies, Washington, D.C., 1986).

9. Philip Martin, *Illegal Immigration and the Colonization of the American Labor Market*, CIS Paper No. 1, (Center for Immigration Studies, Washington, D.C., 1986).

10. Frank Bonilla and Ricardo Campos, *Industry and Idleness* (New York: Centro de Estudios Puertorriquenos, 1986).

11. Leo M. Romero and Luis G. Stelzner, "Hispanics and the Criminal Justice System," in Pastora San Juan Cafferty and William C. McCready, eds., *Hispanics in the United States: A New Social Agenda* (New Brunswick, NJ: Transaction Books, 1985), p. 228.

12. George J. Borjas, "Jobs and Employment for Hispanics," in Cafferty and McCready, *Hispanics in the United States*, p. 153.

13. Ibid., p. 150.

14. George J. Borjas and Marta Tienda, "The Economic Consequences of Immigration," *Science*, February 6, 1987.

15. Kevin F. McCarthy and R. Burciaga Valdez, "Current and Future Effects of Mexican Immigration in California: Executive Summary" (Santa Monica, CA: Rand, 1985) pp. 20–21.

16. Michael Teitelbaum, "Right vs. Right: Immigration and Refugee Policy in the United States," *Foreign Affairs*, Fall 1980, pp. 39–40.

17. For a succinct argument of this position see Sen. Alan K. Simpson, "Mining the Golden Mountain," Letter-to-the-Editor, *Wall Street Journal*, September 3, 1987.

18. Frank Villalobos, *Housing Needs of Hispanics*, Subcommittee on Housing and Community Development, 99th Congress.

19. Ernani Bernardi, "The Need for Immigration Reform," *Los Angeles Herald Examiner*, April 28, 1986.

20. Stephanie Chavez and James Quinn, "Garages are Homes to Low-income Thousands," *Fresno Bee*, May 24, 1987.

21. Michael Batutis, "New York's Housing Squeeze," *American Demographics* (April 1987), pp. 53–54

22. Congress has mandated that $1 billion a year be set aside for four years in order to reimbuse local governments for welfare costs stemming from legalization.

23. Richard Tostado, "Political Participation" in Cafferty and McCready, *Hispanics in the United States*, p. 244.

24. David Sedeno, "Hispanics Seek Political Arenas," *Corpus Christi Caller-Times*, May 27, 1987.

25. Gallup Poll, Gallup Report No. 306 (November 1982), as cited in George Grayson's *Patterns of Influence* (New York: Praeger Publishers, 1984), p. 75.

26. July 1983 opinion poll conducted by V. Tarrance Associates and Peter Hart Research Associates and commissioned by the Federation for American Immigration Reform.

27. "SIN Texas Polls," *Hispanic Link Weekly Report* (May 4, 1984), p. 2.

28. Dr. James Dyer, "Texans Oppose Amnesty for Illegal Aliens, Favor Law Prohibiting Their Hiring," *The Texas Poll*, August 18, 1986.

29. Douglas S. Massey and Felipe Garcia Espana, "The Social Process of International Migration," *Science*, August 14, 1987, p. 737.

III

IMMIGRATION AND NATIONAL UNITY: IS HISTORY OUR GUIDE?

The unspoken question about the immigrants is, *What are they doing to us?* Will they divide and diminish the nation's riches? Will they accept its language? Will they alter racial relations? Will they respect the thousand informal rules that allow this nation of many races to cohere?

       —James Fallows,
        "Immigration: How It's Affecting Us,"
        Atlantic, November 1983

Ellis Island:
The Building of a Heritage
By Eric Sevareid

Ellis Island stands as a symbol of our immigrant past. Plans for its restoration are just as cloudy as our policies regarding future immigration.

Last summer the tall ships sailed around the tip of Manhattan and passed by the colossus holding the lamp, and Americans again wondered at the story of their country's creation and continuity. The Statue of Liberty was a hundred years old. The Constitution became two hundred this year. No piece of statuary has ever acquired a meaning and spirit of its own like Miss Liberty. No document for the governing of men has ever lasted so long, so effectively, as the Constitution.

The vast migration to the United States was almost biblical in its scope, its joys, its hopes, its heartbreak and its torments.

What was the dream of those millions? It came down to this: rebirth, the eternal, haunting craving of men to be born again, the yearning for the second chance. Rebirth occurred. America became the first new thing in history in the relations of man to man, on a mass scale.

The Statue of Liberty and Ellis Island lie close together, and we all think of them together. They were, indeed, officially put together by President Lyndon Johnson and are now administered together. But in the beginning of things, in the nineteenth century, the two had nothing to do with each other.

What attracts Americans right now is that the great lady has been shined up after years of neglect, and Ellis Island, through which some seventeen million migrants moved to their new life, will be transformed to modern usages. The early Dutch picnicked on the island, the British hanged pirates there and the Americans fortified it, all before it became the funnel through which the immigrants passed.

What should be done with it now?

The debate over Ellis Island has reopened the question of the purpose of historic preservation as well as the proper role of the National Park Service.

Ellis Island, between 1892 and 1954, was the nation's largest immigration station—millions entered the United States there. But most people don't even know that a debate is taking place. Had it not been for the firing of Lee A. Iacocca by Interior Secretary Donald P. Hodel from Iacocca's job as chairman of a federal advisory commission on the restoration of the Statue of Liberty and Ellis Island, which raised $230 million for the project, most of the debating would still be taking place behind closed doors.

The debate has revolved around proposals to develop two-thirds of the island next to the Great Hall, where immigrants were processed. The hall is being restored and converted into a museum.

The island's southern seventeen acres are dotted with small, decayed hospital buildings and other dilapidated facilities that only a few immigrants used.

In 1981, the National Park Service sponsored a competition for proposals for that part of the island. The agency selected a $60 million plan for a conference center and three hundred-room hotel.

The Center for Housing Partnerships proposed that the Sheraton Corporation operate the hotel. But Iacocca described the hotel as a luxury facility and dubbed the plan a commercialized "tax break for the rich."

Iacocca spoke of establishing "an ethnic Williamsburg" on Ellis Island. Plans developed for Iacocca by architect John Burgee call for an exhibition center filled with displays of ethnic arts and permanent exhibits showing the contributions of various ethnic groups. But critics derided the plan as "an ethnic Disneyland."

And Park Service officials said the new exhibition hall would dramatically alter the appearance of the island, which is still much as it was when many immigrants first saw it.

Ten acres on the northern side of the island have undergone $100 million in restoration work, which is being financed by the $250 million Statue of Liberty-Ellis Island fund-raising effort. The center of this work is the restoration of the immense Great Hall, and its conversion into a museum of immigration.

To me, the museum part of the proposal makes all the sense in the world. A museum, certainly, to tell the story in word, picture and sound of those who passed through, and what they made of themselves and their new home. It should make visitors think. It should make them laugh and make them cry.

It was a tremendous number of immigrants who came in the great waves in the latter part of the last century. But it is not quite right to say that we are a nation of immigrants. Even at the height of the incoming, a majority of the people in the country were nativeborn Americans and a big proportion of that majority had American roots going back to Washington's time—including, of course, black Americans. Strictly speaking, we are a nation *from* immigrants.

The Statue came simultaneously with one great wave of immigration, in 1886. The target date was ten years earlier—for the centenary of the Declaration of Independence. Twenty-one years had passed between the birth of the idea and the dedication of the Statue.

There was a wonderfully enthusiastic professor in Paris named Edouard de Laboulaye. He loved America, or the idea of America, which, in fact, he never saw in person. He was chairman of the French Anti-Slavery Society. What he and his fellow French liberals wanted directly was freedom from the rule of Emperor Napoleon III. What Frederic-Auguste Bartholdi, the sculptor of heroic statuary, wanted directly was freedom for his beloved Alsace from the Teutonic brutes who wrenched it away from France in their war of 1870.

De Laboulaye and Bartholdi talked endlessly about de Laboulaye's idea of a colossal statue in New York Harbor. On the eve of Bartholdi's first lobbying trip to the United States, he wrote to de Laboulaye and said the prospective monument was to be "in honor of American independence." It was to be called Liberty Enlightening the World. That is what the giant lamp was meant to represent. Apparently, there was no thought that it was to be a beacon welcoming newcomers from abroad. There was no "door" until the "golden door" appeared in Emma Lazarus's poem much later. "Give me your tired, your poor," she wrote, and poet James Russell Lowell told Emma that her lines had given the Statue a reason for being. Thus, Bartholdi's triumph of engineering (more than of art) became something less abstract, more human, something that evoked love and reverence from the native born as well as the newcomers.

So now Miss Liberty is refreshed, repaired and shining again and the island is thronged with visitors from the mainland, not from the foreign ships. But much, if not all, has changed forever. This is a different America, and it may be that the Statue's symbolism will slowly revert to what Bartholdi and de Laboulaye had in mind—freedom for human beings everywhere.

Immigrants do not arrive in the steerage of great ships anymore. They fly in to a dozen airport cities from Boston to San Francisco. The huddled masses of today are Haitians huddling in rickety boats, Miami bound; or Mexicans huddling in the ravines and sagebrush south of San Diego.

But there are far more significant changes than those. In 1886, Lazarus's words of welcome were not only a deeply moving expression of compassion, they were a very practical argument. There were fifty-eight million people in our country then and it urgently needed settling by people from anywhere. Today, we are four times that number and the open, arable land is gone. The overwhelming majority of immigrants are in the cities, forming new and rapidly growing communities with those like them.

I believe we are becoming a crowded country—surely a silly thought to a stranger looking at the map of America's expanse. But a vast proportion of our land is desert, forest and mountain where human communities can only be sparse. In five years, the total population has grown by some twelve million and immigration accounts for about 40 percent of that.

Playwright Israel Zangwill's melting pot did melt most of the ingredients in the pot, though not all. But now the lumps appear to be forming again. There now seems to be a spreading movement, from ethnic group to ethnic group, supported by many well-intended native-born Americans, to actively resist melting, or assimilation.

If I am biased about this, it would be, I suppose, because I grew up in the light of a different vision. I was taught that the idea was for everyone to become as American as possible, that a distinct American identity and personality would arise. Out of the many, one—as our coins say. But we were also taught, though mostly by politicians, that our national strength came from our racial and cultural diversity. I no longer think so. Diversity enriches the cultural landscape, but it does not make for social cohesion and thus national strength. Today, certainly, with these ethnocentric movements going on, social cohesion is getting weaker.

Two-thirds of the people in the world who are trying to migrate from their homelands are aiming at the United States. No nation takes in as many as we do. Entry has come to be in the minds of millions, not a privilege, but a right.

I am convinced that the immigration flow must be drastically reduced and the place to begin, of course, is with illegal immigration. No nation can readily be a nation without a border. And in effect, we have no borders.

No one is sure within millions how many illegal aliens are now in the country. Legal and illegal together, the total inflow must be at least a million a year. Most, of course, are poorly trained or utterly untrained, illiterate at least in English. How do we get on top of the poverty problem alone with this going on?

One vitally important aspect of the phenomenon is that we have never before had such a massive influx of people speaking foreign tongues.

But it goes beyond that. We now have a lobby of native-born Americans who fervently believe in bilingual education. These lobbyists and teachers are insisting on "cultural maintenance." That is, tax-supported public schools should see that the newly arrived children shall also be immersed in the culture of their homeland. That, surely, should be a matter only of later elective courses. Otherwise, one of the basic purposes of our public school system—assimilation— is being violated.

Those who deny the dangers in the present rate of immigration turn their minds away from one overwhelming fact—the rate will greatly increase. We haven't seen anything yet, compared to what is coming. The truth is that by the year 2000 the total population of Latin America is going to increase by 100 million to 150 million souls. The human pressures on North America will become enormous. It will be a sad day when we have to put an army on that southwestern border and hundreds of squads of special police and inspectors at our airports, seaports and highway points of entry.

I hope we will never shut our doors to those who are true political refugees, endangered men and women, though I also hope we will pressure other nations to do their part. The Japanese, whose nation was enriched by the Vietnam War, refused to take in more than a handful of their fellow Asians, the Vietnamese refugees.

In the long, mysterious process of assimilation, of becoming American, forces in our society seem bent on retracing their steps on retrogression. More than ever, ethnic groups become not just cultural repositories and memory banks, but economic demand groups. It is a way to get things from government.

Does all this mean that a genuine, solid Americanism never did take hold, so that millions feel incomplete, emotionally lost, and are seeking to establish their own identity by clinging to or retreating to the culture of their origins abroad? If so, what I was taught as a boy is jeopardized, and, I believe, the cohesion of my country is threatened. Pluralism, which we ritually hail in our speeches, means weakness when carried to extremes.

There is no question in anyone's mind that immigration in the sixteenth, seventeenth, eighteenth and nineteenth centuries helped build America. Let's be sure that immigration in the twentieth century doesn't tear America down.

Various intelligent friends feel I exaggerate these worries and I hope they prove to be right. But one thing I know. We cannot fool around on the question of language. I would support the proposed constitutional amendment making English the only official language. Language is heart and mind, values and visions of life. It is "the nerve of a nation," said Dr. Samuel Johnson.

America has been called "the last, best hope of earth," but it ought not become the only hope. America has great muscles, but it is neither a Colossus bestriding the world nor an Atlas shouldering the world.

We, too, are only human, after all.

Reprinted from Popular Mechanics, July 1986.

Immigration and the National Interest
By Otis Graham, Jr.

The test of a nation's immigration policy is whether it serves the national interest. That statement sounds like a truism, but in the United States it is not the principle upon which we operate. Approximately 90 percent of the decisions about who will be allowed to immigrate on the legal side—and 100 percent on the illegal side—have been turned over to individuals and families. Immigration serves their interests, as they see them. We do not ask, in the normal course of events, and at the levels of government or national discussion, whether this adds up to a policy which is in the national interest. We assume it, or ignore the question.

But these are not normal times. Immigration levels in absolute terms match or exceed the great volume of immigration which came across our shores in the half century prior to World War I. With immigration now contributing nearly one-half of the nation's population growth, about half of that immigration illegal, the policy and academic communities have begun to ask if immigration as currently experienced and immigration policy as now feebly enforced serve the national interest. They began this questioning with something tangible in which the nation has an obvious interest, a healthy economy.

The economic impact of immigration is a very complex matter, much studied but elusive, especially since so much of immigration is illegal and resists accurate assessment. The answer to this question is, however, reasonably clear in broad outline. Immigration, as the United States experiences it in the contemporary setting, is on balance injurious to the economic well-being of the nation.

This reality has eluded some, who for reasons either of ideology, a trained incapacity to see things in wholes, or out of identification with those few groups or sectors which derive short-term benefits, have reported that current immigration has beneficial impacts for society at large. The theoretical basis for such a conclusion seems to be the notion that more (and therefore cheaper) labor of any kind is a benefit without costs, or at least exceeding any costs. This astonishingly narrow view of how an economy works has received official endorsement in the 1986 report of the President's Council of Economic Advisors. Much is made of some empirical evidence that large-scale immigration into the state of California in the late 1970's and 1980's has coincided with expanded employment and small business formation, two signs of economic vigor.

But there is too much on the other side for this optimistic view to withstand scrutiny, either as a valid conclusion for California or the larger society. One cost of this process is significant job displacement among resident and potential resident citizens, as a 1986 GAO report concluded from a review of fifty-one relevant studies. This displacement, often operating across entire industries by a process of "network recruitment," enlarges the pool of what is now more than seven million unemployed Americans who draw upon public assistance without finding a productive economic role.[1] The demographic and educational characteristics of immigrants vary enormously, but the largest segment of the illegal population is composed of young, low-skilled Mexicans and Central Americans, a labor supply which is good economic news for some employers but whose broader labor force impact is to retard the structural evolution of the U.S. economy toward higher technologies and a higher value-added labor contribution. Even in California, an expansion of certain jobs under the impact of immigration could at best be called a form of economic growth. It is doubtful whether it deserves to be called economic progress, until the structural impacts of immigration are better understood.

Beyond these issues, immigrants enlarge the U.S. population, increasing the domestic population growth rate by 50 percent, thus adding to the current and future numbers of residents of a nation which leads the most environmentally damaging and resource-depleting lifestyle in human history. Economic well-being is not in the long run compatible with endless population expansion. As against such costs, the economic gains from infusions of entrepreneurial energies, or financial and education capital brought in from abroad are only minor offsets, and do not make immigration's net impact positive.[2]

Not all reasonable people reach exactly these conclusions, and the economic impact of immigration will and should continue to be a matter of study and discussion. But immigration is much more than an economic force. It changes the host society in multiple ways—not just its demography, but also the racial and ethnic composition of the population, indeed its culture in the broadest sense.

Since the 1965 immigration act, legal as well as illegal immigration flows overwhelmingly from non-European and from the lesser-developed or Third and Fourth Worlds. Demographic, economic, environmental and political trends indicate that we can readily project immigration to the United States to continue in these channels, and with increasing volume and momentum, for at least the next three generations. The United States will surely be transformed in important respects. But what changes are we to expect, and will their impact be on balance beneficial to the national welfare? Certainly this is the standard to which immigration should be held.

The policy and academic communities do not customarily approach the matter in just this way. They are more concerned with whether equity is being dealt to the immigrant, an important and complicated question. But the social impacts? Some attention is paid to labor-market effects of immigration. Beyond this, there is a faith that the future will take care of itself. This is a legacy of our national history. Immigration transformed the nation, but in desirable ways. The possibility that this might have changed is a thought tainted by a nativist past, not to be entertained.

Fortunately, outside the policy and intellectual circles, average citizens continue in ever-growing numbers to do what they have always done, speak out bluntly about things that do not seem to them to be going well in their communities. Average citizens may not be knowledgeable about the macroeconomic impacts of immigration on that abstraction, the U.S. economy. But they do have first-hand knowledge of what might be called the broader socio-cultural impacts of immigrants from abroad (or from the other parts of the United States) who settle in their neighborhoods. They know a good bit about the local fiscal impacts of immigrants upon public services, and especially the schools. While slower to face the issue, in recent years a number of economists and demographers have published several path-breaking academic studies of the long-term impacts of immigration upon American society in general and California in particular.[3]

It was demographer Leon Bouvier who, in 1981, looked ahead to tell us that immigration alone, if it continued for another century to add one million people a year to the U.S. population (a conservative number in view of the current rate), would prevent the population stabilization that would otherwise occur at approximately 260 million (assuming a total fertility rate [TFR] of 2.0). Immigration would force population growth by 2080 to 409 million, with considerable momentum to continue its climb.[4] Then Bouvier and economist Philip Martin, in a pioneering work, were the first scholars to take up the issue which California's former Lt. Governor, Mervyn Dymally, raised so frequently in the 1970s, the inevitable transformation of California into "America's first Third World state." Dymally, himself an immigrant from the Third World, clearly thought this was a good thing, though he was apparently interested only in its political ramifications. In any event, he initially could not get any discussion going. Bouvier and Martin calculated that "minorities" would be a majority in California by 2010; and, as their assumptions about immigration totals were extremely conservative, probably underestimating immigration flows by a factor of two, the future they sketched is nearer than their estimate.[5]

In brief concluding passages, they went beyond economic impacts to consider the likely implications for educational systems, politics, and social cohesion. They tended to see problems. In Martin's words, "If the immigration status quo persists, the United States will develop a more unequal society with troublesome separations."[6] In the concluding passages of another recent study of California, the state which is the harbinger of tomorrow in terms of immigration's impacts, Thomas Muller and associates acknowledge that large-scale Hispanic and Asian immigration is "contributing to an increasingly bilingual society in the Southwest," creating substantial problems in the schools and generating much resentment that the national identity may be changing in unwelcomed ways. "Social, political, and cultural issues," the Urban Institute authors judged, are now "uppermost in the minds of many Americans concerned with the consequences of immigration."[7]

Thus the research community has discovered what ordinary citizens have long been saying, that immigration is altering the society and that these alterations deserve discussion. One naturally expects them to be a blend, though hardly an equal blend, of that which is welcome and that which is unwelcome by residents; one also expects disagreement about these categories. It is difficult to generalize about the complex impacts made by 600,000 legal immigrants arriving each year from abroad, along with the unknown number of illegals who come (judging by apprehension data at the Chula Vista station, the world's busiest border, in 1985) from ninety-three different countries. Some positive impacts are generally agreed upon: the delights of a more international cuisine, the evidence of entrepreneurial energies. What impacts may be negative, outside the economic?

While scholars have had little to say on the matter, citizens have been a source of information we have been reluctant to use. They communicate through letters to immigration reform organizations such as the Federation for American Immigration Reform (FAIR), notes to congressmen and local public officials, calls to radio talk shows, letters to newspaper editors and in public forums. And, in time, the American people always project their deepest concerns into electoral politics. In 1986 public concern about immigration surged strongly into political campaigns in Texas, Florida and especially in California. The absence of border control was a major theme in the 1986 race for the Republican nomination for the U.S. Senate. The three to one margin by which an initiative confirming English as California's official language carried the day in 1986 and verified the growth of public concern that assimilation might be falling behind immigration flows.

Listening to what is said at all levels, one hears an over-arching fear of a society becoming Balkanized, deeply divided along ethno-cultural, and to some extent corresponding class lines. (See especially Sevareid, this book) In California, with a substantial Asian population, this perceived division is complex. There are four major and several numerically less significant Asian nationalities which are to some degree physically and culturally distinct. But still the decisive ethno-cultural stratification in California, as well as in the rest of the Southwest and in Florida, is the visibility of the large and growing Hispanic community, diverse in many ways but knit together by a common language and similar cultural inheritance, with the majority of Hispanics united by the fact of Mexico as their country of origin.

The fear of social division is not a new theme in American life, and in a nation of functioning pluralism, is understandably suspicious that it repeats an unwelcome pattern of the past. The United States has easily survived all the centrifugal forces of diverse nationality, ethnicity, religion, region and class— apart from one narrow escape from social schism in the mid-nineteenth century. Of course we are divided, even along the important lines of ethnicity and culture; what difference does it make?

In response, one hears a catalog of worries that the new immigration is making differences that citizens who love this society do not want and should resist. There is an instinct to place the labels "exaggerated" or "unworthy" on concerns from this quarter. But a society that ignores them all is not only unresponsive to its citizens, but may be a helpless witness, even accomplice, to the erosion rather than the desirable augmentation of its cultural inheritance, perhaps jeopardizing those priceless things we so take for granted—social cohesion and comity, the grounds of a successful pluralism. The role of those privileged with leadership is, at the least, to listen carefully.

In political life, certain worries are occasionally sensationalized. We hear of a border that is porous to entering terrorists, drug traffic, and crime, as well as to to any alien who can walk. There is little good data, but there is talk, of the public health implications of a large flow of unexamined people carrying diseases long-since controlled in the United States. There is discussion of the mounting evidence that the host society cannot absorb, or at least is not absorbing, enormous numbers of immigrants on terms of mutual benefit. The schools, whose rate of success with the English-speaking children born to American citizens has lately been seen to falter, face staggering additional difficulties in their task of educating the non-English-speaking children arriving at their doors, especially those from families without legal permanency.

In the complex literature on educational achievement and the links to social mobility, the failure of the schools with Hispanic children cannot be disguised. In a report of the National Commission for Employment Policy, "Hispanics and Jobs," we learn that 40 percent of Hispanics are reported as having "difficulty in English." Most do not finish the twelve-year school sequence, and the dropout rate among Hispanics of the age when high school should have been completed was 1.5 times that of blacks and three times that of whites.[8]

Such evidence exposes to view a social segmentation that reflects both class and ethnic disadvantage. While the school systems may be "local," the social problems they encounter and are finding so obdurate are national problems. Joined to these concerns, which are linked in one way or another to large-scale immigration, are others: strains on public facilities for social services and recreation, as well as housing, and, by historic standards, high levels of intergroup tensions and conflicts. All of these problems resist, or do not adequately receive, measured and reasoned assessment. One welcomes the thoughtful treatment by author Michael S. Teitelbaum of another element that may be found in the question of the implications of immigration, in his "Latin Migration North: The Problem for U.S. Foreign Policy." There, for example, one finds again the remark of Eduardo Morga, then Chairman of LULAC, words that convey troubling implications that their author may not have intended: ". . . we are all ready to help Mexico in the United States. We feel that in the future, Mexico can use us as Israel uses American Jews, as Italy uses Italian-Americans, and so on."[9]

High levels of immigration to the United States have always strained and slowed the assimilation process, and prompted a renewed search for that elusive bond, national identity. That immigrants are different from natives is to be assumed; that we welcome some differences and tolerate others is accepted as the norm. Yet, on those matters thought to make America distinctive and precious, of which we have a powerful if poorly defined and always evolving conception, the host society has always cared fervently that newcomers change toward national norms.

While there have been some differences of view on these matters, most would say that America remains herself through successive changes so long as there vigorously survives the commitment to individual freedom—religious, political and economic—as well as to the rule of law, and a basic commitment to the principles of the Declaration of Independence, the whole resulting in an elemental national loyalty.

We do not test for these commitments at the border that separates the United States from a world in which many societies are organized around very different and even antithetical beliefs and behavior patterns. We protect and extend what seems to make America distinctive and valuable through the assimilation process, that many-faceted Master Teacher. For long periods we have flatly opposed the workings of the assimilationist principle as applied to some groups, most notably those of African descent; but in modern times we have granted it a more universal authority.

We have never agreed upon exactly what it means to be an American, but the discussion itself is a valuable part of our common life. There is broad agreement that it begins with command of the English language, and with an acceptance of political democracy and the rule of law. Its measures are thought to be full participation in economic and political life, social mobility and patriotic acceptance of the obligations of citizenship.

This discussion only hints at the complexity of that vital engine of national cohesion, justice and individual opportunity—the assimilation process. Now, more insistently than at any time in the lifetimes of the most senior of us, we hear that the assimilation process may be faltering under the pressure of immigration upon the very institutions that most make it possible—an open economy, public schools, the political process, the media, voluntary associations of a bridging character, intermarriage, universal military service.

Americans have heard before, and many of them have believed at earlier times, that immigration was too large in volume, that its economic impacts were importantly negative, as were its cultural and social impacts, and that the assimilation process could not absorb the influx. As a Southerner, a Scot-Irish and an historian who has lived for half a century, this author, too, has heard these concerns. My Scotch and Protestant Irish forebears had a easier time of it than the Catholic Irish, the Jews and others, but still we were seen as clannish, allegedly violent, and resented in some places and times.

The South, which has long been the Third World of the United States—rural, economically backward, poorly educated, its people by national standards ill-nourished, in ill health, and fecund—has also been viewed as foreign by people from other regions of the country. The South was the region with large families, holding on to traditional attitudes toward women and the patriarchal family, slow to question environmental exploitation, tending toward an authoritarian politics with low voter turnout, constrained in our intellectual life, defensive and proud.

The twentieth century has been for the South, until very recent times, one long season of out-migration. We migrated to the Northeast, with a major stream through Oklahoma to California; and we were resented, often enough. It was far, far worse for Southerners who happened to be black. Who, in the first four decades of this century, would have been confident that the economy and society possessed the capacity to absorb the millions of migrating Europeans, black and white Southerners, and growing numbers of Mexicans into a functioning though never a perfect pluralism? Yet migrants were absorbed and society flourished. The assimilation of past generations of immigrants, while imperfect and incomplete, has been nonetheless admirable—but it would be a misapplication of history to dismiss the immigration worries of today as a repetition of needless anxieties.

One misconception in much current thinking about American history is that ethno-cultural conflicts, whether exacerbated by immigration or not, have been deplorable aberrations, their roots only in a psychological illness called "nativism." But a major achievement of modern American historical writing, associated with the work of Lee Benson, Samuel Hays, Robert Kelley, Paul Kleppner, Joel Silbey and many others, has been to reveal and chart the presence and power of conflicting cultural and ethnic traditions in the American past. The discovery has not been simply a matter of the persistence and shaping power of ethno-cultural difference, but a growing appreciation that immigration—that disturber of the existing ethno-cultural balance—brought great and legitimate, as well as psychological and arguably far less legitimate, costs to those who had come before. A classic statement of this evolution is the commentary the distinguished historian John Higham has made upon his own *Strangers in the Land: Patterns of American Nativism 1860-1925*. Were he to write that book again, said Higham, he would give more weight to the real costs of immigration which were levied in the competition for jobs, housing and public facilities. This, too, was part of our historic experience with immigration.[10]

Another misreading of our history comes with the assumption that this society's assimilation of the millions who came prior to restriction in 1921 is somehow proof that this performance may be repeated in the decades ahead, as the incoming numbers again reach and exceed a million annually. Such an analogy is flawed in several respects.

About twenty million immigrants who came to the United States from the 1890s to 1921, and their subsequent children, made their way into English-language fluency, into the economy, and, slowly and with considerable difficulty in cases where ethnic discrimination was pronounced, into social life generally. But they did so in the decades between World War I and mid-century, when certain fundamental conditions obtained, facilitating the difficult and always imperfect social absorption of alien peoples. These conditions no longer obtain in the same way, if at all.

The first is perhaps most important. In 1921 this society made the decision to sharply restrict immigration, and to conform the allowable entries to approximate the national origins of the existing society. We have some reason to believe that the national origin quotas were a policy mistake, but the restriction itself was wise policy. Economic historians point out that income distribution in America improved thereafter, and probably chiefly because of, restriction of the labor supply through immigration reform. Large capital investments were substituted for labor, driving up productivity and allowing real wages to increase.[11]

Another view of the benefits stemming from immigration restriction has been developed recently by black sociologist William Julius Wilson, who views the "flow of immigrants" as "the single most important contributor to the varying rates of urban racial and ethnic progress in the twentieth century United States." Wilson, drawing upon the work of Stanley Lieberson and others, argues that the early curtailment of Asian immigration allowed Asians in America to move upward. The process repeated itself with the European immigrants after the restriction of 1921, but the mass internal migration of blacks continued for decades. Heavy migration intensified discriminatory feelings as well as economic competition, impeding the processes of group advancement. In this view, mass immigration does not "drive up the group next in line," but hampers the progress of previous arrivals from the migrating population. Hispanics in the decades ahead may therefore expect to experience restricted economic mobility as well as the intracommunity pathologies of crime, teenage pregnancy and welfare dependency. When society's assimilative mechanisms are given a breathing space through immigration restriction, there are immediate benefits, and these flow disproportionately to the most disadvantaged Americans.[12]

Judging by the record of immigration reform in the past decade, much of the leadership of this society expects the assimilation process in this stage of our national life to perform its prodigious labors of absorption without the crucial curbs on entering numbers which facilitated the process earlier in this century. Another great difference between that America and our own is the stage of industrialization, and especially the role of industrial cities. The great waves of pre-war immigration to the United States coincided with the robust expansion of industrialism in America, based in and around the cities of the Northeast and the Midwest. Those cities and their factories and associated distribution networks had a huge appetite for low- and semi-skilled labor, as America entered its glory days as the pre-eminent industrial power. Industrial cities, especially, functioned as a great machine for the integration of millions of foreign arrivals as well as internal migrants. Entry-level jobs were abundant, wages and living standards rose, and the cities proved to be a springboard to upward mobility for millions who had been cut adrift from rural life by mechanization. The costs were of course high, yet from this distance we see that the overall result was a powerful voyage toward economic progress which carried millions of aliens into American nationality with all of its benefits. Perhaps there was another, better way, but history took this path—once.[13]

That America is gone. We are predominantly and increasingly a service-based economy, deindustrializing at least as measured by employment, and deconcentrating both population and jobs out of the older urban cores. Two implications flow from these structural changes. We may not agree, after the industrial policy debate, upon the best private and public measures to adopt in adjusting to an altered world economy, but it is quite clear that we are in a new and lasting era of international industrial competition. America's economic future depends upon adaptation, and, if we are to retain a substantial industrial capacity, as for many reasons we must, it must be through a shift toward those knowledge-intensive sectors in both manufacturing and services, leaving many of the low-wage, massproduction industries to take root abroad. This will require a labor force of high educational and skill levels and aspirations; it does not imply a larger labor force, and certainly not one recruited primarily from the mass populations of the Third World.

At the same historical moment when the nation is forced toward these structural changes, the cities have lost their earlier function as industrial engines of assimilation. Factory and blue-collar jobs have slipped away, employment patterns have shifted to knowledge-intensive services, the white and small minority middle class has moved to the periphery, leaving behind low-income minorities and the old, facing a huge gap between existing job opportunities and the skill levels of this disadvantaged population. There is an economic and social function for America's cities, and some are struggling toward new forms more rapidly than others; but the contemporary city cannot perform the function it served in the era of mass immigration which coincided with our industrialization a hundred years ago.

These are great changes in the economic base and in the function of industrial cities. But immigration still delivers to America a similar input as it did eighty to a hundred years ago—a million or more a year from countries basically poor, less developed and culturally very different from the nation's current majority and its heritage. While many institutions contribute to the assimilation process, we can no longer count upon Frederick Jackson Turner's democratizing frontier, or the robust industrial cities that formerly heated the melting pot. The national economy is normally a force for social interchange, the acquisition of national norms and English language skills. But here we encounter the first of many signs that the assimilation process is becoming impaired. There seems to be a spread of ethnically-secluded work sites, entire assembly lines in auto plants where only Arabic is spoken, and entire job sites and industries in the Southwest that have become exclusively Hispanic—fruit and vegetable agriculture, parts of construction, ethnic-owned restaurants and other businesses, janitorial firms, food and poultry processing plants, race tracks. For the first time in U.S. history, a majority of migrants speak just one language—Spanish—and most of them live in ethnic enclaves served by radio and television stations carrying the messages of American advertising as well as all other communication in Spanish. In such settings the assimilative impulses of the national economy have a fainter influence.

Other institutions shouldering the assimilative role appear also to be losing vitality or effect. I have already noted, briefly, some aspects of what many see as the faltering ability of the public schools to convey to non-English-speaking children (in truth, to a lesser extent, also for all children) the language and other educational attainments required for social success. Even where the schools are effective, it is well known that curricula have in recent years been drained of their attention to American and Western history and culture. A subtle but far-reaching shift in values over many decades seems to have carried the majority culture into a zone of self-doubt, leading to the operating conclusion that the new and desirable appreciation in the United States of non-Western cultural backgrounds rules out any publicly-sponsored cultural reaffirmation of the nation's originating inheritance as derived chiefly from Western Europe and in the English language.

And, on the side of recent and incoming immigrants, some have detected a shift in attitudes affecting the process of "becoming American." Assimilation, of course, has always been a process of losing as well as gaining, and thus painful to individuals and resisted by immigrant-group leadership. Is there a trend toward a more widespread or vigorous resistance to assimilation? John Garcia reports that Mexican immigrants naturalize at a rate considerably lower than that of other immigrants, and attributes this to the absence of feelings of identity as Americans. Surveys of Hispanic business leaders in the United States have found that the majority feel themselves to be equally Hispanic and American. A national poll in 1984 found that "most Hispanics think of themselves as Hispanics first, and Americans second" and that the trend was increasing.[14]

Memories of the American past have a reassuring quality, buoying our hopes with the reminder that these questions of national cohesion, assimilative capacity and the benefits and limits of separateness are not new concerns. I have chosen to stress the new conditions which call into question any complacency—an economy shifting out of mass-production manufacturing into knowledge-intensive services and goods production, with different requirements of the labor force, the greatly reduced capacity of our cities to provide millions of immigrants economic entry points to the next convoy of economic advance, as they had through most of the last century; the apparent faltering of other elements of the assimilation process, such as public schools, the self-confidence of the host culture, the receptivity of current immigrants to undergoing the beneficial discomforts of assimilation.

The most striking new feature of our circumstances is, of course, the physical proximity across a 2,000-mile land border of Mexico, the state at the northern tier of a Latin America experiencing rapid population growth within economies in varying degrees of difficulty. In the more than three centuries of immigration which built the current United States there has never been such a circumstance where immigrants in mass numbers arrived from a society to which they could continually return for cultural reinforcement by the mere turn of a dial or by the briefest land journey.

And we should not conclude even so brief a survey of the workings of assimilation in today's United States without looking beyond immigrant populations to the trapped underclass composed of American citizens, so many of them blacks whose efforts to mount the ladder of social mobility go back many generations and whose condition should humble those who still believe that either our economy or our government's remedial efforts constitute singly or together assimilative mechanisms of reassuring power.

Today's America gives many and sharply conflicting messages to any analyst of its economic and social direction. Mr. Reagan's slogan, "It's morning in America!," is a formulation available to uncompromising optimists; but one knows that he has left out much in this view from the white affluent top—the urban underclass, teenagers having or begetting and abandoning children, the dependencies on chemical substances or welfare, the ghettos that do not yield to the strategies of Democrats or Republicans. Uncontrolled immigration makes its own, and mostly a problem-enlarging contribution to these strains upon the social fabric.

In a meeting in San Diego in the Spring of 1986, which included public officials, academics, knowledgeable professionals, and that scholar/journalist, the late Theodore White, a vivid pair of scenarios emerged from discussion of the future of that most immigration-impacted state, California. One possible California, in the year 2000 or 2020, was of a society of forty to fifty million people. Apart from some crowding in Yosemite, it was a happy checkerboard of ethnic enclaves offering the best of the world's cuisine, a composite of the Pacific basin where thousands of rural peasants moved northward across the Mexican border each day to take up the menial chores shunned by successive preceding groups. Faith in this scenario required a suspension of disbelief for those who know immigration trends and reflected upon the economic and social realities.

The other, a far different scenario, was built upon economist Philip Martin's projections:

> If the immigration status quo persists, the U.S. will develop a more unequal society with troublesome separations. . . . the California work force will be mostly immigrants or their descendants by 2010. These working immigrants, mostly non-white, will be supporting mostly white pensioners with their payroll contributions. Is American society resilient enough to handle the resulting tensions?[15]

Other elaborations came forward—a two-tiered society was in prospect, the one young, overwhelmingly Hispanic or black and low-income, the other largely older whites and Asians, affluent, with a woefully small intermixing of these categories. It is a segmented society: the rich who work in high-technology enterprise or are retired to Palm Springs or coastal watering places, move uneasily among a mass population with low educational attainments and income levels; those who own businesses communicate to the work force through foremen who translate from English.

If we evade this second scenario, in California and the Southwest and Florida, in New York and Detroit and Chicago and Denver, and in many other places, it will not be because immigration ceased of its own accord to drive us in this direction. This society has admirable capacities, in its private and public realms, to promote that degree of economic and social assimilation required to bind this heterogeneous society into a working whole. But only an audacious and unthinking hubris would fail to recognize the sobering and apparently intensifying defects of our mechanisms of social integration, and persist in our current policy of permitting uncontrolled immigration. There is much that we do not know, but the immigration realities of tomorrow we do know much about. The Mexican population of over eighty-one million will double in twenty-seven years, the rates of population growth in most of Central America are even higher, and the pressures upon our southern borders grow yearly, apprehensions at Texas and California borders increasing 50 percent between 1985 and 1986. The only major uncertainties in this future are not demographic, but the likelihood, indeed one would now be tempted to say the timing, of the collapse of the social order in Mexico or more intense civil disturbance in societies to her south, loosening floods of refugees whose impact we have not included in even the most pessimistic of our assessments.

And who would be the chief victims and bearers of the social costs of a world without immigration reform? They would not, at least in the short run, be the affluent, who enjoy slight reductions in the cost of motel rooms, tomatoes and restaurant meals, due to a subsidy in the form of alien labor. The poor and the Hispanic American (see Richard Estrada) have the most to lose from uncontrolled immigration, was the blunt summary of Hispanic writer Richard Rodriguez.[16]

The policy recommendations that flow from this analysis begin with the reiteration of one of the most consensual, soundly researched and widely debated policy reforms of recent times, that the U.S. government take effective steps to curb and as nearly as possible to end illegal immigration into this society. The first steps toward that end lie in full and fair enforcement of the Simpson-Rodino immigration reform act of 1986. Second, when we turn to the other half of the immigration reform assignment, also well studied by the Hesburgh Commission and in the legislative process leading up to the 1984 version of the Simpson-Mazzoli bill, the United States should move its legal immigration away from near complete reliance upon the principle of family reunification. An attractive alternative principle, which should weigh more heavily in our own immigration law, is a guiding element in Canadian immigration policy to our north, the labor force needs of the national economy. Immigration decisions should not be made in the future as they have been in the past, by employers who sustain illegal immigration and by individuals, whether citizen or alien, who claim the benefits of family reunification. We should shift the principles of selection toward a nationally determined need for augmentation of our inventory of skills, as well as toward the ends of a national policy on population size, a vital but now lacking instrument for securing the national welfare.

NOTES

1. Philip L. Martin, *Illegal Immigration and the Colonization of the American Labor Market* (CIS Paper 1, 1986), pp. 12-23.

2. For citations to the literature on economic impacts, see Otis L. Graham, Jr., "Uses and Misuses of History in the Debate Over Immigration Reform," *The Public Historian*, 8 (Spring 1986), esp. pp. 46-48, and footnote #7.

3. Leon Bouvier, *The Impact of Immigration on U.S. Population Size* (Population Reference Bureau, 1981); Leon F. Bouvier and Philip L. Martin, "Population Change and California's Future" (Population Reference Bureau, 1985); Philip Martin, "Illegal Immigration;" Thomas Muller et. al. *The Fourth Wave: California's New Immigrants* (WDC: The Urban Institute Press, 1984).

4. Bouvier, *The Impact of Immigration*, p. 4.

5. Bouvier and Martin, "Population Change."

6. Martin, *Illegal Immigration*, p. 45.

7. Muller et. al., *The Fourth Wave*, p. 187.

8. National Commission for Employment Policy, "Hispanics and Jobs," 1982, p. 10.

9. Michael S. Teitelbaum, *Latin Migration North: The Problem for U.S. Foreign Policy* (New York: Council on Foreign Relations, 1985), p. 34.

10. John Higham, *Strangers in the Land: Patterns of American Nativism 1860-1925* (New York: Atheneum, 1954), was followed by his reflections in "Another Look at Nativism," *Catholic Historical Review*, 44 (July 1958), pp. 147-158.

11. Stanley Lebergott, *Manpower in Economic Growth* (Chicago: University of Chicago Press, 1964); Jeffrey Williamson and Peter Lindert, *American Inequality* (Princeton: Princeton University Press, 1980).

12. William Julius Wilson, "The Urban Underclass in Advanced Industrial Society," in *The New Urban Reality* (WDC: Brookings Institution, 1986); Stanley Lieberson, *A Piece of the Pie: Black and White Immigrants Since 1880* (University of California Press, 1980).

13. John D. Kasarda, "Urban Change and Minority Opportunities," in *The New Urban Reality* (WDC: Brookings Institution, 1985).

14. John A. Garcia, "Political Integration of Mexican Immigrants: Exploration into the Naturalization Process," *International Migration Review* 15, (Winter 1981), p. 6; Yankelovich, Skelly and White (Spanish USA, 1984) p. 9. See also Gerda Bikales and Gary Imhoff, "A Kind of Discordant Harmony: Issues in Assimilation," (U.S. English, 1985).

15. Martin, *Illegal Immigration*, p. 45.

16. Richard Rodriguez, "Hispanics in Changing, Change America," *Los Angeles Times*, May 23, 1986.

A Kind of Discordant Harmony:
Issues in Assimilation
By Gerda Bikales and Gary Imhoff

More so than in most other societies, the assimilation of minorities has been a subject of burning interest in the United States. Attempts to define it measure it, explain it and influence it have given rise to that most American of academic disciplines, the *sociology of assimilation.*

In most societies, assimilation is a matter of concern primarily to the minority. In those societies that are receptive to assimilated members of the minority, the major problem for the elders of the minority group is how to minimize cultural loss over the course of generations. Minority leaders constantly search for that elusive point when their group's members have assimilated sufficiently to partake of the opportunities found only in the economic and social mainstream, but are not yet detaching themselves emotionally from the culture of origin and endangering its survival.

In closed societies, those that offer their minority members no rewards in return for assimilation, the likelihood of losing minority cultures is much diminished. In those countries, the minority leadership's major responsibility is to find entry to the broader opportunities of the mainstream society, without unleashing antiminority sentiments.

In both receptive and closed societies, minorities carry almost all the burdens and anxieties of adjustment. The majority societies, secure in their position and confident of their cultural relevance, are largely oblivious to the painful cultural struggles going on within their minority communities.

But in the United States, as in few other countries, the majority is intimately involved in and even responsible for assimilating minorities. In this sense, the majority and the minority uniquely shared the experience. Our national identity was shaped by our immigrant fathers and grandfathers and by their adjustment to those who came here before them, just as surely as that of our children and grandchildren will be shaped by immigrants coming today and by their adaptation to us. Both immigration and assimilation have defined our history and our sense of ourselves as Americans.

And as long as large numbers of immigrants continue to settle in our midst, their adjustment and that of their young will continue to be a subject of serious interest to the American public.

THE EXPECTATION OF ANGLO CONFORMITY

The degree of cultural assimilation which American society has expected of immigrants has changed significantly over time. These expectations have ranged from full conformity to British norms in the colonial and early national periods, to the melting pot model formulated during the large immigration waves in the early years of this century, to the later reaction of cultural pluralism and its present manifestation as the "salad bowl."[1]

The current political debate, in which the assimilation of culturally different groups is equated with intimidation and coercion, tends to obscure the fact that bilingualism and biculturalism actually have had a very short history as philosophic movements in this country. In the colonial and national periods of the United States, the British impulse was toward neither assimilation nor toleration of those with cultural differences. The overwhelming sentiment was instead what we may call European; it combined suspicion of the outsider with conditional forbearance of him, and had only limited provisions for the culturally variant to enter fully into the polity. Colonists insisted upon Anglo conformity. British colonists assumed that native American Indians were neither to be assimilated into British culture nor to be treated as equal participants in the British colonies. They were, rather, separate nations with which the British either had a treaty or were at war. The French and Spanish colonists on this continent were treated similarly.

BLENDING INTO THE MELTING POT

The United States was not confronted with a significant flow of non-English speakers other than Germans until the 1880s, and the reaction toward these foreign language speakers initially followed the earlier pattern: rejection of their foreignness combined with a provisional willingness to accept them if they thoroughly assimilated. But the heavy immigration of many southern and eastern Europeans from the 1890s through the 1910s eventually resulted in a different, an identifiably American, attitude toward the strangers in our midst. Israel Zangwill's plays about Jewish immigrants to the United States, "Children of the Ghetto," "Dreamers of the Ghetto," and "The Melting Pot," produced between 1892 and 1903, came to symbolize the change and gave us an enduring metaphor. America, ran the new mythology, was a place where people of many nationalities and many languages could come together and live in a kind of discordant harmony while they assimilated to the national norm. People of many cultures could shed their old mores and tongues, learn the new ways and new language of the new country, and become a new people, not just an extension of the English colonies.

For newcomers, this positive myth promised easier acceptance in the new country and illuminated a path of achievement which led toward that acceptance. For native Americans, it showed how tolerance for the newcomers' differences could eventually help the process of their Americanization. Coming to America meant entering into a covenant: the immigrant would learn English and a skill useful in the United States, and he would participate in our political system by becoming a citizen and a voter. In return, he would be accepted as a political equal, and his temporary differences from native-born Americans would be tolerated. Zangwill's title permanently labeled this contract, this pattern of assimilation and toleration, as "the melting pot." It lasted for well over a half-century, from sometime before the turn of the century until the 1960s. And though it has come under constant political attack since the 1960s, most Americans are still committed to the melting pot as the most viable principle for integrating immigrants into a society ever renewed by their arrival.

The melting pot worked because of the immigrants' expectations. America was the Promised Land, the land where the streets were paved with gold. The typical migrant to the United States intended to make his future here and expected to sever most of his ties to his home country. Many migrants failed to find success in the wide swings and uncertainties of the competitive economy, and many disappointed migrants eventually left the United States. Contemporary studies suggest that perhaps a third of those who came to this country around the turn of the century, during the first peak years of immigration, returned to their home countries.

But return was not the expectation; success was. The migrant committed a good deal of money to his passage. The distance, the difficulty and the crushing expense of an ocean voyage to the United States restricted migration to those who were willing to take a very large gamble on achieving a permanent future in this country. The difficulty and the expense of communication across the Atlantic tended to wither the ties to family and friends left behind in the Old Country. An exchange of letters between the United States and Europe was not significantly swifter or easier in 1890 or 1900 than it had been in the colonial period.

In return for what seemed a nearly irrevocable commitment to life in this country, the migrant received the liberty which the new world offered as well as tangible economic rewards. The opportunity to participate in a dynamic, growing, seemingly limitless economy was open to him—if he learned English, learned a skill and worked hard. And even if he failed to find a more comfortable life for himself, he was at least confident that his children would do better.

The United States, too, was rewarded in several ways. First, it got cheap labor, workers to clear the fields as the frontier moved westward and workers to staff the factories which opened in urban centers. Second, it received important psychological gratification from being regarded as the land of opportunity, the land to which people wished to migrate. The accommodation of migrants which the melting pot symbolized was essential to the self-image of the United States as a land of opportunity and freedom. And, at first almost against its will, the United States started to appreciate and enjoy the pungent mixture of cultures which its migrants brought to it. By becoming more open and welcoming to the cultural contributions of migrants, the United States gained richness of color and texture for its own. Melting pot immigration brought a new cosmopolitanism to America that softened the austerity that had long been a cultural norm.

THE RISE OF CULTURAL PLURALISM

Though the cultural climate must have been more congenial for newcomers during the era of the melting pot than in the days of Anglo-conformity, many did not accept the "melting" process gracefully. In 1915 Horace Kallen was the first to academically challenge the notion that immigrants must abrogate their ancestral loyalties and undergo a gradual process of complete cultural metamorphosis in America. Kallen was a Harvard-educated professor of philosophy of Jewish descent. He advanced the concept of "cultural pluralism" as the organizing principle most befitting American nationality. Cultural pluralism, Kallen said, would encourage the maintenance of the individual's ethnic group ties and culture of origin; the American nation would be an amalgam of its many separate cultural parts.

Until the 1960s the melting pot and cultural pluralism may have been somewhat in intellectual opposition, but in practice they complimented each other quite well. Melting pot ideology did not demand a total meltdown, and tolerated a full range of melting rates. By acknowledging that immigrant cultures had valuable contributions to add to the pot, it left space and time for a variety of cultural expressions to flourish.

TOSSING IN THE SALAD BOWL

In the 1960s there was a revolution in the unwritten pact between Americans and the aliens who came here. This revolution did not begin at the volition of new immigrants. It began, rather, in the civil rights movement of black Americans. While generation after generation of migrants had come to the United States and assimilated, native-born American Negroes had not been readily accepted into the body politic. The physical distinctiveness of blacks and their history of slavery in the United States had acted as barriers, keeping white Americans from extending to them the acceptance they granted to white migrants. Blacks, whose families had been thoroughly Americanized for generations, did not receive the toleration or the basic rights of citizenship that first-generation European migrants enjoyed.

In the 1960s the painfully slow progress toward full civil rights for blacks provoked a reaction against this rejection. There were variations within this outgrowth of the civil rights movement, denoted as "black rights," "black pride," or even "black separatism," but they all emphasized both their differences from white Americans and the virtue of being different. In fact, at the height of the black pride movement, it was common to be proud only of these distinguishing characteristics.

The black pride movement provided a model and a basis upon which other ethnic groups could build. Hispanic Pride, Native American Pride, Asian Pride, Polish Pride—in general, Ethnic Pride—is an invention of the 1960s and 1970s. Certainly, ethnically identifiable neighborhoods existed prior to this period; and ethnic celebrations based on religious or national holidays preceded these decades, as did exaggerated expressions of the value of being Irish, or Italian or whatever. But what has been different about the last two decades has been the shift in the relative importance accorded to being "American," as opposed to belonging to a distinct racial, cultural or ethnic subgroup in American society.

While Kallen asked that minority cultures be given tolerance and understanding, the Ethnic Pride Movement demanded that they be accorded equivalent standing in the society. This was, in effect, a demand that the United States become a multicultural society as a matter of conscious public policy. There was no longer to be an officially sanctioned culture, loosely based on the heritage and language of the Republic's founders.

The melting pot would no longer serve as the model of American society and accommodation to it. It would be replaced by the "salad bowl," a metaphor that conveys a mixture in which the elements combine without losing their individual character.[2] A carrot exchanges flavor with a stick of celery in a stew, but remains distinctive in a salad. A thin dressing, in the salad metaphor, is all that is necessary to unite the many different ingredients and to reduce friction between them.

BARRIERS TO ASSIMILATION

In the era of the salad bowl, the majority culture of the United States faces serious challenges to its chosen mission of continually reintegrating itself through the assimilation of its new immigrants. Along with the rejection of the melting pot, a combination of powerful forces are at work weakening the impulse towards assimilation:

—immigration (combined legal and illegal) is at the highest level in our history;

—a majority of migrants speak just one language— Spanish. This majority concentration of Spanish speakers among new migrants has already lasted for more than a decade and promises to continue for the foreseeable future;

—the nearness of the countries from which many Spanish-speaking migrants come, and the relative convenience and low cost of travel and telephone communications, ensure that many new migrants will maintain their ties with their home countries;

—the pattern of concentrated settlement of Spanish-speaking migrants in this country creates Spanish-speaking enclaves in some cities, a few cities in which Spanish is the dominant language and entire regions of this country in which Spanish is already a viable language;

—the growth of Spanish-language communications within the United States enables migrants who prefer not to speak English to receive their information and entertainment solely in Spanish while they live in the United States. They can use an ever expanding radio and television Spanish lan-

guage network, and major English language networks eager to use new technologies to provide Spanish translations of regular programs;
—the growth of a distinctly Hispanic consumer market has made it profitable, not only for ethnically oriented products but also for mainline goods and services, to advertise in Spanish;
—the change toward a more sluggish economy, marked by chronic job shortages, has lessened the certainty of economic rewards for English-language proficiency;
—the presence of vocal Hispanic leadership which gives lip service to the need of Hispanics to learn English while excoriating any practical English-language instruction that does not also reinforce the native language;
—the definition of the inability to speak English as prima facie evidence of membership in a disadvantaged and discriminated-against group entitled to affirmative action benefits, has rewarded limited English-language ability;
—the breakdown of institutional support for assimilation, symbolized by the growth of bilingual education and bilingual voting and the controversy surrounding seemingly innocuous Congressional proposals to recognize English as the official language of the United States, has eroded the moral position of those who urge the integration of Spanish speakers into an English-language nation.

THE AVAILABLE EVIDENCE ON ASSIMILATION

In view of these impediments to assimilation, is there any reliable evidence to indicate that today's immigrants are not assimilating into our society as rapidly as previous migration streams? There were, after all, widespread complaints against the first generations of Italians and Eastern Europeans—claims that they were obviously indigestible lumps which would never melt in the melting pot. Looking back on this rhetoric, we see that the complaints originated in the difficulties any society has in dealing with the first generation of any group of migrants. The pessimistic predictions of the period proved baseless—the children and grandchildren of those settlers have been thoroughly woven into the fabric of our national life for decades.

In the search for answers about the workings of the assimilative process today, we can draw upon information from several studies of Spanish speaking migrants which appeared in the last few years. Regrettably, there has been no comparable output of studies on other migrant groups, even of those which have been sizable.

In reviewing these studies, our first and most important question is whether Spanish-speaking immigrants are reluctant to identify themselves as Americans. We are, after all, able to tolerate wide disparities among the life styles, languages and even ideals of people who have made an emotional and political commitment to being American. But those who have a basic reluctance or inability to identify themselves as part of this polity inspire less tolerance in us. The following are some of the available study results on this and related questions.

John A. Garcia's "Political Integration of Mexican Immigrants: Explorations into the Naturalization Process" in *International Migration Review*, examines several earlier studies of the political integration of Mexican immigrants into U.S. society since 1920. Garcia reports that annual rates of naturalization for Mexican-origin migrants varied between 3.9 to 5.9 percent, as opposed to 30.2 to 50.6 percent for non-Mexicans, and that "consistently few Mexicans choose to become naturalized when they satisfy the eligibility requirements."[3] (A 1987 draft report by the GAO, "Immigration: The Future Flow of Legal Immigrants to the United States," concludes that 18 percent of Mexican migrants naturalize, which is significantly lower than the naturalization rate for immigrants from more distant countries.) Garcia's review of the reasons for such low levels of naturalization found that the most significant one was simply that many Mexican migrants didn't identify themselves as American: "Not too surprisingly, the most 'critical' variable for Mexican-born respondents proved to be the extent of social identity with being American (or not identifying as an American). . . . Individuals with continued attachments to Mexico are more than likely to remain non-naturalized."[4]

James W. Lamare's important, though limited, study appeared in *International Migration Review* in 1982. Lamare, an English sociologist, began with the assumption that "At the core of political integration is widespread popular psychological identification with the political system. Without a strong sense of political community within the population, the persistence of the political system is in doubt."[5]

To test the identification of Mexican-Americans with the United States, he studied 700 Mexican-American children aged nine through fourteen residing in El Paso, Texas, in 1978. The children represented first through fifth generation immigrants. What he found is disturbing! "Overall, Mexican-American children, regardless of generation, show only limited commitment to the American political community. To be sure, each generation professes a preference for living in the United States, but only the mixed and second generation consider this to be the best country. None of the five cohorts prefers the label 'American' over identification tags more reflective of their national origin. Lastly, no generation exhibits a strong sense of trust in others."[6] The ambivalence toward the United States, the reluctance to break with the country of origin—these seem to persist through the generations.

This detachment is seen again in the 1983 Hispanic Policy Development Project survey of elected and appointed Hispanic officials. The survey found that the low percentage of voter turnout among Hispanics was a major concern of these officials, as could be expected—68 percent rated it as either a serious or a very serious problem. Interestingly, the officials did not blame this low voter turnout on several alternative explanations which the survey offered: discrimination, an Hispanic "tradition of individualism" or differences among Hispanic groups. Instead, the report notes: "Several respondents offered similar explanations of why voting rates are lower among Puerto Ricans than among other Hispanics. One man, an advisor in the mayor's office in New York City, put it this way: '[Puerto Ricans] feel that they are here as transients. Because of that, there's no reason to get involved.' Because they think they are only going to be here for a while, they don't think of legislation as being important to them.''[7] The Southwest Voter Registration Education Project of San Antonio, Texas, and the Hispanic Population Studies Program of the Center for Mexican-American Studies at the University of Texas at Austin are cooperating on a series of studies of the Mexican-American electorate. One of their published works has found a high degree of political alienation among Mexican-American citizens. Over 71 percent of their *citizen* respondents agreed with the statement that "politics is too complicated," and fewer than 32 percent ever attempted to talk others into voting a certain way. They also found an extremely strong correlation between English-language ability and alienation from political involvement: "First, Spanish monolinguals participate less, regardless of age, on all measures of political involvement. . . . Second, Spanish monolinguals—regardless of age— are less interested in politics and generally more alienated from the political system than are bilinguals and English monolinguals. . . . Third, Spanish monolinguals—both younger and older—are less likely to identify with one of the two major political parties than are English speakers.''[8]

The *Miami Herald* conducted an extensive survey of Dade County, Florida, residents in October and November of 1983. It found that an overwhelming majority—78 percent—of Cuban-Americans in Miami wanted official brochures and signs to be printed in Spanish. It also found that only 39 percent of Cuban-Americans said they frequently had a social conversation, ate together or played sports together with people of other races or ethnic backgrounds—well below the 50 percent of Dade County whites and blacks who answered that question affirmatively. On the other hand, the paper noted in its generational breakdown of Cuban-American attitudes that younger members of the group supported official bilingual material by a somewhat smaller percentage, 64 percent, and that nearly two thirds of them said that they socialized with non-Cubans, compared with only a third of those over thirty-five years old.[9]

The May 1984 issue of "Hispanic Business" surveyed one hundred Hispanic U.S. "influentials," including corporation executives, chosen by its editors. That survey found that seventy belonged to more than one group which fostered cultural identity. Sixteen belonged to only one cultural identity organization, and only fourteen belonged to none. The reinforcement from these groups must be effective: sixty-eight Hispanic influentials said they were equally Hispanic and American; twenty-three felt more Hispanic than American, and only nine felt predominantly American. It should be noted that seventy-nine of the respondents were American by birth.[10]

Another study of the Hispanic elite yielded similar conclusions. The Cultural Communications Group, which carried out a 1983 survey of the "Hispanic Business Agenda," commissioned by the Coca-Cola Company, reported that its "results indicate that corporate representatives should use Spanish when speaking with Hispanic retailers and small business persons. Roughly half claimed no language preference, while 43 percent preferred Spanish. . . . In Miami, many of the Hispanic leaders preferred Spanish because they spoke little or no English. In this market it appears that even the leaders must be reached via the Spanish language."[11]

The only longitudinal survey of the Hispanic general public which has used the same questions and survey methods consistently covers a short period of time. Yankelovich, Skelly & White, a nationally known marketing research firm, conducted a study of the Hispanic market for SIN, the Spanish International Network, in 1981 and again in 1984. It found that "In 1984, compared with 1981, more Hispanics think of themselves as Hispanics first, and Americans second."[12]

It also found that "There was a significant increase in the desire to perpetuate Hispanic traditions through succeeding generations."[13] "We should pass on to our children a sense of belonging to our religious and national tradition."

While the Spanish language is becoming the most important mechanism for preserving Hispanic culture/identity,[14] most other traditions associated with Hispanic culture are seen as weakening.

Finally, a very extensive study on the *U.S. Hispanic Market 1984* by the Strategy Research Corporation of Miami, New York and San Juan, examines the trends and concludes that:

Assimilation has been slow because of the large numbers of recent arrivals and will never equal the absorption of other earlier groups of immigrants for several reasons: The importance of multi-language capabilities, pride of individual roots

Table 7.1   National allegiance/orientation

	1981	1984
"Hispanic first, American second	46%	50%
"Equally Hispanic and American	42%	36%
"American first, Hispanic second . . ."	12%	14%

It also found that "There was a significant increase in the desire to perpetuate Hispanic traditions through succeeding generations."[13]

"We should pass on to our children a sense of belonging to our religious and national tradition.

	1981	1984
Agree	89%	94%
Strongly agree	37%	46%

Table 7.2   Aspects of culture or traditions most important to preserve

	Total Hispanics	
	1981 %	1984 %
The Spanish language	81	84
Religion/church	51	53
Care or respect for elders (net)	58	52
Respect for elders or parents (stay with family)	53	47
Music	54	49
Commitment to family	50	43
Holidays and celebrations	41	37
Food and beverages	46	36
Love for life or know how to enjoy life	42	28
Art and literature	48	28

and heritage, increased flow of tourists and business between the United States and Latin America, the ability to return home and the proximity of Latin Countries. Recent studies indicate that there is an increasing use of the Spanish language in the United States, especially in the Miami area. With increased use of the language, the probability of assimilation decreases.[16]

It seems fair to say that the polls uniformly show that Hispanic-Americans prefer to associate with and to be approached by Spanish-speakers in personal and business relationships and that Hispanics are highly ambivalent about making a commitment to political identification with this country. Yet many of these studies, it must be pointed out, have been conducted for commercial interests: their conclusions are perhaps too comfortably congruent with the case that there is an established and separate Spanish market that must be reached in its own tongue.

When these polls' conclusions are stated so bluntly, they seem to be at odds with other, more anecdotal evidence. They make light of the trend toward Americanization which—perhaps only as a matter of faith—we believe must still be taking place. The best evidence, perhaps, of the continued assimilative power of America may be the fiery young Hispanic leaders who, in halting Spanish, exhort new immigrants to hold on to their separate identity—and who lobby Congress for the new multicultural society in impeccable English.

ASSIMILATION AND DISCRIMINATION

The studies we have reviewed strongly suggest that the assimilative process is slowing down, and point to the possibility of an alternative society, operating in another language, arising within ours. This is clearly good news for the advocates of the "salad bowl" school of cultural pluralism such as Professor of Spanish Robert Cordova, who recently wrote:

> To prepare American youth for America and the world of the not-too-distant future, the present monolingual, monocultural Anglocentric public education system must be replaced by a multilingual, multicultural, pluralistic one. . . . The Hispanic population is becoming larger and Hispanic culture is becoming stronger. . . . American society and ideas of old no longer exist.[17]

This vision of America would not be without its attractions—if people could feel comfortable and function easily while continually criss-crossing cultural borders. But in truth this balancing act is very unsettling, and few can perform it gracefully on a sustained basis. Cultural pluralism is inherently unstable over time. It is not an organizing principle for a society; but rather a phase from which it must move either toward greater integration or toward fragmentation. The individual caught between cultures must also move forward toward the mainstream culture of the host society, or retreat from it into uncomfortable alienation.

The process of individual assimilation is not easy, and it can often be unpleasant. The individual immigrant who assimilates does experience a sense of loss and, at times, a sense of being lost. It is this individual pain which gives the reaction against assimilation its force and which gives champions of the multicultural state their emotional sway. The discomfort of children learning a new language through immersion and the bewilderment of adults getting a first job in a technological society can be interpreted as complaints against the inhospitality of the new country and harnessed as the energy to run ethnic organizations.

The host society has two possible responses when confronted with the resentment of migrants: in the past, America retained confidence in the value of its own culture and in the validity of immigrants' assimilating to it; at present, however, America seems bent on creating a system which will lessen the need for migrants to assimilate.

In the United States the natural and inescapable pain of assimilation has been confused with the actual discrimination which has been practiced upon blacks in our society. But the process of assimilation is not discrimination. Antidiscrimination remedies cannot help the difficulties that those who are in the throes of assimilation encounter.

Some of the large income differential between whites and blacks in the United States is undoubtedly due to discrimination, for example. But the lesser wages that Hispanics who are unfamiliar with English earn are a result not of discrimination but of their lesser ability to function in this country. This is not to deny that there is actual discrimination against Hispanics in the United States, of course; it is merely to point out that one must distinguish migrants' difficulties from the disabilities suffered by the victims of discrimination. (There is no significant wage differential between white Americans and Hispanics who have good English-language skills.)

It is politically useful, however, for ethnic leaders to confuse the beneficent motivations behind assimilation with racism, to erect a wall of separatism around their particular group by a false analogy to discrimination against blacks. Because the problems of assimilation have been confused with discrimination, the United States has responded to the ethnic pride movement not by asserting the value of American culture and the rewards of assimilating to it, but by encouraging a pattern of cultural separatism. We have become vulnerable to the argument that the pain of assimilation is not the inevitable cost, the price of moving from one culture to another, but rather a social wrong that a needlessly cruel society visits upon migrants.

The bilingual education movement and bilingual voting laws originated in the mistaken belief that the difficulties of assimilation were the result of social discrimination, and that the path of migrants in the United States could be smoothed not by requiring (and assisting) them to adapt to their new country, but by altering the country to fit them. But this course ultimately leads to a dead end. The dominant culture in the United States will be changed by new migrants—it always has been—but it will not shift so radically, so swiftly and so completely that new migrants need not adapt to it.

The truly open and accepting society will work hard to facilitate the assimilation and integration of immigrants into itself; it will not create special exemptions, special ghettos designed to isolate immigrants and preserve their differences. Bilingual education programs can isolate non-English-speaking children for years within special classes; bilingual voting programs can encourage non-English-speaking adults not to enter into the mainstream of political discussion and debate. They are the programs and symbols of a country which has chosen to divide itself, to adapt to and preserve division, rather than to integrate and be whole.

There is a fine line between cultural enrichment, to be gained from our many immigrant streams, and cultural chaos. One cannot precisely identify the point at which one becomes the other, but, when we meet the demand for equality of immigrant languages and acceptance of uncertain loyalties, we have definitely passed the point of enrichment.

If we abandon the basic direction of this country's melting pot, its acceptance and integration of migrants from other cultures, and continue in the direction of separation and division, the future of American unity becomes problematic. The clearly stated goal of American society must be the integration of ethnic minorities within the mainstream culture of this country. The current course of unwise governmental policies in support of separatism and division is not inalterable; it can be changed.

If it is, we shall all benefit.

NOTES

1. For the classification system used in this paper we are indebted to the pioneering work of Milton Gordon, though we have altered and adapted his categories. See especially Milton Gordon, "Models of Pluralism: The New American Dilemma," *The Annals of the American Academy of Political and Social Sciences*, Vol. 454 (March 1981) pp. 178-189.

2. The salad bowl concept has been popularized by a highly visible Miami-based Cuban-American organization, the Spanish-American League Against Discrimination—S.A.L.A.D.

3. John A. Garcia, "Political Integration of Mexican Immigrants: Explorations into the Naturalization Process," *International Migration Review*, Vol. 15, No. 4 (Winter 1981) p. 611.

4. Ibid., pp. 620-621.

5. James W. Lamare, "The Political Integration of Mexican American Children: A Generational Analysis," *International Migration Review*, Vol. 16, No. 1 (Spring 1982) p. 173.

6. Ibid., p. 174.

7. The Public Agenda Foundation, "A National Survey of Elected and Appointed Hispanic Officials," (in three volumes: *Moving Into the Political Mainstream, Moving Up to Better Education and Better Jobs*, and *Recent Hispanic Polls: A Summary of Results.*), Hispanic Policy Development Project, (1984); Vol. 1, p. 11. Available from the Hispanic Policy Development Project, 717 Fifth Avenue, 23rd Floor, New York, NY 10022.

8. Robert R. Brischetto and Rodolfo O. de la Garza, *The Mexican American Electorate: Political Participation and Ideology* (Austin, Texas: The Southwest Voter Registration Education Project and the Hispanic Population Studies Program of the Center for Mexican American Studies, 1983), p. 31.

9. Special Supplement, "The Cubans: A People Changes," *Miami Herald*, December 18, 1983.

10. D. Carlos Balkan, "100 Influentials and their Critical Issues Agenda for the Eighties," *Hispanic Business*, Vol. 6, No. 5 (May 1984), pp. 20, 23.

11. The Cultural Communications Group, *The Coca-Cola National Business Agenda*, n.d., p. 6. (Available from Coca-Cola U.S.A., P.O. Drawer 1734, Atlanta, Georgia 30301.)

12. Yankelovich, Skelly & White, *Spanish USA, 1984*, (New York: Yankelovich, Skelly & White, 1984), p. 9. Available from Yankelovich, Skelly & White, 575 Madison Avenue, New York, NY 10022.

13. Ibid., 1984.

14. Ibid., 1984, p. 10.

15. Ibid., 1984.

16. Strategy Research Corporation, *U.S. Hispanic Market 1984* (Miami: Strategy Research Corporation, 1984) p. 34. Available from Strategy Research Corporation, 100 N.W. 37th Avenue, Miami, FL 33125.

17. Robert H. Cordova, "Bilingual U.S. by the Turn of the Century?," *Houston Chronicle*, March 11, 1985.

IV

CALIFORNIA: AMERICA'S IMMIGRATION LABORATORY

San Diego faces West, looks resolutely out to sea. Tijuana stares north, as towards the future. San Diego is the future, secular, soulless. San Diego is the past, guarding its quality of life. Tijuana is the future. On the Mexican side there is a flux, a vast migration, a camp of seige.

—Richard Rodriguez,
"Across the Borders of History,"
Harper's, March 1987

Immigration, Population Change and California's Future
By Leon Bouvier

In 1909 the then Ambassador from the United Kingdom to the United States, Lord James Bryce, asked upon visiting the State of California: "What will happen when California is filled by fifty millions of people? . . . There will be more people—as many perhaps as the country can support—and the real question will be not about making more wealth or having more people, but whether the people will then be happier or better than they have been hitherto or are at this moment."[1] In 1987 with a population of some twenty-five million, California is half-way towards the population level that so worried Bryce.

A few years ago the then Lieutenant Governor Mervyn Dymally, himself an immigrant from the Caribbean, expressed a different kind of concern about population change when he predicted that by the turn of the century a majority of the state's population would consist of "Third World" peoples.

This article examines population growth and composition for the fifty-year period 1980-2030 and looks at the broad picture—social, cultural, economic. From the projections one can examine each ethnic group, and address difficult broad-based questions—questions that must be answered if the state is to maintain cultural, social and economic progress as it enters the twenty-first century.

Three points will be emphasized: (1) the number and types of Californians in the years 2000 and 2030; (2) the size and composition of the labor force and the related issues that result from changes in population size; and (3) the effect of such demographic shifts on the social and cultural environment.

PAST POPULATION GROWTH

Rapid population growth has always prevailed in California. During the century beginning in 1860, a fortyfold increase in numbers took place. At the same time the nation grew only four and a half times. In the 1960s the population increased by 27 percent to twenty million in 1970, while the country added 13 percent of its 1960 population. According to the 1980 census, California's population totaled almost twenty-four million reflecting an addition of some 3.7 million over 1970 or a decennial increase of 18 percent. This is notably larger than the national increase of 11 percent, though the difference is less than in earlier decades.

POPULATION CHANGES 1970 TO 1980

California is the nation's most urban state with 95 percent of its population living in cities and a concentration in the southern section. Fully 60 percent live in Los Angeles and adjacent counties. The state's second largest urban center is the San Francisco Bay Area, comprised of nine counties that contain 5.6 million people, or 23 percent of the state's population.

With more than 15 percent of its population foreign born, California's cultural diversity cannot be overstated. The evolution of the state's heterogeneity began during the 1840s when Chinese as well as Americans from the East came to find work and fortune in the gold mines. There they joined the Native Americans and Hispanics already in California and were later joined by Japanese immigrants. Early in the twentieth century Mexicans streamed in as civil unrest in their country pushed them out, and a demand for unskilled labor pulled them over the northern border. Blacks did not reach the state in great numbers until the Second World War when their labor was needed.

Migration from other states remained a contributing factor to California's growth until the 1970s. However, in that decade more people left the state than moved in from other states. Since 1980 net internal migration has once again been positive.

In recent decades immigration from a number of Asian and Latin American countries has contributed significantly to the state's growth in both size and cultural diversity. Because of changes in Census definitions, comparisons by ethnology are not always accurate. Nevertheless, the 1970s did witness major shifts in the state's ethnic composition. (See Table 1.2)

Substantial in-migration and differential fertility among ethnic groups have contributed to a reduction in the majority proportion in California. In 1970, 77 percent of Californians were non-Hispanic whites while ten years later this group constituted only two-thirds of the state's population. The proportion of blacks changed little during the 1970s; most of the population growth of minorities occurred among Asians and Hispanics.

Since 1970 the proportion of Californians from Asia and the Pacific—then 3 percent—has climbed each year as the number of Southeast Asian immigrants and refugees has accumulated; in 1980 Asian and Pacific Islanders made up 5.5 percent of the state's population. Of these, 27 percent are Filipino, followed by 25 percent Chinese and 21 percent Japanese.[2] Latin Americans are even more visible in California. Hispanics—80 percent of whom are of Mexican origin—

Table 8.1 Population by ethnicity 1970 and 1980 (in thousands)

	1970	%	1980	%
Non-Hispanic white	15,392	77	15,704	67
Black	1,400	7	1,783	8
Hispanic	2,369	12	4,544	19
Asian & other	792	4	1,575	7
Total	19,953	100	23,608	100

make up 20 percent of the population of the state and in 1980 numbered 4.5 million. Though its size enables California to accommodate more people than most states, it contains disproportionately more of the newest immigrants. Fully one out of every four foreign-born persons living in the United States resides in California as do one out of ten Americans. The foreign-born population in California includes nearly one-third of all Hispanics and close to 40 percent of all Asian-Americans in the United States.[3]

Immigration has spawned cultural diversity in California and sustained a relatively young age structure. Internal movement has brought mobile young adults from all states, especially from the North Central and South between 1975 and 1980. Concurrently, an influx of young immigrants with large families and relatively high fertility has skewed the age distribution so that California's median age remains slightly lower than the nation's. The state's median age has edged up since 1970, however, from 28.1 to 29.9 in 1980 as the proportion of elderly (sixty-five years and older) rose to 10.2 percent in 1980 from 9 percent a decade earlier.

California has been undergoing radical alterations in its population size and composition, be it ethnic makeup or age—all the result of demographic behavior. People are born; people move; people die. Shifts in the rates of fertility, migration and mortality are the causes of variations in ethnic distribution as well as in age composition. In turn these shifts affect every aspect of society. This report deals with both the demographic changes and the societal impacts of these changes over the next fifty years.

THE FUTURE POPULATION OF CALIFORNIA

To peer into the demographic future of California we must develop population projections. Projections are not to be confused with predictions. The latter are simply the author's views about the future situation in any given area; the former are mathematical calculations based on a series of assumptions about demographic behavior (fertility, mortality and migration).

This discussion concentrates on demographic assumptions and does not consider the often tenuous assumptions sometimes used in econometric models. For example, rather than projecting the number of jobs in future years and then adjusting rates of migration to that total, we will limit ourselves to purely demographic projections, assuming that the level of migration will in turn determine the number of jobs or the extent of unemployment.

The population of California as enumerated in the 1980 Census is the base population for all projections. In turn this population is subdivided into ethnic categories, all by age and sex composition. Assumptions about future demographic behavior are then applied to these base populations and the projections are derived according to the cohort-component method.

Data is available to construct population projections for four basic groups: Non-Hispanic whites, blacks, Hispanics and Asian and Pacific Islanders (simply referred to as Asians). All others are primarily Native Americans and a few unidentified individuals. No further analysis will be done on this group except to determine its future size and include it within the total population.

THE DEMOGRAPHIC ASSUMPTIONS

For the past thirteen years, fertility in the United States has been at historical lows. Women have been averaging 1.8 live births during their reproductive years, an insufficient number to replace the population in the long run without immigration. California's fertility closely resembles that of the nation. Because of its large Hispanic population, some scholars set fertility at slightly higher than the national average. However, as separate projections are to be made for each ethnic group, this assumption is not appropriate to this study.

Non-Hispanic white fertility is assumed to be 1.7 live births per woman; black fertility reflects that of all blacks in the nation, that is, 2.3 live births per woman. Estimating current Hispanic fertility is more difficult given the limited data. According to the most recent statistics on births of Hispanic parentage in 1982, "Mexican women and 'other Hispanic' women had the highest fertility rates [among Hispanics], 102.8 and 108.8 per one thousand women fifteen to forty-four years of age, respectively."[4] This is approximately 62 percent higher than the overall rate for all women. Thus we assume that Hispanic fertility in 1980 was 3.0 live births per woman.

Similarly, data is rare on Asian fertility. A recent analysis of the 1980 census by Robert Gardner et al. yields interesting information on the larger Asian groups in the United States.[5] Japanese and Chinese fertility is somewhat below the national average, while that for Koreans and Indians approximates the national average. Filipino and Vietnamese fertility are higher. Fragmentary reports indicate that other Southeast Asians may exhibit even higher fertility. We assume the 1980 fertility for these groups to be as follows: Chinese and Japanese 1.7; Indian 1.8; Korean 2.0; Filipino 2.5; Vietnamese and other Southeast Asian 3.0; All Other 3.0.

Fertility for all groups is assumed to converge at 1.8 by 2030. During the period of convergence, average age of mothers at birth of children will also be gradually adjusted toward that reflected by lower rather than higher fertility. That is to say, average age at birth of children will increase slightly as fertility falls. Furthermore, future immigrants will be assumed to have the same fertility as their fellow country persons in California at whatever future date they arrive.

Mortality patterns are easier to assess with some confidence. While we cannot be certain that fertility will not increase in the future, progress in extending life expectancy for all Americans is highly likely. For Non-Hispanic whites and for blacks, we assume that life expectancy will increase from that registered in 1980 for the total United States and will converge at eighty years (for both sexes combined) by 2030. In 1980 life expectancy for whites was seventy-two years; for blacks sixty-seven years. Hispanic life expectancy is assumed to increase from seventy years in 1980 to eighty by 2030. Among the Asian groups, Japanese and Chinese as well as Korean and Indians will follow the same path as Non-Hispanic whites; the other Asian groups will more likely follow that of Hispanics. Differences are slight among the various groups being studied and convergence is assumed for 2030. Projections will be done separately for males and females. In any case, slight variations in life expectancy have little effect on the eventual size and age distribution of a population.

Future migration, whether internal or international, is more difficult to estimate than either fertility or mortality. International movements depend on many imponderables such as the economy and political stability of the sending countries as well as the economic and the legislative mood of the United States. Future and, as yet, unpredictable political disturbances in Latin American or Asian countries could lead to massive refugee movements in the direction of the Pacific Coast. On the other hand, new legislation could drastically curtail illegal movements and limit legal and refugee movements.

Interstate migration is almost totally dependent on economic conditions. Jobs attract people; unemployment sends people away from an area. Will continued high levels of immigration into California mean fewer jobs for other Americans from other regions of the nation? If so, will out-migration from California become the normal pattern? On the other hand, if immigration is substantially reduced at the same time that the state's economy improves, will that lead to significant increases in the number of Americans moving to California? We have seen that during the 1970s the better educated were more apt to move to California, while those in lower occupations tended to move away from the state. Such a pattern may continue in future years.

The number of legal foreign entrants into California depends on the number entering the nation. Since 1980 that number has averaged about 600,000 annually, with about 27 percent settling in California. In addition, two movements have no reliable data bases upon which to make informed estimates: the number of persons entering the country illegally in any given year and the number leaving the country, both legals and illegals.

A recent study has estimated the number of legal emigrants from the United States (thus not including the circular movement of illegal migrants) at about 100,000 per year.[6] Most of these people are Non-Hispanic whites returning to their motherland. Estimates of the number of clandestine settlers in any given year range from 100,000 to more than one million.

The Urban Institute has estimated that more than one million people came to California illegally to settle during the 1970s and that "for the state as a whole, almost 60 percent of the recent immigrants have come without proper docu-

mentation."[7] A 1985 study by the National Academy of Sciences estimates the
number of illegal residents in the United States at between two and four million;
however it says nothing about annual entries.[8] It is thought that a significant
majority of illegal migrants are from either Mexico or Central America, with
many making California their desired residence in the United States.

Given the unreliability of data on immigration patterns, no single assumption
will satisfy all readers. We have a strong predilection for erring on the conservative side. We assume that 750,000 people immigrate annually to the United
States, 600,000 legally and 150,000 illegally (Editor's Note: The Census Bureau
estimates annual illegal immigration at 100,000 to 300,000 yearly). If about
150,000 leave the country, legally and illegally, this means that net migration
into the United States is 600,000 per year. That is our assumption. About 32
percent of all net migration, legal and illegal, 190,000 migrants, is assigned to
California. (This is higher than noted above because the proportion of illegal
immigrants from Latin America coming to California is thought to be more than
35 percent, and a certain amount of secondary migration to California on the
part of some refugees has been observed.) Based on recent patterns of immigration by population size, country of origin, age and sex composition, as well
as on intended place of residence of legal immigrants, the distribution of annual
net immigration into California by racial and ethnic categories is:

Asian	75,000
Hispanic	100,000
Central America	35,000
Mexico	65,000
Non-Hispanic white	10,000
Black	5,000

Interstate migration is also a factor when making projections for the state of
California. Again, to be deliberately conservative, net migration in future years
is assumed to be zero. In other words, over the long run as many U.S. residents
will leave California as will enter the state as has been the situation for about
the last decade. With foreign immigration remaining high, massive surges of in-
migration from elsewhere in the nation are unlikely.

Yet another special type of internal migration must be considered: secondary
movements by refugees. Numerous groups of Southeast Asians, as well as other
refugees, have been resettled in various areas of the nation. Hmongs, for example,
are located in Minneapolis, MN as well as in Providence, RI. Evidence suggests
that over time many such refugees will relocate in California, where many of
their fellow nationals reside.[9] These numbers are not inconsiderable. As noted
above, our assumptions on international migration indirectly take into consideration such secondary moves on the part of refugees. Thus no further attempt
to measure this phenomenon is undertaken.

These assumptions are admittedly conservative, whether in fertility, mortality or migration. Fertility is assumed to decline among future immigrants; mortality levels will fall but not dramatically; migration, both international and internal, will not be as enormous as some predict. By taking this lower approach, the actual projections should be more acceptable and reasonable than they would be if higher fertility and migration assumptions were used.

THE DEMOGRAPHIC PROJECTIONS

By the turn of the century, California's population will be approaching thirty-two million. This represents an average annual rate of growth of about 1.5 percent. Such growth, based on the assumptions described above, is consistent with other projections developed by California agencies.[10] Despite declining fertility after the turn of the century, growth will continue at a fairly high level. By 2030 the population of California will exceed forty-two million. Between 2000 and 2030 more than ten million people will be added, representing an annual growth rate of about 1 percent. We can expect that California's population will almost double from twenty-three to forty-two million between 1980 and 2030. By then, fertility for all groups will be well below the level needed for replacement. However, the momentum for growth combined with continued net immigration will lead to additional numerical gains, albeit at an ever slower rate. Lord Bryce's concerns for fifty million Californians may well come to fruition by the mid twenty-first century.

Numerical increases are important for many segments of the society; equally important are changes in the composition of that growing population. Variations in the racial and ethnic composition as well as the age and sex distribution of the state must be considered along with changes in population size.

In 1980 about two-thirds of all Californians were white, non-Hispanics. In future decades that proportion will decline considerably. By the turn of the century, Non-Hispanic whites will represent just over half the total population of the state. Dymally's comment will be proven correct, although at a later date than originally predicted. By 2010 a majority of Californians will be of Third

Table 8.2   Projected population of California 1980 to 2030 (in thousands)

Year	Population	% Change
1980	23,600	—
1990	27,880	18
2000	31,883	14
2010	35,869	13
2020	38,466	7
2030	42,665	11

World background, if that background is defined to include Asians, Pacific Islanders, Hispanics and blacks. In 2030 Hispanics and Non-Hispanic whites will be numerically equal, each representing 38 percent of the total population. Asians, in the meantime, will exhibit steady growth, reaching 10 percent of the population by 2000 and more than 15 percent by 2030. The proportion of blacks will decline slightly in future years, from 7.5 percent of the population in 1980 to less than 7 percent by 2030. Thus the next few decades will be marked by major shifts in the proportional distribution of the state among its various ethnic groups.

The number of Non-Hispanic whites will grow, though very slowly, until 2010 when it will peak at just under 17 million. Beyond that date some declines can be expected, and by 2030 they will total 16.4 million, or slightly more than noted in 1980. The combination of continued very low fertility and low levels of immigration contribute to this almost zero growth situation. It should be recalled, however, that the assumptions do not include any net domestic immigration. Should such occur, the Non-Hispanic white total would be larger.

Although the proportion of blacks will fall slightly, their numbers will increase from 1.8 million in 1980 to 2.4 million at the turn of the century to 2.8 million in 2030. Most black Californians are American-born. Throughout the nation, however, increases in the immigration of blacks from the Caribbean and from Africa have been observed. Some of these movements are to California. Thus it can be expected that in the twenty-first century the black population will be somewhat more heterogeneous than it is today and will contain small pockets of immigrants and their descendants from certain African and Caribbean countries.

Table 8.3   Projected population by ethnicity 1980 to 2030 (in thousands)

	1980	1990	2000	2010	2020	2030
Non-Hispanic						
white	15,704	16,410	16,704	16,859	16,856	16,388
%	66.5	58.8	52.4	47.0	43.8	38.4
Black	1,784	2,098	2,353	2,578	2,761	2,862
%	7.5	7.5	7.4	7.2	7.2	6.7
Hispanic	4,544	6,736	9,085	11,548	12,799	16,273
%	19.2	24.2	28.5	32.2	33.3	38.1
Asian	1,312	2,312	3,371	4,471	5,598	6,667
%	5.6	8.3	10.6	12.5	14.6	15.6
Other	263	322	368	411	450	472
%	1.2	1.2	1.1	1.1	1.1	1.2
Total	23,668	27,880	31,883	35,869	38,466	42,665
%	100.0	100.0	100.0	100.0	100.0	100.0

The Hispanic population will increase 3.5 times between 1980 and 2030, from less than five million in 1980 to ten million around 2005 to fifteen million in 2025. By 2030 more than sixteen million Hispanics will be living in California. Soon thereafter, Hispanics will be the largest ethnic group in the state. Hispanic immigrants come predominantly from Mexico and Central America. Given the projected growth in Mexico in future years, a growth that will be replicated in most Central American nations as well, the future Hispanic population in California should continue to be overwhelmingly of Mexican and Central American heritage. Furthermore, its immigration level should not decrease. Recall that net immigration of Hispanics to California is assumed to be 100,000 per year which includes both legal and illegal movements. Some might argue that this is too low an estimate of current let alone future patterns. For example, Victor Urquidi, noted Mexican economist, estimates that 200,000 Mexicans emigrate more or less permanently each year. Most of these would be destined for the United States. On the other hand, IRCA could lead to lower levels of immigration.

Percentagewise, Asians will grow more rapidly than Hispanics. Their numbers will increase more than five fold over the fifty year period between 1980 and 2030. Asians numbered only 1.3 million in 1980 but will increase to 3 million before the turn of the century and 6 million by about 2025. The growing heterogeneity among Asian immigrants will result in some remarkable shifts in ethnic proportions. In 1980 Filipinos became the largest Asian ethnic group in the state, passing the Chinese. Following closely behind were the Japanese. Almost three-quarters of all Asians in California were either Chinese, Japanese or Filipino.

By the turn of the century, Filipinos will constitute by far the largest Asian ethnic group, but the Vietnamese will be second and the fastest growing. Indeed, by 2030 the Vietnamese will pass the Filipinos and become the largest Asian group in the state. Many other significant changes will take place within the Asian community. Numerically, the Vietnamese will grow from 85,000 to almost 1.8 million over the fifty year period; the Koreans will increase from 102,000 to 685,000. The number of refugees from Kampuchea and Laos, who only numbered 19,000 in 1980 could grow to more than 600,000. The Japanese, on the other hand, will exhibit extremely slow growth, reaching only 387,000 in 2030 as compared to 269,000 in 1980. Thus the combination of Chinese, Japanese and Filipino will drop from almost 75 percent of the Asian population in 1980 to 45 percent in 2030. Southeast Asians (Vietnamese, Laotians including Hmongs and Kampucheans), a mere 8 percent in 1980, will comprise more than 35 percent of the Asian-Californian population in 2030.

Immigration assumptions should also be kept in mind. Will the current levels from Southeast Asia be maintained for the foreseeable future? Will immigration laws continue to encourage family reunification? Will this result in growing numbers from Korea, the Philippines and eventually Vietnam? Will possible political unrest in the Philippines lead to massive refugee movements? Will the

Table 8.4 Projected Asian population by ethnicity 1980 to 2030 (in thousands)

	1980	1990	2000	2010	2020	2030
Chinese	325	465	591	709	817	906
%	24.8	20.2	17.6	15.8	14.6	13.6
Filipino	358	620	896	1,181	1,466	1,731
%	27.3	25.8	26.6	26.4	26.2	26.0
Indian	59	81	103	125	144	159
%	4.6	3.5	3.1	2.8	2.6	2.4
Japanese	268	309	335	355	374	386
%	20.5	13.4	10.0	7.9	6.7	5.8
Korean	102	215	333	452	569	684
%	7.8	9.3	9.9	10.1	10.2	10.3
Vietnamese	85	356	674	1,026	1,405	1,785
%	6.5	15.4	20.0	22.9	25.1	26.8
SE Asian	18	111	221	343	475	608
%	1.4	4.8	6.6	7.7	8.5	9.1
Other	93	151	213	278	345	406
%	7.1	6.6	6.2	6.4	6.1	6.1
Total	1,312	2,312	3,371	4,471	5,598	6,669
%	100.0	100.0	100.0	100.0	100.0	100.0

1997 shift in political power in Hong Kong mean an increase in the number of Chinese coming to California? These questions remain unanswered, but such future non-demographic developments could affect the projections.

One thing is certain: the ethnic composition of the state of California will become ever more complex and diverse in the next century. Non-Hispanic whites will no longer comprise the majority. They will be replaced, not by another majority group, but by a combination of significant minorities—Asian and Hispanic as well as black and Non-Hispanic whites.

CHANGING AGE COMPOSITION

Changing demographic behavior, whether fertility, mortality or migration, contributes to variations in the age composition of a state's population. Declining fertility causes an aging of the society by reducing the proportion of younger people and thus increasing the proportion of older people. Ironically, when mortality begins to fall, the average age of a society does not increase; indeed, it is more likely to drop. Early declines in mortality are likely to occur among infants and children, thereby increasing their proportion of the total population. Only when mortality is already quite low can any further improvements in life expectancy contribute to a society's aging. Then, progress occurs among the older segments of the population rather than among the youth.

Migration also affects age composition. A significant influx of young adults into an area will obviously contribute to a "younging" of the population. On the other hand, in some retirement colonies, the in-migration of older people results in an aging of the population. For the United States as a whole, immigration from out of the country made up primarily of young adults and their children has retarded the aging of the population that has been underway since the end of the baby boom in the early 1960s and it will continue to do so. Immigration, however, will not stop that process; because of both very low fertility and increased life expectancy among the elderly, we are inevitably an aging nation.[11]

AGING OF THE STATE

California is also aging. In 1980 9.5 percent of all Californians were sixty-five or over and 23 percent were under age fifteen leaving 67.5 percent in the so-called active ages between fifteen and sixty-five. This distribution was slightly younger than the nation's in 1980, and is explained by the relatively high proportion of young adult immigrants settling in the state during the 1970s. By the turn of the century, over 10 percent of California's population will be sixty-five or over, while 22.5 percent will be under fifteen. The big change will occur after 2020 when the baby boom generation begins to enter the retirement stage of life. In 2030 almost 17 percent of the state's population will be sixty-five or over, compared to 19.2 percent under age fifteen. California will nevertheless be younger than the nation which, by 2030, may see the elderly representing one-quarter of its population.

Interestingly, this age shift will not affect the active age population; the proportion between fifteen and sixty-five will remain close to 65 percent throughout the fifty-year period. However, the shifting emphasis from school and preschool expenditures to those involved with aging and retirement promises some interesting issues in future decades.

All four ethnic groups will age. However, all did not have the same age composition in 1980. Almost 12 percent of Non-Hispanic whites were sixty-five or over, with less than 20 percent under fifteen. By contrast, fewer than 4 percent of Hispanics were elderly, while almost one-third were children under age fifteen. Blacks and Asians fell between these two age extremes. By the year 2000 the proportion of Non-Hispanic whites aged sixty-five or over will climb to 13 percent and by 2030, it will reach almost 23 percent; the share of children will decline in turn. The percent of elderly persons among Hispanics will also climb to 6 percent in 2000 and 12 percent in 2030.

Table 8.5 Percentage distribution by ethnicity 1980, 2000, 2030

	Non-Hispanic White	Black	Hispanic	Asian	Other	Total
1980						
0–14	19.7	26.6	32.6	23.2	28.0	23.0
15–64	68.5	67.1	63.6	70.1	67.4	67.5
65+	11.8	6.3	3.8	6.7	4.6	9.5
Total	100.0	100.0	100.0	100.0	100.0	100.0
2000						
0–14	18.3	23.2	29.4	24.3	27.6	22.5
15–64	68.7	68.6	64.6	57.0	65.4	67.4
65+	13.0	8.2	6.0	8.7	7.0	10.1
Total	100.0	100.0	100.0	100.0	100.0	100.0
2030						
0–14	16.1	18.1	22.1	20.3	20.6	19.2
15–64	61.3	64.2	65.8	65.8	67.6	64.0
65+	22.6	17.7	12.1	13.9	14.8	16.8
Total	100.0	100.0	100.0	100.0	100.0	100.0

CHANGING ETHNIC DISTRIBUTIONS BY AGE

Combining projections of age composition with those of ethnic composition reveal some interesting distributions. As noted, by the turn of the century, Non-Hispanic whites will constitute just over half of California's population; Hispanics are projected to be 28.5 percent; Asians, 10.6 percent, and blacks 7.4 percent. These proportions, however, will vary substantially in different age groups.

For example, among children under fifteen, Non-Hispanic whites will make up less than half the total—42.6 percent—while Hispanics will constitute 37.3 percent, Asians 11.4 percent, and blacks 7.6 percent. Even among young people just leaving school or entering the labor force (those aged fifteen to twenty-four), Non-Hispanic whites will not constitute a majority. Only among persons twenty-five and over will Non-Hispanic whites be a majority. Among people between twenty-five and forty-four, they will represent just over half the population. Among those sixty-five and over, almost 70 percent will be Non-Hispanic whites while only 17.3 percent will be Hispanics. Asians will represent 6.1 percent and blacks 6.2 percent of the elderly. (See Table 4.2)

In 2030 Non-Hispanic whites and Hispanics will each be 38 percent of the total population of California. Asians will comprise 15.6 percent; blacks, 6.8 percent. Variations from this overall average will be substantial among age groups. Almost 44 percent of all children under fifteen will be Hispanic compared to 32.1 percent Non-Hispanic whites. About 17 percent will be Asians compared to 6.3 percent black. Similar distributions are projected for the fifteen to twenty-four year-old age group. The heart of the labor force consists of persons between twenty-five and forty-five. In that category, 41 percent will be Hispanic; almost 35 percent Non-Hispanic whites; 16.5 percent Asian; 6.6 percent black. Only among the elderly will Non-Hispanic whites remain a majority (51.6 percent).

These changes in demographic behavior will drastically alter the ethnic mix of California's population in the next fifty years and at the same time the population will age, resulting in growing numbers of elderly and reduced proportions of youth. The following chapters address the challenges these shifts present.

IMMIGRATION AND THE CALIFORNIA ECONOMY

Introduction

California accounts for 10 percent of the United States economy. Its twelve million workers produced goods and services worth $400 billion in 1983. California's economy employs more than 10 percent of the nation's professional, technical and kindred workers. High tech computer and aerospace manufacturing require engineers, biogenetics firms employ scientists, and diverse businesses from motion pictures to wine-making require specialized professionals. These highly educated workers are well paid. Over 12 percent of California's households had incomes of $40,000 or more in 1979, compared to 9 percent of the nation's households, and these affluent consumers make California the trend-setting marketplace for gourmet foods, foreign cars and expensive recreational goods.

California businesses also employ more unskilled and semi-skilled workers than do firms in other states. A disproportionate share of the nation's janitors are found in the state and California farmers employ about 25 percent of the nation's migrant and seasonal farmworkers. Many of these less-skilled workers earn $4 to $6 hourly, making it difficult for them to buy expensive California homes and live as middle-class Americans. Since 1970 many of these low-skilled workers have been immigrants who come to California in search of a better life.

California's Work Force

In 1980 California's civilian labor force counted about 12 million persons, of whom 10.7 million were employed. The state's work force had increased by an average of 340,000 workers annually during the 1970s and the state's un-employment rate has traditionally been higher than the United States' average.

California's work force will continue to grow at a rapid rate in future years. According to the Bureau of Labor Statistics, the United States labor force will increase by 1.6 percent annually during the 1980s and by 1.0 percent between 1990 and 1995. Such rates will be exceeded in California. Between 1980 and 2000, the annual growth rate will approximate 2.0 percent.

For projecting the California labor force, we have relied on the labor force participation rates (by age, sex and racial/ethnic groups) prepared by the Southern California Area Governments (SCAG) and extended to 2030. By 2000 a total of 17.5 million persons will be in California's labor force. The number will increase to 22.7 million by 2030.

Along with growing numbers, the age composition of the labor force will change over time. Between 1980 and 2000 the number between sixteen and twenty-four will increase only slightly from 2.9 to 3.1 million. By 2030 this age group in the labor force will total 3.9 million. On the other hand, the twenty-five to fifty-four age group will grow quite rapidly, reflecting both the aging of the baby boom generation and the continued immigration of young adults. From only 7.6 million in 1980, the number of persons these ages either working or looking for work will increase to some 12 million by the turn of the century and will almost double to 14.5 million over the following thirty years. The number of persons in the labor force aged fifty- five and over will also increase in future years from 1.6 million in 1980 to 2.4 million in 2000 and 4.3 million in 2030.

In recent decades two major changes have been experienced in California's work force: More women, especially married women, have decided to participate and immigrants, legal and illegal, have accounted for an increasing share of the growth in the work force. As of 1985 about 54 percent of all adult women participate in the work force; this compares to 52 percent nationally. Men can

Table 8.6 Labor force by age groups 1980, 2000, 2030 (in thousands)

	1980	%	2000	%	2030	%
16–24	2,933	24.8	3,115	17.7	3,912	17.2
25–54	7,340	62.3	12,086	68.9	14,488	63.9
55–64	1,206	10.2	1,795	10.2	3,000	13.2
65 +	316	2.7	570	3.2	1,287	5.7
Total	11,795	100.0	17,566	100.0	22,687	100.0

expect to work an average of thirty-seven years; a twenty year old woman entering the work force in 1960 could expect to work nineteen years on average; by 1977 this average was up to twenty-six years, and the average continues to rise. Immigrants now account for half of the California annual work force increase of almost 350,000. Illegal immigrants may well outnumber legal immigrants in the state's work force.

The major trends expected to affect the state labor force during the next few decades include a slower growing and older work force and an easier school-to-work transition for most Non-Hispanic white adolescents, but persisting minority youth unemployment.

These trends must be interpreted cautiously. We know how many eighteen year-olds could enter the work force in 2000 because they were born in 1982. If fewer eighteen year-olds than expected enter the work force while economic growth occurs at expected rates, then these adolescents should experience less unemployment. However, immigration and domestic migration patterns could alter these trends: for example, California teenagers might experience more difficult school-to-work transitions if immigration persists at high levels.

Immigrant Workers

Since California receives some 25 to 30 percent of all immigrants to the United States, the effects of such immigration should be particularly marked in California. Different groups of immigrants have different economic experiences: Asians tend to be legally in the United States and are likely to earn above average incomes within fifteen years of their arrival, while Hispanic immigrants are more likely to be illegal and unskilled.

Immigrants and the Future California Economy

California is a haven for immigrants and entrepreneurs because its expanding economy offers a variety of jobs to workers without language and job skills and its infrastructure promotes the formation of new businesses. Waves of immigrants helped to shape the California economy, and these immigrants are at least partially responsible for its heralded flexibility and entrepreneurial vigor.

Table 8.7 Labor force by ethnicity 1980, 2000, 2030 (in thousands)

	1980	%	2000	%	2030	%
Non-Hispanic white	8,198	69.5	9,576	54.5	8,610	37.9
Black	792	6.7	1,262	7.2	1,478	6.5
Hispanic	2,026	17.3	4,701	26.8	8,716	38.4
Asian & other	784	6.5	2,032	11.5	3,894	17.2
Total	11,800	100.0	17,571	100.0	22,698	100.0

Projections of California's population and labor force participation indicate that 5.8 million workers will be added between 1980 and 2000. Many of these will be ethnic minorities. By 2000, 27 percent of the labor force will be Hispanic and another 12 percent Asian. Thirty years later these proportions will be 38 and 17 percent respectively. Meanwhile the shares of Non-Hispanic whites and blacks will decline. By 2030 Non-Hispanic whites will comprise just 38 percent of the labor force, on a par with Hispanics. (See Table 5.3)

Will a dual economy be maintained, given the large growth in both the Hispanic and Asian groups? To be sure, many other factors could intervene. As we will see below, educational attainment levels differ substantially among groups. Will Hispanic educational attainment levels improve, thereby enabling them to compete with others for the high technology occupations that will blossom in the future, or will they remain relegated to lower status jobs in competition with uneducated Americans, both black and white, and some of the more recent Asian immigrants?

Asians have exhibited great enthusiasm for education, as will be noted later. Such enthusiasm may be necessary to assure a continuation of upward mobility within the economic system.

It is quite possible that enclaves of economically successful ethnic minorities will become permanent fixtures of the California scene in future years, given the growth of the minority population and the tendency for some ethnic groups to carve out niches in certain occupations.

One thing is certain, the California labor force, now less than 70 percent Non-Hispanic white, will change dramatically over the next few decades. Indeed, the major test for a multiethnic society in which no single group is a majority will be faced on the assembly lines, the farms and the high-technology industries of the future. Whether California, or the nation for that matter, passes the test depends to a considerable extent on how employment policies are administered in future years and how the newest immigrants adapt to American and Californian society.

Non-Hispanic whites in the California labor force will increase from 8.2 million in 1980 to only 9.5 million in 2000 and then fall to 8.6 million in 2030. Who will replace them in the high status positions traditionally filled by this group? The eventual answer to this question will help to determine the future social structure of the state.

The educational challenge posed by the newest immigrants, mostly Hispanic and Asian, has led to much controversy over bilingual education.

Bilingualism has become one of the most emotionally and politically explosive issues in American education. Secretary of Education William Bennett, in September 1985, pronounced the bilingual-only program "a failure, responsible for a range of ills besetting Hispanics in education." To this a spokesman for the Mexican-American Legal Defense and Education Fund (MALDEF) countered: "They're slowly walking away from the responsibility to teach limited-English children English."[12]

Language will be one of California's most vexing issues as the state adjusts to a population changing rapidly in both age and racial and ethnic composition. Should the California of the years 2000 and 2030 be an English-speaking or a multilingual state? Should Anglo customs continue to predominate, with some adjustments to accommodate the newest immigrants, or should a multicultural society be encouraged? We will return later to this issue, but for now, let us examine the demographics involved.

Currently, over four million boys and girls are enrolled in the public elementary and secondary schools of California. That number will increase in the coming years despite the "baby bust" of the 1970s. As a surrogate for actual numbers of students in primary and secondary schools, our projections focus on the population aged five to nineteen, on the assumption that most persons in this age range are students. The number of persons aged five to nineteen will increase by 27 percent between 1980 and 2000. In the following thirty years the growth will be limited to 15 percent, reflecting our assumption that the fertility of most minority groups will decline. The number of potential students aged five to nineteen will increase from 5.7 million to 8.4 million over the fifty-year period. Beginning about 2000 the nation may well witness a decline in school enrollments as the baby boom "echo" children, born in the late 1970s and 1980s, begin to pass beyond this age range, but this will not be true for California, primarily because of the projected high level of immigration.

Among Non-Hispanic whites, school enrollment will decline as the number of boys and girls aged five to nineteen declines from 3.5 million in 1980 to 3.3 million at the turn of the century and 2.7 million in 2030. This trend will mirror that expected for the nation as a whole if fertility remains at the present low level. Perhaps we are too conservative in assuming net immigration of Non-Hispanic whites of just 10,000 per year. If so, future enrollments will be higher for this group. Nevertheless, some decline is likely over the next few decades.

Black enrollments are likely to be quite stable at somewhat over half a million as the number of potential students aged five to nineteen increases slightly between 1980 and 2000 and then declines gradually to 536,000 in 2030, compared to 517,000 in 1980. This pattern is to be expected, given apparent future trends

Table 8.8   Persons of school age 5–19 by ethnicity 1980, 2000, 2030 (in thousands)

	Non-Hisp White	Black	Hispanic	Asian	Other	Total
1980	3,431	517	1,428	324	81	5,741
%	59.3	8.9	24.7	5.6	1.5	100.0
2000	3,274	571	2,571	789	107	7,312
%	44.7	7.8	35.2	10.8	1.5	100.0
2030	2,731	536	3,665	1,374	102	8,408
%	32.5	6.4	43.6	16.3	1.2	100.0

in California's black population; it will continue to grow numerically while becoming a smaller proportion of the overall total.

Between 1980 and 2000 the Hispanic student-age population will almost double, from 1.4 to 2.6 million. Thirty years later it will pass 3.6 million and outnumber Non-Hispanic whites and blacks combined in this age group and thus, probably, in school enrollment. Such growth results not only from continued high levels of immigration but also from Hispanics' high though falling fertility, as well as from the youthful age distribution of the group. Because a high proportion of the Hispanic population is in or about to enter the childbearing ages, there is a built-in momentum for growth that would yield increasing numbers of school-age persons regardless of immigration levels. The greater immigration is, however, the higher future enrollments will be. One caveat is important regarding Hispanic school enrollment: drop-out rates are particularly high among Hispanic adolescents. Our figures are for the population between five and nineteen and thus overstate present Hispanic enrollments somewhat if not necessarily those of the future.

The Asian population aged five to nineteen will more than double by the turn of the century and by 2030 will approach 1.4 million, almost 4.5 times the number in 1980. At the same time, the ethnic makeup of the school-age population will shift markedly as the Japanese numbers decline while Filipino and Vietnamese numbers in particular rise dramatically.

Simply stated, by the year 2000 Non-Hispanic whites will constitute about 45 percent of all the potential students in California. Thirty years later two of every three students will be Hispanic, black or Asian. But it is important to keep in mind that Hispanics, and blacks to a certain degree, are more likely to drop out of school prematurely than most Asians and Non-Hispanic whites and the latter two groups are more apt to extend their education well beyond the secondary level.

These are the bald statistics that make the bilingual question so critical and yet difficult to answer. The state's educational system will continue to experience a massive upheaval because of recent high levels of immigration. What kind of bilingual (or is it multilingual?) education is the most appropriate response to these demographic projections? Even more important is the larger question: What kind of society do Californians want over the next century? Is cultural assimilation preferable to cultural pluralism? Should bilingual education concentrate on structured immersion into the English language or should it emphasize bilingual/ bicultural maintenance? Again, a difficult issue must be addressed if the state is to proceed into the next century with a society that will be to the benefit of all Californians without the racial and ethnic conflicts that marred the late nineteenth century.

Retirement

At the other end of the life cycle is retirement—the ultimate life goal for most Americans. The nation's retirees will increase in the coming decades, particularly after 2020 when the baby boom generation has begun to enter this stage of life. The economic and health problems associated with a rapidly growing population of retired persons have been addressed elsewhere and need not be considered here. California will have more than its share of such problems over the next half century.

Between 1980 and 2030 the California population sixty-five and older will grow three and a half times, from 2.2 to 7.1 million. That statistic alone should prompt serious planning for the future. To this must be added inevitable changes in the racial and ethnic composition of the elderly population.

In contrast to the student age group, elderly Non-Hispanic whites will not decline in numbers. From 1.8 million in 1980 they will increase to 2.2 million in 2000 and 3.7 million in 2030. Current and continued low fertility will have no effect on the number of elderly Non-Hispanic whites, even in 2030, since the retired people of that year are already born. Similarly, black elderly persons will increase from 113,000 in 1980 to over 300,000 by 2030.

Growth will be far greater for the elderly population of Hispanics and Asians, both because of the aging baby boom generation and because of the continued immigration of young adults—the elderly of the twenty first century. Hispanics aged sixty-five and older will increase elevenfold, from 170,000 in 1980 to 1.9 million in 2030. Asians will experience similar growth, from 89,000 to 926,000.

In sum, the Non-Hispanic whites will remain a majority of the retired population over the next fifty years, but in declining proportion. As already noted, Non-Hispanic whites accounted for 83 percent of California's population, aged sixty-five and older, in 1980 and are projected to be just under 70 percent in 2000 and down to 52 percent in 2030. Hispanics and Asians will be an ever-growing proportion of this group, while the black proportion will increase only minimally.

The sheer growth of the elderly population, particularly after 2020, will pose serious issues for the state, exacerbated by the changing ethnic composition of this age group. Will Hispanic and Asian elderly persons require services different from those provided for Non-Hispanic whites and blacks? Will language barriers and resulting poor communication become a problem in providing health care for the elderly? Will cultural differences in how families cope with care of the elderly become an issue? As we enter the twenty-first century, will a still predominantly Non-Hispanic white middled-aged and elderly population be amenable to the expense of a growing bilingual educational program aimed at the newest minorities? On the other side of the coin, will an ever-growing population of young adults, many of them so-called minorities, consent to growing state expenditures on care of a still predominantly Non-Hispanic white elderly population?

Culture

How will California's culture be affected by these dramatic changes emanating from the demographic behavior of millions of people, both in and out of the state? A good indicator of this is language, which is closely related to culture and can serve as the "glue" that keeps a society together. Currently, in the greater Los Angeles area, for example, students speak some eighty languages in the public schools.[14] Our projections suggest that language will become an even more complex issue in California's future. Should English be the sole language of public communication, or should multilingualism for all Californians be taught and encouraged? Preserving ancestral languages and norms is to be encouraged and certainly Americans, particularly Non-Hispanic whites would do well to become more proficient in foreign languages. It is difficult, however, to visualize a society without a common language through which all its members can communicate. Sociologist Nathan Glazer recently pointed out: "In a society where all aspire to equal participation, all must undergo education in the same modes: the language in use in the society, the methods of calculation that have universal validity, the science that is everywhere the same."[15]

The newest immigrants to California have much to offer artistically, culturally and otherwise. Can these new ingredients be melded into the state's present culture without destroying or radically altering either it or the new influences? Or should California foster a new, diverse, multiracial culture reflecting its many groups, none of which will be a majority thirty years hence.

Social differences are marked among the newest immigrants. Already noted are the educational differences between Hispanics and Asians. The variations are similar within the heterogeneous Asian community. Many Hmongs and Laotians, for example, are barely literate, while half of all Indian adults have completed both four years of college and at least one year of graduate education. Is a new kind of segregation on the verge of becoming institutionalized along newly defined ethnic lines? While over-simplified, a two-tier economy with Asians and Non-Hispanic whites at the top and Hispanics and blacks at the bottom, is a distinct possibility, as seen in an earlier chapter.

How will blacks fare in this new melange of groups? Long the doormat of American society after three hundred years of slavery and discrimination, blacks should finally be moving up the socio-economic ladder, particularly after the anti-discrimination laws passed since the early 1960s. There are now some success stories to be told, but most blacks are still consigned to low-paying jobs and competing with the newly arrived minorities for those that are available. How can such injustice be finally ended while making certain that other groups are not also prey to discrimination?

CONCLUSION

California is just entering what may be its most crucial decade since the Mexican War ended in the 1840s. Demographic changes have always played a key role in its development. Streams of migrants have fueled its soaring economy, beginning in the latter part of the nineteenth century. Even then, and earlier, the racial/ethnic composition of its population was shifting. Native Americans were first joined by Spanish and Mexican conquistadors and their countrymen. Later came the so-called Anglos and the first Asians, Chinese and Japanese, recruited to perform the labor touched off by the Gold Rush and building of transcontinental railroads in the mid- and late nineteenth century. Blacks began to migrate from the south after World War II. More recently have come the growing waves of migrants from south of the border and from Asia. These migrants and their distinct fertility and mortality patterns are helping to mold the future size and composition of California's population. The state will never be the same; yet, as with the nation, it remains unfinished. This could have been said in the nineteenth century, however. The important question is: How will the state adjust to these demographic changes and all their repercussions?

NOTES

1. As quoted in "California's Changing Population," unpublished manuscript, *California Tomorrow*, May 20, 1984.

2. *California Almanac*, pp. 1–2.

3. Thomas Muller, *The Fourth Wave: California's Newest Immigrants (A Summary)*. (WDC: Urban Institute Press, 1984), p. 6.

4. National Center for Health Statistics, S.J. Ventura: "Births of Hispanic Parentage, 1981." *Monthly Vital Statistics Report* (July, 1985).

5. Robert W. Gardner, Peter C. Smith and Herbert R. Barringer, "The Demography of Asian Americans: Growth, Change and Heterogeneity," Paper presented at the Annual Meeting of the Population Policy, *Population Reference Bureau*, Washington, D.C. (1984).

6. Robert Warren and Ellen Percy Kraly, "The Elusive Exodus: Emigration from the United States," *Population Trends and Public Policy*, (WDC: Population Reference Bureau, 1984).

7. Muller et al, *The Fourth Wave*.

8. Daniel Levine, Kenneth Hill and Robert Warren, eds., *Immigration Statistics: A Story of Neglect*. (WDC: National Academy Press, 1985).

9. Department of Finance, Population Research Unit, *Estimates of the Southeast Asian Refugee Population in California Counties and the State: July 1, 1983*, Report SR-84-1 (Sacramento, CA, February 1984).

10. See, for example, *Population Projections for California Counties 1980-2020*. Department of Finance, Sacramento, CA, October 1983; see also, *Projections of Ethnic Total Population in California*. Center for Continuing Study of the California Economy, Palo Alto, CA (1985).

11. Leon Bouvier, "The Impact of Immigration on U.S. Population Size," *Population Trends and Public Policy*, Population Reference Bureau, Washington, D.C., (January 1981).

12. Ford Foundation, *Hispanics: Challenges and Opportunities: A Working Paper*, New York, (1984).

13. Keith Richburg, "US Stirs Up Debate on Bilingual Education," *Washington Post*, September 27, 1985.

14. P. Spencer, as quoted in "Impacts of Present and Future Immigration," *Southern California: A Region in Transition*, Vol. Two: Los Angeles, CA (December 1984), pp. IV-1.

15. Nathan Glazer, "Immigrants and Education," in Nathan Glazer, ed., *Clamor at the Gates*, (San Francisco, CA: ICS Press, 1985), p. 239. *Clamor at the Gates*, (San Francisco, CA: ICS Press, 1985), p. 239.

Two Views: The Impact of Massive Immigration on Southern California

California has become America's immigration laboratory. It is the first choice by far among the fifty states as a place of settlement for legal and illegal immigrants and refugees. California's experience with its many foreign new-comers was the subject for the major study of immigration of the 1980s: The Fourth Wave: California's Newest Immigrants, by Thomas Muller and Thomas Espenshade (Washington, D.C.: The Urban Institute Press, 1985). The study offers expansive data, thoughful interpretation and a range of conclusions on the most debated issues of immigration policy: labor displacement and wage depression, costs and contributions to the public treasury, effect on domestic minorities, burden on public services and implications for population and as-similation. While it identified some of the harmful consequences of rapid illegal immigration on the region in the 1970s, it concluded that the overall effects were on balance positive and indeed even stimulating for southern California's economy.

The following two articles present alternative views of illegal immigration's effects on southern California. The first, Mexicans: California's Newest Im-migrants is the Urban Institute's distillation of the experiences and findings discussed in far greater detail in The Fourth Wave. Then, former Labor Secretary Ray Marshall examines some of the less benign consequences of massive illegal immigration in California apparent in The Fourth Wave and in a shorter study of immigration's effects on California released by the Rand Corporation in 1985.

Mexicans: California's Newest Immigrants
Urban Institute*
Policy and Research Report, May 1986

For nearly a century the history of immigration to the United States has been symbolized by Ellis Island and the Statute of Liberty on the eastern seaboard of America. Today Los Angeles, at the western edge of the continental United States, has a larger proportion of foreign-born residents than New York City has—close to one-third by conservative estimates.

From 1970 through 1983 more than one million Hispanics, Asians and other foreign-born persons settled in Los Angeles County, accounting for nearly half of California's total immigration for the period. Given the many public programs and policies affected by immigration—especially illegal immigration—it is important to understand the extent and the effects of immigration and to identify the opportunities and difficulties it creates for public policy and for private initiatives. The Institute's program in demographic studies, directed by Thomas Espenshade, includes a series of studies on the effects of immigration in California. Much of the recent work has focused on the social and economic impacts of the Mexican presence in southern California.

A PROFILE OF RECENT IMMIGRANTS

According to data from the 1980 U.S. Census of Population and the Immigration and Naturalization Service, an estimated 781,000 legal immigrants entered California during the 1970s and an additional 1,087,000 immigrants entered the state in an undocumented (illegal) status. Moreover, estimates of census undercounts suggest that several hundred thousand foreign-born persons not enumerated in the 1980 Census also came to the state during the decade.

Special computer tabulations from the Current Population Survey indicate that the rate of immigration to California in the early 1980s has continued at a pace at least equal to that of the previous years. In 1983 about 4.7 million persons in California—almost 20 percent of the state's residents—were foreign-born.

Contrary to some popular conceptions, Mexicans do not constitute a majority of the immigrant population in California. Only one-third of all foreign-born residents in California and 37 percent of the people arriving after 1970 are Mexicans. Even Hispanics as a whole—Mexicans and non-Mexican Hispanics—make up less than half the immigrant population. Asians constitute one out of four immigrants to the state and one out of three recent arrivals.

*By permission of The Urban Institute, Washington, D.C.

The economics, demographic and social characteristics of new immigrants differ sharply by their country of origin. For example, while almost 75 percent of recent Mexican immigrants have completed no more than eight years of schooling, almost one-half of recent Asian immigrants have attended high school or college, and over one-third have four or more years of college.

The differences in the educational level of recent Mexican and Asian immigrants are reflected in their occupational status. Whereas most Asians hold skilled, white-collar jobs, Mexicans typically gravitate toward low-skill, low-wage, blue-collar and service jobs. Many of these jobs are in the manufacturing sector, which employed half of the recent immigrants during the 1970s. The Mexican presence is particularly large in food, apparel, textile and furniture industries.

LABOR MARKET IMPACTS

No immigration-related issue arouses greater fear among Americans, particularly blue-collar and service workers, than that their jobs may be jeopardized by an influx of aliens who undercut them by being willing to work at lower wages. In a 1983 survey of southern California residents, nearly half of the respondents believed that illegal immigrants take jobs from citizens, thus contributing to unemployment. Among the blacks surveyed, 58 percent believed that jobs were threatened.

What is the evidence? Do immigrants take jobs away from Americans?

The effect of Mexican immigration on black employment was analyzed not only because blacks constitute a sizable population in Los Angeles, but also because blacks have had below-average incomes and above-average unemployment and poverty rates in southern California. They may, therefore, be vulnerable to the effects of Mexican immigration. However, no statistically significant relationship has been found between black unemployment rates and the concentration of Hispanics in a cross-section of the local labor markets in 1980. Thus, the results do not show that an increase in the Hispanic population raises black unemployment rates.

Another concern that emerged in the 1983 poll of southern California residents was that undocumented workers brought down the overall wages in selected occupations. More than two-thirds of all respondents and more than four-fifths of black respondents expressed this belief. Overwhelmingly, respondents identified low-skill jobs as those more affects.

In discussing the wage effects of immigration, the effect of immigrants on average wage levels of particular occupations and industries must be distinguished from their effect on wages of individuals within those occupations and industries. An examination of relative wage growth in selected industries in Los Angeles shows that average wages in low-wage manufacturing industries in Los Angeles increased only about three-fourths (76.7 percent) as fast as average wages in those same industries nationwide between 1972 and 1980. In these industries Mexican immigrants represented nearly half of all production workers. Thus, there is some evidence that immigrants depress the average level of wages in some industries.

However, an examination of the effect of immigration on black workers nationwide shows that increasing the proportion of Hispanics in a metropolitan area has little effect on black family income. For example, raising the share of Hispanics in an area from an average of 5 percent to 7.5 percent produced a fall in average black family income by just $85 in 1980—from $15,818 to $15,733, or by one-half of one percent. In the Southwest, however, increasing the proportion of Mexican immigrants in local labor markets raised average black family income slightly. Taken together, these results point to a general conclusion that the presence of Hispanic immigrants in local labor markets has little effect, positively or negatively, on black family income.

FISCAL EFFECTS

Concerns over the economic effects of immigrants are focused not only on employment, wages and income but also on public section revenues and expenditures. What effects do Mexican immigrants have on state and local governments in California? Do Mexican immigrants receive more in public services than they pay in taxes?

Estimates of the fiscal effects of Mexican immigrant households in Los Angeles County were confined to state and local governments in California; taxes paid to and services provided by the federal government were excluded. For Mexican immigrant households in Los Angeles in 1980, the gap between services received from and taxes paid to state and local governments is very pronounced. Estimates of the combined fiscal effects at the state and local levels show that each Mexican immigrant household received an average of $4,842 in government services in 1980 but paid just $2,597 in taxes. Thus, benefits received outweighed taxes paid by a factor of nearly two to one, producing a deficit of $2,245 per household, nearly four-fifths of which arose at the state level.

This substantial gap between revenues and expenditures for Mexican immigrant households is traceable to several factors, but the two most important are low Mexican earnings and large Mexican families. An analysis of households in Los Angeles County, for instance, shows that 220,000 households—one out of every twelve households enumerated in Los Angeles County in 1980—were headed by a Mexican immigrant. the average size of these Mexican immigrant households was 4.25 persons, considerably larger than the average (2.54) for non-Mexican immigrant households. The average income of the Mexican immigrant households was $15,256, two-thirds of the $22,480 average for all households in Los Angeles County.

The conclusion that Mexican immigrants cause fiscal deficits to state and local governments must be tempered in two ways. First, these deficits are largely the product of the low socioeconomic status and large size of Mexican immigrant households, rather than of their immigrant status per se. Households with similar demographic and economic characteristics and having native-born household heads would have similar fiscal impacts. Second, there is some information suggesting that the fiscal deficit attributable to Mexican immigrant households decreases with length of stay in the United States.

It is also important to note that the exclusion from the study of undocumented persons (not counted in the 1980 census) could affect the fiscal-balance picture for immigrants. Because many of these undocumented persons are single, have jobs and demand fewer public services than other immigrants, they probably produce small fiscal surpluses. Including their contribution in the estimates, however, would probably not change the deficit balance produced by Mexican immigrant households in 1980, particularly at the state level.

THE FUTURE

Looking to the early 1990s and beyond, what role will both legal and illegal immigrants play in southern California's economy? Declines in birth rates, the gradual aging of the baby-boom generation, and the rising educational attainment of the U.S. population have prompted some economists to speculate that the nation as a whole may face a shortage of unskilled workers before the year 2000 if the economy continues on a course of modest expansion. Because California is expected to experience faster economic growth than other parts of the country, its projected demand for unskilled labor and its projected work-force shortfalls will be greater.

For example, economic growth in southern California is expected to create a demand for an additional 1.6 million workers through the 1980s. Based on the Institute's projections of population and labor force participation rates to the year 2000, labor-force growth from within southern California will be able to meet only 40 to 45 percent of the region's projected labor needs during the 1980s, assuming a 6 percent unemployment rate. Thus, as in the past, the region will require a substantial influx of workers from other parts of the country or from other nations in order to maintain its growth rate.

On the basis of southern California's share of immigrants to the state during the 1970s, about 760,000 legal immigrants can be expected to settle in the region during the 1980s, with about 350,000 finding jobs. Thus, legal immigration combined with internal labor force growth can be expected to meet two-thirds of southern California's labor needs during the 1980s.

How will the remaining one-third be met? The high demand for professional white-collar workers, especially in the technologically advanced defense industries and in other high-tech sectors, is projected to continue in southern California through the 1980s. Any residual demand for these workers can be met by internal migration, continuing the trend of the 1970s. The remaining gap between supply and demand, primarily for low-skill employees, will have to be met from other sources. In the absence of immigration reform, undocumented workers would probably take most of these jobs—perhaps as many as 390,000.

POSSIBLE REFORM

Will the influx of immigration to the United States—concentrated dispro-portionately in California—continue at its current pace, or will it soon peak in response to the tighter immigration controls of the 1986 Immigration Reform and Control Act? To answer this question it is necessary to examine the factors that pull immigrants to California and push people to emigrate from other nations as well as to assess the potential effectiveness of new proposals for immigration reform.

California's geographic location, its perceived quality and style of life, eco-nomic opportunitiers and its already large immigrant population will most likely continue to attract new immigrants. Moreover, in many of the developing coun-tries from which they come, rapid population growth combined with economic and political difficulties act as a powerful push to emigration. The inability of the economies of poorer nations to provide enough jobs for their rapidly ex-panding labor force stimulates the unemployed and under-employed to look elsewhere for improved economic conditions. Over the next two decades, these factors pushing migrants to the United States and California are likely to accel-erate rather than diminish. Also, the political instability plaguing Central America and many other regions of the world is likely to increase the refugee flow to the United States.

The Immigration Reform and Control Act contains provisions for civil and criminal penalties against employers who knowingly hire undocumented workers. The intent of the employer sanctions is to reduce job opportunities for illegal aliens in the United States, thereby removing a major motivation for workers to enter without proper documentation. The inclusion of criminal penalties in the law is important from the standpoint of increasing the ability to control undo-cumented immigration. The experience of other nations—West Germany, for instance—suggests that fines alone have little effect on the use of undocumented workers. Many employers consider the fines part of "the cost of doing business." Even with stiff employer fines and criminal penalities, it will be virtually im-possible to police millions of employers. Whether the new law will actually curtail the flow of undocumented immigrants rests ultimately with the employers themselves as well as on the rigor with which employer sanctions are enforced.

Immigration in the Golden State:
The Tarnished Dream
By Ray Marshall

There was a time when the defenders of the status quo in immigration policy spoke more bluntly than they do today.

"The more slaves, the more produce," Charles Cotesworth Pinckney told the other delegates at the Constitutional Convention as that slave-owning South Carolinian successfully defended slavery and fended off the termination of the slave trade.

Pinckney's grasp of the economics and politics of the issue was exactly right. If you disregard such matters as labor standards, personal liberty and the like and your sole concerns are the volume and the costs of production, it was plausible to argue that preserving slavery meant more cotton at a lower price. Substantial supplies of low-cost cotton, it was argued by Pinckney's South Carolina colleague John Rutledge, would be helpful to the thirteen colonies as a whole: "If the northern states consult their interest they will not oppose the increase in slaves which will increase the commodities of which they will be the carriers."[1]

Massive illegal immigration is a political and economic issue that has some parallels to the question of the slave trade, America's first widely-debated immigration policy issue. Today's illegal immigration and yesterday's slave trade both relate to the supply of labor, the organization of labor markets, workers' rights and production. But the defenders of the status quo, the Rand Corporation in this case, have lost Pinckney's pungency. In a recent report for the California Roundtable (a business group), Rand states "Overall Mexican immigration has probably been an economic asset to the state, in that it has stimulated employment growth and kept wages competitive. Potential displacement effects have been relatively minor *except perhaps among low-skilled, native-born Latinos.*" (Emphasis added)

In other words, there is more product, it costs less to produce, and the only losers are low income American citizens with Hispanic names. Rand dismisses the impact of such migration on disadvantaged, legally-resident workers as it presents its abstract and largely benign view of the subject.

Since Rand is a well known California think tank, and presents its economic analysis smoothly, and since this line of argument is all too common in the immigration field, a closer examination of the Rand study, and a more substantial one produced simultaneously by the Urban Institute is necessary for a better perspective on the complex and controversial illegal immigration question.

The two studies deal with the nature and effects of legal and illegal migration from Mexico to California, particularly southern California.[2] Reading the summaries, one gains the impression that the effects range from nil to beneficial, but if one looks deeper, particularly in the Urban Institute study, one finds a more disturbing situation.

These studies have a number of similarities: both virtually ignore the all-important difference between legal and illegal immigration, and both presented their summaries, with much press coverage, apparently designed to minimize the adverse effects of immigration, before the full reports were available. The publication-publicity maneuver is very misleading, because the reports' policy conclusions are presented but without the underlying data, seriously hampering careful critique. The rush to the media is particularly troublesome with the Urban Institute report, because so much of its apparently carefully collected, often groundbreaking data appear to have only the vaguest connection to the report's generally cheerful conclusions.

Digging more deeply into the Urban Institute's *The Fourth Wave*, one finds revealing data on southern California's immigration-distorted labor markets, where the poor get poorer and the rich get richer, and on the burden that the immigrant families place on other taxpayers, including those beyond the borders of Los Angeles County (where most of the migrants cluster). Further, one finds that resident blue-collar workers have been forced to leave the area, with Los Angeles County's population growth coming largely from other nations. Finally, there is the bloodless nature of both reports, heavy on statistics and light on the labor market realities; all of the Rand report, and much of the Urban Institute's, appears to be written by people oblivious to such concepts as exploitation, grim working conditions and worker docility brought on by grinding poverty in their native lands and fears of *La Migra*.

THE SUBSTANCE OF THE REPORTS

These reports describe, in varying detail, the following:

—the large amount of migration, legal and illegal to southern California;
—the labor market effects of this migration: little job displacement, both reports argue, but substantial depressing of blue collar wages.
—the effects of this migration on the industrial mix of southern California; in sum, a boom in low-wage manufacturing which is declining in the rest of the country.
—the slowing of migration from elsewhere in the United States to southern California (particularly Los Angeles County), and the out-migration of resident blue-collar workers; the increase in Los Angeles County's population is no longer driven by migration from other parts of the United States, it is caused by international migration and high migrant birth rates.
—the extra costs to state and local taxpayers caused by the low level of tax payments and heavy use of services by the newly arrived migrants.
—the differential impact of international migration on black workers (said to be minimal) and on legal Hispanic residents (substantial).

What we are *not* told by either report also is interesting:

—the extent of unemployment in California, and how different it might have been with lower levels of international immigration;

—the impact of illegal migration to California on jobs and businesses *outside* California;

—the indirect costs to taxpayers of welfare rolls burdened with those elbowed out of jobs by illegal immigrants, and

—the ironic impact of illegal immigration on legally-admitted, jobless refugees.

EXTENT OF IMMIGRATION

Using conservative approaches and relatively sturdy government statistics (largely from the Census Report), the Urban Institute estimates that about one-fifth of California's population in 1983 was foreign born. Dealing with the period 1970-1980 the authors estimate some 1,868,000 census-enumerated post-1970 immigrants, of whom the majority, 1,087,000 were illegally present. In addition, census undercount data suggest that another 493,000 undocumented aliens were present but missed by the census. Thus, the Urban Institute finds that there were more than 1.5 million undocumenteds in California in 1980, with that population rising by about 100,000 a year. This would bring the total to over two million in 1986. These are large, serious numbers, carefully handled; and while the techniques used probably understate the size of the illegal immigrant population, they do give us a reasonable lower limit for the size of this population in California.[3]

LABOR MARKET EFFECTS

Many people believe, as I do, that there are two different but related impacts of illegal aliens on American labor markets: the displacement effect, in which legal residents lose their jobs (or do not secure new ones) because of competition from the undocumenteds; and the depression effect, in which low-productivity marginal jobs are perpetuated and legal residents work for lower wages than they otherwise would have had there been no undocumented workers. Unfortunately, neither of these studies addresses either of these problems as I have stated them, because both studies refuse to pay much attention to the legal-illegal distinction. This is unfortunate, because the basic public policy issue before us is the question of *illegal* immigration. What these studies do is to consider the consequences of recent (post 1970) immigration from Mexico on California (more narrowly Los Angeles County in the case of the Urban Institute's *The Fourth Wave*).

What do these studies tell us about the impact of recent immigration from Mexico on labor markets? Both argue that they could detect little evidence of resident-worker displacement, and both show (the Urban Institute with stunning effect) that these immigrants depressed wages in the segments of the labor markets where they clustered.

On the question of displacement, the Urban Institute study presents one of the many inconsistencies between its summary and the full text; the summary states:

> To what extent did the influx of immigrants entering southern California in the 1970s reduce the jobs available to non-immigrants [i.e., resident] workers? The answer for the 1970s is little if at all.[4]

The text, on the other hand, points out that the newly arrived Mexican immigrants largely worked in blue collar jobs and ". . . in Los Angeles County between 1970 and 1980. Mexicans held 116,000 such jobs and other immigrants another 52,000. *Clearly the number of persons other than recent immigrants holding these jobs actually declined.*"[5] (Emphasis added)

Similarly, "Net manufacturing employment [in Los Angeles County] rose by 113,000 during the 1970s but because immigrants arriving since 1970 held 168,000 manufacturing jobs in 1980 there must have been a net decline of 55,000 jobs among other workers."[6] Looking at the entire labor market in Los Angeles County the report tells us that recent immigrants absorbed fully two-thirds of the 645,000 jobs added to the economy during the decade. Further, as noted subsequently, large numbers of blue collar workers migrated *out* of Los Angeles County during the 1970s.

Little or no displacement? It sounds as if the authors' own data suggest a lot of it. Further, what would have happened if the immigration law had been better enforced, or we had a strong employer sanctions program in place? Even if the Los Angeles County illegal alien work force had been reduced by only 100,000 or 200,000 would that not have opened up scores of thousands of jobs for legal residents?

Looking beyond the numbers in these studies, I checked that old reliable, the *Statistical Abstract of the United States*, to see whether California, with such heavy immigration, had unemployment rates above or below the national average for the fourteen years covered by *The Fourth Wave* (1970-1983). I found in twelve of those years California's unemployment rate was higher than that of the nation as a whole, sometimes by more than two full percentage points.[7] While factors other than international migration undoubtedly played a role, those data tend to support *The Fourth Wave*'s text rather than its summary.

Both reports agree on the second labor market effect, the depression of wages, with *The Fourth Wave* presenting new and convincing data on this point. The Urban Institute has measured the apparent impact of heavy migration on Los Angeles County in an interesting way. The authors noted the average increase in wages in several labor market sectors for the nation as a whole between 1972 and 1980; then, sector by sector, they compared these data to the wage increases recorded in Los Angeles County. If international migration had made no impact on local wages, it is assumed that wage increases, on a percentage basis, would have been about the same for the county as for the nation. This was clearly *not* the case in several sectors of the labor market where massive migration from Mexico (much of it illegal) depressed wages substantially.

The first of the two following tables (Table A), a reproduction of one found in *The Fourth Wave*, shows that in low-wage manufacturing Los Angeles County workers received only 76.7 percent of the wage increase recorded nationally; further, in this sector immigrants from Mexico accounted for a remarkable 47.1 percent of the county's work force. In contrast, when dealing with all Los Angeles County workers, vis-a-vis all U.S. workers, county wages increased 8.78 percent faster than those of the nation at large. In the whole county recent Mexican immigrants constituted only 9.9 percent of the labor force.

Examining the data another way, the report states: "relative average wages of unskilled workers in the Los Angeles manufacturing sector have declined dramatically—from 2 percent *above* the U.S. metropolitan average in 1969 and 1970 to 12 percent *below the average a decade later*."[8] (Emphasis in the original)

The direct relationship between relative wage increases in Los Angeles County and the percentage of Mexican immigrants in a given sector of the labor market is shown in an adaptation of *The Fourth Wave* table presented by Frank Loy, president of the German Marshall Fund.[9] Loy's recasting (in Table B) shows that as the percentage of Mexican immigrants in a labor market sector falls, the wage increases rise to meet, and then pass, the national average. In this instance, at least, the more migrants, the lower the wage increases.

While factory workers' wages were lower in California than in the nation on average, this does not seem to indicate that their productivity was comparably lower. The Urban Institute report says that the rate of wage increase for Hispanic, low-wage factory workers in Los Angeles was 16 percent less than the national average, but that worker productivity was only 6 percent less than in the nation as a whole, so Los Angeles employers secured more for their wage dollar than their competitors elsewhere in the nation.[10]

Rand's report for the California Roundtable notes that "overall, the immigrants provide economic benefits to the state, and native-born Latinos may bear the brunt of competition for low-skill jobs."[11] A little later Rand continues: "Our evidence suggests that Mexican immigrants may actually have stimulated manufacturing employment by keeping wage levels competitive."[12]

EFFECTS ON THE INDUSTRIAL MIX OF CALIFORNIA AND THE NATION

As the Rand report points out, correctly:

In the United States as a whole, manufacturing employment grew modestly during the 1970s—significantly less than in California or in its principal manu-

Table 10.1 Comparison of wages in Los Angeles County and the United States, 1972 and 1980

Industry	Los Angeles Wages 1980	Increase in L.A. Wages, 1972–1980, as a Percentage of U.S. Wage Increase	Mexican Immigrants as Percentage of All Workers 1980
All workers	$15,594	108.8	9.9
Low-wage manufacturing[a]	5.06[b]	76.7	47.1[b]
High-wage manufacturing[c]	7.97[b]	90.7	19.5[b]
All retail	9,469	108.3	9.5
Eating and drinking establishments (restaurants, bars)	5,591	89.1	16.8
All other retail	11,196	108.4	6.6
All services	14,099	115.8	5.5
Hotels, etc.	7,312[b]	95.1	15.0[d]
Personal services	8,069	92.2	15.2
All other services	14,659	117.2	3.9
Finance, insurance and real estate	15,590	104.4	2.6

Sources: Bureau of the Census, *Characteristics of the Population* (1970) and 1980 Censuses of Population); 1980 Census, Public Use Microdata Samples; *County Business Patterns* (1972 and 1980). Bureau of Labor Statistics, *Employment and Earnings, States and Areas and Supplement to Employment and Earnings, States and Areas, Data for 1977 to 1980.*

[a] Includes leather goods, apparel, textile mills, lumber and wood, and furniture and fixtures industries.

[b] Hourly wages include only production workers.

[c] Includes metals; machinery; stone, clay, and glass; food; and transportation equipment industries.

[d] Estimated.

Source: This is reproduced from Table 3 from Thomas Muller and Thomas Espenshade, *The Fourth Wave: California's Newest Immigrants A Summary;* The Urban Institute Press, Washington, D.C., 1984.

facturing center, Los Angeles. Although several factors may have contributed to California's and Los Angeles' superior performance, one factor that certainly played a significant role was slower wage growth.[13]

If manufacturing, particularly apparel and furniture, has grown rapidly in Los Angeles while shrinking elsewhere, someone has been hurt: the workers, managers and owners of these firms which had formerly operated outside California. There are adverse effects, throughout the nation, growing out of the massive migration to migration to southern California, but these off-stage victims (like most off-stage victims in much of life) receive scant notice in either of these reports.

As labor economist, Vernon Briggs of Cornell University and others have pointed out, illegal immigration shapes labor markets as well as responding to them.[14] In fact, illegal immigration restructures the very nature of the local and the national economy, distorting, for example, the investment decisions made in labor-intensive industries such as garments, tilting investment toward Los Angeles and away from the rest of the country. In the short run the winners would seem to be the Los Angeles factory owners who are getting the de facto wage subsidies from the presence of the undocumenteds; but in the long run the situation does not bode well for healthy economic growth in the nation, the state of California, the county of Los Angeles and perhaps even in the firms now relying on the illegal immigrants. These investment decisions retain, temporarily, some marginal low wage jobs in the United States that otherwise might disappear or move to the Third World. The alternatives, if there are economic reasons for having these jobs in the United States, would be to raise wages, improve management or to mechanize.

It is very unrealistic to assume that the United States can compete in even minimum wage jobs in those products where wages constitute the principal source of competitive advantage. The only hope for competitiveness in the international market on terms that will maintain American living standards is to improve productivity and quality through mechanization, skill upgrading or improved management and production systems, all of which are discouraged by a steady flow of illegal, low-wage migrants.[15]

INTERNAL MIGRATION

One may have the image of southern California, generally, and Los Angeles, specifically, as the magnet for Americans living in less blessed places—Okies, would-be movie stars, ambitious professionals and unemployed factory workers all heading for the land of opportunity. The Urban Institute suggests that this is only partly accurate, that blue-collar workers, both Anglo and Hispanic, presumably legal residents for the most part, are leaving Los Angeles in droves, apparently largely because of competition from the newly arrived immigrant workers.

Table 10.2 Comparison of wages in the Los Angeles labor market and the percentage of Mexican immigrants in the Los Angeles labor market (an adaptation of a table from *The Fourth Wave*)

Industry	Mexican Immigrants as percentage of All Workers 1980	Increase in L.A. Wages, 1972–1980, Compared to U.S. Wage Increase	Los Angeles Wages 1980
Low-wage manufacturing	47.1	− 23.3%	$5.06/hr.
High-wage manufacturing	19.5	− 9.3%	$7.97/hr.
Eating and drinking establishments	16.8	− 10.1%	$5,591/yr.
Personal services	15.2	− 7.8%	$8,069/yr.
Hotels	15.0	− 4.9%	$7,132/yr.
All workers	9.9	+ 8.8%	$15,594/yr.*
All retail	9.5	+ 8.3%	$9,469/yr.
All other retail	6.6	+ 8.4%	11,196/yr.
All services	5.5	+ 15.8%	$14,099/yr.
All other services	3.9	+ 17.2%	$14,659/yr.
Finance, insurance and real estate	2.6	+ 4.4%	$15,590/yr.

The Fourth Wave reports that while in the five year period 1955-1960 there was a net migration to California from other states of more than 1,122,000, in the thirteen years, 1970-1983, the net migration to California fell to a statistically insignificant 11,000. Who was leaving? During this time there were, among other movements, a *net inflow of 205,000 white-collar workers and a net loss of 134,000 blue-collar workers.* The report concludes: "The similarity between the socioeconomic characteristics of the people leaving California and the characteristics of Mexican immigrants suggests that the flow from Mexico may have substituted for internal migration."[16]

TAXPAYER COSTS

Both reports deal with the taxes paid by and the public services used by immigrant households. (The Urban Institute report carefully analyzed Los Angeles County households headed by Mexican immigrants, with the understanding that some to many members of such households are native-born children of such immigrants.)

The Rand reporting on this subject can be dismissed quickly, but not before quoting it:[17]

> In general, immigrants contribute (sic.) more to public revenues than they consumed in public services; however, the youthfulness of the population, their low incomes, the progressiveness of the state income tax structure and the high costs of public education produce a net deficit in educational expenditures.

As Roger Conner, executive director of FAIR, has commented, "saying that illegal aliens contribute in taxes more than they use in benefits 'except for education' is like saying the U.S. budget is balanced except for defense spending."[18]

Using a variety of data sources, the Urban Institute study estimated the costs incurred and taxes received by state and local governments during 1980 for Mexican immigrant households in Los Angeles County. Their summarized findings were:[19]

	State	County	Total
Revenues	$1,425	$1,172	$2,597
Expenditures	3,204	1,638	4,842
Fiscal gap	−1,779	− 466	−2,245

These data do not take into account substantial amounts of federal funds passed through state and local government. Even so, as the report says, "Benefits received outweighed taxes paid by a factor of nearly 2 to 1."[20] Another point made in the study is that California taxpayers *outside* Los Angeles County are helping to foot the bills caused by these Los Angeles County families.

Three comments seem to be called for regarding the study's findings. First, the Urban Institute has managed, apparently with considerable effort, to secure extremely useful, believable data on the subject of immigrant taxes and service-utilization; it is to be commended for its work, and for the detail in which it displays (in the full text) what it found. The Urban Institute's careful work here is in sharp contrast to efforts by some analysts to use government statistics selectively to show the reverse.[21]

Second, even if immigrant-headed families are not paying their own way at the state and local level, this is not to suggest that all immigrants be barred from the nation, or that poor people should be assessed stiff "user fees" for enrolling their children in the public schools. Legal immigration is a fundamental part of this country's tradition; similarly, America made a very important and commendable commitment early in the nineteenth century to make sure that low-income children are educated at public expense without a means test. It is no argument for illegal immigration that people do not use services they or their families need.

But it does bring us to our third point, that there is no free lunch. Those who argue that illegal immigrants pay more in taxes than they use in services miss two points:

A) We, as a nation, should not condone a harmful, disruptive, and essentially illegal activity (illegal migration) on the grounds that it is a bargain to some taxpayers.

B) The Urban Institute study seems to suggest that even though some parts of the private sector are profiting extensively from illegal immigration, in Los Angeles County, at least, the costs of this group of illegal and legal immigrants (many of whom used to be illegal ones) thoroughly outweigh the taxes paid.[22]

IMPACTS ON HISPANIC AND BLACK WORKERS

While both reports indicate that resident Hispanic workers, particularly those with blue-collar jobs, were paid less than they would have been otherwise because of heavy immigration the Urban Institute study suggested that this statement could not be extended to blacks. The explanation offered is that many blacks had moved into clerical jobs, where there is relatively little competition from Mexican immigrants. The report's analysis of labor force participation rates of black adults and teenagers shows few adverse effects from immigration;[23] similarly, rates of wage increases for L.A. County blacks were close to the national norm (over the period studied), unlike those of Hispanics, which were often only 60 percent or so of the country-wide averages.[24]

I would argue, however, from the Urban Institute's data, that black blue-collar workers suffer indirect displacement because of the extensive international migration to Los Angeles County. The in-migration rate of blacks to California is slowing according to *The Fourth Wave* statistics, and those migrating currently are highly self-selected to deploy in the white-collar sections of the labor market still unencumbered by Hispanic newcomers. Further, elsewhere in the United States blacks are well represented in some of those industries that employ large numbers of undocumenteds in Los Angeles. Because many of those industries are in decline elsewhere in the nation (e.g., textiles in the Carolinas), blacks may be shut out from these jobs when the work, in effect, moves to southern California. Hispanic illegal immigration has thus foreclosed an option for unemployed black, blue-collar workers, but again, they are off-stage victims, ignored in these studies.

WHAT THE REPORTS IGNORE

This suggests another difficulty with these studies—they tend to ignore the impact of California immigration on the rest of the country. We know that people in the United States move from place to place to seek employment, that we are one nation, and that the presence or absence of job opportunities in one jurisdiction affects labor markets elsewhere. California is not an island unto itself.

I am also aware, as are most Americans, that in the period studied we often had as many as seven to ten million Americans out of work; unemployment in California varied from half to close to a million during much of this period. These numbers are not taken from these reports, because extensive unemployment in the nation, and in California, is simply not discussed.

Similarly, as noted before, the spill-over effects of illegal immigration in California, the adverse effects on low-tech manufacturing establishments elsewhere in the nation, are barely mentioned.

Finally, if one is writing about immigration and California, about labor markets and governmental costs, one might want to say somewhat more about one other large group of aliens in California, the refugees from Southeast Asia, who are treated very differently by our government than are the illegal immigrants from Mexico, and who, consequently, play a very different role in California economics.

To oversimplify, the United States has decided to divide all aliens into three categories when it comes to distributing welfare and food stamp benefits. There are the refugees, who for the first eighteen months in the country, have more rights to those programs than citizens; then there are the legal immigrants who, for their first three years in the country, have fewer rights than citizens to these programs; and finally, there are the illegal immigrants, who have, under law, no rights to these programs. These distinctions are particularly important in California where benefit levels are high, and a large newly-arrived refugee family, for instance, can secure much more income from AFDC and food stamps than they could if one member of the family worked full time at, or a little above, the minimum wage (which is still $3.35 an hour).

The availability, or non-availability, of welfare has a direct and inverse relationship to labor force participation, and it is quite clear that the incidence of jobs among legal aliens (green card holders) is about that of citizens, while illegal aliens have no choice but to work.[25]

One of the principal obstacles to greater refugee employment in California, and other high welfare benefit level states, is a ridiculous federal regulation that denies all AFDC (and therefore all medical) benefits to families whose head works more than one hundred hours a month. Instead of reducing benefits gradually as the worker increases his income, this regulation sets up an all or nothing choice; as a result, workers who cannot immediately earn more than their monthly benefits refuse jobs, and do not work, or do so in the underground labor market.[26]

Now how do these systems relate to Mexican immigration to California? In the last two decades, the U.S. government has been busily supporting legal aliens with transfer payments while, in effect, permitting undocumented aliens from another part of the globe to occupy jobs which legal workers might otherwise take. Refugees in California, however, are much less likely to work than citizens. Now, with the passage of the Immigration Reform and Control Act of 1986, the United States has the opportunity to make available to refugees jobs once held by undocumented workers. The employer sanctions provision of the law could reduce the drain on the tax fund due to social service spending for refugees.

THE ABSTRACT APPROACH

I have pointed out the very real contributions of new data offered by *The Fourth Wave*. But both of these reports reflect such a remote and quantitative approach that they miss many nitty-gritty realities of honest-to-God jobs, employers and working conditions. Nobody sweats, nobody gets fired and nobody gets hurt on the job in these reports. I emphasize this point because I believe it is wrong for policy analyses to abstract entirely from human conditions.

As a glaring instance of the genteel, ivory tower approach, let's see how the Urban Institute describes the acquisition of California by the United States. According to the summary the "state seceded from Mexico."[27] There apparently was no Mexican-American War, and there were no invading armies.

Similarly, these reports all but ignore two sets of realities, the all-important question of legal status in the United States and the realities of the labor market.

Legal status makes a major difference, even if the immigration law is not enforced as carefully as it should be. This is both an important and complex issue. There are at least four levels of legal status which bear heavily on the impact of immigration on California:

—at the bottom are the illegal aliens, who have few rights in the labor market, and who cannot, legally, draw welfare benefits.
—next are the legal (green card) immigrants, with many labor market rights and after a few years full rights to welfare benefits.

—then there are the refugees, with the same labor market rights as the immigrants, but even more complete access to welfare than citizens.

—finally there are the citizens, both native-born and naturalized, who have more access to welfare systems and jobs than anyone else (in that they are the only class that can work in government offices and in defense plants, which are numerous in California).

One of the reasons blacks living in California have apparently been less harmed than resident Hispanics by the massive immigration to southern California is their legal status. Virtually all blacks are citizens. They can and do work in government offices (federal, state, and local) and in defense factories, and they vote, join unions and otherwise attempt to protect their rights. Mexican nationals, on the other hand, even if present in the country legally and for many years, are much less likely to seek naturalization than other immigrants. Hence, many of them cannot compete for jobs in the public sector. That the blacks are English-speaking is, of course, another advantage.

Similarly, one of the reasons there is little visible competition between the Hispanic immigrants and the refugees is the refugees' superior access to welfare benefits. They, unlike the illegal immigrants, do not need to work to survive, at least for the time being. Moreover, the refugees came to the United States to avoid political oppression, not to work. Their legal status, family structure, education and skill levels and their assets will cause the refugees' economic effects to be very different from those of illegal immigrants who come mainly for economic, not political reasons.

The downside of the legal status equation is experienced by the illegal immigrants. They know that they do not have any rights, that they can be thrown back across the border if they are unlucky, or if someone deliberately turns them over to the Border Patrol. As a result they can be forced more easily to work hard and scared. One of the reasons why wages are lower where the illegals concentrate than elsewhere is because they are less likely to join unions or to complain about labor standards than workers with full legal rights. These are important realities, if hard to quantify. Similarly, the authors of these studies have apparently not factored into their work any understanding of the often unattractive rules of life in the secondary (low wage) labor market. They apparently do not have any gut feeling for the difference between loose and tight labor markets, or perhaps they feel that these real life mechanisms are reflected in their numbers, as to some extent they are. Let me discuss a few examples of what I have in mind.

Bob Glover, my colleague at the University of Texas, and I spent some time looking at labor-management practices in another border area, the citrus groves of Hidalgo County, Texas, where there were both resident Hispanics as well as those from the other side of the Rio Grande, some legal, some not. The first thing we learned was with a combination of piece rate wage payments (for picking grapefruit) and a loose labor market that there was never much incentive for management to maximize workers' productivity. Under the piece-rate system if a crew was idle because they were out of baskets or waiting for trucks to return from packing sheds, they lost wages. Similarly, workers lost wages when they had to walk long distances to dump fruit in trucks that could not come into the groves; these inefficiencies did not appear to cost management anything. Had the crews been on an hourly basis, however, the owners would have lost money. Had the labor market been a tight one, such workers might have gone to work for other better managed companies in the area, but with heavy immigration from Mexico and high unemployment levels, employers had little incentive to improve productivity.

Moving up the border a few miles, David North told me about another loose labor market. In this case the workers were legal (green card commuters who lived in Mexico and worked in the United States). North was at the Eagle Pass Bridge early one morning, working with an immigration inspector on some project. He talked to a number of green card commuters and found that many of them were driving to Uvalde, sixty-five miles away, to pull carrots. "How long will you work when you get there?" he asked. "Four hours" was the consistent answer. North later realized that the grower had a choice—he could hire x number of workers for a regular eight-hour day, or, given a loose labor market, he could hire twice as many workers for four-hour days, and then he would have to supervise them for only half a day.

In short, loose labor markets not only affect wages (which can be measured), but also the very nature of work and the labor market, in ways that resist measurement. Both of these stories show how large numbers of willing Mexican immigrants have fundamentally affected the very nature of the labor market. There is a circularity at work here; if the labor market is loose enough, and those working in it are desperate and without rights, then the labor market will soon be structured in such a way that the immigrants will "take jobs that no Americans will accept." The Rand report notes the existence of such conditions, but fails to link the situation to the migrations that cause them.

If there is a discrepancy between work that needs to be done and the labor supply available there are two possible approaches. One is to adjust the labor supply (enlarge it by bringing in migrants) and this is the only option that these reports apparently care to address. Another approach is to change the nature, the organization, the technology and the compensation for the job; make sure that the grapefruit pickers always have a tree to pick and a box to pick into, in order to eliminate a lot of wasted time, or otherwise improve the work environment.

THE PRESENTATION

I have already pointed out the impropriety of trotting out your conclusions before you show your basic data. This strikes me also as an odd reversal of genuine scholarship. Typically researchers frame their questions, get somebody to support the work, buckle down to the data collection, look over what they have found, and then write the findings, with the conclusions, logically being the last part written. That's the way most of my colleagues work, and I do not see why Rand and the Urban Institute should so otherwise.

These reports also—particularly the Rand summary—violate another scholarly tradition to tell us exactly where they got their data; they should tell their readers where to go if they want more information. Rand's tables in the summary are almost totally without sources. The Urban Institute is more careful about such matters, but as our note to Table B suggests, it often lays down a path that is hard to follow.

CONCLUSIONS

Since these reports undoubtedly will continue to be used in the debates over controlling illegal immigration, and since their conclusions often do not follow from their evidence, we will summarize the evidence about the impact of immigration on employment contained in these and many other studies:

1. There can be little doubt that immigration displaces workers, though not on a one-to-one basis. The degree of displacement clearly depends on the looseness or tightness of labor markets and the nature of those markets. When unemployment is very low, as during World War II, there is less displacement. In fact, it could be argued that in very tight labor markets, or where the immigrants have skills not available among unemployed legal residents, immigration facilitates economic growth. In loose markets, by contrast, there is little question that immigrants displace other workers, as both the Urban Institute and Rand studies show.

2. It is very important to distinguish between legal and illegal immigration. Whatever its economic effects, there is no justification for illegal immigration in a society that believes in the rule of law. If immigration is in the national interest, it should be done legally.

3. As noted, no study of the economic effects of immigration is able to hold everything else constant. In particular, some employers prefer immigrants to long-time residents and citizens because they are, at least for a time, less likely to be dissatisfied with wages and working conditions that are bad by American standards. The basic policy question is whether or not legal residents and refugees should be subjected to this kind of competition. I do not think they should be. It is, moreover, very hard to protect labor standards in situations where workers are afraid to complain. That is the reason I favor vigorous enforcement of labor standards as well as tighter controls of illegal immigration.

4. Elementary economics suggests that at a time of high unemployment, increased labor supplies depress wages and reduce employment opportunities for legal residents, unless you assume completely segregated labor markets.

Advocates of continued illegal immigration often argue that the immigrants only take jobs legal residents will not accept. There are several things wrong with that argument. First there is no job category in the United States filled entirely by illegals. Secondly, employers have other options—they can raise wages, mechanize or go offshore or out of business. My view is that it would be better for firms that cannot pay prevailing U.S. wages at the low end of the scale to go offshore. If there are reasons these companies should have access to American markets, they should improve management, mechanize or otherwise increase productivity. In the long run these industries can only be competitive if they are subsidized by American workers or if we decide to protect them from international competition by consumers. I believe that in most cases marginal low wage industries hire illegals because they gain a competitive advantage and higher profits thereby, neither of which is a social justification for their existence. Forcing them to pay prevailing wages would therefore cause them to either improve productivity or reduce their profits to the levels they would be without the illegals. Improving productivity is particularly important. The United States has done fairly well in job creation. We have done less well relative to other countries in maintaining productivity and real wage growth. We will not be able to reverse this situation so long as we perpetuate marginal industries that depend on easily exploitable people for their existence.

5. Some try to justify illegal immigration on the grounds that these workers pay more taxes than they burden public revenues. There are some studies that suggest that for selective public programs this might be true, but the more careful Urban Institute work described above suggests that this is not so, at least for Los Angeles County. Moreover, even those studies that do show net positive fiscal effects miss several important points: the effects of displacement and depressed wages on legal residents and the dynamic nature of the immigration process. Studies assuming that illegals always will be young, unmarried people without families have a strange view of human behavior and demographics—people will get families and grow older, and many illegals will be legalized. So, a snapshot at any time misses this dynamic. But from my perspective this argument misses the main point—it is not whether or not illegals produce net fiscal benefits, but whether people use the services they need. It is not at all comforting to be told that because of their illegal status undocumented workers are afraid to use public services. This is one of the reasons there is absolutely no justification for illegal immigration. If people come into the United States they should do so legally, with the full legal rights of residents of the United States.

Finally, we should note that some defend illegal immigration because of their concern about the welfare of Mexican and other workers who are compelled by conditions in their home countries to come to the United States illegally. I fully share this concern and believe the United States and other developed countries should pay much more attention to this problem than they do. We should work with the developing countries to produce the kind of economic development that is in our mutual interests, which generally means a full employment, human resource development strategy. A broader view of our own self interest requires that we support efforts to improve economic growth, fight joblessness, and improve working conditions in these countries. But this should be done through national and international economic institutions; it definitely should not be done at the expense of those low wage American workers who can least afford to extend aid to these developing countries.

NOTES

1. W.E.B. Du Bois, *The Suppression of the African Slave Trade to the United States of America, 1638-1870* (New York: Russell & Russell, 1965), pp. 54-57.

2. Kevin McCarthy, R. Burciago Valdez, *Current and Future Effects of Mexican Immigration in California: Executive Summary* (Santa Monica: Rand Corp. 1985); and Thomas Muller, Thomas Espenshade (with D. Manson, M. de la Puente, M. Goldberger, J. Sanchez) *The Fourth Wave* (WDC: The Urban Institute Press, 1985). The summary of the latter report had been published by the Urban Institute Press in 1984.

3. As opposed to the often casual use of statistics by the leadership of the Immigration and Naturalization Service which, for example, persists in not figuring out how many *people* it apprehends each year, while telling us that the number of *apprehensions* is rising to more than 1.5 million a year.

4. *The Fourth Wave* (summary), p. 13.

5. *The Fourth Wave* (full text), p. 56.

6. *Ibid*, p. 58.

7. *Statistical Abstract of the United States 1985* (WDC: GPO, 1985), table 657, and predecessor tables in previous volumes.

8. *The Fourth Wave* (full text), p. 110.

9. Presentation by Frank Loy to the Ninth Annual Conference of the Center for Migration Studies, held in WDC on March 20, 1986.

10. *The Fourth Wave* (full text), p. 113.

11. *Current and Future Effects of Mexican Immigration in California: Executive Summary*, p. vii.

12. Ibid., p. 20.

13. Ibid., p. 20.

14. See, for example, Vernon Briggs *Mexican Migration and the U.S. Labor Market* (Austin: Center for the Study of Human Resources, University of Texas, 1975).

15. The extent of our wage competition problem is suggested by a recent report on Korean wages. In a modern VCR factory near Seoul, Korea, relatively well educated Koreans work twelve hours a day, seven days a week, with two days off a year for $3,000 a year. United States based companies will surely lose any competitive race based on low wages alone. Carnegie Forum on Education and the Economy, *Report of the Task Force on Teaching as Profession*, (WDC: Carnegie Forum on Education and the Economy, 1986).

16. *The Fourth Wave* (full text), p. 53. The out-migration of workers from Los Angeles County in the 1970s to other parts of California and to other states is estimated as 372,000 by the Urban Institute.

17. *Current and Future Effects of Mexican Immigration in California: Executive Summary*, p. vii.

18. Conner's point is well taken even though the Rand statement appears to deal with all immigrants from Mexico, legal and illegal, rather than with illegal immigrants as such. FAIR "News Advisory" (Federation for American Immigration Reform, Washington, D.C., February 5, 1986), p. 1.

19. *The Fourth Wave* (full text), table 24 on p. 143.

20. Ibid. (full text), p. 143.

21. See, for example, Julian Simon, "What Immigrants Take From, and Give to, the Public Coffers," in *U.S. Immigration Policy and the National Interest, Appendix D to the Staff Report of the Select Commission on Immigration and Refugee Policy—Papers on Legal Immigration to the United States* (WDC: SCIRP, April 30, 1981), p. 259.

22. The principal gainers would seem to be the employers of the illegals (who secure labor at bargain rates) and the migrants themselves, who, while exploited, are earning more than they could in Mexico or in Central America.

23. *The Fourth Wave* (full text), p. 96.

24. Ibid., p. 115.

25. For more on the interaction between income-transfer programs and various classes of aliens, see various reports written by David North, notably *Refugee Earnings and Utilization of Financial Assistance Programs* (Office of Refugee Resettlement, Dept. of Health and Human Services, Washington, D.C., 1984) and *Immigration and Income Transfer Policies in the United States: An Analysis of a Non- relationship* (New TransCentury Foundation, Washington, D.C., 1982).

26. The approach of other programs, such as food stamps, and pensions for Social Security beneficiaries, is to reduce benefits slowly as earned income expands, to encourage employment.

27. *The Fourth Wave* (summary), p. 3. That process is described more accurately in the full text.

V

DEMOGRAPHIC CENTRIFUGE BELOW THE BORDER

Until 1972, in fact, Mexico followed a pronatalist policy . . . Then one fine day the Escheverria government discovered that it had a full-blown population problem on its hands . . . . births outstripped deaths by nearly two million, a gain that exceeded the combined natural increase of the population in the United States and Canada that year by 370,000! . . . By 1972 close to a thousand Mexicans were said to be illegally crossing over every day into the United States—annually, the equivalent of Vermont's entire population!—in search of employment.

> —Pranay Gupte,
> The Crowded Earth: People and
> the Politics of Population
> (New York: W.W. Norton, 1984)

Mexico's Dilemma:
Finding a Million Jobs a Year
By David Simcox

The rapid growth of Mexico's labor force in the last three decades of the twentieth century has critical implications for the country's social and economic order. The demographic and social consequences of that growth will be no less critical for the United States in the years to come.

Mexico's labor force in 1985, according to the International Labor Organization (ILO), was twenty-six million. Between 1970 and 1985, it increased by 54 percent, an average annual increase of 3.7 percent. Growth peaked in the 1970s when yearly growth reached 4.4 percent. Some of the decade's increase reflected the rising participation of Mexican women. ILO projects Mexico's labor force to continue expanding by 3.2 percent yearly throughout the 1980s and 2.9 percent yearly in the 1990s.[1]

As Mexico moves into the late 1980s, the number of new entrants each year will grow to more than 900,000, and surpass one million by the end of the century. Mexico's labor force will have risen from 14.4 million in 1970 to 40.4 million in the year 2000, an increase of 180 percent. Mexico's total population over the same three decades will increase by 113 percent—from fifty-one million to a projected 109 million. After the turn of the century, Mexico's labor force will continue to grow by more than one million a year until 2010 when the changing age distribution will begin to slow the pace of labor force growth.

This surging growth is more remarkable when contrasted with trends in the United States in the same period. The U.S. labor force grew from 82.7 million in 1970 to 117.1 million in 1985, an average annual 2.3 percent growth rate. High historically for the United States, this rate was still less than two-thirds of Mexico's average growth rate during the same period. The gap between U.S. and Mexican growth rates will widen considerably in the late 1980s and early 1990s. The United States will add only fourteen million workers to its labor force between 1985 and 1995, a yearly increase of 1.3 percent.[2] Mexico's labor force will grow at two and a half times that rate, adding nearly ten million candidates for jobs by 1995, though its population is only one-third and its economy one-twentieth the size of those of the United States.

The fifteen million young Mexicans reaching working age by 2000 are prospective claimants on Mexican society for jobs that are reasonably stable and satisfy basic needs. If their claims are unmet, they may follow several possible routes: apathy and withdrawal, joining millions of other underemployed Mexicans already in the country's shadowy subsistence economy; crime, vice or political extremism in pursuit of revolutionary change; and seasonal or permanent migration to the United States.

Table 11.1   Labor force growth in Mexico 1960–2020

Year	Labor Force Total	Growth Rate	New Entrants Yearly
1960	11,056,000	2.74	340,000
1970	14,489,000	4.38	775,000
1980	22,248,000	3.23	820,000
1990	30,487,000	3.17	1,000,000
2000	40,442,000	2.87	1,050,000
2010	51,014,000	2.35	935,000
2020	60,358,000	1.70	700,000

Source: International Labor Organization (ILO).

BACKGROUND: A CENTURY OF MEXICAN MIGRATION

Although Mexicans have migrated northward in appreciable numbers since the 1880s, Mexican legal and illegal immigration began to climb sharply in the mid-1960s, as indicated by immigrant visa applications and issuance, INS apprehensions, deportations and the estimated overstays of visaed visitors. In 1965, the year the U.S.-Mexican Migrant Labor Agreement (Bracero Agreement) was concluded, the INS made only 110,000 apprehensions. Within ten years this number had increased seven-fold to more than three-quarters of a million. By 1977 apprehensions exceeded one million for the first time. Arrests of illegal border crossers, 97 percent of them Mexican, reached 1.3 million in 1985 and 1.7 million in 1986.

There are many explanations for the sharp climb: 1) the end of the Bracero Agreement which simply drove much of what had been legal labor migration underground; 2) the after-effects of the twenty-two- year agreement, which created networks and migration channels that gave illegal immigration a momentum of its own; 3) the explosive growth of the Mexican labor force stemming from the post war surge in population, with rising education levels nurturing new expectations; 4) the demand for cheap flexible labor in the booming U.S. economy of the Vietnam era, when between 1965 and 1974 unemployment averaged below 5 percent.

Changes inside Mexico in the 1960s were also beginning to push out more migrants. While the Mexican economy was registering impressive growth rates statistically through much of the 1960s and 1970s—over 6 percent per year—agriculture was beginning to stagnate, driving more small farmers and day workers into the cities or to the United States in search of work. The labor force in the 1970s was growing at an unprecedented 4.4 percent annually, but the poor education and training of millions limited their utility to Mexico's changing economy. For much of its impressive growth, Mexico's industrial sector did not match the growth of output. The labor force grew by about 750,000 a year, but new jobs approached only 400,000 a year through most of the 1970s.[3]

RISING IMMIGRATION DEMAND

Legal immigration from a particular country can be both an indicator of overall immigration demand and often a stimulant to illegal immigration, as families and friends seek to reunite. Legal Mexican immigration in the decade of the 1960s rose by 50 percent over the 1950s. In the decade of the 1970s legal immigration jumped again by another 41 percent, reaching an average of 64,000 a year. Legal immigration in the 1970s probably would have gone even higher, but in 1976 Congress placed an immigration ceiling of 20,000 on each western hemisphere country, but exempted close family members. Each year Mexico has filled its 20,000 ceiling and in addition sent about twice as many more close family member immigrants exempt from the ceiling. As 1987 began 381,000 Mexicans were on the waiting list for U.S. immigrant visas. The American

Table 11.2   INS apprehensions, Mexican economic growth and U.S. unemployment

Year	INS Apprehensions[a] (1000s)	Mexican Economic Growth Rate[b]	U.S. Unemployment Rate[c]
1965	110	6.5	4.5
1966	138	6.9	3.8
1967	161	6.3	3.8
1968	212	8.1	3.6
1969	283	6.3	3.5
1970	345	6.9	4.9
1971	420	4.2	5.9
1972	505	8.4	5.6
1973	655	8.4	4.9
1974	788	6.1	5.6
1975	756	5.6	8.5
1976	866	4.2	7.7
1977	1,033	3.4	7.1
1978	1,047	8.3	6.1
1979	1,069	9.2	5.8
1980	910	8.3	7.1
1981	975	8.1	7.6
1982	970	-0.5	9.7
1983	1,251	-5.3	9.8
1984	1,246	3.7	7.5
1985	1,300	3.0	7.1
1986	1,700	-5.0	7.0

Sources: [a]INS.
[b]Department of State.
[c]Bureau of Labor Statistics

Embassy in Mexico estimated that 80 percent of the registrants were already living illegally in the United States.

The heavy migration from Mexico since the 1960s may well be only the leading edge of a far vaster wave of migrants that will seek to sojourn or to settle in the United States between now and the end of the century. Many of the demographic, social and economic factors driving this wave are already at work. Major lures are the presence in the United States of large welcoming Hispanic communities, village and ethnic networks to provide jobs and support to migrants, and important U.S. industries that have accepted dependence on Mexican workers. The pulling power of these networks is suggested by INS figures showing apprehensions, when adjusted for the diversion of border patrol manpower to Florida during the Mariel Boatlift in 1980- 1981, leveled off but did not appreciably decline during the 1979-1982 period of peak job creation performance of the Mexican economy. This period also witnessed a sharp rise in U.S. unemployment (1980-1983) and, until 1982, an exchange rate favorable to the peso.

To some degree, the Mexican migration has acquired a dynamic of its own. Yet long term migration pressures will depend greatly on the health of the Mexican economy, as well as the quality of Mexico's political life and its success in improving the distribution of income.

What are the prospects that Mexico can spur the creation of new jobs for at least 14 million additional workers between now and the end of the century?

MEXICO'S INVESTMENT PRIORITIES: CAPITAL OVER LABOR AND SMALL FARMERS

Mexico's strategy of economic development for more than three decades has favored investment in costly state-owned industries, in highly protected and inefficient import-substitution industries or in large scale commercial agriculture for export, to the neglect of small farmers. Heavy investment in the capital-intensive petroleum and electricity sectors, other state-owned heavy industry, and irrigated farming boosted growth figures, but produced relatively few jobs for the amount of capital invested. Proliferation of state-owned enterprises in the 1970s created some jobs, but with high costs and low productivity. Employment, particularly in services, showed significant growth between 1978-1981. But much of this growth came as temporary jobs and was nourished by foreign borrowing as Mexico's foreign debt ballooned.

The drastic decline of the petroleum prices from a high of $32 a barrel in 1981 to $14 a barrel in mid-1986, the heavy burden of servicing a foreign debt of $100 billion, and debilitating capital flight have made it impossible for Mexico to continue high levels of investment and subsidies to the public sector.

Mexican economic policymakers now face the most serious challenge to the country since the revolution. The economic development policies of the last three decades are no longer sustainable in an era of austerity. For the foreseeable future debt payments will continue to syphon off nearly two-thirds of export earnings. The country must develop new export products and expand existing exports to replace the $9 to $10 billion earnings lost annually from the collapse of petroleum prices.

Recovery of oil prices to their 1981 peak is an uncertain prospect. But even with optimistic assumptions about future oil earnings, Mexico's large debt burden and its poor prospects for quickly spurring non-oil exports will rule out resumption of massive public investment and subsidies.

A major potential alternative source of capital and technology for growth, foreign investment, remains suspect in the nationalistic outlook of many Mexican leaders. Mexico's elites have ignored or neglected less glamorous sectors of the economy that elsewhere are major sources of new jobs. Tourism has not received a priority consistent with its job-creation potential. Small business entrepreneurs labor under the handicaps of scarce credit, direct competition from the state-owned sector, over-regulation, and official corruption.

Small scale, rain-fed agriculture has suffered the greatest neglect of all, though it now employs—or more often underemploys—28 percent of Mexico's labor force. Mexico's small communal farmers, or *ejidatarios* have generally received insufficient credit and technical and marketing assistance, and have seen their products often underpriced by the government's low support prices and reliance on subsidized food imports. Additional woes in the 1960s and 1970s were chronic drought and the declining availability and quality of new arable lands. All these factors have added up to heavy underemployment on Mexico's small farms, low productivity and drift to the cities.

RESTRUCTURING THE ECONOMY FOR GROWTH AND JOBS

At least rhetorically, President Miguel de la Madrid, elected in 1982, recognizes that the economy must be restructured. The national development plan for 1983-1988 stresses job creation. The plan accepts that the protectionist industrial policies of the past have contributed to high levels of underemployment. The government intends to push for more efficient industries and for more growth in those areas that are competitive internationally.[4] Some barriers to foreign investment have been lowered.

Some analysts foresee a period of significantly lower growth in industrial employment in Mexico because of the need to eliminate non-competitive subsidized firms and reduce padded payrolls. The government's paring down of state firms since 1982 has already taken a heavy toll in unemployment. As industry recovers, keeping Mexican products competitive will require further devaluations of the peso. A central question here for Mexico's own political and economic stability, as well as for future immigration flows, is whether additional labor-intensive jobs, even if adequate in numbers, will offer the remuneration, security and satisfaction necessary to hold young Mexican workers who might perceive far more attractive work above the Rio Grande. With the difference in potential real earnings between the U.S. and Mexican economies likely to grow, the "holding power" of new jobs in Mexico becomes a critical migration factor.

Boosting productivity and employment in Mexican agriculture is even more problematical for Mexico's leaders, whose most urgent concern is to get more homegrown food and potential exports from the farm sector. Under present circumstances, agriculture will provide few of the extra jobs needed. However, an increasing percentage of the 4.5 million workers expected to remain in agriculture in 1990 will be wage workers, a trend that may help to narrow Mexico's rural-urban income inequalities and slow, but not stop, the exodus from the countryside.

Before the 1982 collapse of oil prices and the debt crisis, the Mexican government was counting on the services sector to create two-thirds of all the new jobs in the 1980s. The optimistic estimates foresaw creation of new service jobs starting at the rate of 400,000 a year early in the decade, rising to one million a year by the end of the decade. But one-third to one-half of these newly created jobs would have come from expansion of government employment—with six million Mexicans directly or indirectly employed by the government by 1990.[5] In fact, government employment has actually fallen, a victim of the country's shrinking revenues.

ESTIMATING CURRENT AND FUTURE UNEMPLOYMENT

Mexican unemployment estimates, based on surveys of major cities, are at best sketchy. Data for such sectors as agriculture and services are often rudimentary or unavailable. The figures understate the extent of underemployment. Many Mexicans, when lacking regular paid employment, either make do through self-employment, part-time or irregular work, return to farm work or to some other form of family employment, thus joining the ranks of the under-employed, or they withdraw from the labor force entirely. Mexican officials define an underemployed worker as one who does not earn annually at least the minimum wage, currently the equivalent of about $1,000 a year.

Noted Mexican economist Victor Urquidi stated in March 1986 that 3.5 million of what he estimated as Mexico's 24 million labor force were unemployed and nine million of the remainder were underemployed.[6] By his reckoning, 52 percent of Mexico's labor force lacked work. The Mexican magazine *Proceso* reported similar figures in June 1986, noting that unpublished government data showed open unemployment at 3.6 million—up 2.4 million since 1981—and underemployment of eight million, totaling 48 percent of the labor force unemployed or underemployed.

But poor economic performance in 1986 has made these bad figures worse. Mexico's projected decline in output of 5 percent in 1986 will result in the creation of no new jobs for the year's 900,000 new entrants to the labor force, and a shrinkage of existing jobs by as much as 3 percent. (One Mexican economist estimates an employment "multiplier" of .6 of 1 percent for each 1 percent change in Mexico's gross domestic product.)[7] Thus, Mexico would begin 1987 with a labor force estimated by ILO at 26.9 million, open unemployment of about 5.1 million—19 percent of the labor force—and underemployment of nine to ten million. CANACINTRA, a major Mexican industrial employers federation, released similar figures in mid-1986, projecting unemployment of 18 percent by the end of 1986.[8]

PROSPECTS FOR JOB CREATION UNTIL 2000

Predictions of Mexico's future job creation rate are risky, as they depend on such unknowns as future growth rates, the mix of labor and capital in investment decisions, investment priorities and labor force participation rates. Since Mexico's present economic crisis began in 1982, its GNP has shrunk by 39 percent in dollar terms, with virtually no net increase in employment. Unemployment has grown from about 1.7 million in 1982 to the 5.1 million estimated for the end of 1986. Projection of the negative employment growth trend of the past five years to the year 2000 would foretell economic and social chaos, with twenty-seven million Mexicans unemployed or underemployed in a labor force of 40.5 million. Such an extreme outcome can be avoided if Mexico, as expected, resumes modest economic growth as current economic reforms take effect. Yet, the structural changes contemplated in these market-oriented reforms may well further increase unemployment in the short and medium-term.

But even under more optimistic growth projections, Mexico will be unlikely to create the more than 900,000 jobs it needs annually. Applying the optimistic job creation multiplier of .6 for each percentage point of growth—and with equal optimism applying the multiplier to current employment in the traditional as well as modern sectors of the economy—a healthy and sustained annual growth of output of 5 percent would yield yearly employment growth of 3 percent— 700,000 to 800,000 new jobs a year in the late 1980s. Impressive by any standard, this rate of job creation would still barely match the projected rapid growth of the labor force. Under this optimistic projection Mexico would still reach the year 2000 with 7.7 million unemployed, 19 percent of its labor force, and an additional nine million still underemployed.

A more discouraging picture emerges if projections up to 2000 are based on the highly respectable job creation experience of the U.S. economy since World War II. From 1948 to 1983 the U.S. economy added jobs at an average rate of 2 percent a year, among the best performances of industrial economies. Only in five of those years did job growth exceed 3 percent. A 2 percent average job growth rate for Mexico over the next thirteen years—a rate that would gladden most industrialized countries—would leave Mexico in the year 2000 with nineteen million members of its labor force unemployed, underemployed or, seeking

a life outside the country. Joining this prospective pool of 19 million job seekers
as candidates for migration would be their current and future spouses and children, some of whom would be enticed at some point to join them by the prospect
of superior U.S. education and social services.

At the 2 percent rate Mexico would have created only 55 percent of the jobs
needed each year. (Table 11.3 projects the gap between labor force growth and
job creation to the end of the century at projected employment growth rates of
2 percent and 3 percent annually.)

Worth repeating is that these discouraging job creation projections are based
on growth assumptions that are optimistic in light of Mexico's current economic
performance. Data Resources Incorporated, for example, sees Mexico's annual
economic growth averaging below 4 percent for the remainder of this decade,
with industrial employment—where the greatest job gains are hoped for— expanding by only 2.3 percent annually by 1990.[9] Merely to maintain unemployment and underemployment at present levels, Mexico must add new jobs
at over 4.0 percent a year. If Mexico were to both hold unemployment at current
levels and substantially eliminate underemployment by 2000, the country would
have to create 1.3 million new jobs a year, a 6 percent annual increase. The U.S.
economy in 1985, growing by about 3 percent, added two million new jobs, a

**Table 11.3   Projected growth of the labor force and
employment in Mexico — 1985–2000.**

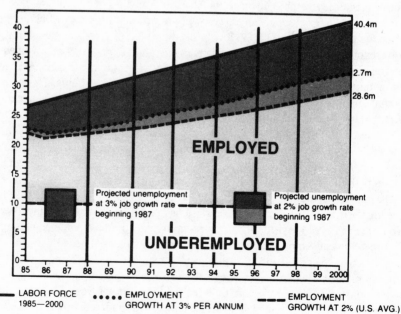

job creation performance only slightly below the average for the past quarter century. But the U.S. economy is more than twenty times larger than Mexico's.

In the absence of major and unforeseen social and economic changes, all conditions in Mexico point to heavy incentives for migration northward: a dizzying growth in the younger population (ages fifteen to thirty-four) most prone to migration; the availability of jobs to only half to at best three-quarters of those entering the labor force, and the declining economic appeal of the available jobs compared to alternatives in the United States as the value of the peso declines.

MEXICO: THE POLITICAL FUTURE AND MIGRATION

The course of Mexico's politics may affect immigration as much as will economic trends. The political outcome over the next decade and a half will both shape and be shaped by the performance of the Mexican economy. Widespread, unyielding joblessness is politically corrosive. Political events could become the critical variable in the decisions of millions of Mexicans whether to try migration. The single party system, the Revolutionary Institutional Party (PRI), is hard pressed by the political stresses of five years of austerity and the growing resentment of much of the middle class. Charting Mexico's political future is no easier than forseeing the course of its economy. Recent history and current events suggest four possible directions for Mexican politics to the year 2000, with varying potential to shape migration trends.

Outcome One—The Status Quo

Continuation of the present highly centralized, corporate authoritarian model represented by the PRI system, with slow and uneven evolution toward greater participation and more latitude for legal opposition groups. Such a trend would be unlikely either to ease such push factors as Mexico's serious maldistribution of income, corruption and desultory human rights abuses, or to overcome the prevailing sense of apathy and cynicism among large numbers of Mexicans about the regime. Discouraging prospects for greater political participation could deepen alienation and pessimism among younger Mexicans. It is unlikely that the cautious and dogma-bound current system would encourage the economic innovations conducive to strong growth. Planned reforms of the economy may delay political reform because the system can't handle both at the same time. On balance, the political outcome of "more of the same" would be likely to reinforce other existing incentives to migrate, such as lagging economic performance and rapid growth of the labor force.

Outcome Two—Democratization and Reform

This outcome, more unlikely than the previous one, would involve a rapid opening of the Mexican political system to greater participation, including movement toward a genuine multi-party system with authentic competition for power, greater respect for human rights and political dissent, and greater responsiveness to rank-and-file demands. The system's transition toward greater pluralism and political competition would be unsettling in the short run, heightening insecurity among some sectors that could harm the business climate and encourage out-migration. But over the longer term, democratization could stimulate progress toward a more open economy, curbing corruption and overcentralization. Job creation could improve. Many Mexicans might be encouraged to view their country's future with greater optimism and choose to remain part of it.

Outcome Three—Dictatorship of the Right or Left

Serious political unrest could lead to a more authoritarian, repressive regime of the right or, more unlikely, of the left, as a way of dealing with economic decay and unmanageable public demands. A rightist regime could have somewhat better prospects of spurring rapid economic growth by gaining foreign invest-ment, quashing ideological obstacles and enforcing labor peace. But a right-wing authoritarian government would probably give lower priority to remedying the country's maldistribution of income or human rights abuses. The less likely alternative, a repressive regime of the extreme left, on the other hand, would risk the loss of major sources of foreign investment and financing and traditional markets for Mexican products. A state socialist model of development over the longer term could reduce income inequalities, but would risk deep disaffection among Mexico's middle and upper classes, as in Castro's Cuba. In either case, a likely environment of instability and insecurity, and tensions in relations with the United States, would encourage emigration. A radical reorientation of the Mexican economy, or attempts at abrupt changes in the distribution of income, could profoundly chill economic growth and investment, and the economic ex-pectations of millions of wage earning Mexicans, spurring out-migration. A hostile regime in Mexico City—or even a weak and troubled one—might well be less cooperative in curbing pressures for non-Mexican illegal migration across the common border.

Outcome Four—A Breakdown of Order

A clear worst case with an even lower probability would be the collapse of political stability in Mexico, with widespread insurgency, violence and govern-ment counter-violence. Disorders might take many forms: rural insurgencies, rising urban rioting terrorism and politically motivated crime, or internecine conflict within the armed forces and allied civilian factions. The economy would suffer accordingly. This "doomsday" outcome could be expected to spark huge outflows of Mexicans seeking either physical safety or economic survival in the United States, particularly from the most strife-ridden areas. While the number of Mexicans who would seek refuge in the United States can only be guessed, it is worth recalling that the 1910 Mexican revolution spurred at least 500,000 Mexicans out of a total population of 15 million to move to the United States. Then Mexico's population was concentrated in areas distant from the U.S. border. Now some six million Mexicans live within ten miles of it.

SHORT-TERM PRUDENCE AND LONG-TERM ENLIGHTENMENT

The interest of the United States at stake in Mexico's rapid population and labor force growth and its economic stagnation are as formidable as they are diverse. They range from satisfaction of basic humanitarian concerns to the security of its sea lanes in the Gulf and Caribbean; from control of its southern border to the preservation of its massive trade and investment in that country; from the prospect of massive welfare and resettlement costs for hundreds of thousands of migrants to the physical security of southwestern communities.

Facile answers to the dilemma, the rapid economic and social development of Mexico—virtually leap to the lips with an ease that belies their complexity. Over decades policy planners on both sides of the border and in international organizations have produced a vast literature about what needs to be "done about Mexico," but the proposed economic, political and demographic remedies are all beset with enormous built-in difficulties and little promise of rapid results.

Proposed economic solutions carry staggering price tags, now compounded by Mexico's onerous debt burden in its low investment rate, which fell by 38 percent between 1981, the peak year for its job creation, and 1984—a decline of nearly $40 billion a year. Thomas Espenshade of the Urban Institute estimates that the total amount of additional investment needed by 2000 to keep labor demand simply from falling further behind supply in the Caribbean Basin could exceed $1 trillion, more than half of it in Mexico.[10] Financial commitments of this magnitude will require a national political will in the United States that is clearly missing.

While not a guarantee of economic growth, political reforms in Mexico could ease migration pressures. More open political process could set the stage for a more equitable distribution of income. Curbing Mexico's renowned corruption would relese entrepreneurial energies and make public investment more efficient.

By Third World standards, Mexico has already made remarkable progress in lowering its rate of population increase. Its growth rate has fallen from 3.2 in 1973, when the government first openly abandoned its pronatalist policy, to about 2.5 percent now. Fertility is likely to continue declining rapidly, further lowering growth rates. But the immediate problem remains unresolved, since those entering the labor force for the next fifteen to twenty years are already born. Even so, Mexico would gain in two ways from stepped up family planning: The employment problems of the early twenty-first century would ease somewhat; and fewer children now would permit redirection of funds for schooling into job-producing investments.

There is broad assent to the principle that the United States should maintain enlightened trade aid and investment policies to encourage healthy growth and job creation in Mexico. But this lofty principle too often stumbles over political, ideological or protectionist objections on both sides of the border. Mexico has been a major beneficiary of the trade and financial concessions to Third World nations developed by the United States and other industrial nations in the North-South dialogue, including commodity agreements, trade preferences such as the Generalized System of Preferences (GSP), and the transfer of labor-intensive manufacturing processes to the so-called *maquiladora* plants along the border. But the *maquiladoras*, which assemble U.S.-made components for re-export to the United States, and which currently employ more than 250,000 Mexicans, are now meeting renewed resistance from labor unions and other protectionist forces in the United States.

Easier terms on Mexico's $100 billion debt would clearly strengthen Mexico's political stability and economic health. Enlightened trade, aid and investment policies toward Mexico deserve support if for no other reason than simple humanitarianism and their contribution to a sounder world economic order over the longer term. But there should be no illusions that even the most enlightened economic policies will have significant effect on rising migration pressures from Mexico in the next decade. A greater risk is that special interests will hold up such enlightened policies as a false alternative to the prudent but difficult steps the United States must take in the short-run to contain migration pressures.

The United States rarely has sought seriously to enforce its immigration laws. There are a number of options for reducing the lure of the pull factors and blocking illegal entry. They deserve a trial. The United States must commit itself without delay to further tightening immigration enforcement at three lines of defense: 1) At the border and ports of entry with a larger, properly equipped and funded border patrol; 2) at the work place, by strictly implementing sanctions against employers of illegal aliens, and vigorously enforcing high labor standards; and 3) at the diverse and expensive safety net of social welfare benefits, using effective identification systems for citizens and legal residents. These tasks are made no easier by the blurring in the public mind of the distinctions among immigrants and refugees and asylees. U.S. policymakers must define and maintain rigorous criteria for distinguishing authentic refugees from economic migrants, for winnowing out those escaping the truly life-threatening from those leaving the merely uncomfortable. Implicit here is the willingness to "think the unthinkable" about the prospects of a major immigration emergency from Mexico that could dwarf Mariel in numbers and complexity. While the U.S. government has made some progress in planning the logistical and bureaucratic aspects of immigration emergencies since Mariel, there are few signs of any serious consideration of the wrenching political decisions our national leaders must face as to who shall be admitted and under what terms in the case of a sudden major outflow of Mexicans fleeing political turmoil or economic collapse, or how those choices will be enforced.

Demographic, economic, political and law enforcement approaches must be taken together if U.S. interests are to be safeguarded and Mexico and the increasingly mobile, restive people of the Caribbean Basin are to survive its current population eruption without upheaval. Effective and lasting multilateral solutions would be the ideal. But the United States must be prepared to take prudent unilateral steps in exercise of its sovereign right to protect its borders.

NOTES

1. International Labor Office, *Economically Active Population—1950-2025*, Volume III (Geneva, 1986).

2. U.S. Department of Labor, *Employment Projections for 1995*, Bulletin 2197 (Washington, D.C., March 1984).

3. Francisco Javier Alejo, "Demographic Patterns and Labor Market Trends in Mexico," *Mexico's Economic Crisis: Challenges and Opportunities* (La Jolla, CA, Center for U.S.-Mexican Studies, 1983); and, U.S. Department of the Army, *Mexico: ,A Country Study* (Washington, D.C., 1985), p. XXXVII.

4. William Glade, "What are the Likely Strategies and Effects of Economic Distribution Policies," Paper presented at U.S. Department of State conference on *Mexican Trends: The Next Five Years*, Washington, D.C., December 1985.

5. Robert E. Looney, *Development Alternatives of Mexico—Beyond the 1980's* (New York: Praeger, 1982), p. 33.

6. Victor Urquidi, "Population and Employment at the End of the Century" (Mexico, DF, March 1986. Unpublished).

7. Alejo, *Mexico's Economic Crisis*. The job growth multiplier of .6 to .7 for each percentage point of growth posited by the author appears high for Mexico—the job growth ratio for the United States since 1960 averages .63—in view of the country's low absorption of labor in the 1960s and 1970s when growth rates were over 6 percent annually. Given the annual job creation of 300,000 to 400,000 during those two decades this rate would appear to apply only to job growth of Mexico's wage sector, which is covered by government surveys, and not to the subsistence agriculture and urban informal sectors that contained nearly 50 percent of the labor force.

8. Salvador Cono, "More than 4,000 Persons a Day Out of Work as Businesses Close," *Proceso*, July 7, 1986.

9. *Latin American Review*, Winter 1985.

10. Thomas Espenshade, "The Cost of Job Creation in the Caribbean," unpublished (Washington, D.C., 1986).

VI

BUILDING A MORE RATIONAL, ENFORCEABLE IMMIGRATION POLICY

This is actually a continuing, running gun battle with tunnel vision, short-term special interests constantly cutting—I think the word actually would be slashing—across the long-term national interests. We must recognize that the American public continues to overwhelmingly support immigration reform.

—Senator Alan K. Simpson's
address to the U.S. Senate, April 28, 1983.

Employer Sanctions in Europe:
Deterrence Without Discrimination
By Mark Miller

"Employer sanctions have proven to be ineffective deterrents to illegal immigration in at least twenty nations, according to the GAO, reported the May 30, 1985 *Wall Street Journal*."[1] Reports such as this have fueled opposition to adoption of employer sanctions in the United States, even though a follow-up GAO evaluation in 1985, noting that its 1982 conclusions had been misinterpreted, found that officials in seven of nine countries surveyed believed illegal immigration would be worse without sanctions.

The wisdom of imposing employer sanctions was hotly debated in the United States during the decade and a half that Congress considered the immigration reforms finally enacted in November 1986. This situation contrasts sharply with continental Europe where employer sanctions were adopted with little or no public debate and a broad consensus in favor of the concept exists. In the United States, critics have warned that employer sanctions would lead to additional employment discrimination against Hispanics. Fear of employer sanctions possibly leading to additional discrimination against immigrants and minorities was a factor in the British decision not to adopt them. And there have been concerns expressed in other European countries with significant minority populations comparable to Hispanics in the United States. In the single most illuminating case, however, employer sanctions in France do not appear to have resulted in additional discrimination against the French citizenry and legally-resident alien population of North African background.

In marked contrast to the American and, to a much lesser extent, the British situation, employer sanctions are widely understood in continental Europe to be a means of preventing the discrimination inherent in the exploitation of illegal immigrants by wayward employers. The possible discrimination-engendering effects of employer sanctions simply have not been an issue in France and other continental European countries with which the author is familiar. The transatlantic contrast in perceptions seemed sharpest when all major Democratic candidates for the U.S. Presidency in 1984 declared their opposition to the Simpson-Mazzoli legislation on the ground that the legislation, and in particular employer sanctions, would lead to additional discrimination against Hispanics. At roughly the same time, the Socialist government in France was announcing steps to enhance enforcement of various laws intended to curb illegal immigration.[2]

Despite important dissimilarities between the various major migrant-receiving countries of Western Europe and the United States, Western European experiences with employer sanctions may have important implications for U.S. views on employer sanctions and their implementation. Several continental European nations have had employer sanctions for a decade now, most notably France and the Federal Republic of Germany (FRG). This time span permits tentative analysis of possible repercussions of employer sanctions and of their effectiveness in curbing illegal immigration.

THE FRENCH EXPERIENCE: STRONGER ENFORCEMENT SINCE 1982

In 1975, the French government set up a "judicial mission" to coordinate the actions of public authorities aimed at suppressing illegal immigration and employment.[3] An interagency group, the Interministerial Liaison Mission to Combat Manpower Trafficking, was officially instituted in 1976, the same year in which employer sanctions became operative. In July 1976, a law went into effect that reinforced penalties against individuals who aided illegal immigration and created an administrative penalty for employers of irregular-status migrants, requiring them to pay to ONI, the French immigration agency, a sum equivalent to five hundred times the minimum hourly wage for each worker illegally employed. In 1980, the fine was 4,275 francs (about $1,000).[4] This administrative fine was automatic in principle, above and beyond any penal sanction that might be imposed on an offending employer, including imprisonment from one to two months and longer in the case of repeat offenders. For many years, actual collection of the administrative fine was haphazard as complaints against employers were not communicated properly to the ONI and many offenders were not located. Enforcement of the fine, however, has improved in recent years. According to the first annual report of the Interministerial Liaison Mission (ILM), the government chose to emphasize control over the employment of aliens more than other possible solutions to illegal migration and employment because limiting the entry of aliens into France was impractical.[5]

One of the major functions of France's ILM is to keep track of enforcement of the panoply of laws aimed against illegal immigration and employment. Employer sanctions are only part of an impressive legal arsenal that has built up. An overview of overall legal enforcement since 1976 as measured by legal complaints (*proces-verbaux*) made by various enforcement agencies reveals a 1976 upsurge in enforcement followed by a decline, precipitous in 1977, 1978, and 1981, prior to a dramatic resurgence in 1982 and 1983. The upsurge in enforcement since 1982 mainly can be attributed to the police and labor inspectors.

The number of infractions by employers against section L341-6 of the Labor Code, which specifically penalizes employers for hiring irregular-status aliens, in 1976 and 1977 amounted to 1,624 and 2,208 respectively.[6] The level of enforcement of employer sanctions strictly speaking correlates closely with ups and downs in overall enforcement of laws against illegal immigration and employment.

The annual report for the year 1979 by the ILM summarized the first four years of enforcement of the 1976 law reinforcing employer sanctions as follows:

> After four years of functioning, it is necessary to recognize that the objective was not totally attained and that irregular-status alien employment remains an important problem both with regard to the employment situation and on the social and human level of those workers themselves. On the other hand, it is difficult to evaluate the number of clandestine foreign workers and thus to know whether it is more important in 1980 than it was in 1976.[7]

Evaluation of the effectiveness of employer sanctions over the 1976-1979 period was complicated by a number of factors. Among them was the continuation of France's legalization of certain classes of foreign residents. A number of "exceptional" collective legalizations occurred during this period, particularly in the spring of 1980 when some 4,000 Parisian garment industry workers, primarily Turks, were granted legal status.[8] The legalizations diverted enforcement manpower as a good number of labor inspectors, who are always in short supply, were involved in carrying it out.[9]

INITIAL OBSTACLES TO ENFORCEMENT

Among the barriers to more effective enforcement during this period, certain problems stood out. Many employers adapted to employer sanctions by masking their activities. Hence, enforcement became an increasingly complicated matter requiring close cooperation among various agencies—cooperation that was not always readily forthcoming. There also was a dearth of specialized agents, particularly labor inspectors, to enforce the laws. Many labor inspectors were uncomfortable with employer sanctions and other laws aimed against illegal migrant residency and employment. In 1978, only a little more than 1 percent of the total legal complaints filed by labor inspectors concerned infractions pertinent to foreign labor.[10] There appeared to be a large gap between the perceived threat of illegal immigration on the governmental level and perception of the phenomenon by the judiciary and local officials. Employer sanctions simply were not enforced in many areas in southern France,[11] and judges often did not punish offending employers.[12] Still, the concept of employer sanctions was far from discredited. Employer sanctions had only been in existence for a few years, and one would normally expect quite a number of initial coordination and implementation problems. The Socialist victories in the 1981 presidential and legislative elections would have important effects upon enforcement.

INITIAL GERMAN ENFORCEMENT PROBLEMS

Similar barriers to more effective enforcement of employer sanctions were also apparent in the German context by 1981. As in France, there is a panoply of German laws concerning illegal immigration and employment. The German employer sanctions, strictly speaking, are provided for by paragraphs 227 and 229 of the Employment Promotion Act, and include fines, prison terms, and a requirement for employers to pay for an alien's trip home.

A large number of employers of irregular-status aliens receive warnings only. Prosecution is focused on employers who repeatedly flout the law and who most exploit aliens. Enforcement of employer sanctions is limited to specific individuals, as firms cannot be prosecuted.

By 1981, the estimated number of irregular-status migrants in the FRG ranged from 200,000 to 300,000, about the same size as the estimated irregular-alien population in France at the time.[13] The problem of illegal alien employment was particularly severe in the FRG's construction industry and in hotels and restaurants. Employers of illegal aliens often realized huge profits, particularly in the construction industry, as much of the work was off the books (*Schwarzarbeit*), and therefore employers would not pay high German payroll taxes. In some instances, the 50,000 deutsche marks ($25,000) penalty foreseen for employment of each irregular-status alien worker did not stop employers. They simply made so much illegally that the employer sanction fine was derisory. Poor coordination and communication among various agencies dealing with illegal alien employment hampered follow up prosecution for violation of social security laws. Prohibitions against the sharing of information between various agencies also hampered enforcement. The official in charge of enforcement of employer sanctions in the German Federal Ministry for Work and Social Order requested authorization to hire three hundred additional inspectors in 1981.[14] While there certainly were numerous obstacles to enforcement of employer sanctions in the FRG apparent in 1981, there also seemed to be broad agreement that employer sanctions were a necessary component of any strategy to curb illegal alien residency and employment.

STRICTER FRENCH AND GERMAN LAWS

In 1981, both the French and the German governments passed new laws reinforcing employer sanctions. The Germans increased the maximum fine per alien employed to 100,000 deutsche marks, ($50,000) effective January 1, 1982. To improve coordination among various agencies and levels of government, the Federal Labor Office established a network of twenty-five priority offices for combatting illegal employment.[15] An important difference between France and the FRG arises from the broader, more inclusive German approach to combatting illegal alien employment. In France, illegal alien employment is seen as a specific aspect of the broader problem of the underground economy, but the Interministerial Liaison Mission's authority is restricted to coordinating measures against illegal alien residency and employment only. In the FRG, the agencies involved are authorized to coordinate enforcement of law against employment in the underground economy in general.

In France, the law of October 17, 1981, made employment of irregular-status aliens a criminal offense subject to fines of 2,000 to 20,000 francs ($285 to $2,850) and imprisonment from two months to a year. For repeat offenders, the prison term could reach two years and the fine 40,000 francs. Separate fines could be imposed for each individual alien involved.[16] The French government, however, simultaneously announced a legalization program and employer sanctions were not to be enforced until it ended. The legalization period took longer than expected as additional categories of aliens, such as seasonal workers, were permitted to apply. Hence, the marked drop in enforcement of employer sanctions in 1981 is a direct consequence of French legalization policy.

Enforcement of employer sanctions did not resume in France until well into 1982. Still later, on August 31, 1983, the French government adopted a series of measures proposed by the ILM which simultaneously aimed at reinforcing the effort to curb illegal alien residency and employment while promoting the integration or ''insertion'' of legally resident alien communities in France. It is important to stress the linkage made by the French government between curbing illegal alien employment and residency on one hand, and the integration of resident alien communities on the other, as it closely resembles the rationale behind the immigration control legislation in the United States. Illegal alien immigration and employment is recognized as jeopardizing the status of legally resident aliens. This linkage was made explicit in the 1983 annual report of the ILM:

> Stopping clandestine immigration, combatting employers of irregular-status aliens, and controlling migratory flows effectively constitute a priority objective (for the French government). Failure in this case would put in doubt the insertion of legally resident alien communities in France.[17]

The August 31, 1983, measures increased the administrative fine for employers of irregular-status aliens from 500 to 2,000 times the minimum hourly wage for each alien illegally employed. As of January 1, 1985, the administrative fine was 26,340 francs.[18] The ILM staff was increased, allowing the Mission to open up a regional office in Marseille. The number of specialized labor inspectors was authorized to increase to fifty-five. Police forces were also authorized to assign higher priority to immigration law enforcement, particularly in areas of the south with large concentrations of illegal immigrants.[19] In September, the senior French judicial official reiterated to all public prosecutors the government's view of the grave consequences of illegal alien employment and called upon prosecutors to step up enforcement of laws prohibiting illegal alien employment. Prosecutors were also asked to ''rigorously apply'' the text of the laws concerning penalties.[20]

In June of 1984, the French created the first of twenty-three priority department-mental (county) coordinating committees, which had been previously authorized by a government memorandum of November 21, 1983.[21] Their objective was to facilitate the exchange of information so as to more effectively detect and sanction violations stemming from illegal alien employment.

IN FRANCE, AN "ENCOURAGING ENFORCEMENT BALANCE SHEET"

The end of legalization in France combined with the measures taken in 1983 and 1984, have resulted in a marked increase in enforcement of laws against illegal immigration and employment as measured by legal complaints communicated to the ILM. The total of 2,245 *proces verbaux* communicated to the Mission in 1983 was the highest ever. The number of *proces verbaux* for infraction of the Labor Code provision which prohibits employment of irregular-status aliens, rose from 549 in 1982 to 947 in 1983. The record number of 2,266 total *proces verbaux* had already been surpassed by mid-1984 as some 2,519 legal complaints had been communicated to the Mission by March of 1985.[22]

The increase in legal complaints was matched by increased court action, enforcement of the administrative fine, and penalties against employers of irregular-status aliens. About 1,300 court decisions ordering employers to pay fines of at least 2,000 francs were made during 1983. In Paris, the first six months of 1984 witnessed a 50 percent increase in the number of persons found guilty of employing illegal aliens relative to the 1983 period.[23] The director of the ILM summed up the judiciary's handling of employer sanctions over the first six months of 1984 as follows:

> The sampling of judgments rendered during the first half of 1984 by various courts appears to us as very indicative of the current tendency toward hardening of legal counteraction *vis a vis* employers of irregular-status aliens. The great majority of fines are to be found from now on above the minimum provided by the law, which denotes a clear-cut understanding by the courts of matters connected to manpower trafficking.[24]

The tone of recent French government assessments of their policy against illegal immigration and employment has been quite upbeat. There clearly is an official perception that enforcement of employer sanctions is beginning to bear fruit. The 1981-1983 period is seen as a stage where the policy instruments decided upon in 1981 were "broken in;" the policy outlined in 1981 on paper has since taken concrete form. In March of 1985, Mrs. Georgina Dufoix, the Minister of Social Affairs and National Solidarity and the spokesperson for the French government, declared that the results of enforcement of laws against illegal immigration and employment have a ". . . very encouraging balance sheet."[25]

WESTERN EUROPE'S COMMITMENT TO ENFORCEMENT

The French government clearly intends to pursue its current strategy against illegal immigration and employment. Employer sanctions play an important role in that strategy. Much the same can be said for the rest of continental Europe. The Swiss decision to adopt employer sanctions in 1984 seems to confirm the trend. The most recent German government report on enforcement of laws against black market or illegal employment in general suggests that the number of illegal aliens in the FRG may have decreased in recent years, but that it would be difficult to attribute any decrease to enforcement of laws such as employer sanctions.[26]

In September, 1984, the Parliamentary Assembly of the Council of Europe adopted a recommendation to the Committee of Ministers on "Clandestine Migration in Europe" which strongly endorsed the concept of employer sanctions. The recommendation called for ". . . laying down severe administrative and legal sanctions for employers of clandestine workers, intermediaries and traffickers, so as to impose the same charges on all firms and to prevent illicit migration by providing equal treatment and working conditions for migrant workers."[27]

Employer sanctions are components of broader strategies to curb illegal immigration and employment. Alone, they are not seen by Western European governments as a possible panacea for the profoundly complex phenomenon of illegal alien immigration and employment. They are, however, generally perceived as a valuable, indeed necessary, deterrent. Illegal immigration and employment is viewed as a long-term and likely increasingly severe problem in Western Europe. Employer sanctions are valued as a medium-term public policy instrument, but there are few illusions that employer sanctions alone could "solve" the problem over the long run.

The Western European experience with employer sanctions over the past decade reveals a number of problems and issues associated with laws penalizing employers for hiring irregular-status aliens. Perhaps the most important of these problems is a lack of general understanding of the phenomenon of illegal migration. Insufficiently understood is that employer sanctions represent only a stop-gap measure in the absence of an intelligent, long-term public policy response to the problem of illegal immigration. Enforcement of Western European employer sanctions has been hampered by a lack of understanding of the sociopolitical and labor market mechanisms which, in a sense, create illegal alien immigration and employment. The most recent annual report of France's ILM, however, suggests progress toward understanding the complex reality of the phenomenon.

PUBLICIZING THE COSTS OF ILLEGAL IMMIGRATION

The gap between governmental perceptions of the social disorder created by illegal immigration and employment on one hand, and the indifference of some institutions and elements of the public at large to the problem on the other also has hindered enforcement of employer sanctions. A key component in the overall strategies of several Western European governments is publicizing the gravity of the threat posed to society by illegal immigration and employment. Western European governments have found that their judicial systems in particular have been slow to regard illegal alien employment as a serious matter. Officials in both the FRG and France complain that judges have often been too lax with offending employers. However, the publicity campaigns undertaken to sensitize judges and the public at large to the perceived prejudicial consequences of illegal alien employment seem to have had an effect in both countries. Judiciaries now seem to be reponding to calls for firmer enforcement of laws prohibiting illegal alien employment.

Employer sanctions, like other laws, are expected to deter certain kinds of behavior. Most European employers comply with the laws voluntarily. It takes considerable manpower and other resources to penalize those employers who do not comply. In France and the FRG, enforcement of employer sanctions has been limited by manpower constraints. Hence, early enforcement strategies have emphasized exemplary cases to encourage voluntary compliance.

EMPLOYER TACTICS FOR EVASION

A minority of employers have responded to employer sanctions by going underground or concealing their activities through dummy or front businesses. The growth of subcontracting in particular often makes it difficult for labor inspectors and other agents to sanction employers of irregular-status aliens. Enforcement is complicated by legal, logistical, and physical constraints, but Western European governments have increased the manpower available for enforcement and have taken steps to improve coordination among various agencies and levels of government so as to prosecute employers hiding behind subcontractors, who often are themselves aliens, or using other devices to disguise their employment of illegal aliens.

The complexity of detecting, charging, and prosecuting many offending employers hinders enforcement. This is why specialized agents concentrate their enforcement activities on so-called exemplary cases, which are likely to be publicized and perhaps deter some employers from engaging in similar unlawful employment practices. Enforcement is also targeted against the worst offenders, those employers who most exploit irregular-status aliens. In general, the growth of the underground economy has weakened the deterrent effects of employer sanctions.

In a number of instances, political considerations have limited or precluded enforcement of employer sanctions. According to one observer, Swiss officials frequently "look the other way" if irregular-status aliens perform employment services regarded as necessary or vital.[28] Much the same has been true in agricultural areas of southern France, such as the *Midi*,[29] although the French government has brought charges against a number of farmers. Some industries with political clout and well-entrenched traditions of using illegal alien labor have been exempted from enforcement of employer sanctions. In cases like these, a long-term approach to eliminating the structural causes of illegal alien employment is needed. In these instances, foreign policy and trade practices become important components of a comprehensive approach to immigration policy. Most Western European employers, it should be stressed, view illegal alien employment as harmful to society and as an unfair labor practice.

EMPLOYER SANCTIONS AND DISCRIMINATION

The United Kingdom ruled out employer sanctions in part because it feared they might lead to additional discrimination against minorities. Fears of possible discriminatory effects of employer sanctions have been voiced in France as well.[30] Nonetheless, putative discriminatory effects of employer sanctions have not been an issue in continental Europe. In the United Kingdom, the Select Committee on Race Relations and Immigration actually recommended that employer sanctions be adopted.[31]

In France, there is little or no evidence that employer sanctions have increased employment discrimination against citizens and legally resident aliens of North African Arab background. Under the 1972 anti-discrimination law, a citizen or legally resident alien could seek redress if he or she were discriminated against by employers. Issues of discrimination are usually well publicized and often are quite politicized in France. Unfortunately, discrimination against persons of Arab background is a deadly serious and quite pervasive phenomenon; but employment discrimination against them appears to arise from factors other than employer sanctions. It cannot be ruled out that employer sanctions have contributed to a certain stigmatizing of North African Arabs which may indirectly affect their employment opportunities. Hence, there might be some unintended linkage between the French government's campaign against illegal immigration and the growing unemployment of Algerians and other North African legal residents in France.[32] But the government views the relationship differently. Control of illegal immigration and employment is seen as a necessary pre-condition to better integration of France's legally resident alien communities.

Racism is a problem all across Western Europe and most observers would agree that racism and racial tensions have grown in recent years. The French government's viewpoint that continued illegal immigration exacerbates discrimination and resentment against foreigners makes sense in this context. Employer sanctions, however, do not appear to have triggered this phenomenon. The causes of employment discrimination against persons of North African descent in France appear to lie elsewhere. The reorientation of French industrial policy in recent years, which has fostered mechanization and robotics, is a major factor in the rising unemployment of Algerians and other North African workers.

Many Western Europeans view the issue of discrimination and employer sanctions in terms other than those most commonly heard in the United States. They see illegal alien employment as inherently discriminatory and abusive of the aliens involved. Consequently, employer sanctions are viewed as a means of combatting discrimination and exploitation. It seems improbable that the ILO, in Convention 143, would adopt a concept that was inherently discriminatory against minorities and against the resident alien populations which are the ILO's special responsibility to protect.

IMPLICATIONS FOR THE UNITED STATES

There appears to be little factual basis for an argument that employer sanctions have not worked in Western Europe, so they will not work here. Such an argument grossly overstates what can be learned through comparison and conveniently ignores or distorts the actual Western European experience with employer sanctions. Employer sanctions simply have not been a major issue in Western Europe. Many Western European countries have them and view them in a generally positive light. The fact that the ILO recommends adoption of employer sanctions and that most continental European countries have them has had the effect of creating an international norm or expectation of some significance to the past U.S. debate over their enactment and the current discussion over their implementation.

The Western European experience with employer sanctions suggests that employer sanctions are not inherently discriminatory against racial or ethnic minorities. There is some potential for possible employment discrimination associated with employer sanctions in societies such as France and the United States, but the possibility of legal remedy and public vigilance should limit this potential problem. This potentiality should be weighed against salutary effects that can be expected from penalizing employers who exploit irregular-status aliens.

Employer sanctions and labor law enforcement often appear as elements of a zero-sum game in the U.S. approach to immigration reform—either you have one or the other. The United States clearly should take note that labor law enforcement and enforcement of employer sanctions go hand in hand in continental Europe.

Employer sanctions can be a valuable component of a broad strategy to combat illegal immigration and employment. Their effectiveness, however, is contingent upon a number of factors including, for example, the obvious need to commit sufficient personnel and financial resources.

But the effectiveness of employer sanctions also is linked to a comprehensive approach to illegal immigration and employment. If the wrong choices are made in a host of related policy areas—of taxation, trade, foreign affairs, and manpower policy—employer sanctions may only achieve Pyrrhic results.

This analysis of employer sanctions in Western Europe has attempted to illuminate the strengths, weaknesses, and limits of the concept of employer sanctions. Employer sanctions are a possible medium-term solution, or more appropriately, partial solution to the illegal immigration problem faced by industrial democracies. The long-term solution is to be found in policies which restructure labor markets and industries so as to eliminate the root causes of illegal immigration and employment.

NOTES

1. *Wall Street Journal*, May 30, 1985.
2. A series of measures adopted by the French cabinet on August 31, 1983, were implemented from late 1983 through 1984. See *Lutte Contre Les Trafics de Main d'Oeuvre*, (Prefecture de Paris, June 1984).
3. Mission de liaison interministerielle pour la lutte contre les trafics de main-d'oeuvre, *Bilan . . . pour l'annee 1979*, (Paris: Secretariat d'Etat aupres du Ministere du Travail et de la Participation, August 1980).
4. Ibid., p. 17.
5. Mission de liaison . . ., *Bilan . . . pour l'annee 1979*, 1.
6. Mission de liaison . . ., *Bilan . . . pour l'annee 1980*, (Paris: Secretariat d'Etat aupres du Ministre de la Solidarite Nationale Charge des Immigres, August 1981), 9.
7. Mission de liaison . . ., *Bilan . . ., pour l'annee 1979*, 2.
8. "Immigration Clandestine," *Bulletin Mensuel des Statis- tique du Travail*, number 106, (1983), 12.
9. Mission de liaison . . ., *Bilan . . . pour l'annee 1980*, 5.
10. Ibid.
11. See, for example, Jean-Pierre Berlan, "Labor in Southern French Agriculture," in Paul Martin, ed., *Migrant Labor in Agriculture: An International Comparison*, 61-62.
12. Mission de liaison . . ., *Bilan . . . pour l'annee 1980*, 10-13.
13. See respectively, R. Rist, p. 78 and Jacqueline Costa- Lascoux and C.W. de Wenden-Didier, "Les Travailleurs Immigres Clandestins en France," *Etudes Migration*, number 63 (1981), 7.
14. Interview, November 1981.
15. *Illegale Beschaeftigung und Schwarzarbeit duerfen nicht sein.*
16. ONI, *La Lutte Contre l'Emploi Irregulier et les Trafics de Main d'oeuvre etrangere*, Paris: ONICLASSEUR document, E.8.
17. Mission de liaison . . ., *Bilan . . . pour l'annee 1983*, 19.
18. Ibid., 19.
19. Ibid., 15.
20. Ibid., 21.
21. *Liaisons Socials*, Number 34/85, (March 25, 1985), 3.
22. *Le Quotidien de Paris*, March 26, 1985.

23. Ibid

24. Ibid.

25. Agence France-Presse dispatch, March 25, 1985.

26. *Fuenfter Bericht der Bundesregierung ueber Erfahrungen bei der Anwendung des Arbeitnehmerueberlassungsgesetzes*, 7, 34-35.

27. Unclassified U.S. Department of State telegram, September, 1984 and Mission de liaison . . ., *Bilan . . . pour l'annee 1983*, 159-161.

28. Remarks made by W.R. Bohning at a GMFUS - sponsored seminar in March 1985.

29. Op. Cit., Jean-Pierre Berlan, 61-62.

30. See, for example, Mission de liaison . . ., *Bilan . . . pour l'annee 1980*, 72.

31. "Immigration" Survey, April 1978, 112.

32. Jacqueline Costa-Lascoux expressed such a concern to the author in a recent letter.

Europe's Lessons for America
By Malcolm R. Lovell, Jr.

It took the United States fifteen years of legislative travail to enact in late 1986 penalties against employers of illegal aliens, a legislative concept that major continental European democracies have accepted and regarded as unexceptional for over a decade. The INS, the Department of Labor, and involved U.S. agencies are now on the unfamiliar ground once trod by European officials as they search for enforcement strategies that make employer sanctions deter illegal immigration effectively, economically, and humanely when they become fully effective in June 1987.

Most Western European states enacted employer sanctions in the mid-1970s (the FRG in 1975, France in 1976), but effective enforcement did not come immediately or automatically. This is the first important transatlantic lesson for the United States. Major European governments went through their own pro-longed period of trial, error and adaptation in making the same legal concept an effective means of immigration control and protection of labor standards. Most of them faced such predictable enforcement obstacles as unforeseen loopholes, bureaucratic confusion or indifference, inadequate enforcement resources, public apathy and toothless penalties. Each country dealt with these problems in its own way with varying degrees of success. And for most of them, it took five years or more to make the changes needed to make their laws begin to work. Now, of the eight European countries surveyed by the GAO in 1985, only one, Italy, still reports that its sanctions laws have failed to help. Not surprisingly, the Italians give as the reasons weak penalties and too few enforcement officers.[1]

Before turning to the European experience with employer sanctions it is fair to ask what is its validity for the United States? Are the historical, social, and economic conditions of the Western European industrial nations comparable? Or are they so different from our own as to be irrelevant? There are no doubt some great differences between our societies; but there are many similarities too, and we can learn from both.

SIMILARITIES IN THE MIGRATION EXPERIENCE

Many Americans are surprised to learn how much we have in common with Western Europe when it comes to immigration, both legal and illegal. Both Western Europe and the United States are advanced industrial societies with high standards of living, high employment by Third World standards, and low rates of population growth. Both societies have long-standing close ties, including past colonial relationships, with extensive areas of the Third World where population growth has often far outstripped economic growth. Both societies have high discretionary income, maturing populations, and a taste for leisure, which feeds demand for many labor-intensive, low-skilled personal services. Both societies have actively recruited foreign low-wage labor in the past, or tolerated heavy inflows of it, even allowing certain industries to become dependent on it. Growers and some service industries in France and Italy see workers from North Africa as essential, just as agricultural and light manufacturing interests in California and the Southwest feel an overriding need for Mexican workers. Both societies in the past had legal foreign labor recruitment policies—braceros in the United States and gastarbeiter in Europe—that fostered the dependence of certain industries and built networks of illegal immigration for use once those programs ended.

Beginning in the early 1960s, German and French employers were permitted unlimited access to foreign workers. Their governments encouraged and participated in recruiting foreign workers. By 1973, when the Arab oil embargo triggered a recession and an end to foreign labor recruitment, net legal immigration into France and the FRG was more than twice as large as into the United States, with the total foreign born population approaching eight million.

As in the United States, European employers had discovered that aliens are a very desirable work force; they will accept low status, dirty jobs ungrudgingly and at lower pay than native workers would demand (though foreign workers in the French automobile industry were becoming increasingly militant). The "push" factors—poverty, population growth, unemployment—mounted as fast in Turkey and Northern Africa as they did in Mexico or the Caribbean.

Past immigration practices in both Europe and the United States have spawned large welcoming foreign ethnic enclaves and employment networks that both attract and help accommodate further illegal immigration. With decolonization since World War II, and the widening income gap between have and have not nations, the United States and Europe have become huge cultural and economic magnets for restless and ambitious young Third World migrants, further enticed by cheap and easy international travel. Both the United States and Europe have huge populations of foreign students from the Third World, many of whom have used higher education as a path to permanent settlement. Both the United States and European states confront a vast surge of asylum claims as Third World migrants seek alternatives to more selective immigration procedures.

In both Europe and the United States, concern for individual rights, privacy and due process, and a tendency to regard illegal immigration as benign, have trammeled immigration law enforcement. At the same time, the United States and Europe have traditions of racial discrimination, though they have often differed significantly in the targets of their discrimination or in the way that discrimination is expressed.

America's dilemma of controlling a long and unguarded border is not unique. Despite their considerable efforts to regulate entry at borders and airports, the continental European states are quite permeable. Their frontiers are difficult to monitor, and their volume of international travel by air, sea, and land is high.

France's long borders with Spain and Italy are important entry points for illegal aliens from Africa and the Middle East. Senegalese and Malian illegal immigrants are smuggled in by Spanish "coyotes" in a fashion very similar to that on the Mexico-United States border, though the volume is much lower. The perilous route across the Pyrenees into France has its parallel in the rugged desert stretches between Mexico and the United States. And, like the United States, France has had little success in getting cooperation from its border neighbors, Italy and Spain, in suppressing illegal immigration.[2]

It was recognition of the ease of illegal entry that helped to convince first the European states, and then the United States, to adopt employer sanctions. When open industrial democracies cannot implement air tight border and port of entry controls, they must rely more on interior controls, particularly at the work place.

UNITED STATES-EUROPEAN DIFFERENCES

There are significant differences as well between United States and European societies, and they too can give us insights for effective enforcement. The United States is far larger in size and population than any single Western European nation. Within our huge nation exist broad regional, ethnic, and racial differences. Mining, lumbering, labor-intensive agriculture and the production of other raw material have greater relative weight in our economy than in Western Europe's. The demand in the U.S. economy for unskilled workers for low-wage, dangerous, high turnover jobs is greater than in Europe, a trend that has been amplified by the rapid growth of the service sector in the United States.

Most European nations are unitary. But our federalism goes well beyond that of even Europe's federal states such as the FRG and Switzerland, in affirming a stronger tradition of decentralization and state and local autonomy. These traditions, while revered, make for greater unevenness in the application of national laws and policies and often inhibit an active state and local role in such federal concerns as curbing illegal immigration.

Europeans have tended to regard immigration primarily as an option to meet labor needs, though France has encouraged it in the past for demographic reasons. But in the United States immigration has acquired a numinous character in our popular history, coming to be seen as a vital rite in our national self-expression. Thus, in U.S. politics, immigration at times becomes an end in itself rather than a practical instrument of manpower or population policy.

Fear of centralization in the United States and a heightened concern for personal rights and privacy have blocked the use of the secure, uniform government identification documents that are now taken for granted in much of

Western Europe. By European standards, America's entire non-system of personal identification is a crazy-quilt with basic vital statistics documents—the "breeder documents" on which all other ID documents are based—now issued by more than 8,000 jurisdictions with few safeguards against counterfeiting or fraud.

THE TRADITION OF VOLUNTARY COMPLIANCE

Offsetting some of the enforcement handicaps in the United States, is a stronger tradition among Americans of voluntary compliance with laws, even those that are burdensome or inconvenient.

This spirit of voluntary compliance may offer the best hope for effective implementation of employer sanctions. Critics of employer sanctions have argued that they will blizzard businesses under massive record-keeping requirements, or that large numbers of businesses will simply ignore the law. But the historical record of U.S. employers' cooperation in enforcing other federal laws is encouraging. On three occasions in the last four decades, America's employers have been called on to cooperate extensively with the federal government in enforcing far-reaching federal legislation affecting their work forces: the collection and remittance of social security payroll taxes in 1939, the introduction of the federal minimum wage laws beginning in 1938 and the withholding of federal income taxes beginning in 1943. Then, as now, opponents foresaw stifling bureaucratic burdens or protested against making employers become law enforcers. But the rates of voluntary compliance by employers, and the efficiency of these largely self-enforced systems, are commendable. A 1977-1979 congressionally ordered study found only 4.9 percent of the nation's 2.6 million employers then subject to the Fair Labor Standards Act to be in violation of the minimum wage provision—some of them unintentionally. Ninety-three cents of every tax dollar collected by the Internal Revenue Service comes in through voluntary compliance.

For employer sanctions as well, enlightened self-interest and civic spirit can work together in favor of legality. With proper encouragement and leadership from the U.S. government, American employers can come to accept employer sanctions—as have many of their European counterparts—as simply a good business practice, a safeguard ultimately for themselves against unfair competition or unearned business advantages for their competitors. It was enlightened self-interest that convinced Western Europe's most powerful employer group, the German Employers Federation (BDA), to endorse employer sanctions as needed to prevent exploitation of workers and to deter employers from unfair labor practices that undermine the German concept of a social state and social partnership.

EMPLOYER SANCTIONS AND LABOR LAWS: AN ENFORCEMENT PARTNERSHIP

A clear message of the European experience is that enforcement of employer sanctions gets best results when closely coupled with enforcement of labor laws. The German government requires agencies and institutions responsible for social security, job placement, industrial health and safety, unemployment compensation and disability insurance, and taxes along with immigration authorities and the police to share information on illegal alien employment. Special legislation was needed in the FRG in 1982 to make close information sharing possible. A similar commitment to interagency cooperation is apparent in France, which brought together immigration, law enforcement, labor standards, agriculture, social insurance, and revenue agencies together in a high-level interagency group to combat manpower trafficking.

The Department of Labor is a key to enforcement success in the United States no less than are its counterpart ministries in Europe. Congress recognized this in the Reform Act when it authorized in principle, but without specific sums, additional funds for the now seriously undermanned Wage and Hour Division and its Office of Labor's Employment Standards Administration Federal Contract Compliance (ESA) "*. . . in order to deter the employment of unauthorized aliens and remove the economic incentive for employers to exploit and use such aliens.*"[3]

ESA must now have a sizeable infusion of funds if it is to enforce existing labor standards laws adequately, much less be effective in enforcing employer sanctions. This is absolutely critical. But the recent history and current outlook on the Department of Labor's enforcement effort are not encouraging. The Wage and Hours Division now has fewer than one thousand compliance officers in the fifty states to enforce the Fair Labor Standards Act and other major labor laws. The number of covered employers and the division's tasks have grown steadily with the economy, but the division's enforcement manpower has actually declined since its peak in 1979. Newly legalized aliens may no longer fear to press back wage claims, adding further to ESA's workload. The number of unattended complaints of Fair Labor Standards Act violations nearly doubled between 1982 and 1986. Despite the new law's exhortation, Labor's initial budget proposals for 1988 allow further reductions in personnel for enforcement of wage and hour and federal contract compliance. Adding general employer sanctions to the division's overburdened agenda without major personnel additions will risk a massive enforcement failure that could write early doom for the overall credibility of the immigration reform law.

As Europeans learned from early enforcement disappointments, the clearest test of a government's determination to enforce employer sanctions effectively is its willingness to commit the resources in money and trained personnel needed.

A build-up of ESA's staffing would yield the added benefit of improved labor standards for much of our low-wage working population already hard pressed by a changing economy and international competition. Chiefly ESA's wage and hour and federal contract compliance arms should have compliance staff increases of the same order as those ordered for INS by the Reform Act— not less than 50 percent.

The Department of Labor's experience in enforcing the Farm Labor Contractors Registration Act also revealed an institutional conflict of interest: the concern of compliance officers that illegal aliens fearing exposure to INS would be reluctant to complain to them of other labor standards violations.[4] Some European labor enforcement officials were reluctant to enforce employer sanctions because of similar feelings—a reluctance European officials worked to overcome with stronger leadership and more enforcement specialization. Obviously, if such conflicts of interest persist, they must be resolved if the Department of Labor is to contribute fully to enforcement.

Enforcement could also be strengthened if other administrations of the Department of Labor whose activities put them in close contact with the workplace were to share information about patterns of illegal alien employment.

Federal and state employment offices must develop rigorous, consistent and uniform standards for verifying the work eligibility of applicants before making referrals. Current legislation makes verification of referrals optional for state employment services. The prospect of federally supported agencies referring aliens barred by federal law from working would hardly be positive leadership. It would be in the interest of employers to insist that state employment services carry out this responsibility. State agencies would gain by assuming this enforcement role.

Government-Wide Cooperation

The European experience also argues for closer cooperation among Cabinet level agencies. U.S. agencies with much to contribute would be the SSA and the IRS. Consistent with current privacy rules, the SSA should share with enforcement agencies information about presumptive employers of illegal aliens that have come to its attention in the course of its normal investigations. Current working arrangements between INS and the Inspector General of the Department of Health and Human Services should be expanded and strengthened to probe social security non-compliance and identification fraud. The 1976 tax reform legislation curbed the access of INS to SSA and IRS files, weakening an important enforcement tool. INS should be allowed greater use of that data for strict enforcement purposes, consistent with basic privacy safeguards.

The IRS has in the past probed illegal alien employment only to the extent that its revenue collections were affected. Since IRS has seen the leakage of this revenue as small compared to other forms of tax evasion, this has had a low priority.[5] IRS involvement now might yield greater returns. The employment of illegal aliens "off the books" has expanded along with the general growth of the underground economy that now troubles IRS. Legislative and regulatory changes are needed to permit IRS to share information with INS when its audits of employers reveal evidence of persistent employment of illegal aliens. Initial draft enforcement rules for employer sanctions grant INS and Department of Labor officials ready access to an employer's file of eligibility certifications. Similar access should be extended to officials of IRS.

State and local governments have increasingly tended to take a "leave it to the Feds" attitude on immigration control; some have even openly withheld their cooperation from INS. But France and the FRG in recent years have stepped up the involvement of local police forces. Local law enforcement agencies around the United States were warned away from a role in immigration enforcement by a directive of Attorney General Griffin Bell in 1978. While that ban was rescinded in 1983, local law enforcement agencies in many areas of the country are still dissuaded from enforcement cooperation by political pressures from immigrant groups, or because resources once devoted to helping INS have been diverted. Some stopped cooperating because INS was often too overtaxed to respond. State and local enforcement agencies for wage and hour, industrial safety, and other labor laws must be encouraged to share information with federal agencies about patterns of illegal alien employment. Federal cost sharing, training, grants, or other financial incentives would quicken state and local cooperation.

Closing the Loophole of Subcontracting

As their enforcement efforts matured, the Europeans discovered that additional measures were needed to halt the use of subcontracting and dummy fronts to evade the law. Some European employers showed remarkable adaptability. As a result of testimony to Congress about the European situation, our reform legislation showed foresight in applying sanctions to those who knowingly use "contracts, sub-contracts or exchanges" to hire illegal aliens. But the opportunities in sub-contracting for abuse and concealment will remain a major enforcement challenge. Some critics of sanctions have warned that larger firms who feel harassed by INS will subcontract out more work to smaller firms that are typically non-union and which will continue to hire illegal aliens. Unless enforcement is vigorous, the law could accelerate existing trends in industry to sub-contract a greater share of production—first to evade unionism and now labor standards and employer sanctions laws. The hostility of AFL-CIO affiliates to the increasing practice of sub-contracting reinforces the common interest between labor and immigration enforcement.

Employer Cooperation is Critical

The cooperation of employers in the United States is no less critical than it was in Europe. The Department of Labor and INS must continue to work closely with employers, particularly in immigrant-impacted areas, to encourage voluntary compliance and full use of citizens, legal residents, and the newly legalized to meet their workforce needs. INS can build on its experience with "Operation Cooperation" since the 1970s, in which it has worked with nearly 1,100 key employers or employer groups nationwide to encourage voluntary use of legal resident or citizen labor. Voluntary compliance can rely only partly on goodwill and civic spirit, it must be accompanied by both convincing incentives and disincentives.

Because of the chronic shortage of investigators, INS, like European enforcement agencies, must continue to concentrate on notorious violators, targetting its limited enforcement efforts to areas of greatest payoff. As many as four million employers in the United States are estimated to be subject to the sanction legislation. But only about 10 percent of them, INS estimated, now employ illegals.[7] INS's staggering monitoring and enforcement task becomes considerably more manageable if the agency can concentrate its investigative efforts on the relatively small percentage that INS will know from long experience to be likely offenders.

But even after it adds the some 400 additional compliance personnel for employer sanctions planned by 1988, INS will still be hard pressed to cover all potential violators. If INS is to rely on deterrence through convictions of notorious violators, early success is essential to that strategy. INS and the Justice Department must pick the initial cases for prosecution with particular care. Defeat of the government at the outset in major exemplary cases will severely damage the credibility and momentum of the enforcement effort.

INS knows from decades of experience which areas and industries most often use illegal alien labor and where to concentrate its enforcement effort for the greatest payoff. At the same time, it is essential that enforcement be uniform across all industries and geographical regions. The law will lose credibility and business competition would be distorted if, for example, the government enforces the law more rigorously against the New York area apparel industries than those of Los Angeles County; or if growers in the San Joaquin valley receive greater lenience than those of the lower Rio Grande valley; or if construction entrepreneurs in Houston are free to flout the law, while those of that city's hotel and restaurant trade are held closely to account.

It is dismayingly clear from European and American experience that chronic reliance on illegal alien labor has deep roots that cannot be removed overnight. The preference of some employers for illegal workers will not change simply with the implementation of employer sanctions, even if suitable citizen workers are offered. They must accept other changes in their basic approach toward labor and its use, and some of these changes may be disruptive for them.

An illustration of the resistance to change is apparent in "Operation Jobs," a targeted effort by INS in the spring of 1982 that removed nearly 6,000 better paid illegal aliens from jobs at some 560 work sites and encouraged their replacement with legal residents. Subsequent assessments of "Operation Jobs" have shown that the number of replacements by citizen workers was low, or that those citizens and legal residents taking the jobs did not remain in them long. The mixed success of the effort—often exaggerated by opponents of employer sanctions—stems in part from some enforcement restraints that the passage of employer sanctions and an increase in enforcement personnel will now overcome, and in part from entrenched employer attitudes. Chronic employers of illegals at that time, with no legal obligation to hire legal workers, had no incentive to change long-set employment preferences. They simply replaced the illegals removed with other illegals. Delays by state employment services in making referrals for the job openings, or their inability to make referrals without an employer request, prevented the rapid filling of vacancies,[8] suggesting a need for better employment service procedures and closer cooperation among agencies. Complaints of high turnover among citizen replacement workers were often self-serving as they ignored the high turnover rate of illegal workers in those same industries where pay, upward mobility, and working conditions are chronically poor.

With employer sanctions now the law of the land, "Operation Cooperation" has become the Legally Authorized Workers (LAW) program. LAW is a co-ordinated effort of INS, the Department of Labor and other concerned agencies to encourage compliance among employers and help them find legal workers for jobs. The success of LAW will depend on the numbers and effectiveness of compliance officers, cooperation among enforcement agencies and their willingness to give it adequate priority, and employers' conviction that the risk of detection of violations is great and the penalties steep.

An educational approach would be to encourage employers to post notices for all employees, actual and prospective, of the requirements of the immigration law and the penalties that employers and employees risk in violating it. Following the practice used in the 1960s and 1970s in extending Equal Employment Opportunity, employers might also affirm their commitment to hire only lawfully admitted workers in their vacancy notices and advertisements. Employers who make and display such warnings, should have these practices taken into account as part of the grounds for an affirmative defense in the case of prosecution.

But education must go hand-in-hand with convincing disincentives. Fines assessed must be carefully evaluated to see if they are really deterring, or are simply accepted as a cost of doing business. Stronger penalties used by the Europeans might be adapted for use here. In France, repeat offenders risk seizure of tools and equipment, similar to INS's current authority to seize the conveyances of alien smugglers. In the FRG, offending employers who are aliens risk deportation.

Properly enforced, employer sanctions can become a major safeguard for the wages and conditions of millions of immigrants and less privileged U.S. workers. But weakly enforced, as opponents of sanctions have warned, they can become another device for unscrupulous employers to exploit or intimidate illegal alien workers, while shifting the costs of violations to the workers themselves. The new law explicitly forbids employers from seeking indemnity bonds or guarantees from workers. But those determined to evade the law have more subtle ways of covering their risks at the expense of workers that will require enforcement vigilance. The prohibition of indemnity bonds should be interpreted broadly or redefined as necessary to abuses with similar intent such as special check-offs, deductions, kick-backs, or contributions to special repatriation contingency funds.

Creating the Political Climate for Success

Worth stressing is that in the first several years after enactment of employer sanctions, change was slow in Europe. Time was needed to explain the law, and to adapt and educate the bureaucracy and the public. Time will be needed in the United States as well, though excessive delay may risk raising public cynicism or disillusion about the likelihood of change. We should guard against the "quick fix mentality," the tendency of politicians to equate the passage of a law with real change and to turn to other problems. Visible support at the cabinet level of government and continuing congressional interest are needed to sustain momentum. It will take time and patient leadership for the public, employers of illegal aliens, public officials at all levels, smugglers and the illegal aliens themselves to realize that our priorities have changed and that employer sanctions are now the law of the land.

Some of the major steps INS must take to enforce employer sanctions successfully will also have high non-monetary costs in determination, discipline, and political will. INS must have the close and visible backing of the White House, the Attorney General, and Congress for enforcing employer sanctions evenhandedly in major illegal immigrant impact areas. One major handicap in Europe cited in the 1982 GAO study was insufficient zeal among prosecutors who, like some of their U.S. counterparts, tended to see immigration violations as benign or promising only a low pay-off. Strong leadership and clarity of priorities will be needed here as much as in Europe.

If enforcement is successful, it will inevitably pinch some industries, which will cry foul or demand relief. This has been the European experience also. It will take the greatest of discipline in Congress and at the upper levels of the executive branch to resist the temptation to interfere with INS measures or to grant *ad hoc* exemptions.

Secure Identification: An Imperative

Western European societies show that effective tamper-proof personal identification systems are compatible with high regard for individual privacy and rights. The availability of secure, universal identification is the single greatest difference between the United States and most European countries. The new

U.S. law relies for verification on early counterfeited or abused ID documents such as birth certificates, driver's licenses, foreign passports bearing INS authorization stamps and social security cards. The current system of identifiers is an invitation to wide-spread abuse and a defense for ill-intentioned employers, but a source of confusion for the conscientious. The current verification and record-keeping provisions of the law are a burden for employers that could undercut their support for enforcement. The executive branch needs to move rapidly toward a secure universally applicable system for verifying the eligibility to work of all U.S. residents without discrimination, while lessening the verification burden on employers and the attendant risks of discrimination charges.

Current enforcement practices have created nine categories of resident aliens with unrestricted right to work and fourteen more non-immigrant categories with temporary or conditional work authority. The variety of documents invites abuse and confuses the well intentioned employer. INS should move toward a single secure ID document for all with work authorization and should seek reinstatement of the annual alien registration requirement ended in 1981. Both measures would ease monitoring of the alien population and provide vital demographic and labor force data.

Paying for the Enforcement Effort We Need

The INS itself must receive significantly greater resources if it is to make employer sanctions effective. It will require the full $900 million addition called for in the reform legislation over the next two years, with that higher level of spending sustained in ensuing years. While much of the funds must necessarily come from general revenues, more ways must be found to shift more of the cost to both the beneficiaries of our immigration system and those who abuse it. Significantly higher fees would not be unreasonable for those applying for or receiving asylum immigrant visas, change of status, or family or labor preference petitions. Congress should again consider earlier unsuccessful proposals to levy a fee on users of special replenishment and temporary agricultural workers, thus leveling the cost advantage of foreign workers over domestic ones while building a trust fund for underwriting research and training to help foreign labor users develop permanent domestic labor alternatives. The FRG now recovers enforcement costs by, in certain cases, requiring the convicted employer of illegal aliens to pay the repatriation travel cost of aliens hired—a major cost item in the INS budget.

Employer Sanctions: A Safeguard for the Vulnerable Newcomer

Europeans are more inclined than most Americans to see employer sanctions not just as a means of immigration control, but as a way of protecting vulnerable workers, whether native or foreign, against the neglect and deliberate exploitation inherent in illegal alien employment. Labor unions were leaders in the fight in

Europe for employer sanctions. The German Trade Union Federation (DGB), began to appeal sanctions as early as 1968. In France it was the Socialist Party, with its strong identification with the working class, and with the backing of the unions, that gave priority to toughening the enforcement of employer sanctions after it took power in the early 1980s. Unions in Sweden, Denmark and Austria are virtual partners of their governments in enforcing sanctions.

It was the United Nation's oldest specialized organization, the ILO, where trade union leaders deliberate together with government and employer representatives, that in 1975 passed Resolution 143 giving employer sanctions international acceptance. The ILO saw then the need ". . . to avoid the excessive and uncontrolled or unassisted increase of migratory movements because of their negative social and human consequence," and to eliminate the abuses of ". . . illicit and clandestine trafficking in labor." Article 6 of the ILO Convention calls for provisions in national laws or regulations ". . . for the effective detection of the illegal employment of migrant workers and for the definition and the application of administrative, civil, and penal sanctions."[9]

American labor, the AFL-CIO, also has supported employer sanctions legislation since the early 1970s, leading the drive for enactment of California's prototypical employer sanctions law, the Dixon Arnett Act, in 1971. The AFL-CIO, however, has become less resolute in recent years as some key affiliates in apparel, agriculture, hotel and restaurant, food processing, and services have recruited illegal alien workers. Employer sanctions should be seen as the latest in 100 years of labor-backed effort to ensure that United States immigration laws protect the wage and standards of American workers, beginning with the 1885 law prohibiting the entry of foreign contract labor.

While the new United States law indeed aims at curbing the flow of illegal workers, current legal immigration trends can be counted on to bring larger numbers of the less skilled into our economy for years to come. Herein lies a significant and potentially challenging difference between current United States circumstances and those existing in the 1970s when the Europeans adopted employer sanctions. Faced with severe economic slowdowns, the Europeans virtually halted legal immigration. Job growth in Europe at that time was slow and remains so. But the United States has enacted sanctions at a time of fair job growth and with the prospects for burgeoning legal immigration. Estimates range from 100,000 to 750,000 for the number of new workers who will legally enter our labor force under the Special Agricultural Workers (SAW) legalization arrangements of the 1986 immigration reform law. As these new workers tire of their farm job and begin moving into less-skilled urban occupations, they will be replaced with additional legalized foreign workers under the RAW provisions permitted by the law. Thousands more will work seasonally each year under the new law's eased temporary agricultural workers arrangement (H-2A).

Then, amnesty for those proving they entered illegally before 1982 will bring hundreds of thousands more illegal workers out of the shadows, and enable them to seek their full rights and better working conditions. Legal immigration, pulled by the suction pump of family reunification and now surpassing 600,000 a year, will yield rising numbers of less-skilled newcomers.

In making its generous offer of legalization or safe haven, U.S. society undertakes a solemn obligation to give the full protection of its laws to those entitled to be legalized. The European experience shows that without employer sanctions the task of integrating large numbers of vulnerable, newly legalized residents who have built some equity in our system would be more difficult. Their wages and labor standards, the very worth of their legal status, would be most at risk if employers remained free to hire and exploit illegal aliens. Most importantly, employer sanctions can help provide an opportunity for jobs and better wages for the twelve million to fifteen million citizens and legal residents who are now jobless or working part-time because that is the only employment available.

TOWARD AN ECONOMY WITHOUT ILLEGAL ALIEN WORKERS

Critics have often pointed out that employer sanctions were not a panacea in Europe. Indeed they are not. But the European countries that have successfully applied them never regarded them as more than one instrument in an array of policies against illegal immigration. Sanctions have yielded best results when coordinated with a range of manpower, law enforcement, and economic policies.

Among possible complementary steps for the United States, better management of our labor force stands out. For general economic and social progress, as well as to reduce reliance on illegal alien workers, we must make full and efficient use of our potential domestic labor force, including displaced workers, willing senior citizens, the handicapped, women, and minorities, as well as the large numbers who will enter it through the legalization and amnesty provisions of the new law.

Reduced demand for illegal immigrants would be only a byproduct of steps the United States might take to improve the proficiency of the domestic labor force and rationalize its use. While this extensive agenda cannot be discussed in detail here, it is clear that we must:

—Improve the labor market service performance of the United States and state employment services and strive for closer cooperation among INS, the employment services and employers themselves in providing labor market services to legal workers.
—Dovetail our job training and job counseling efforts to meet manpower needs of illegal immigrant-dependent industries.
—Make our present immigration laws more responsive to the country's needs for skills, with less emphasis on reunification of the non-nuclear family and adult children.

The time has also come to consider whether the survival of some industries dependent on foreign labor justifies the high socialized cost of maintaining them. A few of the most egregious examples can be cited. The carefully protected domestic sugar industry relies on H-2 workers and illegals in south Florida, and mostly illegals in Texas and Louisiana. No one can defend an arrangement that compels U.S. consumers to buy U.S.-produced sugar at prices well above the world price, thus underwriting American sugar producers who employ predominantly foreign labor. At the same time, low-cost producers of sugar in the Caribbean or the Philippines, with their U.S. export quotas, now cut to the lowest levels in 100 years, must lay off workers, who then become candidates for illegal migration to the United States.

Advocates of New York garment producers, which are heavily dependent on illegal alien labor, deplore job losses to imports and lobby Congress against admission of lower cost foreign apparel imports. Domestic clothing manufacturers' spokesmen have even argued that the socially beneficial role their industry plays as an avenue of entry for immigrants itself justifies protection.[10]

Strong protectionist impulses once again are aimed at weakening economic development and job creation schemes in the Caribbean basin that not only can help stabilize the area, but can reduce the pool of potential immigrants. Restrictions on the duty free entry of products from Caribbean Basin Initiative (CBI) countries are in effect a vote for more illegal immigration. Mexico's current best source of new jobs, the In-Bond (Maquiladora) industries, which now employ 300,000 Mexican workers, is now under renewed pressures from some U.S. unions and other special interests.

The exceptions for agriculture in the new immigration reform law help perpetuate agriculture's archaic labor policies, invite future immigration abuses, and sap the moral authority of U.S. immigration policies. They should be ended promptly. Western growers have disingenuously but successfully brandished the lobbying appeal of the family farm and low consumer prices to win continuation of the subsidy of foreign labor, thus delaying the mechanization the labor-intensive fruit and vegetable industry needs to meet growing foreign competition. In fact, this labor subsidy goes often not to small or struggling family farms but to large-scale operations owned by banks, conglomerates, and oil companies. The citrus industry, a major employer of illegals, has corporate and absentee ownership of 80 to 90 percent. Citrus has overexpanded because of tax preferences, competition-limiting marketing orders, and subsidized labor and water. Some 10,000 citrus growers stand as a powerful lobby for protection against low-cost citrus from Latin America.[11]

EMPLOYER SANCTIONS: A DISCIPLINE FOR COMPETITIVENESS

Western Europe and the United States have together seen their competitiveness decline in the changing international economy. A significant question for the economic future of both societies is the extent to which the easy availability of cheap, flexible labor has distorted investment decisions, rewarding the over-building of low productivity industries and discouraging technological innova-tion. Faced with the choice between long-term commitments to labor-saving capital improvements and hiring more inexpensive, disposable labor to increase output, too many European and American employers in hard-pressed industries have opted for labor. But even with the implicit subsidy of cheap foreign labor, some such industries have still needed protection to survive over the longer term.

Employers, both European and American, in such sectors have experienced the same "treadmill" effect from their reliance on foreign labor. The availability of foreign workers lowers employers' incentive to restructure wages and working conditions to attract and hold domestic workers. The widening wage gulf between their firms and more technologically advanced ones then causes domestic workers to abandon their industries, creating further "labor shortages" to be met by the importation of still more foreign workers.[12] Getting off the treadmill will be painful for some, but good for the country.

Screening illegal alien from jobs and replacing them permanently with legal residents will often demand changes in the hiring practices, cost distribution and production methods of dependent employers. High among requirements will be greater attention to job content, motivation, training, efficiency and wages. It must be accepted that some marginal firms may not survive this process, or may find that they must change their service or product. Acceptance of the conse-quences of effective employer sanctions means acceptance of the possibility of fewer jobs than might have been created in our economy in the long run, but better ones.

NOTES

1. U.S. General Accounting Office, *Information on Selected Countries Employment Prohibition Laws*, (Washington, D.C., October 1985).

2. Mark J. Miller and D.G. Papademetriou, "Immigration Reform: The United States and Western Europe Compared," *The Unavoidable Issue: U.S. Immigration Policy in the 80s*, (Philadelphia Institute for the Study of Human Issues, 1983).

3. House Subcommittee on Labor Standards, Fair Labor Standards Act: *Hearings on HR6103*, 97th Cong., 1st and 2nd sess., May 19 and June 29, 1981 and April 26 and May 12, 1982.

4. Philip J. Martin and Suzanne Vaupel, *Activity and Regulation of Farm Labor Contractors* (San Pueblo, CA: Giannini Foundation of Agricultural Economics of the University of California, 1986).

5. David North, *Enforcing the Immigration Law: A Review of the Options*, (Center for Labor and Migration Studies, Washington, D.C. 1980).

6. Wayne Cornelius, "Simpson-Mazzoli vs. the Realities of Mexican Immigration," in Cornelius and Anzaldua Montoya (eds.), *America's New Immigration Law: Origins, Rationales and Political Consequences*, (La Jolla, CA: Center for U.S.-Mexican Studies, 1983)

7. INS estimates, 1982.

8. INS Memorandum from Acting Associate Commissioner for Enforcement to Commissioner of October 28, 1983 regarding "Analysis of the Enhanced Interior Enforcement Project."

9. ILO Convention 143 "Concerning Migration in Abusive Conditions and the Promotion of Equality of Opportunity and Treatment of Migrant Workers," Article 6, 1975.

10. Senate Subcommittee on International Trade. *Textile and Apparel Trade Enforcement Act: Hearing*, 99th Cong., 1st Sess., July 15, 1985. 174, 605–606.

11. Philip Martin, unpublished letter to the *New York Times*, September 29, 1986.

12. Philip Martin and Mark Miller, "Guestworkers: Lessons from Europe," *Industrial and Labor Relations Review*, Vol. 3, No. 33, April 1980.

REFERENCES

Conner, Roger: "A View of Employer Sanctions from Europe," Appendix to a Statement before the Subcommittee on Immigration and Refugee Policy, Committee of the Judiciary, U.S. Senate, Washington, D.C., June 18, 1985.

German Federal Minister of the Interior, "Survey of the Policy and Law Regarding Aliens in the Federal Republic of Germany" (in English), Bonn, September 1985.

Martin, Philip, "Germany's Guestworker," unpublished paper, January 1981.

Martin, Philip L and Miller, Mark J., "Guestworkers: Lessons from Europe," *Industrial and Labor Relations Review*, Vol. 33, No. 3, April 1980.

Miller, Mark J. and Papademetriou, D.G.: "Immigration Reform: The United States and Western Europe Compared," *The Unavoidable Issue: U.S. Immigration Policy in the 80's*; (Philadelphia, PA: Institute for the Study of Human Issues, 1983).

Mission de Liaison Interministerielle pour la Lutte contre les trafics de main-d'oeuvre, Bilan, 1983, Paris, 1984.

Power, Johnathan, "Western Europe's Migrant Workers," Minority Rights Group, London, 1984.

Schiffer, Eckart, Ministerial Director, German Federal Ministry of the Interior: "Illegal Employment of Aliens in the Federal Republic of Germany," unpublished paper (in English), Bonn, October 10, 1985.

U.S. General Accounting Office, *Information on the Enforcement of Laws Regarding Employment of Aliens in Selected Countries*, Washington, D.C., August 31, 1982.

U.S. General Accounting Office, *Information on Selected Countries' Employment Prohibition Laws*, Washington, D.C., October 1985.

Werner, H., "Post War Labour Migration in Western Europe - An Overview," *International Migration*, Vol. XXIV - No. 3, September 1986.

Principles vs. Expediency in U.S. Immigration Policy
By Lawrence Fuchs

Many of the great books of the Western tradition, including classical Greek and Roman texts, describe the perils, anguish, adventure and opportunity of migration long before nations had immigration policies. The Old and New Testaments are particularly rich in stories of what we now would call migration. Abraham, following Yahweh's instructions, sought permanent settlement in a new land. Later, Ruth left her people to join her mother-in-law, Naomi, in an example of family reunification. Joseph was sold to the Ishmaelites for twenty pieces of silver by Midianite merchants and was taken to Egypt to be sold again as a slave. When his brothers came into Egypt, Joseph accused them of having entered the kingdom unlawfully as illegal alien spies. Then Joseph's family left Canaan with the thought of staying in the land of Goshen for a while and taking charge of Pharoah's livestock. Today, like the Basque sheepherders of the West, they would receive H-2 visas as temporary workers. But they were enslaved, and their descendants had to remain for more than 400 years until, in the central story of Jewish history and the paradigmatic example of flight from oppression, they crossed the Red Sea out of Egypt and back to the Promised Land to save the lives of their first born sons. Later, the Israelites established cities of refuge for asylees, a phenomenon common to many civilizations, and throughout the Old Testament there are stories of resettlement, exile and temporary migration. Migration stories continue in the New Testament, where Jesus, Mary and Joseph fled to Egypt because of their fear of persecution by Herod; and following the crucifixion of Jesus, the Apostles went as missionaries to Macedonia, Cyprus, Syria and Rome as what our immigration laws today would call non-immigrant aliens.

Continuing into the Christian era, the Muslims, the Crusaders and others carried forward the story of irregular migration. Military campaigns and conquests resulted in the principle population shifts before 1600—one thinks of the displacement of hundreds of thousands before the advancing armies of Genghis Khan and his successors from Mongolia as they marched in the twelfth and thirteenth centuries through what is now the Soviet Union, the Middle East and northern India. Group movements have persisted. The displacement of native American Indians, the transporting of African slaves to the Americas, and the movement of European soldiers sent to conquer and rule in Asia and Africa are examples. But after 1600 with the opening of new lands, particularly in the Americas, Australia and New Zealand, the movement of individuals and family groups who were dissatisfied with economic conditions at home began to dominate a new era in migration. Younger sons, faced with limited economic op-

245

portunity, sought advantage in the Americas. Imprisoned debtors and criminals from England earned their freedom by settling in the American colonies; more prominent citizens were enticed by land grants.

By the nineteenth century a new round of technological innovations made it even easier to traverse vast distances. A transportation revolution—steam vessels, canals, railroads—meant that Germans, Norwegians, Swedes and others from inland states of Europe could take a train to a port, sail to the United States, and then board another train bound for the American heartland. Failing peasant farmers from Austria-Hungary, unemployed agricultural laborers from southern Italy, Mennonites and Jews fleeing persecution in Russia, all began to flock to the United States in the last decades of the nineteenth century. An Italian government report declared that "immigration is a necessity . . . it would be terrible if the safety valve did not exist, this possibility of finding work elsewhere." Most immigrants—whether from Italy, Greece, Poland, Russia, Germany, Scandinavia, England, French-Canada, China, Japan, the Philippines or Korea—came to find work and some even to own land. Only among the Irish did a large proportion come out of desperation due to famine.

The United States was the main but not the only destination of immigrants. Between 1820 and 1940 approximately 5.5 million immigrants settled in Brazil. Almost as many went from Spain, Italy and France to Argentina. In 1889, the Chinese population of French-Indochina was 60,000; fifteen years later, it had doubled. Chinese fleeing poverty and seeking work left for Southeast Asian countries in such large numbers that by 1970 it was estimated that they constituted 34 percent of the population of Malaysia, 30 percent in Kampuchea and 15 percent in South Vietnam, with a total of more than twenty-one million expatriates from China living in Asia outside of China, Taiwan, Hong Kong and Macao.

Two world wars, a worldwide depression and the implementation of restrictionist immigration policies by many countries, including the United States, combined to lessen the worldwide flow of voluntary migrants between 1914 and 1945. But the number of refugees and other involuntary migrants rose dramatically. The movement of most people up to and in the years immediately following World War II had less to do with the economic inequality of nations than with political revolution and persecution. The Russian Revolution of 1917 and its aftermath left about 1.5 million Russians in other parts of Europe and Asia. Large scale expulsion and negotiated exchanges of population in Greece, Turkey, Bulgaria and Armenia occurred after World War I. The rise of dictatorships in Spain, Germany and Italy in the 1930s created new refugees. Over one million people, mostly Jews, fled from Germany during the rise of Naziism before World War II, and perhaps five times this many would have fled if democratic nations had been willing to receive them.

Large population movements occurred during and immediately after World War II, as ethnic minorities were exchanged, expelled or repatriated. Nation building within realigned boundaries often brought about political efforts to oust ethnic minorities, and as a result almost twenty million people in eastern and central Europe, including most of the ethnic Germans in Eastern European countries, were moved, and approximately five million Japanese were repatriated from other parts of Asia following the war. The creation of new states, as colonial powers withdrew from Asia, Africa and the Middle East, also precipitated huge refugee movements. For example, the partition of the Indian subcontinent in 1947 caused the frantic movement of about twelve million Hindus, Muslims and Sikhs in the space of one year, about half going from Muslim Pakistan to Hindu India and the other half in the opposite direction.

Wars and revolutions in the last forty years have continued to produce masses of refugees and displaced persons. In Asia several million Kuomintang supporters left for Taiwan and Hong Kong after the Communist victory in China in 1949; we read almost daily about Cubans in the United States, Ethiopians in Somalia, Afghans in Pakistan, Cambodians in Thailand and Vietnamese in a half dozen industrial countries—driven out of their homelands by tyrannical regimes. In all, there are ten to twelve million refugees in the world, most of whom probably will never go back to their countries of origin.

For the past fifty years we have lived in an age of refugees, not of lawful immigration. Only a small portion of the migration of peoples today is what we define as lawful immigration—that is, the choice of a new permanent residence by individuals who are accepted by a new country as presumptive intending citizens. Apart from the United States, which accepted close to 601,000 immigrants in 1986, and Pakistan, only a few other countries, such as Australia and Canada are nations of immigration. Great Britain received immigrants from Commonwealth countries, especially India, Pakistan and the Caribbean, beginning in the mid-1950s, but recently has become extremely restrictive. Restriction is the norm in European countries with respect to immigration. Yet, they and nearly all developed countries are frightened by two other kinds of migration, each of which presents a different set of issues: first, refugees and asylees; and second, temporary workers to do jobs it is presumed most natives will not do at prevailing wages and working conditions.

REFUGEES AND ASYLEES

The refugee-asylee issue evokes a strong moral interest in most countries in Europe, the Western Hemisphere, Africa and the Near East. Their concern was reflected in the effort to build international institutions to deal with it beginning in December of 1946 when the United Nations General Assembly created the International Refugee Organization. Two years later the United Nations proclaimed the universal Declaration of Human Rights, in which Article Fourteen states that "everyone has the right to seek and to enjoy another country's asylum from persecution."

A year later the General Assembly decided to appoint a United Nations High Commissioner for Refugees, promulgating a statute which authorized that organization to take as its responsibility "any other person who is outside the country of his nationality, or if he has no nationality, the country of his former habitual residence, because he has or had well founded fear of persecution by reason of his race, religion, nationality or political opinion and is unable or, because of such fear, is unwilling to avail himself of the protection of the government of the country of his nationality. . .''

That definition was adopted by the General Assembly in July of 1951 via a text of the Convention Relating to the Status of Refugees, defining the conditions to be fulfilled in order to benefit from refugee status and describing in detail the essential rights which states are urged to extend to refugees. But in this century of the uprooted, nations were reluctant to accept such a broad definition and it took three years to secure the adherence of the first six. The United States did not embody the UN definition of refugee in its own laws until 1980. But the United States did take on the major responsibility for funding the Office of the High Commissioner and led the western nations in admitting refugees, particularly those from Southeast Asia. Today the Convention has been accepted by ninety-seven states and is regarded as one of the major instruments in the field of international humanitarian law. But international law is fragile, a weak reed on which to base our hopes for social justice; and most nations, including the United States, Canada, Australia and France, all of whom have cut back recently on the number of Indo-Chinese refugees they are willing to accept, think much less of international law than national interest in setting refugee policies.

The Indo-Chinese are no longer the major refugee problem in the world. Probably four to five million Afghans have left their homeland since 1978— representing one-third of the Afghan population prior to the invasion of the Soviet Union—and constituting almost one-half of the world's estimated refugee population today. Probably about 3.5 million of them now live in Pakistan, mostly in refugee camps. That their plight is not more desperate is due mainly to contributions from the United States and, to a lesser extent, from other wealthy nations, the goodwill of Pakistan, and the effectiveness of the Office of the High Commissioner. The other great source of refugee migrations, the Horn of Africa, has sent at least 1.3 million seeking asylum from Ethiopia to neighboring countries. The Sudan and Somalia are both desperately poor countries, but between them they hold more than 1.5 million refugees today.

What patterns can we pick out with regard to recent refugee migrations? The first is that the vast majority of refugees have been created by communist dictatorships in Indo-China, Cuba, Angola, Ethiopia, Eastern Europe, the Soviet Union and by the war in Afghanistan, and that communist governments make no contribution to any of the international refugee organizations. A second pattern is that the wealthier democratic countries will take refugees primarily when they have an historic tie, either political or cultural, which encourages them to do so, as the United States has done with the Cuban and Indo-Chinese refugees and as France has done with the Indo-Chinese and China with ethnic Chinese from that same region. A third pattern is that asylum policy is mainly a function of foreign policy. That is particularly true of communist countries but also of the United States, which applies a particularly rigorous test to asylum claimants from El Salvador, and which now has under review a revision of its asylum policy to give special favor to those claiming asylum based on a well founded fear of persecution only in communist countries, a position which would fly in the face of the intentions of the authors of the Refugee Act of 1980.

Sweden has a liberal definition of "refugee" and "asylee." It follows the 1951 Convention text but has added a paragraph which broadens the definition of the term "persecution." It includes as refugees persons who because of political conditions do not want to return to their country and "who can present important reasons in support" of that determination. Sweden had 12,000 persons seek asylum in 1984 and admitted 9,700, which is only 3,000 less than the United States admitted, a country with over ten times as many applicants pending.

But even Sweden—in close proximity to Poland, the German Democratic Republic and the Soviet Union—and with increasing pressure from asylum claimants from the Middle East—is affected in its asylum policy by domestic politics and in 1986 adopted a practice of flying undesired presumptive asylum claimants out of the country before they have an opportunity to claim asylum. All governments in Europe and the United States and Canada are wary of the abuse that intending immigrants, who otherwise would be illegal, are able to make of international asylum law. Just by claiming asylum, such persons acquire basic rights in democratic countries. In the United States, for example, asylum claimants are entitled to an elaborate review process which may enable them to stay in the country for several years.

While the United States should not be expected to have as broad a definition of "refugee" or "asylee" as the Swedes employ, given the proximity of this country to millions of people to the south who live in unstable and dangerous political conditions, neither should it politicize its asylum policy in violation of the 1951 UN convention, the 1961 Protocol of the United Nations on refugees, and its own Refugee Act of 1980 to the extent that it has. It is the politicization of asylum policy which has brought forth the sanctuary movement as an alternative to the failure on the part of the United States to grant extended voluntary departure to those fleeing civil war in El Salvador, a subject to which I will return.

This serious flaw in U.S. refugee and asylum policy should not obscure the fact that the United States has taken the lead on international refugee questions in recent years, in contrast to its behavior in the two decades before World War II when it had no refugee policy and when the United States turned back thousands of Jews fleeing Nazi persecution. The Holocaust produced a new consciousness about the importance of saving refugee lives and a series of special refugee acts that passed after World War II culminated in the passage in 1980 of the Refugee Act. It is reasonable that asylum claimants be expected to make a strong case that they have a well-founded fear of persecution should they be returned to their home countries, but that is a standard which is extremely difficult to prove for individuals who arrive in this country without papers or corroborative testimony from others. Rather than strictly applying that standard in the allocation of refugee numbers, successive American administrations have used the regional allocation system to favor refugees from communist countries despite the elimination in the Refugee Act of ideological and geographic considerations. One consequence has been to adversely affect the admission of refugees from Latin America and Africa, particularly those who are not fleeing from communist dictatorships but from other repressive regimes. To help depoliticize the process of allocating refugees, numbers should be provided—not by statute but in the course of the allocation process—for political prisoners, victims of torture and persons under threat of death, regardless of whether or not they can establish a well founded fear of persecution based on racial, religious or political grounds.

The sharp politicization of asylum law is illustrated by a comparison of the reaction to asylum claimants from different countries. Consider the ratio of asylum applications granted to those denied by the State Department and the INS (the INS has the legal responsibility for making the determination but does so on the basis of State Department advisory opinions). For those claiming asylum from all over the world whose applications were acted on in Fiscal Year 1985, three individuals out of ten were granted asylum. But for those fleeing communist countries, the percentage was always higher: for Soviet citizens, 53 percent; for those leaving mainland China, 44 percent; Hungarians, 50 percent; Romanians, 62 percent; Poles, 42 percent; Afghans, 33 percent; Czechs, 65 percent; Bulgarians, 52 percent; Ethiopians, 35 percent; and Vietnamese, 36 percent.

This chart is based on data for asylum cases filed with INS district directors only. Many applications for asylum are filed with immigration judges, particularly in the context of deportation proceedings. The Office of the Chief Immigration Judge is developing a data system, but asylum statistics are not now available.

The most flagrant example of the politicization of asylum policy has to do with the unusually high rate of denials for Salvadorans, Guatemalans and Haitians over the past several years despite the known facts of instability, killing and oppression in those countries. In Fiscal Year '85 up to August 1985, the percentage of acceptance of total number of applicants acted upon was 0.5 percent for Haitians, 1.2 percent for Guatemalans and 5 percent for Salvadoreans. An obvious problem is that the numbers are considerable: 668 Haitians, 409 Guatemalans and 2,107 Salvadorans were turned down in that period. But the question is not just one of numbers. Iran had the largest number of applications acted upon of any country, and Nicaragua the second largest. In the Iranian case, with action on more than 6,000 applications, 63 percent were granted asylum, mostly students who were already in this country and who were able to prove on an individual basis a well-founded fear of persecution should they return home.

Table 14.1 Asylum cases filed with INS district directors, approved and denied, by nationality, June 1983 to September 1986

Country	Approval Rate for Cases Decided	Cases Granted	Cases Denied
TOTAL	23.3%	18,701	61,717
Iran	60.4%	10,728	7,005
Romania	51.0%	424	406
Czechoslovakia	45.4%	99	119
Afghanistan	37.7%	344	567
Poland	34.0%	1,806	3,495
Hungary	31.9%	137	292
Syria	30.2%	114	263
Ethiopia	29.2%	734	1,774
Vietnam	26.0%	50	142
Uganda	25.3%	75	221
China	21.4%	84	307
Philippines	20.9%	77	291
Somalia	15.6%	74	399
Nicaragua	14.0%	2,602	15,856
Iraq	12.1%	91	655
Yugoslavia	11.0%	31	249
Liberia	8.4%	20	218
Pakistan	6.5%	26	370
Cuba[a]	4.9%	99	1,906
El Salvador	2.6%	528	19,207
Honduras	2.5%	6	234
Lebanon	2.4%	34	1,338
Haiti[b]	1.8%	30	1,631
Guatemala	.9%	14	1,461
India	.3%	1	311
Egypt	.2%	2	703
Bangladesh	.0%	0	403

[a]There were 89,606 cases from Cuba pending at the end of FY 86.
[b]There were 2,042 cases from Haiti pending at the end of FY 86.
Note: Starting in May 1983, the INS kept asylum statistics by number of cases. Each case, or application, may include more than one individual. From June to September 1982 and October 1982 to April 1983, INS asylum figures were for actual number of individuals. To avoid inconsistency, this chart includes data only since INS data was based on number of cases. Nationalities shown are those which had 100 or more decided in any one of the fiscal year periods included. The total includes all nationalities.

But such favorable actions did not serve as a signal for more applicants from Iran since getting here presents enormous problems. That is also why it is possible for the State Department and the INS to have acted favorably on the applications of 105 Libyan nationals already in the United States, whose percentage of total applications acted on favorably was higher than for any other country, at 81 percent. By contrast, the rate of acceptance for Nicaraguans has until very recently been relatively low, 9 percent in 1983, 12 percent in 1984, 10 percent in 1985 for the fiscal year up to August. While the percentage of acceptance has always been much higher than for Salvadorans, with figures of only 2 percent and 5 percent for the same periods, undoubtedly indicating ideological bias, the rate of turndown was higher for Nicaraguans than for any other Communist country with the exception of Cuba, which presents a special case. In fact, Cubans constituted almost 92 percent of all asylum applicants pending as of August 1985, a large proportion of whom are already in a special entrant status awaiting action by the Congress to grant them permanent residency, which is also true for the second largest group of applicants, persons from Haiti, who numbered almost 6,000 in August 1985, or 4.6 percent of the total number of applicants.

The differences between the percentage of acceptance for Cubans and Haitians in the period under consideration—5 percent to 0.5 percent—and between Nicaraguans and Salvadorans—almost 10 percent to 5 percent—indicate bias in favor of persons fleeing communist regimes. But at least until 1986, the United States government was tough on Nicaraguans and even Cubans, although not as hard as on Salvadorans. The United States was worried that favorable decisions on asylum applications from nearby countries would serve as a stimulus to a flood of new asylum applicants, creating a side door to immigration and serious social and political problems.

That changed in 1986 when 60 percent of the asylum applicants from Nicaragua in Fiscal Year '86 (to this writing) gained approval. In Spring 1986 Perry Rivkind, the district director of the Florida office of the INS announced that rather than have Nicaraguans prove the well-founded fear of persecution required of other nationals he would give Nicaraguans asylum routinely because they were fleeing a communist country. The INS director probably would not have taken that position in the face of strong opposition from the State Department and the White House, even though it is technically within his province to do so. His decision may reflect domestic politics in Dade County, Florida, as much as foreign policy in Central America, since Cubans and Cuban-Americans in Miami as well as Nicaraguans have constantly badgered him to take a strong anti-communist stand by approving the Nicaraguan claimants for admission as asylees.

Since civil war and oppression in Nicaragua and El Salvador persist, it would be reasonable to grant EVD to persons from both countries who claim asylum.

In recent years nationals from eleven different countries have been eligible for EVD under certain criteria. Nicaraguans received EVD from July 3, 1979, to September 28, 1980. Ethiopians who arrived in this country prior to June 30, 1980, have it at the present time, as do Poles who arrived before July 21, 1984. In the Nicaraguan case the telegram which went from the Attorney General to all immigration officers specified that "the Department of State has recommended against the forcible return to Nicaragua of Nicaraguan nationals for the remainder of the calendar year, irrespective of the date of arrival in the United States, due to the unsettled conditions in Nicaragua." When Iranians received EVD it was on the ground of "unstable conditions" in Iran, a phrase also used to grant EVD to Poles. Conditions in El Salvador have been at least as unstable as those in Poland in January of 1982, but the United States does not want to encourage Salvadorans to come to this country or to convey the impression that there is persecution and oppression under a government that we strongly support. Unfortunately, our uneven administration of asylum law undermines our claim to moral authority throughout Latin America.

A much better approach for our own interests, in my view, would be to depoliticize the administration of asylum law to some extent by following the recommendations of SCIRP. The Commission urged a narrowing of administrative discretion in the granting of asylum claims. It would do that by having group profiles developed outside of the State Department or INS which would provide information as to how members of a particular religious or ethnic group (or those of a particular political and social affiliation) are treated in different countries. The Commission also recommended that the position of Asylum Admissions Officer be created within INS, for persons who would be schooled in the procedures and techniques of eligibility determination.

In recent months INS has begun to provide special training for asylum adjudications but the efforts to date are not as strong as they should be. These changes, none of which is earth shaking, would help move this country to a position of greater integrity in the administration of its asylum law. But the major action that should be taken now is to grant EVD to Salvadorans and Nicaraguans in this country in an even-handed manner that recognizes the tremendous dangers which a large portion of them would face if they returned home, as has been proposed by Senator Dennis DiConcini (D-AZ), a member of the Select Commission, and Representative Joe Moakley (D-MA).

There are several advantages to such a policy, one of which is that it would bring a great many illegal aliens out into the open under the law; but most important of all it would show that the United States does take action to protect individuals against the possible loss of life, even if not specific political persecution in most cases, when it has the chance to do so. It is not often that a nation can act upon the rabbinic injunction: to save a life is as if one saves the world.

ECONOMIC OPPORTUNITY MIGRATION

Civil war, famine, drought and persecution will continue to produce refugee migrations, but an even larger source of migration in the world today and perhaps for the future is economic opportunity migration by persons who seek work outside of their own homes, not with the intention of immigrating but of returning to their homelands. A considerable amount of sojourner-worker migration was regularized in the 1950s in Europe by receiving countries who wanted workers but not immigrants. The FRG signed its first formal guest worker treaty with Italy in 1955, and during the 1960s signed agreements with Greece, Spain, Turkey, Morocco, Portugal and Tunisia. France also signed agreements with many countries. By 1977, 25 percent of the labor force in Switzerland, more than 11 percent of that in France, and over 9 percent in the FRG was made up of foreign workers.

The oil-rich countries of the Middle East have also attracted foreign laborers. By 1975 almost half of the labor force of Saudi Arabia and Libya and more than two-thirds of those in Kuwait, Qatar and the United Arab Emirates consisted of temporary foreign workers. The United States had its own temporary worker program from 1942 to 1964, under which almost five million Mexican temporary workers came to this country.

For the receiving countries these are not immigration policies but labor recruitment programs, intended to import workers to do the hard, dirty jobs which natives apparently will not do under prevailing wages and working conditions. The idea is to import muscle but not members. The phenomenon of labor recruitment occurs even in countries that send out workers elsewhere. Italians, for example, have sought and found work through temporary worker programs in central and northern Europe, but North Africans, Turks and others have migrated illegally to Italy for the same reason. Just as Mexicans cross the border to the United States in search of economic opportunity, Guatemalans and Salvadorans cross the southern Mexican border to find work in a more highly developed country as illegal aliens. Trinidadians can be found working in New York City, having left the country that provides jobs for persons from Guyana and other poorer countries in the Caribbean. Millions of persons, finding it hard to enter another country legally, use illegal means of entry in order to support themselves and their families wherever they can cross borders or sea lanes easily, as Colombians do to reach Venezuela and Paraguayans and Bolivians do to work in Argentina, as Ghanians do in Nigeria, and as workers from Bangladesh do in the province of Assam in India, and as millions from this hemisphere have done in the United States.

The United States has a *de facto* labor recruitment policy—its illegal aliens— who, according to demographers from the Census Bureau working at the request of the Select Commission, constituted no fewer than 3.5 million or more than six million persons in the United States at any time during 1978. The total number of illegal aliens in the United States as of this writing probably is not higher than six or seven million, and, according to recent studies, may be less; but the accessibility and the perception of an economic opportunity by would-be illegal workers from Latin America and the Caribbean will continue to produce enormous migration pressure. In Latin America it is expected that the number of persons between the ages of twelve and thirty-nine will increase by thirty-eight million between 1980 and 2000. Not all the illegal aliens who come to the United States do so to do dirty, hard jobs. Probably more than one-fourth of all of the illegal aliens who remain in the United States came originally as tourists or students, or through some other legitimate non-immigrant channel before letting their status lapse; but nearly all of them come to work. Mexico, for example, looks to migration as a safety valve for the underemployed and un-employed, who send remittances home as a form of economic aid.

Migration itself cannot do much to bridge the economic inequality of nations. For instance, at a conference at the Academy of Arts and Sciences in Cambridge on population interactions between the poor and rich countries in 1984, little hope was expressed by anyone that migration itself was even a partial answer to the problem of the inequality of nations, however important it may be as an answer to the individuals and their families who perceive an economic gap and do something about it. Mexico is a case in point. The need to create millions of new jobs by the year 2000 cannot be affected substantially by lawful admissions to the United States, even when combined with a continued flow of illegal migration at approximately present levels, something that the United States is highly unlikely to permit for non-economic reasons.

That is why migration is a problem for nations even though it is an opportunity for individuals. The individual Turkish worker and his family in the FRG may have improved their lot. The problem of Turkey remains largely unaffected and the problem of ethnic conflict in the FRG must be faced. Sweden, Switzerland, FRG, France, the Netherlands and Belgium asked for workers and to their great surprise it was human beings who came—human beings with different religions, cultural values and skin color. Even in Great Britain, there have been enormous problems of absorption of relatively small populations from the poorer countries of the British Commonwealth.

Rigid systems of stratification by occupation—nothing new in world history—along ethnic lines will be extremely difficult to break in most European countries, but they are unlikely to see extreme forms of ethnic persecution such as the expulsion of East Asians from Uganda, the driving out of the Ghanaians from Nigeria, or the murder of the Tamils in Sri Lanka and of the Bengalis in Assam. Migrations of the poorest to the poor countries of the world arouse ethnic passions to an extreme degree partly because people already live so close to the margin of survival in the receiving countries.

The contrast in the management of multi-ethnic societies in most of the world with the United States is clearly in our favor because of certain obvious advantages: size, wealth, our history of immigration, and a concept of national identity based upon political and civic ideals rather than religion, race or ethnicity. Those advantages have enabled the United States to admit substantial numbers of immigrants from poor countries since 1965 when we abolished the National Origins Quota System that favored northern European Protestant countries. Jamaicans in New York City move freely back and forth from the United States to Jamaica, feeling comfortable in both places. French-Canadians in New England migrate frequently to French Canada and to Quebec and return. The flow of traffic between Mexico—not just of Mexicans but of other Central Americans—across the border and back again is constant. Of course, many stay in the United States and raise their children here where they become Jamaican-Americans, French-Canadian-Americans, and Mexican-Americans rather easily. My own view, contrary to many of those found elsewhere in this volume, is that the basic values and institutions of American society have been strengthened considerably by recent lawful immigrants from Third World countries, and the United States probably would benefit from slightly higher levels of legal immigration in the late 1980s.

Given the restrictionist policies of European nations and Japan, one would think that the industrial nations of the world would develop trade, aid and investment strategies to minimize migration pressure. The truth is that very little is known about the relationship of trade, aid and investment to patterns of migration from developing to wealthier nations. Simple statements can be made such as: if Americans will buy tomatoes grown in Mexico, the folks who pick them in Mexico are not as likely to come to the United States to pick American tomatoes. Yet, even assuming the growth of labor intensive economic activity in Mexico, it is not easy to conclude what the overall effects will be on migration patterns from other sectors of a Mexican economy. Those who migrate tend to be the more ambitious and adventuresome within whatever sector or whatever level of economic activity they perform.

While receiving nations may gain in remittances and in a reduction of underemployed and unemployed, it is often charged that they lose some of the most energetic and high quality human capital in their nations through emigration. But little is known about the relationship of emigration to capital formation and development in the sending countries. While able and energetic immigrants may take their human capital elsewhere, there is also evidence that the immigration process brings more than remittances back home, that it results in a transfer of technology, knowledge and capital, too, to the sending countries.

The whole question of the relationship of the inequality of nations to migration flows and of the relationship of various kinds of migration to economic development in the sending countries needs systematic research. For the present, the only overwhelming safe generalization is that the inequality of nations will result increasingly in migration pressures in the years ahead. Of these pressures and of migration itself, the following generalizations can be made: Immigration invariably means increased opportunity for individuals and their families; it often means enhanced economic activity and growth in the host countries; and it usually results in serious social and political problems in those countries, with the fewest such problems in the United States. One cannot generalize in a comparable way as to the effects of migration on the long-term development of sending countries; and it is not possible to make significant generalizations about the relationship of international aid, investment and even trade policies to migration.

The entire subject cries out for a transnational response, yet, the world, organized as it is into nation states, is not any more able to deal with this transnational problem than those of energy, food production and distribution or national armaments. Nations are interdependent but are a long way from acknowledging their interdependence through the creation of supernational institutions capable of dealing with these questions, including the problem of transnational migration.

Until that time the United States would be wise to do what the Select Commission recommended by beginning to build a secure system of employee eligibility with sanctions against employers who willfully hire those ineligible to work while at the same time legalizing a large proportion of the illegal aliens already in this country and increasing lawful immigration, including immigration not based on family reunification. Such a policy we call "closing the back door while opening the front door a bit wider." Such a policy would extend the benefits of immigration to the United States and individuals from other countries while protecting our society against the buildup of an underclass of illegal alien workers who not only depress U.S. wages and labor standards and undermine the validity of U.S. laws, but who also will be the scapegoats for harsh enforcement measures and public hostility in the event of an economic downturn.

I believe that more principle and less expediency with respect to both worker migration and asylum claimants will not only bring a larger measure of justice to a world sadly broken by hatred and poverty, but also will serve the interests of the United States.

The U.S. Refugee Industry:
Doing Well by Doing Good
By Barnaby Zall

Jean-Pierre Respail, in 1956, wrote a prophetic book *Camp of the Saints*, about a march of refugees from Asia to Europe; the surge of humanity soon overwhelmed any humanitarian impulses. Father Theodore Hesburgh, Chairman of the 1981 Select Commission on Immigration and Refugee Policy, has taken note of fears of the same phenomenon.

Surveying the world today, we can see that Respail and Hesburgh were not dreamers. Respail was just before his time; Hesburgh is current. Millions of people around the world are on the march, seeking safety or a better life.

We call people who seek safety from persecution "refugees." Refugees have been with the world for thousands of years. Ancient Chinese warlords used to push refugees before them to weaken their enemies. The Old Testament contains several stories about refugees. In popular parlance and in the media the term refugee is used with increasing imprecision, often as a blanket term for any actual or intending migrant from most Third World and communist countries, regardless of his motives or circumstances.

In modern international law, true refugees have a special place. We consider them to be worthy of extraordinary treatment, beyond the bounds of most immigration restrictions. Most western countries have statutory provisions for assisting refugees (most communist countries simply produce refugees, both their own and from Third World countries, without helping any).

International law is clear on which persons are to be considered refugees— those who have been persecuted and who have a well-founded fear of persecution if they were returned to their homelands—and who are not: those who want to move simply for economic or social betterment, or persons who leave areas of unemployment and poverty for a job are not refugees, no matter how desperate their circumstances. They are "economic migrants." We normally think of economic migrants as "immigrants."

American refugee law developed after World War II as a hodge-podge patchwork of individual programs to assist persons from specific areas. In 1980 Congress passed the Refugee Act, consolidating and modernizing our refugee-related laws and creating new programs of assistance. The Refugee Act contains a refugee definition slightly broader than that in modern international law (under our law, a refugee does not have to actually leave his homeland before being considered a refugee; international law requires flight). The U.S. Supreme Court has held that the 1980 Refugee Act's definition of refugee conforms to international law; the Supreme Court also held that the United States was fulfilling all of its international obligations to refugees.[1]

NURTURING AN INDUSTRY

The Refugee Act, however, also created a new series of domestic pressures which have returned to haunt us. The Refugee Act established massive federal payment programs to cooperating private organizations. The Refugee Act thus, in effect, set a bounty on each refugee resettled by these organizations. Since 1980 more than three billion federal tax dollars have been spent on refugee resettlement, and hundreds of millions more by state and local governments and private groups.

The channelling of billions of federal dollars to private organizations spawned a refugee resettlement industry with sizable bureaucracies whose existence is dependent on continued federal money. Key components of the industry are the voluntary agencies, often spin-offs of church, ethic or philanthropic organizations, and to a lesser degree ethnic and emigre organizations and service providers in state and local government. Like any other enterprise, the refugee resettlement industry wants to preserve its source of funding; in this case, the source of money is a continued flow of refugees to resettle. Consequently, the self-interest of these organizations has induced them to push the American refugee program toward questionable policies. Though couched in appeals to humanitarianism and generosity, the resettlement industry's actions raise serious questions under both the letter and the spirit of the Refugee Act of 1980.[2]

The refugee resettlement industry has conditioned the United States to expect a continuing high level of refugee resettlement, with less concern whether the aliens being resettled are actually refugees. This distortion has moved American refugee policy from assistance to refugees to a jobs program driven by internal politics. The effect on the United States and its less fortunate citizens and residents has been discounted in the rush to maintain resettlement programs.

IMMIGRANTS AND REFUGEES: THE VANISHING DISTINCTION

The attitude of the refugee industry threatens gains in refugee programs made over the last ten years by the western world. As actual refugee emergencies diminish around the world, and as western nations learn how to manage refugee problems using alternatives to resettlement, the refugee industry's insistence that the United States take large numbers of refugees in disregard of the law's criteria, undermines the fragile international cooperation mechanisms painstakingly assembled in the last decade.

Preoccupied with current growth, the refugee industry seems at times heedless of future consequences of its present actions. Between 1975 and 1986 the United States admitted one million refugees, an amount equal to those accepted by the rest of the world combined. During the same period the United States accepted five million regular immigrants, far more than all other immigrant-receiving nations combined. Yet the generosity of the American people is not limitless, even for people called refugees. By calling ineligible people refugees and accepting federal grants for any person who claims refugee status, the refugee industry obscures the uniqueness of refugee status and undermines popular American support for any refugee resettlement. If a backlash against refugee admissions is triggered by abuse of our generosity, even legitimate refugees might be hurt.

Southeast Asia has for more than a decade been the largest source of refugees for the refugee resettlement industry. Southeast Asia has been the one place in the world where the mere fact of leaving one's homeland creates the presumption of refugee status for a person. This approach contrasts sharply with the African refugee practice, where departure for temporary refuge means eventual return. But in Southeast Asia departure equals permanent emigration and resettlement.[4] The sharply reduced number of qualified refugees in Southeast Asia is posing the greatest danger the resettlement industry has faced.

If Southeast Asia's recent candidates were considered under international law standards, few would qualify as refugees. International law requires some individualized persecution on certain specified grounds (race, religion, political opinion, membership in a social group or nationality), along with some objective evidence of the factors generating a fear of persecution upon return. Very few current Southeast Asian migrants can meet these tests.

A secret study by the United Nations High Commissioner for Refugees, never released and quickly suppressed, found that very few Southeast Asians in refugee camps meet the international law definition of refugees. Most are simply economic migrants. Independent study groups from the United States have reached similar conclusions.[5] Refugee resettlement interests disagree and their efforts to pressure the United States to take more Southeast Asian refugees continue unabated.

In an internal document, the INS acknowledged a tendency of refugee officials overseas to make presumptive judgments about persons overseas who are part of a large exodus from a country. Immigration law specialist David Martin has observed that Vietnamese boat people benefit from a presumption that all who risked their lives at sea faced persecution at home and therefore meet the refugee definition. But Haitians who risk their lives at sea enroute to Florida and land directly in the United States have enjoyed no similar presumption.[6]

The Soviet Union is the second largest source of refugees, with more than 106,000 coming since 1975. Persons leaving Russia have also enjoyed a less rigorous test of their refugee status. Author Joseph Nocera calls the practice of defining all Soviet Jews as a class of refugees a "fiction" driven by politics in Congress and in the U.S.-Soviet relationship. But he also attributes it to a misunderstanding about what life is like in Russia for Soviet Jews. Nocera writes:

> The notion that Soviet Jews face a great deal of persecution by the state for their
> race and beliefs has not been created out of whole cloth. The Stalinist purges and

261

**Table 15.1 Resettlement of Indochina refugees
April 1975–May 1986**

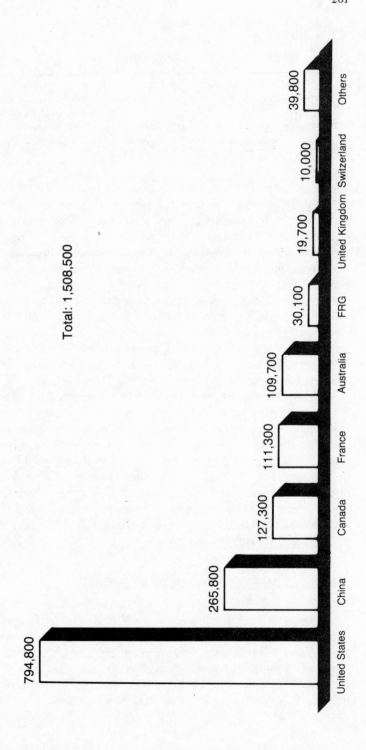

Total: 1,508,500

794,800 — United States

265,800 — China

127,300 — Canada

111,300 — France

109,700 — Australia

30,100 — FRG

19,700 — United Kingdom

10,000 — Switzerland

39,800 — Others

pogroms were very real. . . . But these repugnant cases tend to obscure something equally true about life in Russia today: that most Jews who want to emigrate are not dissidents or refuseniks. They are not even religious. . . . They are not leaving because they face religious persecution. They are leaving in part because they suffer from ethnic prejudice, but primarily because life in Russia is hard for everyone—Jews included—and, unlike most others, they have an escape hatch. . . . The Soviet Jews themselves will be the first to admit. . .that they left Russia for political reasons that have very little to do with "political persecution" and a great deal to do with wanting to find a better life for themselves and their children somewhere else.[7]

The pressures of special interest groups that have inflated refugee admissions and permitted the resettlement of many who are not genuine refugees have blurred the distinction in Congress and public opinion between refugee programs and ordinary immigration. Such perceptions have been behind proposals in Congress to place a ceiling on overall immigration and include refugee admissions under that cap.[8] Clearly, the distorted criteria applied in refugee admissions have contributed to the view that they are merely an alternative, expedited form of immigration. Over time refugee programs progressively take on the characteristics of other immigration as family members try to reunite in resettlement countries. The demographic and labor market effects of mass refugee flows differ little from those of immigrants. The vast majority of refugees soon becomes permanent residents and uses the existing immigration preference system to bring spouses, fiances and family members to the United States.[9]

Not surprisingly, resettlement and ethnic interests have violently resisted initiatives to route refugee flows into immigration channels or to establish a worldwide admissions ceiling in which refugee programs would compete with other forms of immigration for rationed numbers. Refugee interests argue that refugees would lose out under such a system in head-to-head competition with the politically potent demands of family reunification. More compelling, but less often invoked as an argument, is that immigration is often a much slower process. Waiting lines in some preference categories are long, and immigrants must resettle themselves without the help of special social welfare programs or federal dollars routed through voluntary agencies.

CHANGING AMERICAN REFUGEE PROGRAMS

The refugee resettlement industry is a relatively new phenomenon. American refugee programs began following World War II with international programs to resettle persons displaced by the war. Until the 1970s most American refugee programs were part of cooperative international efforts to resolve multinational programs. With the exceptions of the Cuban and Hungarian refugee programs, the United States insisted that other countries resettle proportionate shares of refugees at the same time we accepted our own portion.

Perhaps as important was that, until recently, when the government brought refugees into the United States for resettlement, it did not pay resettlement organizations for their assistance. Yet hundreds of thousands of refugees were resettled using only volunteer help from truly humanitarian organizations.

The enormous number of Southeast Asian refugees spawned a new American effort to resettle hundreds of thousands of refugees in a short period. At the same time, the United States tried to pressure other countries to accept a fair share of refugees (the United States, of course, ended up taking the lion's share).

With the new program, the United States sowed the seeds of its current dilemma. The program had humanitarian origins but was increasingly driven by foreign policy considerations such as a U.S. desire to embarrass Hanoi or to respond to pressures of ASEAN (Association of Southeast Asian Nations) member states to remove displaced Vietnamese, Laotians and Cambodians. The U.S. decision to instigate or encourage emergency movements against the Vietnamese occupation of Cambodia was taken with little thought of the resulting additional refugee flows and the accompanying moral obligation of the United States to assist them. The record leaves little doubt that refugee resettlement decisions have been distorted because of their management by the State Department, an agency whose entire optic is foreign, not domestic.

The efforts by both the public and private sectors to assist vast numbers of refugees spawned a new multi-billion dollar refugee resettlement industry, a curious mix of the humanitarian and the mercantile tinged with real politik. At first, U.S. resettlement was a traditional type, responding to the heartfelt needs of desperate refugees. But soon the program responded solely to demands from abroad and from within to take an unending stream of immigrants, whether they met the definition of refugee or not.

The American program depended on private resettlement agencies, the volunteer agencies, "VOLAG," to assist refugees' transition to U.S. society. But unlike prior refugee programs, the federal government paid the private agencies by contract for their services (in the past the services had been volunteered). As a result, the groups have hired thousands of employees and passed millions of dollars through to local agencies.

These organizations truly do well by doing good. There is now a bounty paid by the federal government for each refugee resettled here, and refugee groups, rather than compete with each other, strive for volume, for more refugees to be admitted into the "pipeline." As a result voluntary agencies now receive $560 in "Reception and Placement" grants for each refugee settled. There are currently about 280,000 Cambodians waiting in Thai resettlement camps; at current rates, those refugees are worth as much as $157 million to the refugee resettlement industry.

As the refugee industry grew, it developed the religious and humanitarian bases for its own legitimacy and permanence. An important source of strength were the growing ethnic lobbies formed by resettled refugees and immigrants who were quick to recognize an identity of interests with the voluntary agencies in a continued heavy refugee flow. Although the industry receives assistance from thousands of sincere Americans, in their business aspects, these organizations are relentlessly efficient. At periodic meetings, called "auctions," the industry divides the available pool of refugees among resettlement organizations.

Advocates for the industry have engaged in bouts of America-bashing. Although the United States takes far more refugees than all other countries, industry spokesmen regularly castigate Americans and their government for being heartless in ignoring individuals or groups claiming to be refugees. Startling ideas to have come out of recent publications are the proposition that American refugee processing is biased against persons from cultures which legitimize lying, and the theory that America was responsible for the Holocaust against European Jews by the Nazis.[11]

Nevertheless these voluntary agencies are powerful and have influential friends in Washington. Questions of policy have often been submerged by powerful economic and political interests.

An example of the power of the refugee industry was the policy presumption that all Southeast Asians who left their homelands were eligible as refugees. The INS still maintains an office in Hong Kong with responsibility for selecting refugees for admission to the United States. The State Department and voluntary agencies try to influence the decisions, but the final choice lies with INS.

Following the passage of the 1980 Refugee Act, the chief INS official in Asia, Joseph Sureck, began to apply the definition of refugee in the Refugee Act (the definition was slightly broader than that in current international law). If an alien who was not eligible under the statutory definition applied for refugee admission to the United States, the INS rejected the alien's application.

Sureck was urged by the refugee industry representatives, and eventually by the State Department officials in the area, to relax his definition so ineligible Southeast Asians would be admitted. Sureck refused, citing the new law.

The State Department sent out a study team, headed by former Ambassador Marshall Green (who in other contexts was for more restrictive management of immigration). The study team, under tremendous pressure from Senator Mark Hatfield (R-OR) and other members of Congress, who were themselves under siege by the refugee industry, recommended that Sureck be removed and aliens ineligible under any reasonable definition be admitted as refugees. An exchange of telegrams, known to insiders as the "Kamput cables," ensued concluding in what some regard as INS instructions to Sureck to break the law and admit ineligible aliens.[12]

Eventually, the White House issued National Security Decision Directive (NSDD) 93. That directive required INS to presume that any alien who left any Indo-Chinese country was a refugee, without further inquiry. A series of six priority groups were outlined, ranging from those with close and continuing ties to the United States to those with no present or past ties to the United States.

Those with close ties to the United States were to be processed immediately and INS was not to inquire further to determine if the aliens described were, in fact, refugees under international or American law.

Sureck, who had put in some thirty honorable years of service to the INS, retired in the Summer of 1984. A new and more pliable INS chief was appointed to replace him; the refugee industry was involved in the selection.

NSDD 93 violates the Refugee Act, as well as international law. It so blatantly ignores the law. Yet NSDD 93 remains in force today.

There are no refugees left in Southeast Asia who fit into any of the higher categories of priority. Only those in the lowest category (P-6), i.e., with no ties to the United States, are left; State Department officials call these refugees the "residue." The euphemism used to cover up plans to bring these ineligible aliens into the United States as refugees is "the changing character of the refugee flow."

These categories now drive the American refugee program. The refugee definition is no longer the test used for Southeast Asians in most cases, only the categories. Since Southeast Asians still make up most of our refugee program (40,500 from East Asia out of 70,000 worldwide in Fiscal 1987), the failure to use the refugee definition means that the entire American refugee program has been distorted.

Just as the Green panel beat down INS resistance to distorting the law, later administration actions defended the diluted refugee program against potential attacks. In 1984 Senator Simpson, chairman of the Senate Immigration Subcommittee, issued a report accurately depicting the refugee program as a backdoor immigration program ignoring the definition of refugee. In response, a 1985 State Department survey team issued a glowing assessment of the refugee program under NSDD 93.

The State Department team, headed by former Iowa Governor Robert Ray, was concerned that the Southeast Asian refugee program would be made into a regular immigration program. The Ray Report's response to a suggestion that the Southeast Asian refugee program be wound down?: Start taking more Priority-Six "residue" refugees with no ties to the United States.[13]

Traditionally, the Department of State had been the advocate for increased refugee admissions while the Justice Department has sought restraint. Within the State Department, the actions of the Bureau of Refugee Programs were heavily influenced by the Bureau of East Asian Affairs, whose primary concern has been the stability and goodwill of allied countries in the region and for the troublesome human rights issues arising from forced repatriations from those countries. In 1986, however, under pressure from Eastern European ethnic groups, the Justice Department sought an increase of 20 percent in the refugee admission quota. Recognizing that few eligible refugees remain in resettlement camps, the State Department in 1986 urged only a modest increase in the admissions level from 1985.

Senator Simpson, concerned about the refugee program, urged the level of admissions be kept the same as in 1985. House Immigration Subcommittee Chairman Romano Mazzoli also went on record as opposing the admissions proposed by the administration as inconsistent with the administration's stated intention of "managing down" the Southeast Asian flow. Mazzoli detailed other chronic congressional concerns: State's failure to commit the resources to monitor the use of the millions it gives to VOLAG's, and State's inadequate pursuit of the alternatives of voluntary repatriation or resettlement in Thailand.[14] The rest of the Congressional oversight committee involved in the refugee admissions process opted for the small increase proposed by State.

The State Department won, receiving a refugee "quota" of 70,000 refugees for the 1987 fiscal year. Refugee officers were doubtful that the United States could find even that many refugees qualified under our laws this year, but they were determined to fill the quota.

EFFECT ON OTHER COUNTRIES

The international legal community has now had five decades of refugee flows in which to refine its responses. Ponderous though international law may be, it seemed in the last few years that we were finally turning the corner on our major refugee programs. Southeast Asia had almost ceased hemorrhaging; the Middle East, though volatile, was being accommodated; African flows had diminished; even European countries and Canada were reforming their policies to deal with abuse.

The international community recognized that its resources were being strained. Nations, working together, accommodated the needs of first asylum countries (where the refugees appeared first before moving on) and resettlement countries (where most immigrants wanted to end up). Even source countries, such as Vietnam, and traditional adversaries such as the two Germanies, accepted the new agreements.

One of the advances in these discussions was the recognition that the African model of temporary refuge, followed by repatriation, was desirable in most parts of the world. Countries, though not completely satisfied, were taking steps to ameliorate the worst situations, to manage the problems.

The new international concept is called "sharing out." Sharing out recognizes the international character of the burden of resettlement. Proponents of sharing out contend that the overall problems of refugee flows have been cauterized, so that each country would have a reasonable idea of what refugee burden to expect. Thus, through future planning, each country could manage a significant resettlement program without internal dislocation.

Unfortunately, the new American attitude, driven in part by the refugee industry's needs and State Department complaisance, imperils international participation. Why should any rational government leader risk internal criticism if the United States will simply take all remaining refugees? They are more likely to advocate popular restriction programs, which are politically cost-free if the United States takes all refugees in any event, qualified or not.

In the last decade, American refugee policy had been addressing the effect of refugees on the countries of first asylum. Now, with that pressure slackening but with internal political pressure growing in refugee resettlement countries, and countries of first-asylum, the change in American policy to a vacuum cleaner approach has endangered that fragile international consensus on refugee matters.

As internal political pressures within the United States keep resettlement numbers high, we are undercutting the international efforts to reduce refugee flows and resettlement burdens. But most U.S. refugee resettlement officials are not concerned: they declare that we fear the United States would sully its humanitarian spirit if it were to accommodate other nations' efforts to manage the problem.

But in the State Department there is concern that events will overtake us. Other resettlement countries will impose tougher measures without us, and we will be left to react to their moves. Over several years, our control over our refugee policies will weaken, as migrants unable to exploit other countries' resettlement systems turn to ours as more vulnerable. That trend will hardly be resisted by the resettlement agencies, understandably anxious to continue doing well by doing good.

EVENTUAL BACKLASH

The refugee industry risks overdoing its relentless demands for more admissions of unqualified persons. The American people are generous; the United States is recognized as pre-eminent in accomodating refugees and immigrants, legal and illegal. Yet the capacity of the American people is not limitless.

By debasing the concept of refugee, and by violating the same laws that gave them legitimacy, the refugee industry and the State Department risk eventual deep reductions in all refugee programs. The current admission of so many unqualified "refugees" at a cost of billions of dollars threatens eventually the political will to admit any refugees, no matter how valid their claim for assistance. Public and congressional skepticism may well shake the political underpinnings of the nation's generous immigration system.

The lessons learned by the rest of the world should guide us in the future. Europe has discovered that generous laws lead to abuse; revisions to avoid abuse result in travail for potentially-eligible claimants. Africa teaches us that even the most massive refugee flows can be managed successfully by regional cooperation and repatriation, but only if isolation and resettlement are avoided. But Asia teaches us that refugee flows can be endless, particularly when other routes for immigration are reduced, and that a significant portion of refugee flows may be ineligible under any legal definition.

The current American refugee system takes no heed of any of these lessons. In fact, our single-minded refugee industry threatens the delicate gains made by all generous countries. We must rein in the self-serving impulses of those otherwise well-intentioned organizations for the good of other countries, for the good of our own country and for the good of true refugees.

NOTES

1. Roger Lemaster and Barnaby Zall, "Compassion Fatigue: The Expansion of Refugee Admissions to the United States," *Boston College International and Comparative Law Review*, Vol. 6, No. 2. Spring 1983.

2. R. Zucker, "Refugee Resettlement in the United States: The Role of the Voluntary Agencies," in *1982 Michigan Year Book of International Legal Studies* (New York: Clark Board Company, Ltd., 1982).

3. Remarks of Senator Bennett Johnson, 128 *Cong. Rec.* S10352 (daily ed. August 12, 1982).

4. "Persons Coming out of Vietnam, Laos and Cambodia . . . are to be presumed to be refugees." Letter for U.S. Secretary of State Alexander Haig to Attorney General William French Smith (April 30, 1981). Unclassified Memorandum from Acting INS Commissioner Doris Meissner to INS District Director Hong Kong (May 27, 1981).

5. *Indochinese Refugees: The Impact on First Asylum Countries and Implications for American Policy*, Study for the Joint Economic Committee, November 25, 1980. Patrick Smith, "Pull Factor Gets the Push," *Far Eastern Economic Review*, July 17, 1981. "The Indochinese Refugee Situation," Report to the Secretary of State by the Special Refugee Advisory panel, August 12, 1981.

6. David A. Martin, "The Refugee Act of 1980: Its Past and Future," in *1982 Michigan Year Book of International Legal Studies*.

7. Joseph Nocera, "Tales of the Vienna Airport," *Harper's*, May 1982.

8. Dennis Gallagher, Susan Forbes and Patricia Weiss Fagan: *Of Special Humanitarian Concern: U.S. Refugee Admissions Since Passage of the Refugee Act*. (WDC: Refugee Policy Group, 1985), pp. 34-36.

9. LeMaster and Zall, "Compassion Fatigue."

10. Senate Committee on the Judiciary: "Annual Refugee Consultation." *Hearing before the Subcommittee on Immigration and Refugee Policy.* 99th Cong., 1st sess. September 17, 1985. (WDC: Government Printing Office, 1986).

11. Kalin, "Troubled Communications: Cross-Cultural Misunderstanding in the Asylum Hearings," and Zolberg, Suhrke and Aguayo, "International Factors in the Formation of Refugee Movements." *International Migration Review*, No. 20 (Summer 1986), pp. 230-238 and 151-162.

12. Unclassified INS Memorandum to District Director Hong Kong.

13. U.S. Department of State, *Report of the Indochinese Refugee Panel*. (WDC, 1986).

14. House Committee on the Judiciary. *Hearing on the Refugees Admissions Program Fiscal Year 1986.* 99th Cong., 1st sess., September 19, 1985.

How Many Americans?
By Lindsey Grant

Passage of the IRCA in October, 1986, has interrupted the immigration debate and changed the terms for the next round of that debate. Having made a clear national decision to try more seriously to enforce our immigration laws, the nation will face a series of problems in making that decision stick. Even more important, we will need to face the more fundamental question: What should be the objective of immigration laws?

THE CENTRAL ISSUE AND THE SECONDARY ISSUES

Let me state the proposition at the outset. The central purpose is demographic: to help regulate how many Americans there will be. It is not simply a question of being for or against immigrants.

I will argue that we should seek as small a population increase as we can decently achieve. Pursuit of this objective will require the control of illegal immigration and the limitation of legal immigration to annual numbers approximating the 1920-1970 rate. It will require that we control the generous tendency to welcome immigrants, and it will require that we think as a nation, not simply as interest groups.

Immigrants are of course individuals and not simply numbers, and the United States is justified in choosing among them, limiting certain kinds and encouraging others. We need to keep alien terrorists out of the United States (a particularly timely issue). We have concerns about health and epidemic control and drug smuggling. We prefer to decide who will come, rather than having others such as Fidel Castro do it for us. We have legitimate concerns about the very illegality of much immigration, and about the strains that concentrated immigration impose on local governments' education, medical and welfare services.

If these were indeed the only issues, most of them could be addressed (as some have suggested), by making all immigration legal and screening out the undesirable individuals.

Some have advocated reduced immigration on the grounds of cultural assimilation problems, particularly the concern that massive concentration of immigration from Spanish-speaking countries could lead to a bilingual society. The problems of Belgium, Cyprus, Canada, Sri Lanka, Yugoslavia and Spain with its Basque minority come immediately to mind. This concern is legitimate and it is not necessarily racist. (American national policies can now be defended as genuinely anti-racist, and current immigration law is in fact intended to diversify the national sources of immigration.)

The possibility of being simply swamped by other cultures is a legitimate subject for examination, given the population pressures in the Third World and

269

the United States' magnetic pull. However, cultural diversity is itself a source of richness and creativity, and we are right to be proud of it. The nation has been remarkably successful in the past in absorbing diverse cultural streams and profiting thereby.

There are environmental, resource and economic constraints on the growth of the country's population that will require limits upon the numbers of immigrants much more stringent than the cultural argument alone would justify. (For the moment, I am assuming that the United States makes the effort to assimilate the immigrants. This is by no means current national policy, and I will return to that question.)

This brings up the question: "how many Americans?"

THE NUMBERS

Let us look briefly at U.S. population trends.

Several years ago, demographers projected a U.S. population peak of 245 million in 2030, assuming that immigration and emigration are in balance and that American women continue to have a total fertility rate of about 1.8 children each. If annual net immigration is steady at 250,000 per year (approximately the annual legal immigration rate for 1920-1970), the population would also peak about 2030 at a level of some 261 million. If immigration continued at a net rate of one million a year—a reasonable guess as to the current level—the population would reach 310 million in 2030 and continue growing.[1] That would amount to 65 million additional people, and 133 million by 2080 (more than the total U.S. population at the start of World War II).

These projections will turn out wrong, because fertility and immigration never stay constant. In fact, we have already reached 245 million. If anything, the calculations have a built-in conservative bias; we will come back to that question.

The point is that—unless the nation goes through another baby boom—the key to the future size of U.S. population is immigration policy. Immigration presently constitutes perhaps 40 percent of America's population growth (depending on one's estimate of illegal immigration and of emigration), and the proportion is rising.

THE DEMOGRAPHIC ARGUMENT

Is there danger in continuing population growth?

We live in a time of explosive technological and demographic change. In two or three generations, the human race has altered its ways of living and its relationships with the earth more profoundly than it did during the transformation from hunter-gatherer to tiller of the soil, which took millenia to accomplish.

More people have been added to world population in two generations than in all preceding time.

In the same fifty years, we have quadrupled the use of fossil energy (which was globally insignificant a century ago), and introduced nuclear energy. In the U.S. and worldwide, the use of chemical fertilizer has increased by an order of magnitude, and pesticides and herbicides by several orders of magnitude. There has been an exponential growth in the introduction of new chemicals.[2]

These changes have brought prosperity to many, and society is tempted to keep playing a winning system.

The problem lies in the by-products—the unintended consequences—of the new technologies. Our activities affect the earth's natural systems in ways unimaginable a century ago.

The technological revolution has been remarkably successful in producing economic goods. It has been even more successful in producing waste. When you drive your car, you use 1 or 2 percent of the energy in the gasoline to move you, 13 percent to move the vehicle, and you discard the remaining 87 percent as waste heats and exhaust gases,[3] which in turn contribute to issues as diverse as human illness and world climate change.

Nobody—literally nobody—understands the implications of the new reliance upon man-made chemicals. Of the chemicals important to commerce "only a few have been subjected to extensive toxicity testing and most have scarcely been tested at all."[4] That statement is about immediate, direct toxicity. Much less do we understand the processes when chemicals and heavy metals are transformed, redistributed and released into nature.

Technological change—automation, computerization, robotics— is fundamentally altering the labor market and the relationships between labor and capital as factors of production.

The energy revolution is acidifying the soils and killing the forests of the northern temperate zone. The damage to conifers in New England, the southern Appalachians and parts of California has been widely enough reported to be well known. The situation is worse in Europe, which does not have the luxury of space. In West Germany, by official count, more than half the forests are suffering "*waldsterben*" (the "death of the forests"). The proportion may be even worse in East Europe.

More profound even than the loss of forests is this warning from a scientific panel convened by the White House:

> We as a committee are especially concerned about possible deleterious effects of a sustained increase in the acidity of unmanaged soils. Its microorganism population is particularly sensitive to a change in acidity. But it is just this bottom part of the biological cycle that is responsible for the recycling of nitrogen and carbon in the food chain. The proper functioning of the denitrifying microbes is a fundamental requirement upon which the entire biosphere depends. The evidence that increased acidity is perturbing populations of microorganisms is scanty, but the prospect of such an occurrence is grave. It may take many years of accumulation of acidity,

from wet or dry deposition, before measurable consequences would be observed. Such an effect is 'long-term' or 'irreversible' . . .[5]

Almost as profound is the prospect of worldwide climate changes resulting from the increase in atmospheric carbon dioxide and trace gases resulting from human economic activities. Among the anticipated consequences are major shifts in agriculture caused by changing rainfall patterns and the flooding of low-lying coasts by rising sea levels. Sea levels are already rising, and the climate is getter warmer. There is debate among scientists as to the timing, speed and specific consequences of the process, but very little dissent as to the direction in which man-made atmospheric changes are driving climate.

When the human race is changing the air it breathes and the climate it lives in, it would seem cause for more concern than is yet evident.

The world has indeed entered a new era, when economic activities may need to be changed or redirected, not because they fail to achieve the results intended, but because of the unintended results. The ban on DDT, the environmental legislation of the 1970s, and recent legislative proposals to reduce the release of nitrogen and sulfur oxides into the atmosphere are perhaps just the precursors of a new process whereby economic activities must be judged, not just in terms of their direct results, but in the context of the earth that supports them, if they are not to destroy us. The U.S. role will be central to this process because of our size and our intensive use of energy and chemicals.

How do population and immigration policies relate to these issues?

The point is that solutions can be envisaged for problems such as I have identified, but population is itself one element of the equation. Population growth intensifies the socio-economic and environmental problems the nation faces. It diminishes the resources available to deal with them.

THE IMMEDIATE AND THE LONG TERM

The argument can conveniently be separated into two time frames:

—The immediate. Employment, opportunity and our obligation to American youth and minorities. "The American dream."
—The long term. Resources, the energy transition and the national patrimony. "The sustainable society."

The immediate issue has been examined in depth elsewhere in this volume. The potential immigrant labor supply is, for practical purposes, infinite.

An increase in the supply of a commodity tends to drive the price of that commodity down. In this instance, the commodity is labor, and the ultimate floor price is subsistence-level wages—a grim return to Ricardo's Iron Law of Wages—such as obtain in much of the world today.

At this stage in our history, America's poor (and particularly its minorities) suffer from an expansion of the labor force. We are no longer a frontier. Technology is driving us. Automation makes possible enormous productivity for a few workers, if the capital is available to buy the technology. Those who cannot gain entry into the modern sector either lower their wages to compete with the machines, or move into the service sector or drop out of the labor force to become part of the floating, restless and frequently alienated permanently unemployed.

We used to speak of the "American dream:" A decent and improving living in return for honest work, with the related ideal of a mass market of prosperous workers. We have gone the other way in the past few years. Income differentials are growing, as is the proportion of Americans below the poverty line.

To acquiesce in a steadily widening income gap would be to abandon an attractive ideal and a source of national strength. It would also probably be dangerous to assume that American workers would remain politically inert through such a process.

Proposals have been made as to how to address the structural changes in the economy. The task is not easy. There is, however, one unassailable observation: The task will be far harder if the labor supply—particularly at the levels at which new American workers seek entry—is indefinitely expansible.

The need to protect the living standards of disadvantaged Americans should be one contraint on permissible levels of immigration.

The long term issues revolve about an inescapable moral choice: are we willing to live by the slogan *carpe diem* and pass a poorer environment to our descendents? To people of that persuasion, there is no future, and ecological arguments are irrelevant.

Most of us would prefer not to take a downward road, and we sense an obligation to pass an undiminished patrimony on to future generations.

Any measurement of resources, seen from that viewpoint, is meaningless unless it is per capita. Let me illustrate by starting with forests. Pronatalists have used total U.S. timber resources as an argument that we need not worry about population growth. Let us look more closely. The U.S. timber stock rose 19 percent from 1952 to 1977 (the last available national inventory).[6] That's the good news. The bad news is that per capita it declined 15 percent. Population growth accounts for the difference.

The problem is not one of absolutes. One can always ameliorate problems through substitutions—in turn raising questions as to the consequences of the substitution—or through technology. We can build with masonry or fiberglass, grow super-trees (at an environmental cost), build flimsier houses or smaller ones, or shift land from cropland or pasture to forests—all of which we have been doing. Technology, substitution and conservation defer problems and sometimes shift them, but they do not dispose of demography. There comes a time when society must face trade-offs between halting population growth or facing

increasingly stringent limits on per capita levels of pollution and resource use—
and this country is into that era.

Let me illustrate by continuing with the example. Partly to save those timber
stocks from acid rain, Congress is considering bills to cut sulfur emissions (mostly
by the power industry) by ten to twelve million tons, or about half. The new
cool water coal gasification technology may help achieve this ambitious goal.
It can be done. It is expensive. It can be done more easily if total energy demand
is not being pushed up by population growth.

The other principal source of acid precipitation is automobiles. We can still
improve mileage per gallon, perhaps by shifting to fuel cell engines, but technical
fixes alone may not be enough. The total mileage driven may need to be constrained. The larger the population, the fewer miles per person. Per capita consumption—your consumption—may be circumscribed by U.S. population growth,
which is determined in turn by the realities of immigration.

The United States' arable acreage is somewhat larger than China's, and one
periodically hears that the United States has no population problem, that it could
support a population as large as China's. Fine, but what does "support" mean?,
at what level? Would you like to pull a plow, personally, as some peasants must
in China? The comparison with China is presumably offered because the comparison appears so remote. That illusion fades if one thinks in terms of generations. China's population has doubled since the communists took charge in
1949, and the United States' has increased two-thirds. Population growth is not
a game one can play indefinitely.

The easing of petroleum prices since the "second oil shock" should not blind
us to the expectation that the petroleum era will be a short one. A few nations
(the U.S., the U.S.S.R., China) have the coal to prolong the fossil fuel era.
Most industrial nations face a starker choice among nuclear energy, import
dependence in a sellers' market or a painful lowering of energy consumption.
Europeans are stabilizing their populations—sometimes to the dismay of anach-
ronistic leaders preparing to fight old wars again—and perhaps their instinct is
right.

But what if it becomes necessary to constrain the use of fossil fuels, not
simply because of a diminishing supply, but because of the intolerable effects
upon acidity and climate?

The United States' relatively low population density per arable acre still gives
us options that most countries do not have. We can make an orderly transition
to a mixed system including biomass (trees and fast-growing annuals) along with
solar and other sources. More crowded countries cannot.

This scenario is built on one issue of air quality. Part of it is already real;
part is conjectural. Similar scenarios could be developed concerning other air,
water and soil pollution as well as agriculture—or simply about the question of
"enough room." In no case do I argue that population will be the sole determinant
of national success in meeting the problems before us, but in every case it is

arithmetically an element of the issue, and slower population growth will make the solution of other national issues less difficult. And immigration is presently the key element in demographic policy.

HOW MANY AMERICANS?

How large should this society be? How many people can the United States' area and resource base support? Should it be an object of policy to maximize the human population within such limits?

Various writers have tried to define the concept of "carrying capacity"—the number of people that can be supported by a given ecological system—but it is a tricky concept. It is easier to apply to, say, a herd of cows on unmanaged range than to humans in a complex modern society. One must make tenuous guesses as to what growth can be sustained in agricultural yields within ecological constraints, what sort of diet people will eat, what techniques are or could become available to mitigate the ecological impacts of economic activity, the need for and availability of capital, the potential role of foreign trade in supplying requirements and so on.

The Canadians a decade ago coined the concept of "the sustainable society." It is an effort to describe how many people the nation can support, with what national policies, for the indefinite future without degrading the resource base. It is a useful concept to apply to "carrying capacity."

By that standard, this country in some respects is already beyond its carrying capacity. I have described the degradation of the atmosphere and its potential effects. We are mining our groundwater resources and polluting them in ways that threaten drinking water supplies. (Half the nation depends upon groundwater for its drinking water.) We are eroding the topsoil off perhaps one-quarter to one-third of our farmland, and degrading our range land. We have yet to agree how to handle our growing mountains of urban sludge and radioactive waste. New York's sewage sludge and solid wastes wash up on the beaches of Long Island and New Jersey.

It is possible to correct all this—to put our activities on a sustainable basis—but it will require both the national will and a major commitment of capital. Those capital requirements will compete with the requirements for accommodating an expanding population.

It would be foolhardy to assign a number to "carrying capacity," to try to defend it, or to suggest that it is immutable. Common sense would seem to justify a simpler rule of thumb: we should try to avoid large population increases until we have arrived at sustainability for the population we have.

Foresight is a rolling process. Such a rule of thumb, if adopted, should be periodically re-examined at the national level to decide whether it is too strict or too lenient. A population appropriate to the fossil fuel era may be too large for the twenty-first century.

Meanwhile, there is valuable guidance to be had from the traditional Rule of the Prudent Person. If you are uncertain of your alternatives, do not commit yourself to the irreversible one. If as a nation we should later decide that we would profit from a larger population, we can always foster immigration. If, however, it becomes apparent there are too many of us, there is very little we can do about it.

And let us agree that this is not a contest to see how many people we can cram in. The object is not to maximize human density, but to provide the most congenial environment for human life—and that goal includes a respect for other plants and animals, even down to the soil micro-organisms whose state of health worried the Acid Rain Peer Review Panel in 1983.

THE POLICY IMPLICATIONS

What kind of immigration policy is suggested by this analysis?

Present national fertility levels would lead to the end of natural increase (excluding migration) in about forty years, at a size substantially like the present. This is a tolerable period. To accept this level as desirable would spare the nation an acrimonious debate, which would certainly erupt if a more drastic policy were proposed.

Stabilization over such a time frame can be expressed in terms of the two-child family, which is a simple and appealing way of expressing the goal of stabilization. (It should be more than a slogan. The government would be wise to watch fertility trends and to monitor the potential effects on fertility of proposed social, welfare and tax legislation.)

What immigration levels are implied by such goals?

Arithmetically, this would require zero net immigration unless fertility levels decline. That means gross immigration at about 100,000 per year (to balance estimated emigration). For a society descended from immigrants, this idea is pretty drastic medicine.

One possible compromise would be to go back roughly to the 1920-1970 legal levels and plan for a net annual flow around 250,000. This would add about 6 percent to our population when it stabilizes about 2030 (see page 270). Dealing as we are with some very broad and imprecise concepts, this increment would seem to be an acceptable exchange for the preservation of the traditional openness of our society.

Any such planning, of course, becomes academic if illegal immigration is not brought under control. However, in most pursuits— whether law enforcement, weapons systems or athletics—the last few percentage points of performance are usually the hardest to achieve. To eliminate 99 percent of illegal immigration might well require border and airport surveillance measures, internal passes and other controls that Congress would find expensive and abhorrent. A compliance rate of 90 percent might be much more easily and happily achieved—

but that other 10 percent must be factored into demographic calculations and decisions about legal quotas.

This can all be done, and with less draconian changes in our present quotas than one might expect. Assuming that, even after better enforcement, residual illegal immigration is still around 100,000 annually, this approximately nets out against the annual emigration of Americans and legal immigrants. The 250,000 figure that I have used is close to the current annual 270,000 ceiling set by U.S. law. However, several adjustments would still be needed to bring them together:

—refugees would necessarily be brought back within the ceiling, as they were before 1980;
—immediate families of American citizens would come under the quota, probably with a special priority; and
—we would need to end a built-in contradiction in present migration policy. Within the present preference system, we still try to accommodate an almost limitless chain of other relatives of immigrants because of the politically potent demand for "family reunification." In fact, migration necessarily implies leaving some relatives, unless entire societies are to migrate together.

TO REBUT THE REBUTTALS

So far, I have sketched out a rationale for stabilizing the United States' population and a set of guidelines for an immigration policy that would help to achieve it. Some readers will agree with the thrust of the argument but differ in detail. There are three lines of argument that would seek to undermine the rationale or would make it impossible to pursue such a national policy by subordinating national to factional interest.

The first of these I would dub the "competitive fertility" argument. There are pronatalists who argue (without addressing the constraints I have discussed) that more people are needed to maintain national power against growing populations in other countries.

The second line of argument I would style the "American conscience" viewpoint that humanitarian concern for others should take precedence over concerns about the effects of immigration upon the United States.

The third is the "salad bowl" view of American policy, which attacks assimilation as colonialism by the existing establishment against minorities and argues for the preservation of linguistic and cultural separateness.

Let me attempt a brief rebuttal of each of these lines of thought.

COMPETITIVE FERTILITY

There have been articles recently suggesting that the industrial world (usually meaning the white world plus Japan) is getting slack about baby-bearing, that it is falling behind the "Third World," and that it had better start breeding or encouraging immigration to avoid being submerged. Of course, the proportion is changing. The industrial world sent through a surge of population growth when death rates fell, before birth rates fell to match them. That phase seems to have ended, but the Third World is now going through a population explosion more virulent than anything the West experienced. This has hardly been a cause for Third World rejoicing. On the contrary, the leaders of the most populous Third World countries say that they must stop the growth for their own well-being. The biggest country, China, is going through a drastic and politically dangerous effort to stop population growth out of the conviction that continued growth would be suicidal.

The pronatalists argue that the West's moral influence will wane as its share of the globe's population diminishes. This argument assumes a correlation where none is demonstrable. Sweden with eight million people is hardly a lesser influence in the world than Bangladesh with 100 million. Nor has their relative influence changed perceptibly in the past fifteen years, although the population ratio has changed by one-half.

Here is the pronatalists' central argument: ". . . it has been generally true that no amount of technical superiority could balance a gross population disadvantage over an extended period of time . . . a large population is no guarantee of great-power status, but it is one necessary precondition . . . The advantages of a large labor force, big military establishments, and the economies of scale and production (sic) are simply too important to lasting global influence."[7]

Even more starkly: "Nations of 225 million people can afford to build submarines and aircraft carriers. Nations of 25 million cannot."[8] This is reductio ad absurdum. It is written to justify high fertility, but a tenfold reduction of U.S. population is hardly a choice under debate. Japan in World War II with a population of 75 million, built both, by the way—with enough energy left over for other enterprises such as the occupation of much of China—and could build them again.

The pronatalists worry about the supply of troops and the industrial base. The need for the former depends upon what kind of war one is likely to fight, and with what weapons. Today, with our wasted assets of unemployed youth, the question is not whether we have enough potential soldiers, but rather how many we could afford to arm, and to what purpose.

As to industrial power: we are today watching the United States' heavy industrial base atrophy in the face of competition from such modest powers as Korea—and for reasons much more complicated than raw census counts.

The pronatalists' generalization concerning power and population has not been supported by systematic reasoning or by a study of history. The idea is beguiling, but a quick mental scan of the histories of China, India and Europe would suggest that the reverse may be true. Smaller tribes and nations have regularly bested larger ones—even before this age of technology. From classical Athens to World

War II, Germany and Japan, one could argue that aggressors have periodically failed because of hubris and the willingness to take on several major adversaries at once, but it would be very hard to argue that population has regularly been an important determinant of military success.

I would urge the pronatalists to examine the constraints I have described before taking us down their road. The Third World has not accepted their suicidal proposal for a fertility race. Neither should we.

THE "AMERICAN CONSCIENCE"

There is something of a dichotomy apparent.

Overwhelmingly, Americans say in opinion polls that they favor enforcement of our immigration laws and a scaling down of legal immigration.

On the other hand, one detects both among liberals and some libertarian conservatives a resistance to the idea of tougher controls on immigration.

The natural and generous impulse of many Americans is to welcome the immigrant, particularly if they know him. If people are crowded elsewhere, if they are driven from their livelihood by economic or political pressures, do we not owe them the chance we have had? Most immigrants seem attractive and hard-working. Why not welcome them?

This reaction arises from a peculiarly American mindset that leads us to universalize our experience. We assume a responsibility for everything and everybody, everywhere. The United States has been a continent and a frontier more than a nation-state. We are not accustomed to thinking in terms of limits. Japan and Europe have had longer experience with limits, as their restrictive immigration policies attest.

This American world conscience comes into conflict with other moral values that should be important to us. Are we to abandon the sense of obligation to our own poor? Are we to reconcile ourselves to a society in which the rich get richer and the poor get poorer? Do we have the right to pass on to our children an ecology that is living beyond its means, passing a progressively impoverished environment on to successive generations?

Each person must resolve this conflict for himself, but I would argue that our conscience begin at home. There are good reasons both altruistic and practical to help others, but in a nation-state system our nation has neither the authority nor the obligation to save them. The President is sworn by the Constitution to "promote the general welfare, and secure the blessings of liberty to ourselves and our posterity," not the world. As other countries periodically make clear, this limitation might not be altogether unpopular abroad.

There is another level to the moral issue. As Americans, we are entitled to believe that the immigrant is happier here than he would have been at home, but it is not so certain that the movement is of benefit to the vast majority who will (one must assume) stay behind. The "brain drain" robs Third World countries of talents they need; some countries such as India have bitterly resisted the drain. Similarly, migration to the U.S., if it provides a safety valve by draining off the articulate and restless, may simply defer the day when their countries address their own problems. And delay intensifies the problems.

The Third World contains 76 percent of the world's population. Even by an optimistic estimate, its growth alone during this quarter-century will be nearly twice the total population of the industrial world and nearly ten times that of the United States. To believe that a permissive view of immigration will significantly contribute to solving a problem of this scope is simply to engage in wishful thinking. Even if such a permissive attitude were shared throughout the industrial world (which it emphatically is not), migration could not accommodate the current surge of population. It must be dealt with, as China understands, at its origins.

To offer haven to the few who escape is to forget the many who cannot, and an expanding American population does not necessarily advance the common good. To those whose conscience stands in the way, I offer this suggestion: your humane instincts may be sending you the wrong message.

THE "MELTING POT" AND THE "SALAD BOWL:" WHERE ARE WE HEADING?

Even if the national interest demands that we limit population growth, the national interest will be politically irrelevant if we look upon ourselves, not as Americans, but as ethnics—if we look at immigration reform as a way of "keeping out my people" rather than as a reflection of national needs.

It is something of a paradox that, at a time in our history when racism was acceptable (the Dillingham Joint Congressional Commission of 1911 is a case in point), the nation was accepting multi-racial immigration and melding the immigrants into a new America. Now, at a more tolerant time when racism is an ugly charge, the pursuit of racial separateness is becoming increasingly accepted. The "salad bowl" has replaced the "melting pot." Ethnic groups are expected to retain their identity and separateness. This very separateness encourages alienation, estrangement and competition.

There are demographic trends underway that may make this sense of alienation increasingly important. I mentioned that the demographic projections earlier in this paper are probably optimistic. They assume that immigrant women, upon arrival, immediately adopt the United States' current very low fertility pattern. In fact, most immigrant women currently come from societies with much higher fertility rates, and we don't know how fast they will adjust. One good benchmark is that Hispanic residents, including American- and foreign-born, have overall fertility rates about 60 percent higher than non-Hispanic white women. The Census count of Hispanics has risen five times as fast as the overall population since 1950. Some of this respresents immigration, but a larger part of it reflects the higher fertility of Hispanic women.[9]

It is axiomatic that (barring sufficient differences in mortality) the more fecund component of the population will become a larger proportion, which in turn will tend to drive overall fertility— and the total population—upwards. If we wish to avoid this result, national policies should encourage a melding of groups and a decline in that fertility differential.

The impulse toward "competitive fertility" exists within the United States. Spokesmen for La Raza (an Hispanic lobbying group) have boasted of the growing power associated with Hispanics' growing numbers. On the other side of the equation, American Jews are concerned that, with their low fertility, Jews may lose their identity.[10]

We may be heading for serious racial problems if the nation does not move systematically to defuse them. In Chapter IV, Dr. Leon Bouvier has described the present transition of California from a "white" to a "multi-racial" society, as those rather slippery terms are interpreted. The nation as a whole is following suit. Depending on one's assumptions, in another two generations whites may constitute only one-half to two-thirds of the population, with very large minorities of Hispanics, blacks and Asians, probably in that numerical order.[11]

There is always a question as to how far the ideological concerns of the articulate actually affect demographic behavior, but it would be a disaster, both demographically and socially, if the United States should become the cockpit of several competing ethnic factions who identify themselves with their factions, not with the country.

The demographic projections are not predictions, but they are mathematically valid statements of the way we are heading. If indeed we are becoming a nation of major ethnic blocs, it would behoove us to blur the differences rather than emphasizing them. Intermarriage is the most enduring solution, but that is a long process. National policies can increase or diminish the sense of ethnic separation.

Nationally and at the state level, we have already opened Pandora's box with policies that promote ethnic and linguistic separateness. A prime example is the promotion of the official use of languages other than English. It would be hard to conceive of a policy more effectively driving ethnic groups apart than helping them to live their lives, side by side, unable to talk with each other.

The wrenching debate over "reverse discrimination" is another case in point. Like our policies on language, it was born of good will, but it has deeply divisive consequences. Does the poor white slum youth feel less bitter toward blacks, if he is the victim of discrimination, than the black feels when the discrimination works the other way? We must seek ways of ending discrimination without letting the process intensify the sense of ethnic separateness.

Color blindness is still the only enduring corrective to racial discrimination, and perhaps we had better take another look at the "melting pot" that fell into disfavor, along with nationalism, a generation ago. Both ideas state shared goals and a common identification. They justify the altruism that leads people to base their judgments on the social good rather than factional interest.

The basis for good immigration policy exists only when the people agree that the shared well-being—the national interest—is a legitimate and indeed the paramount criterion for national decisions. We should balance that thought against our penchant for letting everybody do his own thing. It is legitimate to ask of any national policy, existing or proposed: "does it enhance or weaken the sense of national cohesion?" Only with a sense of shared identity are we likely to be able to take the tough decisions that reason tells us are required, whether it be about economics, the environment, resources, demography or immigration.

NOTES

1. Leon F. Bouvier, *The Impact of Immigration on U.S. Population Size*, (Population Reference Bureau, Washington, 1981).

2. Some six million chemicals have been listed in the American Chemical Society's Chemical Abstract Service since 1965, more than four times the number that the Society estimates had been described inthe preceding 45 years. *Science*, (Vol. 220, April 15, 1983, p. 293).

3. Emmett J. Horton and W. Dale Compton, "Technological Trends in Automobiles," *Science*, (Vol. 225, August 10, 1984, pp. 587-593). The example is a Ford Escort, and I assume that passenger weight approximates 10 percent of GVW.

4. National Research Council report quoted in *Science*, (Vol. 223, March 16, 1984, p. 1154).

5. Executive Office of the President, Office of Science and Technology Policy News Release, June 28, 1983, quoting the report of the Acid Raid Peer Review Panel.

6. USDA, U.S. Forest Service, *Forest Resource Report 23*, 1977, Appendix A - "An Analysis of Timber in the U.S. 1952-2030."

7. Ben J. Wattenberg and Karl Zinsmeister, "The Birth Dearth: The Geopolitical Consequences," *Public Opinion*, December/January 1986, p. 9. Perhaps to their credit, the authors are inconsistent. Having argued the benefits of size, they then propose that industrial nations seek to bring fertility up to replacement level and that the third world bring it down to that level. This is a moderate goal, but it would vitiate the initial argument. The authors have ignored population momentum. If, miraculously, their proposal could be put in practice tomorrow, there would be something like a doubling or trebling of Third World population—if the resource base could support it—and consequently a further dramatic shrinkage of the proportion of the world's population in the industrial countries, before stability were reached.

8. Allan Carlson, "Depopulation Bomb: The Withering of the Western World," (*Washington Post*, April 13, 1986, p. C1).

9. Cary Davis, et al, "U.S. Hispanics: Changing the Face of America," *Population Bulletin*, (Vol. 38, No. 3, Population Reference Bureau, Inc., June, 1983).

10. "Convention to Study Projected Decline in U.S. Jewish Population." *Washington Post*, (March 25, 1984, p. A11).

11. Leon F. Bouvier and Cary B. Davis, "The Future Racial Composition of the United States," Demographic Information Services Center of the Population Reference Bureau, (Washington, August 1982).

APPENDIX

SUMMARY OF IMMIGRATION REFORM AND CONTROL ACT OF 1986 "SIMPSON-RODINO IMMIGRATION BILL"

Title I—CONTROL OF ILLEGAL IMMIGRATION

PART A—Employment

EMPLOYER SANCTIONS:

Sec. 101. CONTROL OF UNLAWFUL EMPLOYMENT OF ALIENS. [new INA Sec. 274A]

Prohibition of Hiring "Unauthorized Aliens"
Unlawful to "knowingly" hire, recruit, or refer for a fee after the date of enactment an "unauthorized alien"

Unlawful to continue to employ an alien knowing the alien was or has become unauthorized to work

Unlawful to fail to comply with requirements for verification of work authorization and identity

"Grandfather" for Current Employees
Employer sanctions do not apply to an individual who was hired, recruited, or referred prior to date of enactment

Employer sanctions do not apply to continuing employment of an alien hired before date of enactment

---

Prepared by Amy R. Novick, Esq. and Warren R. Leiden, Esq. based on the joint Senate/House Conference Report adopted by the House of Representatives on October 15, 1986.

Reprinted with Permission of the American Immigration Lawyers Association

Verification of Identity and Work Authorization/Record-keeping Requirements
For all individuals hired, recruited or referred, requires employers (persons or entities) to verify, by examining existing documents, the individual's work authorization *and* identity, and to attest under penalty of perjury to such verification on the form designated by Attorney General

Documents Required to Establish Work Authorization and Identity
Individuals must present:
U.S. passport, unexpired foreign passport with work authorization stamp, certificate of U.S. citizenship or naturalization, or alien resident or registration card found acceptable to Attorney General
OR
One document evidencing employment authorization—a social security card, certificate of birth in the U.S. or other designated documentation found acceptable to Attorney General—and one document establishing identity—driver's license or other State-issued identification document found acceptable to Attorney General

Requires Attorney General to develop and implement verification procedures to determine employee's work eligibility

Requires employers to comply with verification procedures and to retain the signed verification form for up to three years

Verification requirements are deemed fulfilled if individual was referred to State employment agency and employer has retained appropriate documentation

Compliance in good faith with the verification requirements establishes an affirmative defense against prosecution for violation of employer sanctions

Provisions for More Secure Future Systems
Requires President to monitor and evaluate verification system to determine whether system is secure and to implement necessary changes to establish secure employment eligibility system

Requires two year notice and congressional hearings and review before implementation by President of *major* changes to verification system

Penalties for Employers
Establishes graduated civil penalties for employers who knowingly hire unauthorized aliens:

First offense: $250–$2,000 fine per unauthorized alien
Second offense: $2,000–$5,000 fine per unauthorized alien
Third offense: $3,000–$10,000 fine per unauthorized alien

Establishes criminal penalties for pattern or practice violations: $3,000 fine and/or six months imprisonment per violation

Failure to complete and retain verification form results in fines of $100 to $1,000 per individual

Provides for hearings before ALJ; appeals to U.S. circuit court of appeals

Effective Dates
First 6 months (beginning on first day of first month after enactment) is strictly public education period (no proceedings conducted nor orders issued on basis of any violation)

Second 12 months is first citation period; in the first instance of an alleged violation, Attorney General will issue a citation without further proceedings or orders; second instances of alleged violations may incur civil orders and fines

[Employer sanctions become fully effective after 18 month period]

[Small employers of three or fewer are not exempted from employer sanctions]

Section expressly does not authorize the issuance or establishment of a national identification card

Termination of Sanctions for Pattern of Widespread Discrimination
[Employer sanctions do not automatically expire]

GAO will report to Congress annually for three years on the implementation and enforcement of employer sanctions to determine whether a pattern of employment discrimination based on national origin has resulted from employer sanctions, whether the provisions have been carried out satisfactorily, and whether an unnecessary burden has been created for employers

Requires Attorney General and Chairman of Civil Rights Commission and EEOC to establish Task Force to review each GAO report and to make legislative recommendations if such discrimination has been discovered

Provides Congress with expedited procedures for sunsetting sanctions if, after three years, it accepts GAO report that sanctions cause a pattern of widespread employment discrimination

Requires the Attorney General to conduct a study on the use of existing telephone verification systems for determining employment eligibility and to report to Congress

Requires HHS to conduct study of feasibility and costs of establishing SSN validation system and to report to congressional committees within two years of enactment

Sec. 102.   ANTIDISCRIMINATION PROVISIONS: UNFAIR IMMIGRA-
TION-RELATED EMPLOYMENT PRACTICES. [new INA Sec.
274B]

Makes it an unfair immigration-related employment practice to discriminate against any individual on account of national origin or "citizenship status" (U.S. citizenship or "intending citizenship"); however, it is not an unfair immigration-related employment practice to prefer a U.S. citizen over an alien if the two individuals are *equally* qualified

Exempts employers of three or fewer employees from prosecution for discrimination

Creates an Office of Special Counsel in Justice Department for investigating and prosecuting any charges of "immigration-related employment" discrimination

Hearings on charges conducted before ALJ; appeals to U.S. circuit court of appeals

Individuals may bring private action if Special Counsel fails to bring charge within 120 days

Allows prevailing party (except government) attorneys' fees if the losing party's argument is without reasonable foundation in law and fact

Sunsets antidiscrimination provisions if sanctions are
repealed, or upon a joint resolution by Congress if the GAO reports that no significant discrimination has occurred or if the administration of these provisions has resulted in unreasonable burden on employers

Sec. 103.   FRAUD AND MISUSE OF CERTAIN IMMIGRATION-RELATED
DOCUMENTS.

Imposes additional civil fines and criminal penalties for fraud and misuse of immigration-related and employment-related documents

PART B—IMPROVEMENT OF ENFORCEMENT AND SERVICES

INS FUNDING FOR ENFORCEMENT AND SERVICES:

Sec. 111. AUTHORIZATION OF APPROPRIATIONS FOR ENFORCE-
MENT AND SERVICE ACTIVITIES OF THE IMMIGRATION
AND NATURALIZATION SERVICE.

Establishes sense of Congress that two essential elements of the
immigration control program of Act are (1) increased border patrol
and other inspection and enforcement activities of INS to prevent
and deter illegal entry of aliens into the U.S. and (2) an increase in
examinations and other service activities of the INS to ensure prompt
and efficient adjudication of petitions and applications

Increases authorization of appropriations for INS and EOIR for enforcement and examinations activities, improved services, in-service
training programs, and community outreach programs

Increases the Border Patrol for FY1987 and FY1988 50% higher
than the level of FY1986

Sec. 112. UNLAWFUL TRANSPORTATION OF ALIENS TO THE UNITED
STATES.

Increases up to $10,000 the penalty for transporting or harboring an
alien not authorized to enter the U.S.

Sec. 113. IMMIGRATION EMERGENCY FUND.

Authorizes appropriation of $35 million for INS Border Patrol and
enforcement activities and for reimbursing States and localities in
meeting immigration emergency, as determined by President and
certified by House and Senate Judiciary Committees

Sec. 114. LIABILITY OF OWNERS AND OPERATORS OF INTERNA-
TIONAL BRIDGES AND TOLL ROADS TO PREVENT THE UN-
AUTHORIZED LANDING OF ALIENS.

Provides that an owner or operator of an international toll road or
bridge is not liable for penalty if the person has acted diligently and
reasonably to fulfill duty to prevent the unauthorized landing of
aliens; Attorney General, upon request, may inspect facility for compliance purposes

Sec. 115. ENFORCEMENT OF THE IMMIGRATION LAWS OF THE UNITED STATES

Establishes the sense of Congress that the immigration laws of the U.S. should be enforced vigorously and uniformly and, in the enforcement of such laws, the Attorney General shall take due and deliberate actions to safeguard the constitutional rights, personal safety and human dignity of USC's and aliens

Sec. 116. RESTRICTING WARRANTLESS ENTRY IN THE CASE OF OUTDOOR AGRICULTURAL OPERATIONS

Forbids INS officers from entering farms or open fields without a search warrant or owner's consent

Sec. 117. RESTRICTIONS ON ADJUSTMENT OF STATUS.

Bars adjustment of status to permanent residence in the U.S. to any alien (except an "immediate relative" of a U.S. citizen) who is not in legal immigration status or who has failed (other than through no fault of his own for technical reasons) to maintain continuously a legal status since entry into the U.S.

PART C—VERIFICATION OF STATUS UNDER CERTAIN PROGRAMS

SAVE PROGRAM:

Sec. 121. VERIFICATION OF IMMIGRATION STATUS OF ALIENS APPLYING FOR BENEFITS UNDER CERTAIN PROGRAMS.

[Requires all States to verify through the Systematic Alien Verification for Entitlement (SAVE) Program the immigration status of all aliens applying for certain federally funded public assistance programs to assure alien eligibility to benefits; provides waiver for program where a particular verification program would not be cost-effective

[Provides 100% reimbursement to State governments of the total costs of the SAVE program; hearing available to applicant with unresolved immigration status]

TITLE II—LEGALIZATION

LEGALIZATION OF UNDOCUMENTED AND OUT-OF-STATUS ALIEN RESIDENTS:

Sec. 201. LEGALIZATION OF STATUS

Legalization to Temporary Resident Status
Permits temporary resident status eligibility for aliens who have continuously resided in the U.S. in an unlawful status since before January 1, 1982

Provides eligibility to nonimmigrants who have entered and resided in the U.S. since before January 1, 1982 provided they establish that their authorized stay expired before *that date* or the government knew of unlawful status as of that date; exchange visitors (J visas) subject to two-year residency requirement must have fulfilled requirement or obtained a waiver

Applicants must have continuous physical presence in the U.S. from the date of enactment (brief, casual, and innocent absence from U.S. does not interrupt continuous physical presence)

Application Deadlines
Alien must apply for legalization during 12 month period beginning on date designated by Attorney General (not later than 180 days after enactment)

Aliens apprehended by the INS before application period who can establish a prima facie case of eligibility may not be deported and shall be granted work authorization but must apply for legalization within first 30 days of application period

During application period aliens subject to OSC [deportation proceedings] who can establish prima facie use of eligibility must apply for legalization within 30 days of beginning of application period or 30 days after issuance of OSC, whichever is later; such alien will not be deported and shall be granted work authorization until application is adjudicated

Other Eligibility Requirements and Waivers
To be eligible, the alien must be generally admissible, must not have been convicted of a felony or three misdemeanors in the U.S., must not have assisted in any form of persecution, and must be registered for the military service if required to do so

Requires legalized applicants to submit documents to support continuous residence with independent corroboration of the information contained therein

Waives numerical limitations and grounds of exclusion under Secs. 212(a)(14), (20), (21), (25), and (32); Attorney General may waive other grounds of exclusion for humanitarian purposes, to assure family unity, or in the public interest except under Secs. 212(a)(9), (10), (15) (special rule for determination of public charge provides that an alien is not ineligible as inadmissible under Secs. 212(a)(15) if alien demonstrates a history of employment in the U.S. evincing self-support), (23), (27), (28), (29), or (33)

Newly legalized temporary residents are authorized for employment and may travel abroad under restrictions to be promulgated by the Attorney General

Application Procedures
Applications must contain information pursuant to requirements set forth by Attorney General

Individuals may file application for temporary resident status:

with the Attorney General (the INS)
OR
with a "qualified designated entity"—voluntary organizations, State, local and community organizations—designated by the Attorney General; Attorney General also may designate other persons determined qualified and experienced in the preparation of adjustment applications

Confidentiality of Information
Information (files and records of the "qualified designated entity") relating to an alien's application is confidential; INS and Attorney General are barred from access to files without consent of the alien

Information furnished pursuant to legalization application may not be used by the Attorney General or Justice Department for any other purpose than to make a determination on the application

Imposes criminal penalties for violations of confidentiality provisions

Adjustment to Permanent Resident Status
Provides for adjustment to permanent resident status after 18 months if the alien has resided continuously in the U.S. as a temporary resident, is generally admissible, and meets minimal English and civics requirements

Alien must apply for such adjustment during 12 month eligibility period

Review of Denial of Applications and Limitations on Public Assistance

No review of denial of adjustment application if denial is based on late filing

Provides single level of administrative review; judicial review only after deportation or exclusion proceedings and limited to "abuse of discretion" or findings contrary to clear and convincing facts

Newly legalized temporary and permanent resident aliens (except Cuban/Haitian Entrants) are barred from receiving most federally funded public assistance for five years

CUBAN/HAITIAN ENTRANTS:

Sec. 202.   CUBAN-HAITIAN ADJUSTMENT.

Provides eligibility for permanent resident status for all Cuban/Haitian entrants who have continuously resided in the U.S. since before January 1, 1982 and who are generally admissible

Applicants must apply for adjustment within 2 years after date of enactment

Adjustment under this provision does not reduce the number of immigration visas authorized under INA

Waives grounds of exclusion under 212(a)(14), (15), (16), (17), (20), (21), (25) and (32)

Sec. 203.   UPDATING REGISTRY DATE TO JANUARY 1, 1972.

Updates registry date from June 30, 1948 to January 1, 1972

REIMBURSEMENT TO STATES:

Sec. 204.   STATE LEGALIZATION IMPACT-ASSISTANCE GRANTS.

Appropriates $1 billion federal funds for each year for four years (beginning in FY1988) to reimburse State and local governments for the costs of providing public assistance and medical benefits to newly legalized aliens according to specific formula; unused funds may be expended through FY1994; 30% of funds must be allotted equally among public assistance, health assistance, education agency programs

Requires States to report annually to Secretary of HHS; Secretary to report annually to Congress

TITLE III—REFORM OF LEGAL IMMIGRATION

PART A—TEMPORARY AGRICULTURAL WORKERS

TEMPORARY AGRICULTURAL WORKERS:

Sec. 301.   H-2A AGRICULTURAL WORKERS.

Creates new "H-2A" classification, as amendment to current H-2 program, for temporary agricultural workers

Provides expedited procedures for grower requests for foreign labor and review of denied applications: certification application required not more than 60 days before commencement of labor; seven days for denial; certification 20 days before commencement of labor for certification

Requires employers to provide housing (or housing allowance) and worker compensation for H-2A workers

Requires an affirmative recruitment of domestic farm laborers

"SCHUMER SEASONAL AGRICULTURAL WORKERS":

Sec. 302.   PERMANENT RESIDENCE FOR CERTAIN SPECIAL AGRICULTURAL WORKERS.

[new INA Sec. 210]

Creates "seasonal agricultural worker program": grants temporary legal resident status to any alien who has performed at least 90 man-days in seasonal agricultural services from May 1, 1985 to May 1, 1986; permits adjustments to permanent resident status *after one year* to any alien who has worked 90 man-days in each of the last three years; permits adjustment to permanent resident status *after two years* to any alien who has worked 90 man-days in the last year ending May 1, 1986; permits a total of 350,000 foreign agricultural workers to obtain permanent resident status after one year; the remainder are eligible after two years

Grants seasonal agricultural workers right to travel abroad and work authorization

Provides for adjustment at appropriate consular office for eligible aliens

Requires alien to prove by a preponderance of the evidence that he/ she has worked the requisite number of man-days by producing sufficient evidence that shows such employment; burden shifts to the Attorney General to disprove the reasonableness of the inference drawn from the evidence

Imposes criminal and civil penalties and renders alien inadmissible under Sec. 212(a)(19) for false statements in applications for adjustment of status

Waivers numerical limitations of Secs. 201 and 202 and grounds of exclusion under Secs. 212(a)(14), (20), (21), and (32); Attorney General may waive other grounds of exclusion for humanitarian purposes, to assure family unity, or in the public interest except under Secs. 212(a)(9), (10), (15) (special rule for determination of public charge provides that an alien is not ineligible as inadmissible as under Secs. 212(a)(15) if alien demonstrates a history of employment in the U.S. evincing self-support), (23), (27), (28), (29), or (33)

Provides for temporary stay of exclusion or deportation before and during application period for an apprehended alien who establishes a nonfrivolous case of eligibility; provides work authorization

Provides single level of administrative review; judicial review of the administrative record only during exclusion or deportation proceedings; review limited to abuse of discretion or findings contrary to clear and convincing facts

Disqualifies temporary legal residents from receiving AFDC for five-year period (limited access to Medicaid benefits)

REPLENISHMENT WORKERS:

Sec. 303.   DETERMINATIONS OF AGRICULTURAL LABOR SHORT-AGES AND ADMISSION OF ADDITIONAL SPECIAL AGRI-CULTURAL WORKERS. [new INA Sec. 210A]

Provides for replenishment workers for four years (1990-1993) if the secretaries of agriculture and labor certify that a shortage of agricultural workers exists; determination of number to be admitted based on specific formula of anticipated need minus supply of agricultural workers for that year

Requires Attorney General to admit for temporary resident status the number of aliens equal to the shortage number; requires adjustment to permanent resident status after three year period

Grants replenishment workers right to travel abroad and to work authorization

Requires replenishment workers to perform 90 man-days of seasonal agricultural services in each year for three years to avoid deportation and to become eligible for permanent resident status

Requires Director of the Bureau of the Census to report annually to Congress on the estimated number of special agricultural workers

Disqualifies replenishment workers from receiving public benefits for five-year period (with exception of eligibility under the Food Stamp Act and Housing Act) to the same extent as newly legalized aliens

Waives grounds of exclusion under Secs. 212(a)(14), (20), (21), (25), and (32); Attorney General may waive other grounds of exclusion for humanitarian purposes, to assure family unity, or in the public interest except under Secs. 212(a)(9), (10), (15) (special rule for determination of public charge provides that an alien is not ineligible as inadmissible as under Secs. 212(a)(15) if alien demonstrates a history of employment in the U.S. evincing self-support), (23), (27), (28), (29), or (33)

Requires employers to provide equal transportation arrangements and services to domestic workers as those provided to alien agricultural workers

Makes certain rights, remedies, and penalties under Migrant and Seasonal Agricultural Worker Protection Act applicable

Aliens admitted under this section may not be naturalized as U.S. citizens unless they have performed 90 man-days of seasonal agricultural services in each of five fiscal years

Sec. 304.   COMMISSION ON AGRICULTURAL WORKERS.

Establishes Commission on Agricultural Workers composed of 12 members appointed by the President and Congress (1) to review the impact of the special agricultural provisions on domestic farmworker conditions, the extent to which Schumer workers continue to perform seasonal agricultural work and the industry's reliance on them, the impact of legalizations and employers sanction on the supply of agricultural labor, and special geographical problems and (2) to evaluate the overall program

Requires the Commission to report to Congress within five years of enactment with recommendations for appropriate changes; Commission terminates approximately five years after enactment

Sec. 305. ELIGIBILITY OF H-2A AGRICULTURAL WORKERS FOR CERTAIN LEGAL ASSISTANCE.

Qualifies nonimmigrant alien H-2A agricultural workers for eligibility for legal assistance under the Legal Services Corporation Act but only with regard to housing, wages, transportation and other conditions of employment under H-2A contract

PART B—OTHER CHANGES IN THE IMMIGRATION LAW

Sec. 311. CHANGE IN COLONIAL QUOTA.

Increases colonial quota from 600 to 5,000 immigrant visas annually

Sec. 312. G-IV SPECIAL IMMIGRANTS.

Provides for adjustment of status to special immigrant status for the certain G-IV nonimmigrants who have resided in the U.S. for certain periods: unmarried sons or daughters, surviving spouses, retired officers or employees of international organizations, or spouses of a retired officer or employer; affords nonimmigrant status to their parents or children

Sec. 313. VISA WAIVER PILOT PROGRAM FOR CERTAIN VISITORS.

Establishes a three-year pilot program for the waiver of tourist visas for nationals from certain designated countries who visit for not more than 90 days

Authorizes the Attorney General and Secretary of State to designate up to eight countries that extend reciprocal privileges to USC's as pilot program countries

Pilot program countries must meet specific qualifications according to a low nonimmigrant visa refusal rate formula

Bars pilot program aliens from extending their stay, adjusting to immigrants (except as immediate relatives under Sec. 201(b), or adjusting to nonimmigrants; such aliens waive any right to review or appeal of an immigration officer's admissibility determination

Sec. 314. MAKING VISAS AVAILABLE FOR NONPREFERENCE IMMI-GRANTS.

Authorizes 5,000 additional nonpreference immigrant visas for FY1987 and FY1988, first for natives of certain countries who were adversely affected by Pub. L. 89-236 [1965 Admendments]; waives labor certification requirement in determining eligibility

Sec. 315. MISCELLANEOUS PROVISION.

Equal Treatment of Fathers
Provides that an illegitimate child may gain the same immigration benefits from the natural father as from the natural mother

Suspension of Deportation
Provides that an alien has *not* failed to maintain the seven-year continuous physical presence requirement for suspension of deportation if an absence from the U.S. was "brief, casual, and innocent" and "did not meaningfully interrupt the continuous physical presence" (restores to pre-*Phinpathya* standard)

Sense of Congress Respecting Treatment of Cuban Political Prisoners
Establishes the sense of Congress that visas should be issued to Cuban national political prisoners without regard to Sec. 243(g)

Alien Crewmen Members
Bars for one-year after enactment the admission of alien crewmen to perform services aboard a vessel or aircraft during a strike in the unit in which the alien intends to work; exempt alien employees who were employed before date of strike concerned and who seek admission to continue employment in same capacity

TITLE IV - REPORTS TO CONGRESS

Sec. 401. TRIENNIAL COMPREHENSIVE REPORT ON IMMIGRATION.

Requires the President to transmit to Congress not later than January 1, 1989 and every third year thereafter a comprehensive immigration impact-report, including the number and classification of aliens admitted and who have entered without visas, the impact on U.S. economy, and society, and on governance and to submit appropriate recommendations on changes in the numerical limitations

Sec. 402.   REPORTS ON UNAUTHORIZED ALIEN EMPLOYMENT.

Requires the President to transmit to Congress annually for three years reports on the implementation of employer sanctions including the adequacy of employment verification system, resultant violations, and impact on enforcement

Sec. 403.   REPORTS ON H-2A PROGRAM.

Requires the President to transmit to the House and Senate Judiciary Committees reports on the implementation of the temporary agricultural worker (H-2A) program within two years after the date of enactment and every two years thereafter

Sec. 404.   REPORTS ON LEGALIZATION PROGRAM.

Requires the President to transmit to Congress two reports on the legalization program; one report within 18 months after the end of the application period for adjustment to temporary resident status; second report on the impact of legalization within three years of the date of the transmittal of the first report

Sec. 405.   REPORT ON VISA WAIVER PILOT PROGRAM.

Requires the Attorney General and the Secretary of State to jointly monitor the pilot program and to report to Congress within two years after the beginning of the program

Sec. 406.   REPORT ON THE IMMIGRATION & NATURALIZATION SERVICE.

Requires the Attorney General within 90 days of enactment to prepare and transmit to Congress a report describing the type of resources required to improve the capabilities of the INS to carry out the service and enforcement activities required by this Act

Sec. 407.   SENSE OF THE CONGRESS.

Establishes sense of Congress that President should consult with the President of Mexico on the implementation of this Act and its possible effect on the U.S. or Mexico; President should report to Congress any recommendations for change in legislation

TITLE V—STATE ASSISTANCE FOR INCARCERATION COSTS OF ILLEGAL ALIENS AND CERTAIN CUBAN NATIONALS.

Sec. 501. REIMBURSEMENT OF STATES FOR COSTS OF INCARCER-ATING ILLEGAL ALIENS AND CERTAIN CUBAN NATION-ALS.

Provides federal reimbursement to State and local governments for the costs of incarcerating illegal alien felons, as defined, or Cuban national felons

TITLE VI—COMMISSION FOR THE STUDY OF INTERNATIONAL MIGRATION AND COOPERATIVE ECONOMIC DEVELOPMENT.

Sec. 601. COMMISSION FOR THE STUDY OF INTERNATIONAL MI-GRATION AND COOPERATIVE ECONOMIC DEVELOPMENT.

Establishes Commission for the Study of International Migration and Cooperative Economic Development, composed of 12 members appointed by Congress, to conduct studies in consultation with governments of sending countries concerning conditions contributing to unauthorized migration to the U.S. and to develop trade and investment programs to alleviate such conditions

Commission to report to President and Congress within three years after appointment; terminates when report is transmitted

TITLE VII—FEDERAL RESPONSIBILITY FOR DEPORTABLE AND EXCLUDABLE ALIENS CONVICTED OF CRIMES

Sec. 701. EXPEDITIOUS DEPORTATION OF CONVICTED ALIENS.

Provides for the expeditious commencement of deportation proceedings in a case of an alien convicted of a deportable offense

INDEX